THE 1971 INDO-PAK AIR WAR

REFLECTIONS AND PROJECTIONS

THE 1971 INDO-PAK AIR WAR

REFLECTIONS AND PROJECTIONS

Edited by

Air Marshal **Anil Chopra** PVSM AVSM VM VSM (Retd)

Dr **Shalini Chawla**

Foreword by

Air Chief Marshal **RKS Bhadauria** PVSM AVSM VM ADC

KNOWLEDGE WORLD

KW Publishers Pvt Ltd
New Delhi

in association with

Centre for Air Power Studies
New Delhi

The Centre for Air Power Studies is an independent, non-profit, academic research institution established in 2002 under a registered Trust to undertake and promote policy-related research, study and discussion on the trends and developments in defence and military issues, especially air power and the aerospace arena, for civil and military purposes. Its publications seek to expand and deepen the understanding of defence, military power, air power and aerospace issues without necessarily reflecting the views of any institution or individuals except those of the authors.

Centre for Air Power Studies
P-284, Arjan Path
Subroto Park
New Delhi 110010

Tele: (91-11) 25699131

E-mail: capsnetdroff@gmail.com
website: www.capsindia.org

ISBN 978-93-91490-09-6 Hardback
ISBN 978-93-91490-10-2 ebook

Published in India by Kalpana Shukla

KNOWLEDGE WORLD

KW Publishers Pvt Ltd
4676/21, First Floor, Ansari Road
Daryaganj, New Delhi 110002
Phone: +91 11 43528107
Marketing: kw@kwpub.in
Editorial: production@kwpub.in
Website: www.kwpub.in

Printed and bound in India

CENTRE FOR AIR POWER STUDIES

VISION

To be an independent centre of excellence on national security contributing informed and considered research and analyses on relevant issues.

MISSION

To encourage independent and informed research and analyses on issues of relevance to national security and to create a pool of domain experts to provide considered inputs to decision-makers. Also, to foster informed public debate and opinion on relevant issues and to engage with other think-tanks and stakeholders within India and abroad to provide an Indian perspective.

Dedicated to

All the Air Warriors who participated in the

1971

Indo–Pak War

Contents

एयर चीफ मार्शल आर के एस भदौरिया
प वि से मे अ वि से मे वा मे ए डी सी
Air Chief Marshal RKS Bhadauria
PVSM AVSM VM ADC

वायु सेना मुख्यालय
नई दिल्ली - 110 106
Air Headquarters
New Delhi - 110 106

FOREWORD

The Liberation of Bangladesh was a landmark event in global history. On the signing of the Instrument of Surrender on 16 December 1971 in Dhaka, East Pakistan ceased to exist and the sovereign nation of Bangladesh was born. The largest military surrender after the Second World War shattered the prestige of the Pakistani Military and left 93,000 Pakistani Prisoners in captivity. Pakistan lost a third of its Army, half its Navy and a quarter of its Air Force, bringing an end to the atrocities the Pakistan Army had unleashed with "Operation Searchlight" on the predominantly Bengali population of East Pakistan.

This book is a result of contributions from individual research conducted by various authors and the lessons they have derived from their scholarly perspective. The authors bring out how the Air War was orchestrated with sister services and agencies to achieve national objectives in a unique manner covering almost every element of air operations and decision making with their writings. Historical events can be portrayed in different ways based on the vantage points the author chooses. You would find aspects of the 1971 War being narrated from various intriguing perspectives, providing you a different facet of operations in every chapter. While the opinions of every author are personal, and these drive his subsequent analysis, when read together they provide a comprehensive picture of this pivotal conflict, and serve to fill gaps in our understanding of it.

There is little doubt that the Indian Air Force played a crucial role in this war. After responding to the pre-emptive strikes from Pakistan, the air campaign executed a strategy of enabling the Army to hold ground in the west while running an offensive air campaign in the East. The IAF obliterated the PAF in the East, thereby allowing a free run for the Indian Army towards Dhaka. Joint operations with the Indian Army and the Indian Navy thereafter continued till the end of the war. The IAF dealt the coup de grace with the bombing of the Governor's house resulting in a historical surrender and creation of a nation.

As India and Bangladesh celebrate 50 years of the victory as "Swarnim Vijay Varsh", IAF is very proud of its history and especially the achievements of its Air Veterans who shaped the IAF over the years. This book is being released at an appropriate juncture to aid our understanding of the war and motivate the next generation. I compliment Director General CAPS, and his team for bringing out this account.

Air Chief Marshal
Chief of the Air Staff

31 Jul 21

Preface

Fifty years after the Indo-Pakistan War of 1971, it is time to recollect the great military campaigns and reflect on the lessons and changes that have helped make India a stronger power. The two-front 13-day war began with the anticipated Pakistan Air Force (PAF) preemptive strike on December 3, 1971. Code-named "Operation Chengiz Khan", the PAF targeted eleven Indian Air Force (IAF) air bases and other installations. This also paved the way for India's formal entry into the war for East Pakistan's independence, and ultimately, the creation of Bangladesh. The war ended with the surrender of Pakistan's Eastern Command in Dhaka on December 16, 1971. Over 93,000 Pakistani personnel were taken prisoner. The IAF engaged in every facet of air operations, and air power was a very significant contributor to the historic victory.

Earlier, on March 26, 1971, leaders of the majority political party in East Pakistan had called for its secession from Pakistan. The Pakistan Army had responded with a heavy hand through a full-scale "Operation Searchlight", blatantly killing local civilians, and supporting arson and rape by pro-Pakistani Islamist militias, in one of the worst genocides. Bengali freedom fighters formed the "Mukti Bahini", a guerrilla resistance movement consisting of the Bangladeshi military, paramilitary and civilians. Pakistani atrocities resulted in thousands being killed, and also led to nearly 10 million refugees flooding into the eastern states of India. Facing a mounting humanitarian and economic crisis, India started actively aiding the Mukti Bahini. The PAF was initially reluctant to strike own people in East Pakistan on moral grounds, and had assured the

Bengali PAF staff of their personal safety. The Pakistan Army considered this as treason.

The creation of the Bangladesh Armed Forces was announced on April 4, 1971. The liberation forces secured control over large parts of the Bengali countryside. The Mukti Bahini received training and weapons support from India. The PAF began attacking the liberation forces in support of the Pakistan Army. India had banned over-flights to Pakistani aircraft as early as January 20, 1971, making it difficult for reinforcements from West Pakistan, which had to detour to take the much longer route through Sri Lanka. The PAF's C-130s and the Pakistan International Airlines (PIA) aircraft had to be fully committed to this task. The PAF's Operation "Great Fly-In" was launched between March 26 and May 2. Two C-130B planes were stationed in Dhaka for operations in East Pakistan and also to ferry fuel from Sri Lanka and Myanmar.

At the commencement of the war, the IAF in the East consisted of 13 fighter-bomber, three MiG-21, four Hawker Hunter, three Folland Gnat, one Sukhoi Su-7, and two Canberra squadrons. There were three C-47 Dakota squadrons, two An-12, one DHC-4 Caribou, one DHC-3 Otter and one C-119 Packet squadrons based at Jorhat, Guwahati, Barrackpur and Dum Dum. There were three flights each of Mi-4 and Alouette III helicopters. For air defence, the IAF had nine signals units for communication and radar coverage, and there were three SA-2 squadrons in the East. The PAF had just 16 Canadair F-86 Sabres, two T-33 trainers, and eight helicopters. The IAF had begun flying reconnaissance flights over East Pakistan as early as June 1971. The IAF also helped the Mukti Bahini organise a formation of light aircraft (called the Kilo Flight) which were manned and serviced by Bengali pilots and technicians who had defected from the PAF. The Kilo Flight had launched attacks on targets in Bangladesh on December 3, 1971, before the actual commencement of the Indo-Pak War, and the flight flew several missions through the war.

The IAF commenced operations in the Eastern Sector from December 4, 1971. By December 7, Tejgaon airport had been put out of operation, thus, grounding the PAF in East Pakistan. PAF operational effectiveness had suffered considerably because most Bengali pilots and technicians, almost 50 per cent of PAF personnel in East Pakistan, had been grounded during the political unrest since March 1971. As conflict between the Mukti Bahini and Pakistan Army intensified, the PAF flew 100 sorties in support of the ground forces between October and December 3. Meanwhile, the Mukti Bahini had sabotaged hundreds of bridges and rail lines by November 1971, thus, diminishing transport capacity in East Pakistan to barely 10 per cent of the normal, and crippled daily supplies to the Pakistan Army units. Mukti Bahini naval commandos had managed to sink or damage over a hundred ships and ferries.

As the Indian Army began a lightning campaign towards Dhaka, the IAF achieved total air dominance by destroying the Sabres of No. 14 Squadron, and thereafter carrying out the famous Tangail air-drop and Meghna helilift, defending Indian forces from the PAF and providing ground support. The Tangail air-drop on December 11, involved nearly 50 An-12s, C-119s, 2 Caribous and Dakotas air-dropping 700 troops of the 2nd Para Battalion near Tangail about 15 km north of Dhaka. Gnats from No. 22 Squadron provided top cover for the operation. The IAF also made plans to counter any Chinese incursions into Indian territory in the Eastern Himalayas, but the Chinese remained militarily inactive in 1971. The PAF was conscious that the IAF considerably outnumbered it. Also, the IAF had the qualitative edge in aircraft and technology. Pakistani planners had assumed that the PAF would be neutralised within 24 hours of the IAF launching combat operations in the East. The PAF also lacked the service facilities for sustaining prolonged air operations. Pakistan had neglected the East Pakistani defences since independence, thus had poor ground based radar and Air Defence (AD) weapons cover.

Pakistan had lost two aircraft, with one damaged on November 22, over Boyra, and were already down to 14 operational airplanes by December 1971. The PAF Sabres were not cleared for night operations, therefore, any air defence at night was based on anti-aircraft guns. The IAF fighters mostly flew day-time missions in the East. As PAF bases were being repeatedly attacked by IAF aircraft, the Sabres flew day-time Combat Air Patrols (CAP), resulting in several dogfights with Indian jets. On December 6, four MiG-21s of No. 28 Squadron, flying from Guwahati, led by Wg Cdr B. K. Bishnoi, bombed Tejgaon airstrip with 500 kg bombs, scoring several hits on the runway. The MiGs also rocketed Kurmitola runway. Tejgaon was bombed again on December 7, and throughout the war to prevent repairs, effectively grounding the PAF fighters for the rest of the war. The PAF had considered using the wide roads adjacent to the airport to operate the Sabres but that did not work out. The PAF decided to evacuate the Sabre pilots. One Twin Otter carrying nine Sabre pilots flew to Burma on December 8, and the remaining pilots were flown out of Dhaka on December 10. On December 14, four MiG-21s of No. 28 Squadron attacked the Governor's House in Dhaka with 57 mm rockets, ripping the massive roof off the main hall and turning the building into a smouldering wreck. The East Pakistan governor was so shocked by the incident that he resigned on the spot, hastening the surrender.

As per records, the IAF lost 19 aircraft in East Pakistan, three in air combat, six to accidents and the rest to anti-aircraft fire. Five PAF Sabres were shot down by IAF aircraft. PAF Air Headquarters (HQ) had issued orders to blow up all the remaining aircraft in the East, but the local commander decided to only destroy the ammunition stocks and sabotaged the electric and hydraulic systems of the aircraft on December 15. After the war, Tejgaon airport was made operational by December 25, 1971. The Kilo Flight relocated to Tejgaon. The newly formed Bangladesh Air Force lacked trained personnel and for some time the base was administered by an IAF officer. Eight Sabres, one T-33, three Alouette, and one DHC-3 Otter were made fit for service by March 1972 by the Bangladesh Air Force. These aircraft remained operational until they were replaced by more modern aircraft after 1973.

One of the most important factors for the quick liberation of Bangladesh was the total air supremacy that the IAF gained in the opening days of the war in the East, and the excellent coordination among the Indian Army, Air Force, Navy, and the Mukti Bahini.

The IAF's initial air campaign in the West was to strike PAF forward bases and provide ground support to the Indian Army. The Pakistan Army's military strategy was based on winning an overwhelming, decisive victory over the Indian forces in the Western Front so as to have bargaining power for losses in the East. After the not-so-successful preemptive strike, the PAF adopted a defensive stance in response to the IAF's heavy retaliation. This lack of further PAF retaliation has been attributed to the deliberate decision of the PAF to cut its losses, as it had already incurred huge losses in the conflict in the East. The IAF continued with day and night attacks against airfields and radar, and by fighter jets. There were night attacks against airfields and strategic targets by Canberras and An-12s. The number of sorties flown by the PAF decreased day-by-day. The IAF continued attacks against PAF forward air bases, and deep penetration strikes, until the end of the war. It also maintained interdiction and close-support operations. On December 8, 1971, IAF Hunters of No. 20 Squadron at Pathankot attacked the PAF air base at Murid and destroyed five F-86 aircraft on the ground. IAF aircraft played a great role in supporting the Indian Army's ground battles in most sectors. The IAF's air strikes on Karachi airfield and installations had a serious demoralising effect. The IAF also outclassed the PAF in air combat engagements. The PAF aircraft that survived the IAF's onslaught took refuge at Iranian air bases or in concrete blast pens, refusing to offer a fight. As per official records, the IAF flew 1,978 sorties in the East and about 4,000 in the West, against the PAF's 30 and 2,840 respectively.

This book looks at the full gambit of air operations of the 1971 Indo-Pak War. The detailed chapters covering diverse aspects of the air operations have been authored by some of the veterans who not only excelled in the air operations, but also won gallantry awards. ACM PC Lal was at the helm of affairs as the Air Chief. He carried years of operational and administrative experience when the war broke out. He was known for being a cool, calm, suave and sophisticated task master, with clarity of mind and thought. This book looks at how he saw and orchestrated the air war, which is so well covered in his personal memoirs, *My Years with the IAF*.

Starting from the force levels of the two sides, the book looks at offensive operations in both the Eastern and Western Fronts, and also the joint operations. The air-land operations in the East comprised a game-changer. The vertical envelopment operations by the helicopter fleet and para-drop operations were indeed unique. There is a chapter on the operational approach and psyche of the PAF. During the Battle of Longewala, air power demonstrated its responsiveness and decisive impact. The Canberras were extensively used, mostly for night bombing. Interestingly the An-12s were most effectively deployed in the bombing role. The Forward Air Controllers (FACs) played a very significant operational role in getting the attacking aircraft to their correct targets.

The book also revisits India's national strategy during that period, and also how the 1971 War altered Pakistan's strategic posture. It also looks at the scenarios of conventional war under the nuclear overhang. There is a very interesting interaction with AVM BK Bishnoi VrC & Bar (Retd), who was the then Commanding Officer (CO) of No. 28 Squadron, and had the led the air strikes on the airfields near Dhaka, and also the Governor's House. There is a narrative about the "Kilo Flight" by Gp Capt Shamsul Alam, a veteran of the Bangladesh liberation war. The book covers all this and much more.

The 1971 air war was one of the last in which classic close combat took place between two major Air Forces. The air war saw clear air superiority being established against a major Air Force. The war ended with the birth of a nation. It was also the largest surrender of a force after World War II. While the book records the air operations of the war in the correct perspective, it also looks at the lessons. Undoubtedly, over the years, the capabilities of air assets have greatly enhanced, and their employment changed significantly. The professional approach and culture have also evolved. Clearly, the air superiority of the IAF in the Eastern Sector greatly imparted momentum to the land battle and led to the eventual fall of Dhaka. The war saw many air combat engagements. Clearly, the MiG-21s flown by superior pilots outclassed the technologically superior F-104s. Air combat engagements still remain relevant even in the Beyond Visual Range (BVR) environment as was seen in the PAF-

IAF engagement of February 2019. Air power continues to be employed best in an offensive role. Air-launched cruise missiles and stand-off delivery with Precision Guided Munitions (PGMs) have brought a new dimension to the surface attack. Offensive and defensive air operations supported by long range missiles, Airborne Warning and Control System (AWACS) and in-flight refuelling, have increased capability and combat engagement ranges. With the significant increase in platforms, including unmanned ones, and long-range Surface-to-Air Missiles (SAMs), the challenge of air space management has become more complex. The inherent strength of air power is both its flexibility and ability to act autonomously. It must be used offensively to hit much deeper. Air power continues to influence and support the surface battle in a big way. The missile-armed attack helicopter is a powerful platform for interdiction and close contact support.

Much more capable air and space platforms greatly support the Intelligence, Surveillance and Reconnaissance (ISR) functions, and enhance command and control functions. Space is a great enabler for all networked operations, and for targeting. The capability to hit maritime targets at very long range in some ways gives an advantage to shore-based aircraft. Strategic air mobility not only gives global reach but can quickly mobalise forces across theatres. They are also a great national asset for Humanitarian Assistance and Disaster Relief (HADR). Clearly there still is some level of conventional war under the nuclear overhang, as has been seen in operations in Kargil, Balakot and also the showdown in Galwan.

This book is aimed at putting the air operations of the 1971 Indo-Pak War in the correct perspective, and to record the events as they happened. It explores the myriad dimensions of air operations in a war that created both history and geography. It highlights some outstanding examples of jointmanship. The book should make interesting reading for practitioners of air power, students and researchers of military aviation history, and for strategist and policy-makers.

Air Marshal **Anil Chopra**

Acknowledgements

We would like to earnestly thank the Chief of the Air Staff, Air Chief Marshal Rakesh Kumar Singh Bhadauria, PVSM, AVSM, VM, ADC for his encouragement and support to initiate and execute this book project showcasing the air campaigns and commemorating 50 years of the India-Pakistan 1971 War. We are extremely grateful to all the contributors who not only agreed to our request to share their wisdom, knowledge and experience in a short period but also gave us very detailed and comprehensive chapters which have enriched the book tremendously. We wish to thank KW Publishers, Ms. Kalpana Shukla and her team for putting the book on priority and executing the project not only timely but also smoothly. We sincerely thank Ms. Rehana Mishra for her meticulous help in editing the book. The library staff of the Centre for Air Power Studies and our young scholars, Shantanu Roy-Chaudhury and Rushali Saha, have been very helpful in facilitating the research.

Air Mshl **Anil Chopra**
Dr **Shalini Chawla**

List of Abbreviations

Air Force Ranks

ACM	Air Chief Marshal
Air Mshl	Air Marshal
Air Vice Mshl	Air Vice Marshal
Air Cmde	Air Commodore
Gp Capt	Group Captain
Wg Cdr	Wing Commander
Sqn Ldr	Squadron Leader
Flt Lt	Flight Lieutenant
Fg Offr	Flying Officer
Plt Offr	Pilot Officer

Appointments

CAS	Chief of the Air Staff
VCAS	Vice Chief of the Air Staff
AOC-in-C	Air Officer Commanding-in-Chief
SASO	Senior Air Staff Officer
ACAS	Assistant Chief of the Air Staff
GOC	General Officer Commanding
AOC	Air Officer Commanding
CO	Commanding Officer

Commands

WAC	Western Air Command
EAC	Eastern Air Command

CAC	Central Air Command
TC	Training Command
MC	Maintenance Command

Awards

PVC	Param Vir Chakra
MVC	Maha Vir Chakra
VrC	Vir Chakra
AC	Ashok Chakra
KC	Kirti Chakra
SC	Shaurya Chakra
PVSM	Param Vishist Seva Medal
AVSM	Ati Vishist Seva Medal
VM	Vayu Sena Medal
DFC	Distinguished Flying Cross
VSM	Vishist Seva Medal
M-in-D	Mention in Dispatches

Miscellaneous

COSC	Chiefs of Staff Committee
IAF	Indian Air Force
RAF	Royal Air Force
PAF	Pakistan Air Force
HAL	Hindustan Aeronautics Limited
CAP	Combat Air Patrols
CFL	Cease Fire Line
TAC	Tactical Air Centre
FAC	Forward Air Controller
AEW&C	Airborne Early Warning and Control
AWACS	Airborne Warning and Control System
HADR	Humanitarian Assistance and Disaster Relief

1. ACM PC Lal: The Quiet Orchestrator: The Eagle's View

Anil Chopra

Pratap Chandra Lal, Padma Vibhushan, Padma Bhushan, Distinguished Flying Cross (DFC) was at the helm of the Indian Air Force (IAF) from July 16, 1969 to January 15, 1973, precisely three years, 184 days.[1] Earlier, he had been the Vice Chief of the IAF, directly running the operations in the 1965 Indo-Pakistan War. He not only oversaw the build-up to the 1971 Indo-Pakistan War, but also had time for reflection and to imbibe the lessons of the conflict. The professional standards, capability and flexibility of the much expanded IAF had been put to the acid test. It was the culmination of a long and distinguished career of an outstanding professional, an able leader, yet a very modest, unassuming, and gentle human being.

His book *My Years with the IAF*,[2] was the first time that an Air Chief had penned his life-time experiences and memoirs. It was in a way the story of the evolution and growth of the IAF. The book was forthrightly engaging, and perhaps a few who were on the hot seats then may have found the truth hard hitting.

Plt Offr PC Lal

Source: http://www.bharat-rakshak.com

A Comprehensive Professional Upbringing

To a great extent, leaders are shaped by their exposure and professional upbringing. Born in December 1916, in Ludhiana, PC Lal joined the IAF in 1939 when World War II had just begun, and served till his retirement as the Air Chief in 1973. Young Lal was keen on aviation, and was one of the youngest Indians to get the amateur pilot's licence in January 1934. By 1938, he had a diploma in journalism from King's College, London. By now, he had plans for full-time study of law in England. As the great war broke out in Europe, everyone in India with a pilot's licence was invited to join up. So Lal joined the IAF, and was commissioned in May 1940. Later, Sqn Ldr Lal was the Commanding Officer (CO) of No. 7 Squadron, from July 21, 1944, to September 18, 1945, operating from Peshawar/Imphal. He was awarded the DFC for flying reconnaissance sorties over the Irrawaddy plains in Burma (now Myanmar).[3]

In December 1946, Lal attended a senior commander's course in the UK. In May 1949, he attended the Royal Air Force (RAF) Staff College.

By mid-1950, he was an Air Commodore. Later, he was appointed Senior Air Staff Officer (SASO) of the No. 1 Operational Command (later Western Air Command), a post he held for three years. He was the military secretary to the Cabinet from 1953 to 1955. In October 1954, he led the evaluation team to select a new aircraft for the IAF, which led to the induction of the Folland Gnat, an aircraft that would later become a household name after the 1965 Indo-Pakistan War. Interestingly, he was the first Indian to fly supersonic (in a Mystere IVA) and to fly the Gnat. Later, he took over as the Air Officer Commanding (AOC) Training Command in Bangalore. In 1957, Lal was appointed general manager of the Indian Airlines Corporation (IAC), a post he held for six years. During this period, he served as a member of the Board of Directors of both IAC and Air India. He drove the modernisation of the fleet and ensured profitability.

He had differences with the then Defence Minister VK Krishna Menon over what aircraft must replace the airlines' aging Dakotas. Lal had suggested that India send a dozen accomplished technical officers and technically enabled pilots to the Massachusetts Institute of Technology (MIT), California Institute of Technology (CALTECH) or Stanford University to do their Masters/PhD in aeronautical engineering so that they could spearhead India's military aviation programme in the years ahead. He had reprioritised the roles and missions of the IAF to support the higher directions for war, which looked at deterrence and protection of sovereignty as key drivers.[4] The highly abrasive, staunch socialist, Menon was not amused by the idea. When Lal's tenure in IAC finished on September 30, 1962, Krishna Menon arranged to have him retired from the IAF. Prime Minister Jawaharlal Nehru offered him a job in a public sector steel mill but Lal refused. On September 30, 1962, he left the Service. Immediately after the 1962 China debacle, Krishna Menon was forced to resign, and in December 1962, PC Lal's was reinstated and posted as Air Officer Maintenance in the rank of Air Vice Marshal. On November 24, 1963, he was posted as Air Officer Commanding-in-Chief (AOC-in-C) Western Air Command. And on October 1, 1964, he became the Vice Chief of the Air Staff (VCAS), and oversaw the operations in the 1965 War. For his contributions during the War, Lal was awarded the Padma Bhushan. Later, he was promoted to Air Marshal. In September 1966, Lal took over as the Managing Director of Hindustan Aeronautics Limited (HAL), a post he held till July 1969. He brought about a lot of innovations at HAL, including improved productivity. During his tenure, HAL began the production of the MiG-21 and Gnat fighters, and the HS 748.

Lal became the seventh Chief of the Air Staff (CAS) on July 16, 1969. With an outstanding exposure of combat flying, activities related to aircraft production and maintenance, his contribution to India's aviation industry as the head of IAC and HAL, was most significant. And being at the operational helm during the 1965 and 1971 wars says it all.

The 1965 Indo-Pak War and Lessons for the IAF

During the Indo-Pakistan War of 1965, Lal was the VCAS. In his book, *My Years with the IAF*, Lal recounts how he looked at the build-up to the 1965 War. On October 27, 1958, Ayub Khan had taken over through a military coup. He ran a "Crush India" campaign, and began building an international Muslim block. He courted the USA in 1961, and said, "The only people who would stand by you against Communism are the people of Pakistan". Just four years later, in March 1965, he was singing a different tune in front of the Chinese, "Pakistan and China are united by a common determination to eradicate the last vestiges of imperialism in all its forms."

The military assistance to India from the UK and USA after the 1962 War was limited to a few non-lethal items such as spares for transport aircraft and communication equipment. Meanwhile, Pakistan had got the top end, F-86 Sabres and F-104. India had just got about 12 MiG-21s, and mostly had Mysteres, Hunters and Gnats. So the technical superiority of the Pakistan Air Force (PAF) had somewhat neutralised India's numerical superiority.

Despite an agreement signed after the showdown in the Rann of Kutch, by mid-May, the Pakistan Army had occupied some of the heights overlooking the Srinagar-Kargil-Leh highway. India fought hard and seized some Pakistani posts, but barely a month later, these were handed back, after the signing of a ceasefire agreement. Lal linked such hand back of Indian gains after the 1965 War and also the 1971 War to a lack of Indian strategic firmness and excessive use of "good faith".

In early-August, the Pakistan Army personnel, dressed as Kashmiri locals, crossed the Cease Fire Line (CFL) as a prelude to Operation Grand Slam. The Indian forces crossed the CFL on August 15. On September 1, the Pakistan Army launched a counter-attack "Operation Grand Slam" and struck in force in Chhamb, the most vulnerable area for India. The IAF had been kept informed and was ready. On September 1, the IAF was given the go-ahead by the government. The IAF used the Vampires and Mysteres to attack the Pakistan Army. The Gnats provided cover for the strikes, and early successes against the Sabres in air combat greatly increased the IAF's confidence. The Pakistan Army was already near Akhnoor, and any further advance would have threatened the road to Kashmir. On September 6, India launched a massive ground offensive, opening three fronts in the Punjab sector, and made major gains in the Sialkot and Lahore sectors. A major tank battle was fought at Khemkaran.

The PAF launched a massive attack on IAF air bases in the Western Sector at 5 pm on September 6, destroying some MiGs and Mysteres on the ground. On September 7 morning, at first light, the IAF made a retaliatory strike on most major PAF air bases. Without going into further operational details, suffice to say that though India's gains in the few days' fighting may not have been spectacular, but Pakistan started running out of supplies by the end of the first week. Ayub Khan was a worried man. India's and Pakistan's concepts of defence and offence were different. Pakistan kept its armed forces' strongholds well away from the border. The IAF had to thus strike deep. The PAF had acquired powerful radars and concentrated more on air defence assets while India believed that offence was the best form of defence.

The IAF could not efficiently deliver close air support to the Indian Army primarily because of antiquated air support demand procedures. In fact, the 1965 War demonstrated the deficiencies of the Indian Army-IAF link-up at virtually all levels of command and control. Clearly inter-services cooperation needed to be cultivated throughout the personnel's career, and its importance cannot be overemphasised. Also, the IAF needed an integrated air defence system of anti-aircraft guns, surface-to-air missiles and radars.

The IAF also felt the serious shortcoming of operational air bases in the Rajasthan sector. After the war, the Air Force Academy at Jodhpur was moved out and airfields built at Barmer (Uttarlai) and Jaisalmer. Lal felt that the lack of a joint naval-air plan[5] was a serious deficiency. The Pakistan Navy could bombard the Indian naval base in Saurashtra under the very nose of the IAF base in Jamnagar. This was prevented in 1971 through better joint planning and coordination.

A major lesson for protection of aircraft on the ground was learnt when the PAF attacked the IAF bases at Pathankot and Kharagpur. Many aircraft were destroyed on the ground. Hardened aircraft shelters were then built, and the IAF was better placed in 1971.

After the war, on January 15, 1966, the post of CAS was upgraded to the rank of Air Chief Marshal and that of the VCAS to the rank of Air Marshal. Lal was the first VCAS to hold the rank.

ACM PC Lal

Source: http://www.bharat-rakshak.com

Initial Years as the Air Chief

As the Air Chief, Lal began building and preparing the IAF for better war-fighting capability. He reorganised various aspects of the IAF's training and logistics. He also visited many Army formations to clearly understand the needs of air support at different levels. He improved tactics, training and careful planning, and all these contributed in making the IAF one of Asia's most effective air arms. His efforts did not go unrewarded.

The Three Chiefs and President V.V. Giri

Source: Ministry of Defence, Photo Division.

Higher Command Structure Till 1971

Lal was appreciative of the general higher command structure that evolved after independence. Under the civil control, the three Services had equal responsibility for the defence of the country. The Chiefs were directly responsible for the operational employment of their Service. The equality and interdependence of the Services at the highest level were fundamental for cohesive and optimum operational working. Lal was appreciative that the IAF had played a stellar role in saving Jammu and Kashmir (J&K) in 1947-48, with close and effective collaboration with the Indian Army. The same was not true of the 1962 War. The overconfident Defence Minister Krishna Menon had taken over many functions, including the prosecution of the Army's war, and the Chiefs of Staff Committee (COSC) had ceased to function. When it came to the fight, it was as if the combat elements of the IAF did not exist. Whether or not the IAF would have turned the tide of the war is difficult to say, but it would have made a difference, Lal felt. The Air Chief, Air Mshl A.M. Engineer was a frustrated man. The IAF had only 15 squadrons in 1959. Its approved strength after the 1962 War was 45, writes Lal.

Things had not changed much in 1965. Lal mentions that the Chhad Bet incident of December 1964 had given enough indications to the Army Chief Gen Chaudhuri, and by May 1965, the larger intentions of Pakistan to seize Kashmir were clear. Gen Chaudhuri had discussed the ground situation with the political leadership, and necessary sanctions and approvals were taken. All this was revealed by Gen Chaudhuri during a National Security Lecture he delivered at the United Services Institution (USI) in January 1971.[6] The Air Chief was kept informed through informal meetings. The Naval Chief was not kept in the loop. The Navy's role was not expected to be a very big one.[7] In the guise of security, the Army Chief applied the "need to know" principle to such an extent that even the COSC and the joint intelligence and planning staff were not kept in the picture. Therefore, joint contingency plans were not made, and the three Services were never clearly asked to plan for war. From the General's own statements, it comes out clearly that he treated it as the business of the Army alone, and the Air Force was a passive spectator and Navy out of it all together. When the Pakistani troops and tanks came into Chhamb, he burst into the Defence Minister's office, where the then Air Chief was discussing modernisation plans, and sought air support for his beleaguered forces. Things changed thereafter, and the three Services were activated and worked together. Howsoever able a commander he may have been, as Gen Chaudhuri clearly was, no Service can fight a war alone.

All planning must be done at the COSC level. Contingency plans must be developed together. Otherwise all three will suffer in war, and the Army more so. In all fairness, despite the failures in points of detail, the Indian armed forces succeeded in foiling the Pakistani plans and restored the morale that had been battered by the 1962 China debacle.

Planning for 1971 Operations

Lal felt that the armed forces were blessed to have two outstanding leaders, Prime Minister (PM) Indira Gandhi and Defence Minister Jagjivan Ram. Prime Minister Indira Gandhi[8] "had the ability to understand complex situations, identify major problems, and define clear cut lines of action";[9] Defence Minister Jagjivan Ram, who was cool, unflustered, quick-witted, cheerful, and did not talk down to people. Ram had complete confidence in the Service chiefs and the secretaries. The period between March and December 1971 was well spent in good coordination among the three Services and the Ministry of Defence.

ACM PC Lal Shaking Hands with PM Indira Gandhi, as Gen Manekshaw and Adm Nanda Look on

Source: Indian Air Force.

While one is used to the Staff College exercises like appreciation of war-like situations, in reality there are more imponderables. The build-up in the East was being well reported even by foreign journalists. There were adequate intelligence inputs. Pakistan's confidence to threaten India was bolstered by support from the US and China. The US was too busy in its rapprochement with China. The Soviet Union that had arranged the Tashkent Accord after the 1965 War, had offered a Treaty of Friendship, like that with India, to Pakistan also. Their condition was for Pakistan to leave the Southeast Asia Treaty Organisation (SEATO), and Central Treaty Organisation (CENTO), an offer that Pakistan rejected. That Yahya Khan would open the action in the West was known early enough. The timing was unclear but it was understood that it would be after the monsoon and before the winter. The Indian Army began preparing plans at Army Headquarters level in consultation with the lower formations. The IAF plans were initially meant for the counter-air operations and plans with Army and Navy were to evolve once they had finalised theirs. Unlike the Army, the Navy exercises much more flexibility and mobility. The support to the Navy, out at sea, those days was limited. Joint planning among the three had its own complexities because each Service had different types of operations. Air Force operating environments are more stable.

The objectives defined by the COSC were to gain as much ground in the East as possible, and create conditions for the early establishment of the possible state of Bangladesh. In the West, the target was to prevent the Pakistani forces from making any gains. The war would be short because the UN Security Council was expected to intervene. Operations would have to be executed quickly. Territorial gains in the West would have to be handed back. The kind of collapse that actually happened in East Pakistan was not anticipated. The Indian Navy was doing its first operation. It decided to deploy in an offensive role, attacking Karachi in the West and using the aircraft carrier *Vikrant* in the East.[10]

The IAF's support to the Army and Navy was decided by the IAF itself. The prioritisation was air defence of the homeland first, support to the Army, followed by the Navy next, counter-air bombing third, and para-drops, etc. came thereafter. Commands could change priorities for short periods. While the Western Air Command (WAC) and Eastern Air Command (EAC) looked after their sectors, the Central Air Command (CAC) was tasked for all bombing, transport and support to the Navy. This redefining of duties proved good in the war. The air stations in West Bengal were also put under the EAC, and made it easier to coordinate with the Army. The Advanced HQ with each Army Command were strengthened, down to Tactical Air Centre (TAC) and Forward Air Controller (FAC) level.

War in East Pakistan

In March 1971, East Pakistan (now Bangladesh) declared independence from Pakistan, starting the Bangladesh Liberation War. The Pakistan Army unleashed brutal suppression in an effort to curb the Bengali nationalist movement through "Operation Searchlight." India continued to tacitly aid and prepare the Mukti Bahini. The Pakistan Army kept attacking the Mukti Bahini more viciously. The Indo-Soviet Treaty of Peace, Friendship and Cooperation was signed in August 1971. This twenty-year treaty was meant to neutralise possible Chinese and US support to Pakistan in the case of war. Pakistan had by now, realised that Indian armed intervention in East Pakistan was imminent. By October 1971, the India supported Mukti Bahini was repeatedly attacking East Pakistani military establishments. It was a state of active undeclared war. By November, both sides were known to be violating each other's air space. However, the first real aerial combat between the two Air Forces took place on November 22, nearly 12 days before the actual commencement of the war. Regular Indian Army troops engaged and mauled the Pakistani armour at Garibpur. At 1449 hrs, four Pakistani Sabres[11] attacked Indian and Mukti Bahini forces in the Chowgacha Mor area. Four IAF Gnats of No. 22 Squadron which were operating at Dum Dum airport, Calcutta, were launched. They reached the area of action when the PAF was carrying out the third strafing run. In the air combat that followed, three Sabres were shot down. All the Gnats returned safely. The first round in this air battle over Boyra had clearly gone in favour of the IAF. It was a fair duel, 4 vs. 4. To guard against retaliation, the sector director mounted Combat Air Patrols (CAPs) over many airfields in the area. While it greatly raised the Indian morale, the PAF was not deterred by the loss, and came with vengeance the next morning to attack Indian ground positions. By the time the MiGs scrambled and reached, they had gone back. After this incident, the Pakistani President declared a national emergency on November 23, 1971. He announced that "Pakistan would be at war with India in the next 10 days".[12] It actually happened that way.

The war record of the Kalaikunda based No. 22 Squadron was excellent: 100 per cent serviceability; and all 12 aircraft flew every day during the war, a total of over 250 missions. Other Gnat squadrons also did well. Gnats were also used for strikes against river boats and some other small targets.

The Air Defence Direction Centres (ADDCs) did a great job during the war. The sector directors those days were Flying Officers and Flight Lieutenants. They did a great job, taking timely decisions to identify the threat and scramble. They worked closely with the Army artillery, and no friendly aircraft was ever shot. They handled some classic interceptions.

Many encounters took place across the air space in the next 10 days before the war began on December 3. Air HQ kept the EAC updated on the evolving war plans. Strategic targets were updated in the last 24 hours. The IAF radar cover in the East was good. So was that of the PAF. Every IAF raid was, therefore, anticipated by the PAF.

The IAF fighters achieved early air superiority in the East, and the innovative and considerably accurate MiG-21 strikes on Kurmitola and Tejgaon runways near Dhaka comprised the final nail in the Pakistani coffin. The IAF's air superiority gave freedom for action to both the Army and Navy.

The Hunter aircraft did very well in the East. "Hunters don't need escorts, they fight their own battles,"[13] said Wg Cdr Chatrath, then commanding No. 17 Squadron. No. 37 Squadron under Supy Kaul was the other squadron in Hashimara. No. 14 Squadron under Sunderesan was in Kalaikunda. They had the range to fly from Hashimara and strike Dhaka. They successfully engaged the Sabres. Of course, we lost some Hunters.

The MiG-21s also did a great job. No. 28 Squadron under Wg Cdr Bishnoi operated from Guwahati. His squadron boys flew 2-3 sorties every day throughout the war, logging 320 strike missions. They repeatedly struck Tejgaon. No. 4 Squadron also took part in many bombing missions. The Russian Embassy staff in Dhaka were most impressed with the accuracy of the MiG strikes, all done without computerised gunsight, by just "two Indian eyes in an Indian skull."

Joint Operations in the East

There were many outstanding examples of air support. The IAF worked very closely with the Indian Army's II and IV Corps. No demands were turned down ever. Nearly 60 per cent of the air effort was allotted to the Army. IV Corps under Lt. Gen. Sagat Singh became a highly mobile strike force.[14] Their mobility was to a large extent due to very intelligent and bold use of IAF helicopters. It was a great example of jointmanship, and contributed a great deal to the collapse of East Pakistan. The credit for the airlift of IV Corps must go entirely to the EAC and not to the Air HQ or the Army. Stn Cdr Chandan Singh at Jorhat was a very good organiser, with plenty of initiative and drive. The EAC sent him to interact with IV Corps for a few days. IV Corps was supported by the two MiG squadrons at Guwahati and Hunters at Kumbhigram. There were 409 offensive support missions. All were supported by the ground FAC. Initially, it was hoped that naval aircraft from the *Vikrant* would support the Army in the Southern areas, but the same was not possible because the naval pilots were not trained for such a role, the Navy said. Therefore, the extra load on Kumbhigram.

After the fall of Jessore, the only obstacle in the race to Dhaka was the Brahmaputra river. No. 2 Para was selected for a possible air-drop at Tangail on December 11, at 1600 hrs. Tangail had the advantage of a friendly population. It was on the road from Jamalpur to Dhaka and would help intercept the retreating Pakistani forces who would go back to strengthen Dhaka. Evening, and not night was chosen because the PAF had nearly ceased to exist. A force of 50 transport aircraft (22 Dakotas, 22 Packets, six An-12s, and two Caribous) was marshalled. The Gnats gave the fighter escort. Only one An-12 was hit and damaged by ground fire.

The cooperation between IV Corps and the IAF was exemplary and a highlight of the war. It greatly helped that the General Officer Commanding (GOC) of the Corps was himself a paratrooper, and had lived and operated with the IAF for long. The cooperation with the Navy could and should have been better. When a United Nations C-130 aircraft was flying into Dhaka, the IAF had transferred flight details to the Navy, yet Sea Hawks from the *Vikrant* attacked and fired on it. Providentially, they missed. It could have been most embarrassing.

Gen Sagat's Valid Observations[15]

Gen Sagat Singh made two valid points about air support: first, the Army's training doesn't sufficiently factor in air support – it is to be treated as a bonus. The two must train together much more to understand each other's strengths and limitations to be able to exploit to advantage. Second, he felt that the IAF did not give importance while posting TAC commanders. They should be qualified on the type of aircraft that are likely to be used in close support so that the Army feels more confidence in their advice.

Operation Chengiz Khan: PAF's Preemptive Strikes

With a losing battle in the East, President and Martial Law Administrator Yahya Khan chose to try to protect Pakistan's integrity using Ayub Khan's strategy: "The defence of East Pakistan lies in the West". He said this was to be the "final war". The Pakistan Army had created a myth of invincibility, and propagated obsessive hostility towards India, with total disregard for the ground reality. It was unfortunate for them, and the country that the masses believed their propaganda.

Pakistan Army Chief Gen Tikka Khan had masterminded the offensive against India, and expected the PAF to create a local, limited period air dominance. As a part of the grand design, the PAF launched preemptive strikes on the IAF forward air bases, radar installations, railway stations, Indian armour concentrations, and some other targets on the evening of December 3, 1971. Codenamed "Operation Chengiz Khan", the air strikes began the war in the West. In addition to the 11 forward airfields, the Pakistan Army carried out artillery strikes on Indian positions in Kashmir. In doing so, the PAF was trying to ape the Israeli Air Force "Operation Focus" launched during the Six-Day War of 1967. Friday, the day of the *jumu'ah* (Muslim Sabbath), was chosen for achieving deception, and the time of 1745 h was chosen to coincide with the IAF's radar shift timing.

The Indian air defence radars failed to detect the approaching formations, and final confirmation came only after the air raid actually reached the airfields. The weapons used were unguided rockets and sticks of 125 kg bombs. The runways were the targets. These missions were opposed only by anti-aircraft guns, and no aircraft were scrambled. The Pakistan Army began shelling the Indian Army positions in Jammu and Poonch area immediately thereafter. Having learnt its lessons from a similar air strike in the 1965 War, India had secured it aircraft and air base assets. The PAF had reportedly dropped 183 bombs over 12 target runways. The damage was minor and all the airfields were back to full action within hours.

IAF Strikes Back in the West

The IAF struck back that night. The Canberras flew 23 sorties, and bombed eight West Pakistan air bases, inflicting heavy damage to Sargodha and Masroor air bases. The IAF also attacked the main East Pakistani airfields of Tejgaon, and Kurmitola. Within days, India was able to achieve air superiority.

The CAS was asked by many as to why the IAF took over six hours to hit back, more so when the Indian government had already authorised the COSC as early as October to take proactive action if Pakistani forces crossed Indian territory. The IAF had to strike with Canberra bombers. Unlike the fighters on the Operational Readiness

Platform (ORP), these had to be loaded with bombs. In the East, Tejgaon and Chittagong were bombed that night. Mrs Gandhi returned from Calcutta that evening, and the Defence Minister from Patna. The Cabinet met at 21:30 h and the Chiefs briefed them. They were very satisfied with the response.

The fortnight-long war ended with an unconditional surrender by Pakistan in the East and in the creation of Bangladesh. More than 90,000 Pakistani soldiers were taken prisoner. Pakistan suffered 6,000 casualties against India's 2,000. The IAF finally flew nearly 4,000 sorties in the Western Sector, and nearly 2,000 sorties in the East, averaging nearly 450 sorties per day. The IAF lost 42 aircraft, but in the process, shot down 86 PAF aircraft. The IAF maintained aircraft and systems serviceability in excess of 80 per cent.

Concentration was on interdiction missions, to disrupt Pakistani communications, and destroy logistics nodes and fuel and ammunition dumps. It was also to target the Pakistan Army ground force bridgeheads and concentrations to thwart any offensive action. On the Eastern Front, in addition to keeping the PAF grounded, the IAF supported the rapid advances of the Indian Army, through vertical envelopment. The IAF also bombed the retreating Pakistan Army. In a very important air action in the Western desert, four Hunters of the Operational Conversion Unit (OCU),[16] operating from Jaisalmer air base, destroyed an entire Pakistani armoured regiment at Longewala, thus, stopping a major armour thrust into the desert.

Since the IAF was flying much larger offensive missions, and the PAF was mostly on the defensive, the IAF was bound to suffer some losses. Most of the IAF losses during the war were from the intense anti-aircraft fire. The IAF came out a clear winner in aerial combat. The Gnats had made a great beginning in the East, and the MiG-21s, and other fleets took action to the Pakistani hinterland. Three MiG-21 squadrons operated from Guwahati and Tezpur. They flew counter-air, escort and close air support missions. The MiG-21s were very successful in 500 kg steep glide bombing attacks on Tejgaon and Kurmitola air bases. They also made effective use of 57 mm rockets against military installations and also command centres in the capital Dhaka.

In the West, the MiG-21s primarily flew air defence escort and interception missions. They mounted combat air patrols all across the Western border, defending Vital Points (VP) and Vital Areas (VA). They were on operational readiness missions to intercept intruding PAF aircraft. They escorted bombing and strike missions. The MiG-21 got a chance for the first time to engage its famous old opponent, the F- 104 Starfighter, in air combat. In all four recorded dogfights, the IAF MiG-21s outclassed them.

The December 1971 War also meant the gaining of India's highest award for gallantry to the IAF. Fg Offr Nirmal Jit Singh Sekhon, flying Gnats with No. 18 Squadron from Srinagar, was posthumously awarded the Param Vir Chakra.[17] Notwithstanding the successful historic campaign of December 1971, the IAF had its own lessons to learn. These lessons would later support further refinements.

The Major Air Strikes in the West

The IAF attacked deep inside Pakistan's territory. The targets were the airfields, Karachi harbour, Sui gas plant, Attock oil refinery and Mangla hydroelectric power plant. It made a serious dent in Pakistani oil supplies. While the basic target for air operations is air superiority, the kind that was achieved in the East is rare. Mostly, you have to fight for it throughout the war. The fact that the PAF could not interfere with our surface ground operations in both sectors was evidence that the IAF enjoyed clear superiority. All imports to Pakistan came in from Karachi. The road-rail network in West Pakistan, unlike in India, runs in a narrow corridor parallel to the border and is, therefore, much easier to attack. The granary and major military installations are in the Punjab area. Supplies from the newly opened Chinese Silk Road were still far and few. Attacking the lines of communication, thus, would pay dividends. To make a similar dent, the PAF would have to travel much deeper into India.

Great Operations by Canberra Fleet[18]

The Canberras were at Gorakhpur, Agra and Pune. The bombing targets were decided at Air HQ. The plans were then passed to the CAC. Gp Capt PP Singh (Canberra MVC 1965) was the Air 1. The Canberras were used for bombing from the first night itself, and bombed in every sector of Pakistan. The bombing attack over Karachi on December 9 was coordinated with the Navy's attack on the harbour. Four Canberras each attacked the oil installations and Karachi airfield. While the Navy claimed to have set Karachi on fire, it was actually the Canberras that launched the first attacks on the oil storage in the harbour. Since the CAC had never tasked attacks on the oil installations and these targets were decided by the squadron, this issue remained contentious for times to come. Clearly the attacks on the oil installations gave a big hit to the morale of the Pakistanis. The Canberras of No. 106 Squadron were engaged in strategic reconnaissance. The famous pictures of the criss-cross of Pakistani tank tracks in Logewala comprised the photographic evidence of the desperation of Pakistani tanks trying to escape the Hunters firing at them. The Canberras also carried out reconnaissance missions at Karachi and over Dhaka among many others.

An-12 as a Bomber[19]

On the night of December 3, six An-12s armed with 12 × 500 lb bombs each, including some napalm containers took off to target the Changa Manga forest, which had a massive Petroleum, Oil, Lubricants (POL) dump, with midnight Time-Over-Target (TOT). In the valleys in Poonch area, even the Vampires were too fast to spot any targets. No. 123 Squadron had four Harvard aircraft and six pilots, and were used more effectively. However, using the An-12 as bombers on December 6 was most effective. They took off from home base Bareilly, flying in the moonlight via the Rohtang Pass and Srinagar. They dropped 40 tonnes of old 500 lb bombs over artillery positions near Kahuta. Forty per cent proved duds. In the Poonch area, they caused landslides and virtually ended the battle of Poonch. Two Mirages tried to chase them, but all six returned safely. Later, they flew bombing missions to attack

18 Division HQ at Fort Abbas, and Bahawalpur. They also bombed the Sui gas plant. The bombing of Skardu by An-12s on the last day of war was staged from Chandigarh. Out of the 36 bombs dropped on Skardu, 28 fell on the runway.[20] This was shallow glide bombing from 170 ft above the ground. The accuracy was testified by the Canberra aircraft that followed. All An-12 missions were at ultra-low level and the bombs were dropped in low-level run.

Close Cooperation with Indian Army at Operation Level in the West

For his part, Lal ensured close cooperation between the IAF and the Indian Army. Collocating the IAF Command's Advance HQ, under an Air Commodore, with their respective Army Commands, Tactical Air Centre (TAC), at Corps HQ level, and in the field, FACs directed air strikes called out in support of the Army.

The IAF's immediate air support from Jaisalmer to the Coy Cdr Maj Chandpuri who was understaffed and overwhelmed by the Pakistani tank regiment attack at Longewala, was a classic case of air support. IAF Hunter aircraft destroyed nearly 40 tanks. The Pakistani threat in the region was thus neutralised. Wg Cdr Bawa sent a message to the TAC Commander at Jodhpur: "Not being utilised fully. Request more utilisation". As Gen Fazal Muqeem Khan said: "Mercifully, the Indians did not pursue".[21]

Another factor that played a decisive part was the IAF's support to the Army in Chhamb. The Indian Army had changed its war plan in the region in the last few days prior to the war. 191 Brigade, which was West of Munawar Tawi river, was being continuously attacked by the Pakistanis. The IAF's support was sought. The battle was too close and there was a high risk of attacking our own troops. The IAF had the capacity to provide 45 Close Air Support (CAS) sorties a day. Initially, the demands from the Army were much less at between 20 and 30 sorties because of the changes in the Army's plans. Later, the demands increased. It was decided to attack behind the Pakistani lines to stop support and reinforcements. The front in Chhamb was just 10 miles long. Not more than two fighters could be employed at any given time. The Army initially tried to blame the loss of ground to lack of air support, knowing fully well that it had not asked for more. The moral of the story was that some Army Commanders used the IAF as a whipping boy for their own failures. Wherever they achieved success, the IAF was just a bonus.

In Shakargarh area, the targets given by the Army were not so clear. It wanted the IAF to bomb the minefields. It was done. All close air support effort was provided. The tonnage of bombs delivered was high, but whether they were effective was not very clear. The Pakistani camouflage was good, and the armour was not visible. Our attacks were based on area identification.

The Indian Army's XI Corps was mostly holding in the defensive. The Pakistan Army had planned a massive armour thrust in the Fazilka and Suleimanke headwork areas. The Indian defences were overwhelmed by the Pakistani forces. The IAF stepped in. Over 300 sorties were flown by day. The IAF targeted Pakistani armour, fuel and ammunition dumps, and communication lines in Fort Abbas, Bhawalnagar and Haveli general area.[22] The Mysteres destroyed a train carrying 50 tanks between Okara and Montgomery. The area was also struck by the Sukhois. The Canberras and An-12s did night bombing for three successive nights in the Changa Manga forest area. All these sorties were pre-planned and there was little immediate support sought. The IAF had great success in interdiction. It intercepted many train loads of tanks, and other critical war supplies in the Western Sector to immobilise the Pakistan Army by isolating the battlefields. Clearly, the IAF made the difference.

The two factors that won us the war were the efficiency of each Service in its core competency and cooperation among the Services at operational level.

Army's Air Support Demands

The tendency was for the Army to ask for sorties by numbers. The IAF insisted that the Army define the task. The Army tasks came by Wireless/Telephony (W/T) and book cyphers were cumbersome and time-consuming. This system carried on for some more years after the War.

Lack of Adequate Intelligence

Both the Army and IAF found the intelligence about Pakistani forces lacking. The Indian armed forces fought the Pakistanis with little idea of the force levels and capability pitted against them. Inputs from civil intelligence agencies had little military value. This was a weak area requiring addressing.

Despite many photo-reconnaissance missions, the post mission processing was very slow. The films were developed manually at the station level, interpretation was at Air HQ, with assessment then sent to Army HQ. The process was slow. Not much immediately relevant information could flow to the Army either.

Innovative Ideas

Gp Capt Gole[23] had been commanding Halwara for long before the war. To camouflage his airfield, he started growing wheat within the station right up to the runway dumbbells. This worked well to merge the area with the Punjab fields. Gole's emphasis was on low-level air defence. Halwara had mastered the Base Air Defence Concept (BADC). He evolved a very interesting system of mobile observation posts. There were similar individual initiatives by some other field commanders.

Need for South-Western Air Command

The area of responsibility of Western Air Command was rather large. He had to deal with two Army Commanders, Western and Southern. An The Air Officer Commanding (AOC) Rajasthan was thus appointed to be at Jaipur, co-located with the Advance HQ of Southern Command. He looked after the Gujarat and Rajasthan sectors. The Air Officer Commanding-in-Chief (AOC-in-C) WAC remained responsible for the entire Western border. Learning from the 1965 War, it was clear that there was a need for a South-Western Air Command (SWAC). The plan was prepared but shelved in 1969, and finally, the SWAC came up only in 1980. Rajasthan had been strengthened as it was a weak sector with only Jodhpur as the training base. After the 1965 War, two more air bases at Jaisalmer and Uttarlai had come up. They had no Radio/Telephony (R/T) equipment even for flying control. Each Care and Maintenance Unit (C&MU) had just a jeep and a 3-tonner. The water supply was 15 km away. Both these bases did not have many facilities to fight a war early in 1971. By end August 1971, the facilities started coming up. In September, Wg Cdr Bawa was made Station Commander Jaisalmer. In October, two Hunters were moved from Jamnagar, and later four more in November.

On December 5 and 6, Jaisalmer earned its laurels in Longewala. The Army's 12th Division did little but got many awards for Longewala. The IAF and AOP pilots were also honoured with awards. The HF 24s were used both for counter-air missions and also air interdiction across Rajasthan sector. The HF 24s also got air-to-air kills.

Uttarlai had even less resources. The runway was repeatedly bombed by day and at night by the PAF for three days. The base did a great job clearing the runway and getting back on operations. The HF 24s, Gnats and later MiGs operated from there. The MiGs in Uttarlai shot down two Starfighters using K-13 missiles.

The Kanbi Patels of Bhuj area were a great help in garnering labour at short notice. Men and women worked long hours day and night and then refused to take payment for the labour. This was their way of contributing to the cause of the war.

Reluctance to Share Army Plans at Headquarters Level

Army HQ was most reluctant to discuss its plans in detail with Air HQ, before or during the war. While the broad scope of the defensive operations was briefed, the contingency plans in the case of either offensive or reverses were never shared. This was a failing at the Chiefs of Staff Committee level.

Summary of Air Effort: 1971 War[24]

The IAF flew 7,346 sorties in the 14 days: averaging more than 500 a day. Some 5,400 were combat missions. The Gnats flew the most sorties at 1,275,[25] followed by the MiG-21s, Canberras, Sukhois, Hunters and Mysteres. As per the government press release on December 17, the IAF lost 42 aircraft, against the PAF's 86. A large percentage of IAF aircraft on strike missions were damaged by ground fire.[26] Many were hit by own bomb debris. In the East, every airfield was attacked by the IAF. In the Western Sector, all major airfields were attacked, many repeatedly. Around 50 Pakistani trains were destroyed through air interdiction.

Unlike in 1965, the Pakistanis lacked aggression, and most attacks were inaccurate and seemed insufficiently planned. There was lack of determination, which reflected poorly on the morale and training. A lot of technicians were Bengalis and that brought in maintenance issues.

The IAF's main weak area was lack of low-level radar cover for both air defence and close support. Mobile observer posts were somewhat effective but their introduction was late. Photo recce was very important, but the image processing system was slow and needed an overhaul. Limiting pilots to two sorties in a day helped retain stamina and efficiency.

Unlike the Army which fights in groups, Air Force pilots have to go deep and they are on their own on most missions. To hit the target, pilots fly low and closer to the target. This requires a special kind of temperament and summoning up of the innermost reserves of courage and fortitude. The strike and bomber pilot often would not know the results of his mission, unlike the air combat pilot who can see his target going down or being hit himself.

The War in the East was a classic example of inter-Services cooperation and the importance of this cannot be underscored. Inter-Service personal contacts and friendships work wonders, clearly bringing out the importance of the National Defence Academy and inter-service courses.

PC Lal initiated the case for the establishment of a specialist unit to develop new fighter tactics for both air combat and ground attack. His initiative led to the formation of the Tactics and Combat Development and Training Squadron at Adampur on February 1, 1971. It moved to Ambala in June 1971 and Jamnagar in 1973 and metamorphosed into the Tactics and Combat Development Establishment. He was a cerebral CAS who always had his eyes on the future.

Mrs Gandhi: Courageous and Graceful in Victory

Mrs Gandhi was courageous and cool in adversity, and very level-headed in her moment of triumph. Having achieved Pakistan's surrender in the East, she announced a unilateral ceasefire. She was astute in carrying the entire opposition and the country with her, Lal wrote. She wrote to the US President, "Indian soldiers had shed their blood to uphold the same values that the people of the United States cherished. It would have been far better for Pakistan to negotiate with one man 'Mujibur Rahman' than to wage a ruthless war against his own people". Twice US Ambassador to India, Chester Bowles, wrote in the *Washington Post*, January 30, 1972, that he believed that the "... naïve, weary and poorly informed (US) President was charmed off his feet by a succession of Pakistani Generals with British accents and taste for golf, polo and dry martinis."[27]

Dominance of the Largest Service: Army

The Indian Army being the largest Service always likes to take the credit for all successful operations, as was the case in Bangladesh. The Army Chief made public declarations, as if he and he alone had been responsible for the success of all the operations. Especially on December 14, he made a statement that if the Pakistanis did not surrender, he would unleash the IAF on them. Lal let this be, as being boisterous and a loose expression to intimidate the enemy. There appeared a general thought among the Indian Army that the IAF should be part of the Army, and the Navy reduced in size or liquidated. Maj Gen Habibullah made such a case in his book *The Sinews of Indian Defence*.[28] Ever since, the Army has been pushing the case of the Chief of Defence Staff (CDS). Even though, by chance, Manekshaw was the Chairman Chiefs of Staff Committee, he was just one among equals. In the COSC meetings, he was friendly and cooperative, but there too, he revealed much less information about the Army action, than he sought from the other two Services. He gave an impression that he was using the other two Services for his own personal ends rather than for a collaborative effort. The Naval

Chief Nanda and Lal did not want to make an issue at that sensitive time.[29] In public, he (Manekshaw) would seek personal glory and importance.

Right to left, Defence Minister Jagjivan Ram, Army Chief Gen Manekshaw, Naval Chief Adm Nanda and ACM PC Lal

Source: Indian Air Force

Case for CDS

On March 24, 1972, the Principal Secretary to the Prime Minister P.N. Haskar called Lal[30] who was visiting air bases in Assam, and asked for his views about appointing Gen Manekshaw as the CDS in recognition of the way he had directed the Bangladesh War. Lal wrote back his views, clearly stating that all the three Chiefs and each Service had contributed in its own way in the victory. Undoubtedly, the Army did a good job and Manekshaw as the Chairman Chiefs of Staff Committee did coordinate well, but there was no case for a CDS. In fact, there were risks of having an overbearing CDS who could run roughshod over the other Services. Also, if the Service Chief did not agree with the CDS, that Service would not push through the implementation of orders or would underperform. Therefore, all the Service Chiefs must function as equals. Manekshaw fully deserved the recognition of being made a Field Marshal, Lal said. Lal also felt that on points of inter-Service friction, the Chiefs must display greater understanding, tolerance and good faith.

Honour to Lead and Lead to Win

In the winter of 1971, PC Lal had the honour to lead the IAF in the war against Pakistan. The Air Force had a very significant role throughout the intense conflict that led to the creation of Bangladesh. For Lal, the 1971 War marked the pinnacle of his career. His able leadership was the architect of the IAF's most decisive victory. He had moulded a large and rapidly expanding IAF into an efficient fighting force.

For his services to the nation, and for his leadership of the IAF, Lal was awarded the Padma Vibhushan in January 1972. Lal retired from Service on January 16, 1973 after serving for over 33 years, as one of the IAF's most successful Chiefs and its most highly decorated officer. He handed over charge to ACM Om Prakash Mehra.

The Ford Car

A Ford car (1967 model) manufactured by M/s Ford of the USA was inducted[31] into the IAF for use by the Air Chief on July 30, 1969, by PC Lal. It was used by subsequent Chiefs till 1992. Air Chief Suri presented this car to the Air Force Museum on June 10, 1993.

Post-Retirement

In April 1973, Lal was appointed full-time Chairman and Managing Director (CMD) of the Indian Airlines Corporation (IAC). In August 1976, after falling out with Sanjay Gandhi, he was removed from the Chairmanship. With the change of government in March 1977, Lal was appointed part-time Chairman of Indian Airlines in July. He also served as the Chairman of the Indian Tube Company, a part of the Tata Group. In February 1978, Lal, was appointed Chairman of Air India also.

Leaves Behind a Great Legacy

Lal lived his life for the Service and the country. He played a commanding role in both of India's major wars with Pakistan, as the Vice Chief in 1965 War and as the Air Chief in 1971 War. His contribution in both the wars was most suitably acknowledged and awarded by the nation. When he retired from the Service, he received many touching messages. His favourite was the one from No. 33 Squadron, which read, "You made us touch the skies with glory and paint it with shades of red (Lal). The colours shall be fast forever. Our Pratap shall be our light in all weathers. Farewell, Sir."

Lal died of a heart attack while visiting London on August 13, 1982. His body was flown to India in an Air India flight. He was just 65, and still working on his memoirs and a history of the IAF. He was cremated with full military honours. Among the pall bearers were the former Chief ACM Arjan Singh and the serving Chief ACM Dilbagh Singh. His memoirs *My Years with the IAF*, was finally completed and published by his wife Mrs Ela Lal in 1986. It provides an eminently readable history of the IAF's first 25 years.

Notes

1. ACM Pratap Chandra Lal, http://www.bharat-rakshak.com/IAF/Database/1567. Accessed on May 11, 2021.
2. ACM PC Lal, ed., Ela Lal, *My Years with the IAF* (New Delhi, Lancer International, First Edition 1986), p. 7.
3. Pratap Chandra Lal Padma Vibhushan, Padma Bhushan, DFC, CAS, IAF, https://indianairforce.nic.in/content/pratap-chandra-lal-padam-vibhushan-padam-bhushan-dfc-cas. Accessed on May 13, 2021.
4. AVM Arjun Subramaniam (Retd), "Closing the Gap: A Doctrinal & Capability Appraisal of the IAF & the PLAAF," in Pushan Das and Harsh V. Pant, eds., *An Indian Military Transformation?* ch. 4. Orfonline, Book Defence Primer, https://www.orfonline.org/wp-content/uploads/2018/04/Defence_Primer_2018.pdf p. 37. Accessed on June 22, 2021.
5. Lal, n. 2, pp. 164-165.
6. National Security Lectures, USI 1973, p. 13.
7. Ibid., p. 44.
8. Lal, n. 2, ch. 11, p. 167.
9. Ibid., n. 2, ch. 11, pp. 166-167.
10. Ibid., n. 2, ch. 11, p. 173.

11. The War of December 1971, IAF, https://indianairforce.nic.in/content/1971-ops. Accessed on May 7, 2021.
12. Lal, n. 2, ch. 10, p. 154.
13. Ibid., ch. 12, p. 195.
14. Ibid., ch. 11, p. 177.
15. Ibid., ch. 12, p. 216.
16. Ibid., ch. 14, p. 280.
17. Ibid., ch. 12, p. 227.
18. Ibid., ch. 15, p. 295.
19. Ibid., ch. 15, p. 298.
20. Ibid., ch. 15, p. 303.
21. Gen Fazal Muqeem Khan, *Pakistan's Crisis in Leadership* (Islamabad: National Book Foundation, 1972), p. 212.
22. Pushpinder Singh, *Aircraft of Indian Air Force 1933–73* (New Delhi: English Book Store, 1974), p. 110.
23. Lal, n. 2, ch 12, p. 247.
24. Ibid., ch 16, p. 319.
25. Ibid., ch 16, p. 320.
26. Ibid., ch 16, p. 320.
27. Ibid., epilogue, p. 338.
28. Ibid., p. 325.
29. Ibid., p. 326.
30. Ibid.
31. Delhi Explorer, Facebook, https://www.facebook.com/445607022640891/photos/ford-saloon-car-iaf-1ford-car-1967-model-manufactured-by-ms-ford-of-usa-was-indu/493844781150448/. Accessed on May 10, 2021.

2. 'Squaring Off': The Balance of Forces and its Implications

Vikram Singh

The Pakistan Air Force (PAF) and Indian Air Force (IAF) can trace their lineage to shared history when an unpartitioned India raised an Indian Air Force, at Drigh Road, Karachi, in April 1933. Moving to the North-West Frontier on the Durand Line, the unofficial border between India, and the unsettled tribal territories along the Afghanistan border, the fledgling Air Force cut its teeth against the recalcitrant tribal warriors before being plunged into World War II in Burma. Fighting together, the IAF was home to the strong bonds and camaraderie that come from shared hardship and danger amongst its wildly varied demographics, only possible in India. Post war politics, and deliberate encouragement to divisiveness by the British caused the independence movement to split into a 'Muslim versus the rest' binary. Imagined fears and the rise of political Islam finally led to the demand for a separate land for Muslims. In their final act of poor sportsmanship, the British walked off the pitch with the wickets under their arms, as it were, shattering the dreams of an independent united India. Officers and airmen of the IAF were forced to choose between their faith and war-time brotherhood, loyalty, filiality and a shared history of eleven centuries. Most, of the Muslim faith, understandably chose to transfer to the new PAF, while aircraft and stores were supposed to be shared on a 80-20 per cent rule based on the communal ratios. With the start of the Cold War, Pakistan used its only currency, its strategic geographic location in Central Asia, to throw in its lot with the USA as a pivot against Soviet Russia. The PAF then began to transform from mainly British, to American equipment with large and rapid inflow of American military aid.

As the nation was partitioned into Pakistan and India, Pakistani regulars led *jihadi* tribal hordes in an invasion, hoping to turn their Muslim brethren in the state of Jammu and Kashmir (J&K). The IAF played a significant role, attacking these invaders and helped supply and lift sieges of small localities along the boundary and in the far-flung mountains of the Himalayas while the fledgling PAF played an inconsequential part. It was in the second Pakistani invasion of J&K in September 1965 that the PAF played an offensive role in the West and the East. Initially caught off guard, the IAF played with gloves-on as it assumed it was a limited battle for J&K alone. As the Pakistani plan to cut away J&K from India emerged, the IAF was finally allowed to take off its gloves and responded with resolve and ferocity. The war ended inconclusively for both sides but with the invader's aims emphatically blunted. The IAF, however, emerged somewhat discomfited with the large number of lessons it had to learn.

It was only after the 1965 War that the Government of India declared Pakistan as an enemy state, and serious and focussed preparations to fight Pakistan began. Already overburdened with the huge investments in infrastructure projects in the northeast, Sikkim and Eastern Ladakh after the Chinese debacle, India had chosen to employ Soviet arsenals with their friendly payment/barter terms. Both Pakistan and India had been embargoed by the US at the start of the September 1965 War and their rearmament now depended mainly on the Soviets for India, and the Chinese and French for Pakistan. While the Soviets provided 'civilian' Aeroflot Mi-8 helicopters and training for Pakistan Army officers in armoured warfare, China provided the Shenyang F-6 fighter and T-59 tanks apart from huge caches of small arms and ammunition. In 1967, the PAF received 24 Mirage IIIEP/D/R fighters and in 1970, they would place orders for another 30 Mirage VP fighters. A just-emerging underground market for American weapons, equipment overhaul and spares in the North Atlantic Treaty Organisation (NATO) nations and Iran, Turkey, Israel and Thailand, the seat of the Southeast Asia Treaty

Organisation (SEATO), managed to keep PAF equipment afloat to some extent. On the other hand, the only new additions to the IAF's inventory after the 1965 War were the MiG-21 FL and the Su-7 both of which would carry the day for the IAF.

In 1970, the IAF began looking for an aircraft that would replace the Canberra, Mystere-IVA and Hunter. ACM PC Lal would visit France, the USA and the UK to assess the F-4 Phantom, Jaguar and Mirage V and F-1. In May of 1971, an IAF team was invited to look at the Tupolev, TU-22 strategic bomber at Kubinka outside Moscow. Ultimately, it was seen as overkill and the proposal was not followed up and the Anglo-French Jaguar would enter service in late 1978.[1]

Helmsmen

The PAF received a new Commander-in-Chief (C-in-C), 44-year-old Air Mshl Abdur Rahim Khan on September 1, 1969. His predecessor, Air Mshl Malik Nur Khan, under whom he had served as the Deputy Chief of Staff during the 1965 War had moved as governor Punjab. Rahim had been commissioned in the undivided IAF in 1943 and had served under Sqn Ldr PC Lal flying Vengeances with No. 7 Squadron IAF in Burma. Rahim was married to an Indian princess of Rampur, was well read and well regarded.[2]

Just a month and a half earlier, the IAF had bid farewell to its beloved Chief of the Air Staff (CAS), 50-year-old ACM Arjan Singh (later Marshal of the Indian Air Force). He was replaced by 53-year-old Pratap Chandra Lal an old colleague from the IAF's fledgling years in Burma. Lal had served as the Vice-Chief during the 1965 War and then had been sent off to streamline the many projects at Hindustan Aeronautics Limited (HAL) – the MiG-21FL production line, Avro production, etc. – as Chairman and Managing Director HAL. He returned as the seventh CAS. Lal, like Arjan Singh was a highly regarded, professional man of great talent and drive. He had commanded his fighter squadron in the thick of battle in Burma. His being at the helm of the IAF, prior to, and during, the 1971 War was to have game changing effects in the way the air war was planned and executed.

ACM Arjan Singh, DFC (right) hands over to Air Mshl PC Lal, DFC, on July 16, 1969. Both wear their Padma Vibhushans earned for the 1965 War

Source: Arjan Singh Collection

Air Mshl Nur Khan (left) hands over the reins of the PAF to AVM Abdur Rahim Khan at a Mess function on September 1, 1969

Source: Author's Collection

IAF Early Warning Organisation

The Air Defence (AD) organisation also called the control and reporting organisation revolved around a set of hastily put together Observation Posts (OPs) deployed like a chain along the border as a basic warning of any aircraft crossing or returning to Pakistan. These posts were manned by raw, just-enrolled airmen recruits led by a pilot officer at each OP with rudimentary communications. Behind this chain were the early warning radars with an average of 45 km pick-up of low flying targets based at each of the forward airfields. Station masters of the Indian railways were also trained to report aerial activity over them as they had a better communication system than the IAF and were long deployed in a well oiled pre-Independence network that covered the whole of Punjab. The railway network did an excellent job of reporting these raids. In fact, the IAF was able to establish a pattern that if Gurdaspur railway station reported "sound heard", the raid would proceed to Pathankot and if Patti or Fatehgarh Churian railway stations reported, the raid would be for Amritsar.[3]

Planning for the induction of radars had started some time in the beginning of 1950. The AD concept had been envisaged on the British pattern of Sector Operations Centres (SOCs), Ground Control Interception (GCI) and Early Warning (EWs) units. The first SOC, 11 SU (Signal Unit) was established at Delhi in 1954. From the mid-1950s to the Indo-China War in 1962, the ground radar environment of the IAF consisted of five SOCs (11, 16, 18, 20 and 27 SUs), each equipped with Marconi T-13 (height finder) and T-14 radars, four mobile units 12, 55, 135 and 149 SU with T-15 radars and four EWs 36, 43, 91 and 121 SU with AN/TPS-1E radars.[4]

Full scale modernisation of the IAF began immediately after the Chinese debacle of 1962. Orders for MiG-21s (each MiG-21 Squadron came along with its P-30 mobile surveillance radar for local flying), Mi-4s, An-12s, IL-14s, SA-75 (SAM-II) Dvina batteries and the associated P-12 and P-15 radars were placed with Russia from 1960 onwards and the US was also requested to provide ground radars and training. Six American Star Sapphire units (500 series) with FPS

89 and 100 radars acted as Air Defence Direction Centres and twelve Russian P-30 units (200 series) acting as terminal air defence radars were inducted over the next five years. These were located at Amritsar, Bikaner, Delhi, Jamnagar, Agra, Madh Island, Bombay, Zaffarpur, Calcutta, Jodhpur, Sirsa, Baghdogra, Ahmedabad, Misamari, Tezpur and Patiala. Locations of Star Sapphire units were planned primarily to counter the threat from China but in the West, two units were set up, one each at Delhi and Barnala near Halwara. The rest of the P-30s were located at or around IAF airfields as PAF low level strikes were expected to target mainly IAF airfields. This was, therefore, a reactive set-up that aimed to either intercept raiders overhead IAF airfields or when they were exiting from an attack. Forward radars were set up at vantage points for expected ingress routes and gaps such as 230 SU at Amritsar, 501 SU at Barnala and AN/TPS-1E radars at Ranikhet, Ganganagar and Ferozepur/Faridkot. In an attempt to surprise the enemy and reduce radio traffic to a minimum, several "pop up" points had been designated where own interceptors, when scrambled, would fly at low level and then 'pop up' on call to surprise enemy aircraft ingressing or egressing. These were Dhariwal, Fatehgarh Churian, Patti and Makhu all roughly 70-100 km from Adampur where No. 1 Squadron MiG 21 FLs were on AD alert.[5]

A joint exercise "Shiksha" with the US and the UK was conducted in Western and Eastern India in November 1963. For this purpose, two units (311 and 411 SUs), each with US MPS 11 and 16 radars were also deployed at Patiala and Rampurhat respectively along with American F-100 Super Sabre and RAF Javelin aircraft. The Americans did not take back the radars after the exercise and these units provided good radar coverage during the 1965 Indo-Pak War. By the time of the December 1971 War, the IAF had focussed most of its radars towards China in Eastern, Central and Western India. Shorter range, low-looking radars were positioned at likely PAF ingress routes to IAF airfields in the West. One Air Traffic Control (ATC) radar at Patni Top, a location at 6,500 ft, North of Udhampur, provided some look-across into Pakistan.

Surface-to-Air Guided Weapons

Just five years after its induction in the Soviet Air Defence Forces (1957) the IAF signed up for five independent wings with their technical and combat squadrons of the high altitude surface-to-air guided missile, SA-2, Dvina, in 1964. The wings thus raised were, Chandigarh (Zirakpur) on September 8, 1964, Delhi (Rajokri) on November 9, 1964, Calcutta (Barrackpore) on February 25, 1966, Bombay (Thane) on May 1, 1968, and finally Agra on December 15, 1969. Since, uniquely, no ground training was conducted in the USSR, a complete training centre was set up at Baroda in the Maharaja Baroda's palace at Makarpura on December 7, 1963. In turn, whole squadrons would train together and be deployed and then operationalised together. A missile live-firing range on the Andhra coast at Suryalanka was also set up on September 1, 1967. Training commenced on April 1, 1964 under the school Commanding Officer (CO), Wg Cdr Pundalik Powar.[6]

No. 50 Squadron became the first operational SA-2 Squadron on February 1, 1965 and was based at Rajpura along with Nos 49 and 51 Squadrons at Kalpi and Baknaur around Ambala. Nos 43, 46 and 53 Squadrons were set up at locations defending Chandigarh while Nos 62, 63, 64, 65, 66 and 67 Squadrons were set up around Delhi. Only some of the Chandigarh, Ambala and Delhi Squadrons were operational, some only just, when the September 1965 War flared up. Several adjustments and relocations were made during the Kutch crisis that led up to the war but the fundamental capability limitation of not being able to engage targets below medium altitudes remained. It was only after the lessons learnt from the on-going Vietnam War that the Soviets modified some of the SA-2 systems by the December 1971 War, to be used down to 1,000 ft.[7]

By the time of the December 1971 War, the IAF redeployed Nos 63 and 64 Squadrons (unmodified) from Faridabad and Sohna around Delhi to around Halwara, with a mini tech squadron, No. 36 Squadron from Suryalanka to support missile preparation and delivery. Nos 49 and 50 Squadrons (modified) deployed around Adampur near

Jhandu Singha from Chandigarh area and No. 65 Squadron moved from Rajokri near Delhi to Samalkha South of Chandigarh as it had done in the 1965 War. During the war, as the threat to Koyali oil refinery at Ahmedabad emerged, No. 69 Squadron (modified) at Kanchrapara north of Calcutta was moved to Baroda and then Harni. This squadron itself was replaced at Baroda by No. 68 Squadron from Barrackpore. The moves, however, could be affected only by December 23, a week after the ceasefire. Almost all the squadrons (except those around Delhi) were protected by L-60/70 guns of the Indian Army AD regiments and others by between four to six 20 mm anti aircraft cannon manned by the IAF.[8]

Anti-Aircraft Artillery

Traditionally all the IAF vital installations such as airfields, radars and Surface-to-Air Missile (SAM) sites were defended by the Army Air Defence (AAD) Regiments. A total of nine each regular and Territorial Army Regiments with L-60 and L-70 radar controlled, 40 mm, Bofors, single barrel guns were deployed to protect IAF installations, Army field formations, bridges and other strategic installations. The IAF itself deployed a few World War II 20 mm single barrel anti-aircraft cannons at select airfields.[9] Twelve L-70 guns would be redeployed from Hasimara to the West on December 5, 1971.[10]

PAF Air Defence Scheme

The PAF's Sector Operations Centre (North) was located at Sakesar, the highest mountain on the Western edge of the Salt Range in Pothohar at a height of 1,522 m. It lay on the outer fringes of the Soon valley in Khushab district and was actually closer to Afghanistan than to India, being approximately 320 km from the Shakargarh bulge. Medium and high level radar surveillance in the Northern Sector rested with the high-powered General Electric AN/FPS-20 radar at Sakesar which was also the master GCI, while a modern Marconi Condor radar each at No. 400 Squadron, Chuhar Kana (a radar located just 60 km behind Lahore and much hunted-for by IAF Su-7s), No. 403 Squadron, Muridke (25 km north of Lahore and only 50 km from the airfield at Amritsar, watched every move of the IAF in the area) and No. 410 Squadron Tatepur near Multan (which gave excellent cover from Husseiniwala to Suleimanke to Bahawalpur), provided medium level cover from December 1968. Four AR-1 radars located at Rafiqui (No. 4092 Squadron), Cherat (No. 411 Squadron, halfway between Peshawar and Attock at 900 m elevation), Kallar Kahar (No. 4093 Squadron, at 600 m elevation, 70 km North of Sargodha and on the same spur as Sakesar 70 km West) and Kirana hills (No. 4091 Squadron, 10 km South of Sargodha at 300 m elevation) gave extended low level cover due to the hill-top locations of the latter three from April 1969 onwards.[11]

The PAF's Sector Operations Centre (South) was located at its war-time site at Korangi Creek just south of the historic Drigh road, where the IAF was formed in 1933. High level radar surveillance cover in the Southern Air Defence sector rested upon a FPS-20 and FPS-6A radar at Badin on the old World War II airfield installed on January 27, 1962, 170 km due East of Karachi across the Indus river, which was also the master GCI for the South. A P-35 radar, pulled out from Dacca just before the War started, was positioned at Malir (No. 406 Squadron), a disused pre-World War II airfield North of Karachi. Another P-35 radar, was moved from Malir to Jacobabad mid-way in the War and a Marconi Type-21 radar was located near Khanpur just 20 km Northeast of Rahim Yar Khan, giving good coverage across to Jaisalmer. Low level cover was provided by a civil aviation ASR-4 approach radar at Karachi airport and an AR-1 radar of No. 4082 Squadron at Pir Patho,[12] 70 km West of Badin on a small hill in the Indus delta, named after a local Tableeghi, Pir Patho, also known as Gopi Chand to the local Hindus.

Pakistani Anti-Aircraft Artillery (AAA)

Pakistan had three anti-aircraft brigades to protect PAF installations and the naval dockyards at Karachi. Further units were deployed as organic AAA units to Army field formations. There were also anti-aircraft Mujahid units (akin to the Indian Territorial Army battalions) for tasks other than regular. While PAF airfields and radars received the highest priority, bridges and dockyards came next but oil installations and the railways remained largely unprotected.[13] The AAA units carried a mix of Chinese, American and British guns. The Chinese 37 mm twin barrel was the most effective followed by the Chinese 14.5 mm quadruple barrel guns and then the World War II Bofors 40 mm L-60 guns and American 20 mm cannons. The 37 mm twin barrel was the deadliest, with no comparable gun on the Indian side. It could set up a barrage of 320 shells every second at a height of 3,000 m with a muzzle velocity of 880 m/sec. The 14.5 mm Quad Type 56/58 could set up 600 rounds at a height of 1,200 m every second with a muzzle velocity of 1,000 m/sec. Indeed, by the end of the war, 24 IAF aircraft would be lost to ground fire in the West alone. Eight aircraft would be lost in the East to AAA over Dacca/Tejgaon.

Indian Air Force: Aircraft

Folland/HAL Gnat Mk I

In 1956, Hindustan Aircraft Limited (HAL) and Folland signed an agreement to manufacture the Gnat Mk I in India after several trials of the Midge, an early forebear of the Gnat. The initial order was for 40 Gnats – 25 to be built at Hamble, UK, and 15 to be delivered as kits for assembly by HAL. HAL would also license produce the Gnat from scratch. HAL built 195 Gnats up to early 1974. The first Gnat assembled by HAL flew in Bangalore in November 1959 and the first completely HAL-built Gnat flew in May 1962. The Gnat entered squadron service in March 1960 with No. 23 Squadron, with Sqn Ldr S Raghavendran in command. This was followed in early 1962 with No. 2 Squadron and the following year by No. 9 Squadron, all based in Ambala. Nos 15 and 18 Squadrons would be reequipped just before the September 1965 War. However, with India being the only real export customer, the Gnat was beset with problems from day one. It featured some revolutionary designs to meet the size and weight design goals of a light fighter. Some of the quirky designs to save space were the use of half-extension of the undercarriage as airbrakes and use of nitrogen to charge the base pressure of the hydraulic reservoir as an emergency aid to the lower undercarriage. The Gnat's two, 30 mm ADEN cannons carried 115 rounds each and because of the compact nature of the design, were fed by a very complex, curving-bottom belt feed design that led to routine gun stoppages. Uniquely, the guns were fed by a cross chute mechanism as each gun's ammo box was on the other side of the aircraft. Several gun stoppages at critical moments whilst in combat led to many failed intercepts. At one point, this was seen as sabotage by the IAF and several officers were court martialled. The Gnat could carry up to eight T-10 rockets under wing along with two 300-litre (66 imperial gallons) drop tanks.

In the September 1965 War, the Gnats shot down three PAF Sabres while losing two in air combat. By the 1971 War, the IAF boasted of eight Gnat squadrons of 14 Gnats and one or two Hunter T Mk 66 each with two being raised (Nos 21 and 22 Squadron), and one being reequipped on the type (No. 24 Squadron). Of the 112 on strength, 64 were deployed in the West and 48 in the East. After the War, in 1972, the IAF issued a requirement for an improved Gnat, capable of both air defence and ground attack. The improved Gnat was named Ajeet (Invincible) and flew in September 1976. Deliveries began in 1977, a total of 79 being retro modified by the time production ended in 1982.

Sukhoi-7 BMK (Izdeliya S-22)

After some difficulties in procuring further Hawker Hunters from Britain and the delays in the indigenous HF-24 fighter project, the IAF went in for an ad hoc acquisition of the 'Tactical Fighter Bomber' Su-7BMK (Bomber, Modified, Commercial). The aircraft was evaluated at Lugovaya in the USSR in July 1966 and an initial order was placed for 90 aircraft on January 2, 1967, followed by another order for 32 aircraft signed on May 25, 1967. The deliveries were completed by sea via the Russian Far East (from the Komsomolsk-on-Amur factory) to Bombay. By March 1968, No. 26 Squadron, and then No. 101 Squadron in December 1969, had re-equipped at Adampur. No. 221 Squadron, No. 108 Squadron, No. 222 Squadron and finally No. 32 Squadron had converted by mid-1970 at Bareilly and Ambala. Fourteen trainers had also been received. The Su-7BMK was almost half as heavier than the Hunter at 16 tonnes maximum All Up Weight (AUW) and almost 25 per cent bigger. It could carry 2,500 kg payload against the Hunter's 1,800 kg but had severely short legs as the specific fuel consumption was typically, for Soviet fighters, very high. This would remain its Achilles heel throughout its 14-year service and outweigh it advantages against the Hunter.

Standard armament comprised its two internal Nudelman-Richter 30 mm cannons with 75 rounds each, 500 kg FAB-500 GP bombs or 500 kg M-62 HE bombs. The 16 rocket (S-5, 57 mm) UB-16-57 UMP rocket pods were carried and towards the end of the war, the S-24, 240 kg unguided rocket could be carried in pairs. Initial batches were supplied with 600-litre twin ventral drop tanks. Later batches came with two extra wing stations with a modified adapter of the inboard stations to carry the larger 950-litre (209 imperial gallons) drop tanks.

Every one in five aircraft delivered came with an internal AFA-39 35 mm belly camera. Locally, the IAF would also modify four Su-7s with the UB-16-57 rocket pod modified to carry the Fairchild F-96, Type 536 camera on the outboard pylons as well as on the 600-litre ventral drop tank. Initial aircraft came with French labelling as they were diverted from an Algerian order and it was the first IAF fighter to sport a radar warning receiver (Serena) before the MiG-21 FL entered service. However, like the MiG-21 FL, it lacked the rear view periscope so important for air combat, a role never intended for the type (later Su-7s were fitted with the periscope but no IAF Su-7 was modified).

By December 1971, 80 Su-7s were available in the West and a further 16 with No. 221 Squadron at Panagarh in the East. This squadron would transfer back West to Bareilly on December 16, 1971, too late to take part in operations in the West. The four squadrons in the West would fly 786 sorties while the lone squadron in the East would fly 178 sorties.

Hawker Hunter F Mk 56/56A

The IAF received a total of 206 fighter and 39 two-seat Hunters from 1957 to 1974, with the first 32 aircraft diverted from a cancelled Royal Air Force (RAF) order and the next 16 being overhauled ex-RAF examples. It was the last 112 new examples that were the FGA Mk 9/56A standard with a tail chute and capability to carry the inboard 230 imperial gallon drop tank. The first order of 160 fighters and 22 two-seaters had been received by September 1961. After the 1965 War, 46 fighters and 17 two-seaters, all second-hand, ex RAF, Royal Netherlands Air Force and Royal Belgian Air Force examples were refurbished by Hawkers for the IAF to make up for attrition losses. Of these, all, except five T Mk 66E ex-RAF two-seaters (January 1974) were received by 1970. The Hunter went on to serve with six frontline squadrons (Nos 7, 14, 17, 20, 27 and 37) and one training unit (Operational Training Unit – OTU). Just prior to the War, 1 Base Repair Depot (BRD) modified one Hunter T-66, and five Mk 56A and eight Mk 56 were modified with the three-port camera modification in the nose akin to the Hunter FR Mk 10 mod (1 BRD Report).

By the 1971 War, the IAF fielded 32 Hunters in the West with Nos 20 and 27 Squadrons and an ad hoc raising from the OTU, No. 122 Squadron at Jaisalmer and 64 aircraft in the East with Nos 7 (Baghdogra), 14 (Dum Dum and Jessore), 17 (Hasimara and Kumbhigram) and 37 (Hasimara) Squadrons. No. 7 Squadron, on December 7, 1971, would deploy partly at Hindan, Sirsa and Pathankot after the rout of the PAF in the East. IAF Hunters would fly 360 sorties in the West and 795 sorties in the East.

English Electric Canberra B(I) 6/12/58, PR 57/67, T-4/13

India was by far the largest foreign user of the Canberra after the USA, first ordering the type in 1957. In all, the Indian Air Force received 120 Canberras of eight marks. All the aircraft except the last four B(I) 66 and the 17 ex-Royal New Zealand Air Force (RNZAF) aircraft had been received by December 1971. One B (I) 66, IF1025 just slipped into Bombay from Bahrain at 1750 h on December 2.

- 71 B (I) 58s (The tropicalised interdictor version fitted with a teardrop canopy on the port side, provision for a ventral pack similar to the B(I)6 with 4 x 20 mm (0.787 in) Hispano Mk.V cannon.
- 10 PR.57s (Photo-reconnaissance version based on B6. Tropicalised for India as PR-57).
- 13 T-4s (First trainer variant with dual controls and a crew of three).
- 10, B (I) 66s (Similar to the B (I) 58, ex-RAF attrition replacement after 1965 War).
- 2 PR.67s (ex-RNZAF version of the PR-57).
- 6 TT.18/418s (ex-RAF Target Tugs).
- 8 B (I) 12s (Essentially B (I) 58, ex-RNZAF).
- 2 T.13s (essentially T-4 trainers built for the RNZAF but with ejection seats for the pilots also).

By December 1971, the IAF had 48 Canberras left, excluding the trainers and photo recce versions and they would fly a total of 245 sorties in both East and West. Large numbers were in major overhaul in HAL Bangalore and several had been lost to peace-time and war-time attrition. Two Canberras had been modified to carry K-13 Air-to-Air Missiles (AAMs) on the wing station. Trials at the end of November 1971 by No. 35 Squadron against burning splash targets simulating a ship's smoke stacks were inconclusive and the weapon was not employed operationally.

Mikoyan Gurevich/HAL MiG-21 FL (Izdeliye T- 77)

The IAF had received three MiG-21 F-13 (T-74) and six MiG-21 PF (T-76) by the time of the 1965 conflict. By then, the IAF had already signed up for 37 flyaway MiG-21 FLs and HAL had received the licence to first assemble and then manufacture the MiG-21 series, its engines and accessories at HAL, Nasik, Koraput, Hyderabad and Lucknow. By the time of the 1971 War, the IAF had received an estimated 130 MiG-21 FL T-77 aircraft, excluding the first nine

F-13s and PF. An order for 75 T-77s was under delivery when the war broke out. A further eight MiG-21 U (T-66) flyaway trainers had also been received (HAL never manufactured the two-seater). The MiG-21 rapidly equipped eight IAF squadrons, Nos 1, 4, 8, 28, 29, 30, 45 and 47. The MiG-21 Fl (T-77) was powered by the higher rated Tumansky R-11-F2-200, second generation R-2 L radar, two K-13 AAMs and the ability to carry two 57 mm rocket pods or two FAB 500/M-62 500KG GP bombs. However, the internal fuel carriage was reduced and the single 30 mm cannon was also omitted as in the case of other Western fighters (F-104, F-4 Phantom, EE Lightning, etc.). This was later remedied, to an extent, by carrying the GP-9 gondola with the twin 23 mm GSH-23-2 cannon with 200 rounds as opposed to just 60 rounds for the 30 mm internal cannon of the F-13, T-74. However, the gondola went in place of the ventral tank, making it quite the Hobson's choice for the pilot. The gun was aimed by a fixed, inverted 'ring and bead' sight with no offset computing, a feature, that even the 22-year old Vampire-possessed. No. 1 Base Repair Depot would modify three MiG-21s with the GGS-Mk IVE British gyro gun sight just before the war, and one T-77 would shoot down a F-104 Starfighter with guns using this sight. One MiG-21 (C1110) would also be modified with a Fairchild F-24 camera in a UB-16-57 rocket pod under the starboard wing. When this was found too 'draggy' for long duration sorties, a gondola under the belly was developed for the Flight Reconnaissance (FR) role. This aircraft would ultimately fly eight missions between December 1-12, by day, across Pakistan in the hands of test pilot Sqn Ldr Kirpal Singh of the Aircraft and Armament Testing Unit. One last remaining T-74, BC820 was serviced and provided to fly Combat Air Patrols (CAPs) over Ambala.

Most importantly, the MiG-21 FL came with no rear view mirror. This was later retrofitted in the late 1970s from the Hunter. The MiG-21 with its high performance but typical short legs and unreliable first-generation K-13 AAMs and no guns made a frustratingly good aircraft to fly but difficult to bring to bear. However, in the East, in a pure air-to-ground role the MiG-21 would shine in a secondary role that was never intended for the supersonic high-altitude interceptor. The rapid expansion of the MiG-21 fleet as was the case with the Su-7 fleet, sucked away top, experienced pilots from the Gnat and Hunter squadrons. This left the latter fleets generally less experienced and skilled. However, as the war became imminent, several pilots undergoing MiG-21 and Su-7 conversion would be reverted to their parent Gnat or Hunter squadrons redressing, the balance to an extent. By the time the war broke out, the IAF fielded 64 MiG-21s in the West and 48 in the East, flying 966 and 609 sorties respectively. No. 30 Squadron operating out of Panagarh just Northwest of Kalaikunda, was transferred back to Chandigarh on December 16, 1971, too late to take part in operations.

HAL HF-24 Mk I, Marut

The HAL HF-24, Marut (Wind Spirit), India's first fighter was designed by a HAL team headed by the legendary Kurt Tank, of the Focke-Wulf design centre in World War II Germany. Flying for the first time in June 1961, it entered service with No. 220 Squadron at Poona on April 1, 1967. By the time the war commenced, only two squadrons had converted and 32 Maruts had been taken on charge. However, severe teething troubles, largely based on its very high pressure hydraulic system (4000 PSI/270 bars), lower-than-expected performance due to its unsuitable Bristol Orpheus engines, and unsettled spares supply chain provided an average of only 15 airplanes for flying through the War. The aircraft used the same internal 55 × 68 mm rocket pack as the Mystere IVA, had four stations to carry up to 3,400 kg of payload and sported four Aden 30 mm cannons in the nose. However, as the aircraft's weaponisation was rushed through before the war, it could not completely solve the problem of excessive vibrations caused by four-gun firing and its deleterious effects on the aircraft controls. Indeed, just before the war on November 21, 1971, the test pilot, Sqn Ldr Sapre was killed as the aircraft's controls switched to manual and caused it to crash into the sea off Jamnagar when firing all four guns together. Ultimately, the aircraft used only the two lower guns in service, although all four guns were available during the war. After much refinement, the aircraft would later develop into a "twin engine Super-Hunter" a sobriquet not entirely something to be ashamed of.

While 32 aircraft had been taken on charge, the two squadrons began the war with 18 aircraft only. The average availability after the first three days dropped to 12 aircraft due to significant battle damage and serviceability issues. The Marut fleet would fly a total 127 sorties during the war.

AMDBA Mystere IVA

The IAF had received 110 Mysteres IVA by 1960. The Mysteres had been inducted after the AMDBA Ouragons, their straight wing forbears, and excelled in the 1965 War in their intended ground attack role but by 1971, they were beset with maintenance problems and low serviceability. They still packed a punch with their unique internal pack of 55, 68 mm rockets which fired in five sets of eleven, and external armament equal to that of the Hunter Mk 56 (less two cannons). Nos 3 and 31 Squadrons at Hindan along with the No. 2 Target Towing Flight at Jamnagar had 32 Mysteres between them but poor serviceability kept the number at an average of 13 through the war. Yet they would fly 228 sorties in the plains of Southern Punjab and Haryana.

Transport Types

Transport aircraft included one maritime Recce Squadron (No. 6 Squadron) with six L-1049 Super Constellation aircraft, about 55 C-47 Dakotas of various marks, 24 Fairchild C-119 Packets, 15 IL-14s, 30 An-12s, 25 Otters, 12 HS-748s and 26 Caribou aircraft. Helicopters included about 40 Mi-4, about 30 Allouette III and 12 Bell-47s. While the Mi-8 had been ordered, the first examples were received at Bombay only in January 1972 and the first four examples handed over to the IAF between January 25 and February 6, 1972. The first unit-118 Helicopter Unit (HU) at Chabua had, however, stood up on the first day of the war, December 3, 1971. A table of the transport and helicopter war-time effort is projected in Table 1.

Table 1: Transport and Helicopter Effort[14]

Sl No	Type	Sorties	Passengers	Casualties	Maritime Support
1	SUPER CONSTELLATION	-	-	-	39
2	AN -12	273+44 (Bombing)	680	182	2
3	C-119 PACKET	550	1,604	45	-
4	HS-748	39	29	-	26
5	IL-14	92	264	132	11
6	C-47 DAKOTA	927	164	463	-
7	CARIBOU	206+10 (Bombing)	91	-	-
8	OTTER	301	211	14	-
9	MI-4	1,397	4,065	866	-
10	ALOUETTE II	894	809	282	-
11	BELL 47	113	-	31	-
12	TOTAL	**4,791+55**	**8,917**	**2,015**	**154**

Source: Lessons Learnt from the Planning and Conduct of Air Operations August-December 1971. Air Headquarters, February 1972.
Note: Does not include Indian Airlines flying 28 Boeing-737 sorties carrying 3,003 troops between West and East.

Pakistan Air Force: Aircraft

Pakistan relied heavily on US aid under the US Military Defence Mutual Assistance Programme (MAP). However, following spares shortages encountered during the post 1965 US embargo, they decided to look to China and France for their new equipment, receiving favourable payment terms, in particular from the Chinese government.

Lockheed C-130B Hercules

No. 6 Squadron received its first of four C-130 Bs on March 1, 1963. Based at Chaklala, the squadron was very busy during the 1965 War. The original four aircraft were supplemented by two civil L100s purchased from Pakistan International Airlines in 1965 and a further five C-130Bs from US MAP.[15]

In the run up to the 1971 War, the squadron transported troops back and forth between West and East Pakistan, routing via Sri Lanka in order not to fly over Indian air space. When the civil war broke out in March 1971, two aircraft became permanently stationed at Dacca. This airlift was supported by four ex-Iranian AF C-130Bs and five Turkish AF C-130Es. The Iranian aircraft were never returned.[16] Two of the PAF aircraft were withdrawn to West Pakistan in December. During the 1971 War, the PAF C-130 B/E fleet would fly only 11 sorties by night.[17]

Lockheed F104A/B Starfighter

Fourteen F-104A/B Starfighters were delivered to Pakistan by the time of the 1971 War. First arriving on August 5, 1961, they were operated by No. 9 Air Superiority Squadron at Sargodha air base, just elevated from the care and maintenance role to a full base in November 1959. Two F-104Bs two-seaters (57-1309 and 57-1312) were also supplied. Further, one each F-104A would be received in June 1964 and March 1965. These jets had been refurbished prior to delivery under the MAP funding, having been fitted with C-2 upward-firing ejection seats, arresting hooks and more fuel-efficient J79-GE-11A engines. This uprated power plant gave these F-104As the best thrust-to-weight ratio of any Starfighter variant at the time. M61 guns, removed for US Air Force (USAF) aircraft, were also reinstalled. Removing the gun had enabled an optional 100-gallon fuel tank to be installed. AIM-9B missiles could be carried for the air superiority role on 'Red Dog' wingtip launchers.[18] During the 1965 War, they flew air defence, escort and reconnaissance missions, losing one F-104A to a Mystere IVA flown by Sqn Ldr AB Devayya of the Flying Training Wing (FTW), attached No. 1 Squadron IAF. The unit went into the 1971 War with to eight F-104A/B and a further ten Royal Jordanian Air Force (RJAF) F-104As would be ferried to Masroor on the December 13/14, 1971, beefing up the F-104 fleet to 17 aircraft. Five RJAF F-104As were flown in by Jordanian and PAF pilots on December 13, and another five followed a short while later. Maj Ihsan Shurdom (later the Commander-in-Chief of the RJAF) led the first RJAF Starfighters into Masroor on December 13, and the aircraft were to remain in Pakistan with PAF markings until three weeks after the war.[19] Political constraints officially prevented them from crossing the Indian border on combat missions. However, on December 26, three camouflaged Northrop F-5As, Freedom Fighters in PAF markings passed through Tehran airport en route to Pakistan. They were part of a batch of eight originally destined for Libya but diverted from storage in California to Pakistan, via Iran and Turkey.[20]

During the 1965 Pakistan-India War, the F-104s flew a total of 246 hours and 45 minutes, while during the 1971 War, the F-104s would fly a total of only 96 sorties/103 h and 45 minutes.[21]

Lockheed T33A/RT33A Shooting Star

Between May 4, 1955, and 1956, the PAF received 15, T-33A two-seat jet trainers and six RT-33A single-seat photo-reconnaissance aircraft under the US MAP. They initially equipped No. 2 Composite Squadron and a tactical reconnaissance flight which later became No. 20 Squadron at Sargodha. During the 1965 War, No. 20 Squadron flew 24 tactical reconnaissance missions over enemy territory. During the 1971 War, a total of 12 remained and the squadron maintained a detachment of three aircraft at Tejgaon and the balance was based at Mauripur. T-33s flew a total of 43 sorties during the war.[22]

Martin B-57 Canberra

Pakistan was the only 'real' foreign user of the B-57, with 24 B-57Bs and two B-57Cs passed on in 1959 under the US MAP.

The first 11 of 26 B-57s arrived in Pakistan on November 27, 1959, to be operated at Masroor (Mauripur) by No. 7 Squadron. No. 8 Squadron converted in August 1960. In-country modifications included the addition of, from 1963, the RB-1A "Georgia Peach" all-weather bombing system, giving these machines a longer nose. Some of the Pakistani B-57Bs were also modified to allow them to carry four external tanks, permitting them to conduct strikes deep inside India.

Weapons carried consisted of four Colt M39 20-millimetre revolver-type cannons in the wings, with 290 rounds per gun. The original bomb bay doors of the British Canberra were replaced by a rotating bomb bay door, a scheme that had been developed by Martin for the XB-51. Munitions were actually mounted on the door itself; not only did this configuration reduce buffeting and permit high-speed and dive attacks, but it was also possible in principle to have a "bombed-up" door available at an air base to swap into a B-57 returning from a sortie, permitting rapid turnaround. A total of 2,720 kg (6,000 lb) of stores could be carried internally. There were four stores pylons under each of the B-57B's wings, for a total of eight, each capable of carrying a 225 kg (500 lb) bomb. That gave in principle a maximum warload of 4,500 kg (10,000 lb) of munitions, but in practice, the usual warload was no more than half that. Either 56 × 2.75 inch rocket projectiles or two 750 lb bombs could be carried under wing.[23]

The B-57 force was affected by the US arms embargo that followed the 1965 War, resulting in the number plating of No. 8 Squadron in May 1970. Its assets were passed over to No. 7 Squadron and some of the aircraft were cannibalised for spares in order to keep the fleet going with 17 B-5B/C and one RB-57C. During the 1971 War, No. 7 Squadron was once again committed to counter-air strike missions against IAF airfields by night. Another operator of the B-57 was No. 24 Squadron, based at Peshawar, formed in December 1962, and which operated a mixed fleet of B-57B, RB-57B and RB-57F. They used their aircraft in the electronic intelligence and radar jamming roles. Prior to the 1965 War, one of the two RB-57Fs had returned to the USA for rework. Ownership of the aircraft is unclear but they were originally operated by the USAF in missions against the USSR for Intercontinental Ballistic Missile (ICBM) telemetry signals monitoring.[24] Upon returning from a mission against Amritsar, a B-57B (or RB-57B, 53-3961 was shot down on the September 11, 1965, near Amritsar). The Squadron Commander and the leading Electronic Counter-Measures (ECM) specialist were killed and both sides claimed the shoot down. The remaining RB-

57F was severely damaged on September 21, whilst over Delhi, after a SAM-2 exploded in its proximity. The pilot landed with 170 shrapnel holes at Peshawar where a nose wheel collapsed on landing. It was returned to the USA for repairs and never received back. During the 1971 War, the B-57B fleet would fly just 130 sorties.[25]

North American F-86F Sabre and Canadair CL13B Sabre 6

Following the conclusion of a Central Treaty Organisation (CENTO) mutual defence pact with the USA in 1954, the PAF received a total of 120 F-86Fs under the MAP from June 13, 1956 (the same year the Royal Pakistan Air Force (RPAF) dropped its 'Royal" prefix). No. 15 Squadron PAF was raised on the same date and became the first squadron to become operational on the type. Initially, the PAF received 30 F-86-F-35s without leading edge slats in June 1956 via a US Navy (USN) aircraft carrier at Karachi, followed by 90 of the F40 version, starting in 1957. They were converted in-country with the addition of leading edge slats and wing tip extensions, bringing them up to dash 40 mod status which improved their manoeuvrability and operating altitude. More importantly, later upgrades followed, enabling approximately 25 per cent of the force to be compatible with the Sidewinder air-to-air missile. By the time of the 1965 War, the PAF had nearly 10 years experience on the type and were able to field 7 squadrons which gave them a cutting edge over the IAF.[26]

After the 1965 War, embargoes, 90 surplus Ex-West German Air Force Canadair CL-13B, Sabre Mk 6 aircraft were delivered in 1966 (including the last Sabre to be manufactured by Canadair-Sabre #1815) via Vahdati in Iran to Pakistan via agent Gerhard Georg Mertins of Merex AG (Bonn).[27] The Canadair Sabre Mk 6 was the final variant and was considered to be the "best" production Sabre ever built. It was equipped with a two-stage Orenda engine developing 7,275 lb (3,302 kg) of static thrust, almost 1,500 lb more than the F-86Fs GE J-47GE-13 engine. Its altitude performance and climb rate were enhanced over the Mk 5 and the reinstatement of the wing leading edge slat gave it excellent low-speed characteristics.

Many changes had taken place in the intervening years between the wars. Two PAF squadrons, Nos 5 (Mirage III EP/DP/RP) and 11 (Shenyang F-6) had re-equipped, some had re-equipped with the Sabre 6 and No. 19 Squadron PAF used both. No. 26 Squadron was raised August 1, 1967, to act as an Operational Training Unit for the Sabre force. Initially based at Masroor, they had moved to Peshawar by 1971 and were commanded by the Officer Commanding (OC) No. 16 Squadron whose squadron did not participate. By 1971, the PAF had six squadrons on 65 F-86F and 74 F-86E (Mk 6) including No. 14 Squadron at Dacca. During the war, they would fly a total of 1,452 sorties including 44 in East Pakistan from November 22-December 6, 1971.[28]

For unknown reasons, two other Sabre units were operational leading up to the war but took no active part, other than supplying pilots and aircraft to bolster other squadrons. These were No. 15 Squadron at Sargodha and No. 16 Squadron at Masroor which was finally number plated in 1972.[29]

Weapons carried by the Sabre were four under wing jettisonable pods each containing a combination of seven 2.75 inch or eight 5 inch folding fin aerial rockets. On occasion, three pylons under each wing were utilised for bombs and rockets, plus 100 or 200 gallon drop tanks. For the ground attack role, bombs carried were mainly two, 500 lb or 1,000 lb; 800 rounds were carried in the six forward fuselage mounted 0.5 inch machine guns and the AIM-9B Sidewinder was carried on the two pylons inboard of the main wheel oleos. Strangely, the F-86Es procured in 1966 could not carry bombs, perhaps a legacy of their previous West German Air Force owners who as North Atlantic Treaty Organisation (NATO) partners were not allowed offensive weapons, this shortcoming being only rectified, just in time, on November 23, 1970.[30]

Shenyang F-6

Immediately after the 1965 War, the People's Republic of China supplied the Shenyang F-6 aircraft (Chinese copy of the

MiG-19, called the J-6) to the PAF (December 30, 1965) as military assistance. Initially 72 aircraft were procured, with subsequent additions bringing the total to 253 aircraft. At its peak, the F-6 aircraft equipped ten fighter squadrons of the Pakistan Air Force. By the 1971 War, 90 F-6s had been received.[31]

The F-6 carried three 23 mm cannons with 75 rounds each for the wing guns and 70 rounds for the single nose cannon gun. The major upgrades included the provision of Western avionics, Martin Baker ejection seats, AIM-9 Sidewinder air-to-air missiles in April 1967, and additional under wing tanks in February 1971. After the war, French 68 mm rockets in place of the UB-8-57 mm rockets (August 1979), underbelly 'Gondola' fuel tanks and a special ground-power unit for instantly starting its twin engines to shorten 'scramble' time were introduced. The PAF's F-6s uniquely carried no bombs during the war.[32]

The PAF raised three squadrons on the F-6 by the time of the war. No. 23 Squadron PAF was the first to equip. No. 25 Squadron under Wg Cdr Mohammad Ghulam Tawab (later CAS, Bangladesh Air Force) became the type conversion unit and was split into two detachments of eight aircraft each, based at Sargodha and Mianwali during the war. At the latter base, the detachment had the task of guarding the 'back-up' strike assets including 10 B-57 and 5-odd Mirage IIIE for the all-important phase of the Pakistan Army's main offensive.[33] No. 11 Squadron converted to the F-6 in 1966 and was based at Rafiqui. During the war, it deployed to Sargodha. No. 23 Squadron PAF was stood up on February 6, 1966, after number plating in 1964. It converted to the F-6 at Sargodha and deployed to Risalwala for the war. PAF F-6s would fly a total of 821 sorties during the war.[34]

AMDBA Mirage III EP/DP/RP

In 1967, the PAF purchased 24 Mirages from Avions Marcel Dassault Breguet Aviation (AMDBA) in France. The first batch of six aircraft was ferried to Pakistan, arriving at Sargodha on March 8, 1968. The delivery of these aircraft to Sargodha enabled No. 5 Squadron PAF to convert from the F-86F. 18 Mirage III EP (P-Pakistan), four Mirage III DP two-seaters and four Mirage IIIRPs photo reconnaissance aircraft were delivered.[35] The IIIE was basically the multirole version of the IIIC with Marconi Doppler navigation radar, increased fuel and the Thomson-CSF Cyrano II dual mode air/ground radar. The IIIRP recce version was fitted with a purpose-developed camera nose, which internally accommodated up to five OMERA side and forward looking cameras. Photo flash cartridges could be fired for night photography as well. The armament included two inbuilt DEFA 30 mm cannons plus the choice of one ventral Matra R-530 radar guided semi-active AAM, AIM-9B Sidewinder AAMs, 750 lb American Mk 117 HE bombs and long range or supersonic fuel tanks under the wing. Uniquely, the Mirage III was equipped with two Matra JL-100 drop tanks/rocket packs, each with 19 68 mm (2.7 in) SNEB rockets and 250 l (66 US gallons; 55 imperial gallons) of fuel. One IIIRP was lost to a bird hit prior to the war and the PAF went to war with 23 Mirages, with No. 5 Squadron manning two detachments at Sargodha and Mianwali. During the war, the Mirages would fly a total of 390 sorties.[36] Pakistan had ordered another 30 Mirage VP/DP (the pure ground attack version) with Saudi money but none was delivered before the war. Strangely, the first Mirage CO, Wg Cdr MM Alam whose preposterous and since debunked claim of having shot down five IAF Hunters in 30 seconds, was not in command during the war. Perhaps his Bengali blood weighed heavier than his purported air combat claims.

Assessment

The Indian armed forces had appreciated the following considerations:

- The lack of 'Western' governments' support (although their media was aghast at the West Pakistani excesses in East Pakistan).
- The rather potent threat from West Pakistan based air and land forces.

- The very real danger of getting trapped in an extended battle for Dacca.
- The very real possibility of intervention by the US Navy and supply from outside.
- The threat of Chinese mobilisation in Sikkim and Arunachal Pradesh.

East Pakistan was primarily a riverine country with roughly 700 waterways measuring in excess of 24,000 km in cumulative length. Thus, the main thrusts had to be along these waterways through the ubiquitous flooded paddy fields and wet lands. It was, therefore, decided that any campaign to liberate Bangladesh could not start before October-November 1971, and must be concluded in the shortest possible time before external factors as described above could come to the rescue of Pakistan.

It was well appreciated that the fundamental Pakistani doctrine to protect East Pakistan, a land completely surrounded by India, was that an attack in the East would be met by a Pakistani attack in the West. For all his faults, the Pakistani President and Chief Martial Law Administrator, Gen Yahya Khan was a pragmatic man who perhaps knew that given the force asymmetry, a war with India was unwinnable, especially in both wings, and therefore, East Pakistan was already a lost cause. Certainly, as early as February 22, 1971 the Americans had realised that East Pakistan would not survive when Kissinger, the secretary of state, sent a memorandum to Nixon, "*A realistic assessment would seem to recognise that there is very little left in the fabric of the unity of Pakistan....*"[37] But, America, hoping for a rapprochement with China to counter the Soviets, was hopeful of Pakistan enabling a meeting between Nixon and Chou Enlai, caused Nixon to continue to back Pakistan in spite of immense pressure at home.[38]

Given the smaller size of the PAF, the idea of a preemptive Pakistani attack in the West was a foregone conclusion for the Indians as it was the only rabbit available in the PAF's proverbial hat, with surprise providing the only chance of any success. In the West, contrary to popular belief, the two Air Forces were almost matched in numbers; 215 PAF aircraft versus 245 IAF aircraft. While deployment of the SAM-II by the IAF proved quite a deterrent to PAF day counter-air attacks, the missile itself achieved no success even though seven were launched.[39] On the other hand, Pakistani anti-aircraft artillery, especially the large numbers of Chinese 37 mm and 14.5 mm four barrelled gun proved deadly (Tejgaon alone had 70 guns deployed) as the very large numbers and proportion of IAF losses to AAA would demonstrate.

In the East, with the urgency to reach Dacca as soon as possible, overwhelming numerical superiority was necessary to wrest air superiority at the earliest, 110 IAF aircraft versus 13 PAF aircraft, and then to carry out sustained offensive support to pave the way for the Army as it by-passed enemy garrisons. Large numbers of Mi-4 helicopters and transport aircraft would also help leapfrog the Army East to West across the North-South river systems and para-drop them in the enemy's rear and put them at the doorstep of Dacca.

It now appears that this apparent numerical superiority was the greatest deterrent as the PAF was less than enthusiastic about the outcome of the war from day one. The PAF was probably more interested in surviving the war as an 'Air Force in being' with its 'reputation' intact rather than throw itself at what appeared to be meaningless attrition for a cause whose fate would be, and was, actually decided in East Pakistan, not West Pakistan, quite shockingly opposite to Pakistan's original postulation. The greatest effect of this 'imbalance' of forces and the IAF's demonstrated resolve and almost reckless doggedness in supporting the Indian Army by throwing itself repeatedly at overwhelming anti-aircraft defences was that the much touted and purported Pakistan Army II Corps offensive in the Bahawalpur-Abohar area to relieve East Pakistan fizzled out even before Niazi capitulated in East Pakistan. Table 2 projects the IAF and PAF, holdings, actual average serviceability during the war and sorties flown.

Table 2: PAF and IAF Holdings, Average Serviceability, and Sorties Flown in the West and East[40]

Western Theatre								
PAF[4]					IAF			
Sl No	Type	Holdings	Average Serviceable	Sorties	Sorties	Average Serviceable	Holdings	Type
1	F-86F	65	44	617	624	29	64	Gnat
2	F-86E	74	62	791	360	19	32	Hunter[2]
3	F-104[1]	8	8	96	127	15	32	HF 24
4	F-6	90	48	821	966	51	64	MiG-21Fl
5	Mirage III	23	23	390	228	13	32	Mystere IV A
6	B-57	18	18	130	786	53	80	Su-7
7	T/Rt-33	12	12	43	245	38	48	Canberra[3]
8	-	-	-	-	44	16	40	Vampire
9	Total	290	215	2,886	3,380	234	392	Total
Eastern Theatre								
10	F-86E	14	12[5]	44	492	24	48	Gnat
11	RT-33	2	1		975	38	64	Hunter[2]
12					609	36	48	MiG-21Fl
13	Total	16	13		178	12	16	Su-7
14				44	2,254	110	176	
	Total	**306**	**228[6]**	**2,930**	**5,634**	**344[7]**	**568**	

Source: Lessons Learnt from the Planning and Conduct of Air Operations August-December 1971. Air Headquarters, February 1972.

Notes for Table 2:

1. Ten Royal Jordanian AF F-104As were available to the PAF after December 13, 1971.
2. 10 serviceable Hunters from Nos 20 and 27 Squadrons were withdrawn on December 12, 1971, and No. 7 Squadron from Baghdogra redeployed from the East with 10 Hunters to Pathankot.
3. Canberras numbers and sorties flown are for both fronts, East and West.
4. PAF figures are from Tufail.
5. PAF No. 14 Squadron commenced the war with 14 aircraft and ended with 11. Hence, an average of 12 is depicted.
6. PAF average serviceability was thus 74.5 per cent West and East.
7. IAF average serviceability was 60.5 per cent due to five of the seven types being more than 20-year-old fleets.

Notes

1. Interview with Air Mshl Vir Narain, November 18, 2018.
2. A.Q Hijazi, *The Story of the Pakistan Air Force: A Saga of Courage and Honour* (Islamabad: Shaheen Foundation, 1988). The PAF would drop its C-in-C title with the removal of Rahim Khan on March 3, 1972.
3. Interview with Gp Capt ML Bountra, August 6, 2019.
4. Ibid.
5. Ibid.
6. IAF HQ, *The History of the Pechora*, 2013.
7. Operations Record Book, No. 50 Squadron IAF.
8. *Lessons Learnt from the Planning and Conduct of Air Operations August-December 1971*, Air HQ, February 1972.
9. History of the Corps of Air Defence Artillery, Directorate General of Air Defence Artillery, Indian Army, 2003.
10. War dispatch, Air Mshl HC Dewan, AOC-in-C, HQ EAC, December 20, 1971.
11. Kaisar Tufail, *In the Ring and on its Feet: Pakistan Air Force in the 1971 Indo-Pak War* (Karachi: Ferozsons Pvt. Ltd, 2018), p. 68.
12. Ibid.
13. Shaukat Ria, *Izzat-o-Iqbal* (Nowshera: School of Artillery, 1980), p. 453.
14. n. 8.
15. Hijazi, n. 2.
16. S. Sajjad Haidar, *Flight of the Falcon: Demolishing Myths of Indo-Pak Wars 1965 & 1971 - Story of a Fighter Pilot* (Lahore: Vanguard Books Pvt Ltd, 2009).
17. Tufail, n. 11.
18. Peter E. Davies, *F-104 Starfighter Units in Combat* (UK: Osprey Publishing Limited, 2014), p. 73.
19. The serial numbers of these RJAF Starfighters were as follows: 56-774, 56-775, 56-767, 56-777, 56-799, 56-839, 56-843, 56-845, 56-1787, 56-1789.
20. Usman Shabbir, Yawar A Mazhar, "F-104 Starfighter in Pakistan Air Force Service," Pakdef.info, Pak mil consortium, http://urbanpk.com/pakdef/pakmilitary/airforce/1971war/F104inPAFService.html. Accessed on July 15, 2018.
21. Tufail, n. 11.
22. Ibid.
23. "Martin B-57A," Wikipedia, https://en.wikipedia.org/wiki/Martin_B-57_Canberra
24. https://military.wikia.org/wiki/Martin_B-57_Canberra. 23.5.21. Accessed on June 20, 2021.
25. Tufail, n. 11.
26. Hijazi, n. 2.
27. Via Mr Jagan Pillarisetti, Peter-Michael Gerhardt on Air Britain Information Exchange. Email dated February 27, 2021.
28. Tufail, n. 11.
29. Hijazi, n. 2. However, Tufail, n. 11, states that No. 15 Squadron operated from Murid under Wg Cdr Syed Nazir Ahmed Jilani.
30. Hijazi, n. 2.

31. Tufail, n. 11.
32. Ibid.
33. Ibid.
34. Ibid.
35. Hijazi, n. 2.
36. Tufail, n. 11.
37. Memorandum of April 28, 1971, from Henry Kissinger to President Nixon in FS Aijazuddin ed., *The White House and Pakistan: Secret Declassified Documents 1969-1974* (Pakistan: Oxford University Press, 2002).
39. Rajiv Dogra, *Where Borders Bleed: An Insider's Account of Indo-Pak Relations* (New Delhi: Rupa Publications India Ltd, 2015).
39. n. 8.
40. Tufail, n. 11; n. 8.

3. Offensive Operations in the West: A Calibrated Approach

VK 'Jimmy' Bhatia

The defence of the East lies in the West.

– *Pakistani War Doctrine*

Since its very inception in August 1947 – when India was partitioned to support the two-nation theory – Pakistan's military high command had always believed that the defence of its Eastern Wing lies in the West and adopted it as its war doctrine. 1971 was no different. The strategic role of the forces in the East was to hold out until Pakistan had defeated India in the West. The bulk of the Pakistani forces were, therefore, deployed in the West. As far as the Pakistan Air Force (PAF) was concerned, it had deployed just one squadron of F-86 Sabres – albeit with an augmented UE (Unit Establishment) – in East Pakistan, while the bulk of its aircraft remained in West Pakistan.

India's war philosophy, however, was just the opposite of Pakistan's with the point of decision being in the East. The ACM Pratap Chandra Lal-led Indian Air Force (IAF) in consonance, had deployed its forces with such numerical strength in the East so as to overwhelm the PAF by unleashing an all-out offensive in the shortest possible time and attain absolute air superiority. This not only helped the Indian ground forces to operate freely in enemy territory, but also made possible the famous Tangail drop that resulted in their race to Dacca for its subsequent fall in record time.

In the Western Sector, however, the IAF adopted a policy of a calibrated approach with the aim of causing as much attrition as possible to the enemy but keeping own losses under control. It was appreciated that territorial gain in the Western Sector was not as much of an aim as preventing the enemy from making advances into Indian territory. The air campaign in the West was structured accordingly.

Air Cmde Jasjit Singh in his book 'Defence from the Skies' has listed 35 squadrons of combat aircraft that were available to the IAF for the two-front war with Pakistan in 1971.[1] Out of these, as many as 11 squadrons had been deployed in the East at the beginning of the war. In the West, type-wise breakdown of combat squadrons was: 5 × MiG-21 or Type 77, 5 × Gnat, 5 × Su-7 or S-22, 3 × Hunter, 2 × HF-24 Marut and 2 × Mystere IVA plus a small specialied unit TACDE. In addition, there was a sprinkling of Vampires and Harvards, which were used rather effectively in the Jammu and Kashmir (J&K) sector for Army Close Air Support (CAS) tasks. The bomber force comprising four Canberra squadrons including the Jet Bomber Conversion Unit (JBCU) and the sole Canberra Photo Reconnaissance (PR) Squadron were centrally located to cover both fronts, on an as required basis. Also, aircraft of No. 44 An-12 Squadron had been modified for carpet bombing tasks.

But for the lone squadron of combat aircraft in the East, the PAF had amassed 12 squadrons in the West, consisting of F-104 Star Fighters, Sabres, Mirage-IIIs, MiG-19s and B-57s. In addition, it had received one squadron worth of F-104s from Jordan and 35 Sabres (approximately three squadrons worth) from Saudi Arabia and Iran.[2]

In pursuance of the IAF's overall aims, broadly of defending its bases against enemy air attacks, and, at the same time, conducting counter-air operations to reduce the PAF's effectiveness by destroying its aircraft and bases, as also to provide effective support to the Army and Navy, Headquarters Western Air Command (HQ WAC), under guidance from Air HQ, had carried out meticulous planning months in advance for air operations in the Western Sector. Nothing was left to chance. All squadrons and units had been given specific roles, with their primary and secondary tasks well defined. For example, the MiG-21 and Gnat squadrons were given air defence as their primary role and were deployed accordingly at IAF bases for Air Defence (AD) duties. In a similar fashion, all ground-attack squadrons were given counter-air and counter-surface force targets. The targets were allotted keeping in view the war locations of the squadrons and their lo-lo-lo radii of action capabilities. Selected squadrons such as No. 32 Thunderbirds and No. 20 Lightnings were chosen to exploit their niche deep penetration capability for such tasks that could not be undertaken by other squadrons.

Maps prepared for the missions and pre-briefings done, the IAF waited for the balloon to go up! In the interim, ACM Pratap Chandra Lal, Chief of the Air Staff (CAS) visited a large number of bases for invigorating and morale-boosting pep-talks.

According to the official history of the 1971 War,[3] it was suspected for weeks and months that the Pakistani attack on India would start with preemptive air strikes on a number of forward airfields. Some information was available on December 1 that Pakistan was likely to strike in a day or two. Under the circumstances, the IAF could very well have preempted the PAF, but the Government of India took a prudent decision to let Pakistan 'do the honours', and strike first.

PAF's Preemptive Strikes and Declaration of War

When the sneaky preemptive assault by the PAF's fighters against seven IAF airfields in the Western Sector on the evening of December 3 actually came, it turned out to be a tame affair, as the strikes were carried out in hurried single passes, with the runways as the predominant targets, causing only superficial damage at some airfields. The IAF, which already had an inkling of the possibility of such action by the PAF, was fully prepared with its aircraft generally tucked away in covered blast pens and, therefore, didn't suffer the loss of even a single aircraft on the ground. The half-hearted PAF strikes followed by the declaration of war by the slurring – somewhat inebriated – Pakistan President Gen Yahya Khan opened the doors for the IAF to roll out its well-planned air campaign, without India being labelled as the aggressor.

IAF Strikes Back

Counter-Air Operations

The IAF's counter-air response was swift, all-encompassing but well calibrated, aimed at causing as much attrition as possible during the opening stages of the war while ensuring that the IAF's own losses did not spiral out of control. The first retaliatory strikes were carried out against a large number of PAF airfields on the same night by Canberra bombers from Central Air Command operating out of Agra and Pune. Western Air Command, on the other hand, was entrusted with the task of carrying out attacks on PAF bases at Sargodha, Shorkot Road, Peshawar, Chaklala, Murid, Chander, Chak Jhumra, Risalewala, Masroor, Drigh Road and, the radar stations at Lahore, Sakesar and Badin.[4] As mentioned earlier, fighter squadrons had been pre-selected for specific counter-air tasks depending upon their locations and reach, and the planning had been done in the preceding months before the outbreak of war. For example, No. 20 Squadron Hunters, equipped with the 230-gallon long-range tanks and based at Pathankot were given Peshawar and Mianwali airfields as targets. Similarly, Hunters of the Operational Conversion Unit (OCU) – also equipped with the above-mentioned long-range tanks were given targets in Karachi area. Then, it was No. 32 Squadron with its operation base at Amritsar – the only Su-7 squadron with 900-litre long-range drop tanks – that was given the task to take on Sargodha and the PAF's Shorkot Road base located in some depth in the Southern Multan sector of Punjab province in Pakistan.

There was a lot of mystery attached to Shorkot Road, considered to be a secret base of the PAF. There was no mention of this base during the Indo-Pak War of 1965. Presumably, the base came into being between the two wars. Its existence came to be known for the first time from information revealed by the PAF Bengali defectors during their interrogation by Indian intelligence agencies just months prior to the war.

Even during the planning stage, the squadron was unsure of the exact location of the PAF's base at Shorkot Road. Two probable positions were plotted on the map and navigation planning done for both, which situation remained unchanged till the first operational mission was actually flown on the morning of December 4 – led by the author, then the youngest squadron leader in the unit.

As tasked, the squadron had planned counter-air strike missions, comprising four aircraft each – a Thunderbird formation led by Wg Cdr HS Mangat Commanding Officer (CO) and an Eagle formation led by the author – against PAF bases at Sargodha and Shorkot Road, respectively. The Eagles included young Flt Lts Sathaye (No. 2), Tambay (No. 3 and deputy leader) and Maly Grewal (No. 4). When the balloon went up on the December 3 evening, most of us were in our home base at Ambala. As Amritsar had suffered superficial damage to the runway and a minor landing mishap involving a MiG-21 during the night, the repositioning flights back to Amritsar were postponed till the morning. The Eagles took off at dawn, skimming over the early morning fog – turned into 6/6 low stratus clouds. A little thaw in the weather near Amritsar saw the formation landing in quick succession off LL circuits (150 m above ground level – agl). The stage was set for the first lot of daylight fighter attacks against PAF airfields.

The Eagles carried out a total of three raids against Shorkot Road in the next 24 h – maximum day strikes against a single PAF base during the war. The Eagle formation was lucky to have found its preferred choice of target location to be the correct one, ensuring that the first strike went on as planned. At the end of those three raids, seven enemy aircraft were awarded as confirmed 'kills' to the Eagles, based on gun camera analyses and the lone Battle Damage Assessment (BDA) sortie flown immediately after the first strike. Own losses amounted to two aircraft shot down – one each in the second and third strike – on December 4 evening and December 5 morning, respectively. The PAF seemed to have given utmost priority to this secret air base by deploying as many as 108 AD guns of different calibres for its protection. A description of these raids in some detail by the author can be found in Bharat Rakshak archives.[5] However, a brief description of the first strike is as follows.

Shorkot Road Raids: The 'Eagles' Strike

First Strike

The aircraft were ready by 0930 h. If I recall correctly, the strike Time on Target (TOT) was 1045 h Indian Standard Time (IST). The morning low clouds had lifted by then and the visibility was reasonably good. We flew a loose broad frontage formation. Keeping low all the way though, stepping up our heights just a wee bit to avoid high tension pylons South of Lahore. A strict R/T (Radio/Telephony) silence was maintained. I knew that all the other members had their eyes peeled to spot bogeys (enemy aircraft) while I concentrated on navigation.

The suspense was building up to a climax when I gave the orders for the pull up. It was sheer delight to find the airfield sprawled below in front of us. I rolled into the attack, heading for the nearest Operational Readiness Platform (ORP), where I spotted a Sabre parked just outside a blast-pen. Closing into correct range, I fired the first salvo of rockets.

Flt Lt Sathaye, my No. 2 who was flying 300 m behind me spotted two Canberras that were being refuelled, and fired his rockets at one of them, while the second pair took on other targets.

The second attack was equally successful. It appeared that we had taken the enemy completely by surprise as not a single shell of ack-ack was fired at us.... The strike turned out to be the most successful one with one Canberra with a bowser and three Sabres as confirmed kills.

Pilots downed by enemy ack-ack were Flt Lt Grewal on December 4 evening and Flt Lt Tambay on December 5. Grewal was taken Prisoner of War (POW) and later was one of the three to make a daring escape attempt from the POW camp for IAF pilots at Rawalpindi.

The 'Eagles' became one of the most decorated formations during the war, earning as many as three VrCs, which also included a Bar to the Vir Chakra.

The lone attempt to attack Sargodha by Thunderbirds on the evening of December 4 failed due to the strike's inability to rendezvous with MiG-21 escorts, causing some confusion in subsequent navigation to the target. It also gave the PAF enough reaction time for interception in the ingress mode itself by the lurking Sabres in the vicinity. This resulted in the strike breaking off with scattered late-dusk recoveries at Amritsar. In the melee, the leader's aircraft received a Sidewinder hit, causing considerable damage to the aircraft, but the robustness of the Su-7 was proved beyond doubt, with the aircraft accelerating to near sonic speeds at low level and a normal (though tailchute-less) landing at base. Thunderbird 1, Wg Cdr Mangat was awarded the MVC for bringing the crippled aircraft back in one piece. There were no further attempts to attack Sargodha during daylight hours.

Further north, under the dynamic leadership of Wg Cdr CV Parker, CO No. 20 Squadron, 'Lightnings' were unleashed to attack the Peshawar and Mianwali airfields, Sakesar radar and Attock oil refinery (to be discussed under the 'Energy Sector'). But equally glorious – if not more – moments were the Lightning attacks on Chaklala (Islamabad) and Murid which came within the first few days of the war. Among the air warriors in the squadron was a naval aviator on an exchange posting from the Navy, namely, Lt Arun Prakash [later Admiral and Chief of the Naval Staff (CNS)] who, writing about his many exploits during the war, recounts how he destroyed a twin-engine Beechcraft belonging to US Air Force (USAF) Brig Gen Charles Yeager. The famous 'Çhuck' Yeager (first to break the sound barrier while flying the Bell X-1) who had been assigned to Pakistan to advise the PAF before the war, was livid with the destruction of his beloved aircraft, and accused Mrs Indira Gandhi of having specifically instructed the pilot to blast his plane.[6]

It may be interesting to note that out of the 21 confirmed and a few probable PAF aircraft losses by IAF counter-air strikes, more than two-thirds were shared between just two squadrons – No. 20 Lightnings and No. 32 Thunderbirds.

Like the Hunters and Su-7s of Nos 20 and 32 Squadrons operating from Pathankot and Amritsar, as described above, Su-7s from Halwara, Hunters from Jaisalmer and Jamnagar and HF-24 Maruts from Utterlai also carried out daylight counter-air sorties against PAF airfields in their respective sectors. PAF airfields engaged were Risalewala, Nawabshah, Hyderabad, Drigh Road, Masroor, etc., with varied results. Apart from this, the Badin radar was attacked with reasonable success by MiG-21s of No. 47 Squadron operating out of Utterlai, however, with the loss of its CO Wg Cdr HS Gill.

Canberra bombers continued with the night attacks, joined by fighters from TACDE – a more detailed account of which is covered later under special operations. However, as stated earlier, the main aim of the counter-air campaign was to force the PAF to go on the defensive while causing as much attrition as possible, but without incurring too many losses by own forces. Once the main aim was achieved after the first few days of the war, counter-air missions reduced to a trickle.

AVM Arjun Subramaniam, commenting on the IAF's counter-air strikes against PAF airfields in his epic book, *India's Wars: 1947-71* writes,

> ... it was quite clear that the IAF's counter-response was low key, calibrated and yet effective as the number of sorties reduced from 140 on December 4 to 70 the next day and finally to less than 10-20 sorties after December 10.[7]

While other writers including Air Cmde Jasjit Singh, in his book *Defence from the Skies*[8] differ on the number of sorties flown in counter-air missions – especially during the first 24 h after the war started – they all agree on the greatly dwindling effort in this domain of fighting as the war progressed.

The Official History of the 1971 War records,[9]

> The general concept for gaining air superiority was to mount relentless attacks on the Pak airfields and radar installations, so to force the PAF to deploy a major portion of its resources for their defence. Such a reaction would then enable the IAF to concentrate on special/strategic strikes and on close support to ground forces with relative impunity. In the light of subsequent pattern of PAF reactions, the preferred concept stood vindicated.

It further records that the efficacy of this strategy was confirmed by F.M. Khan in his book entitled *Pakistan's Crisis in Leadership*.

Counter-Surface Force Operations

As stated earlier, the entire gamut of Counter-Surface Force Operations (CSFO), comprising interdiction, close air support – even search and strike missions – had been planned and catered for by the planners. Adhocism was truly a thing of the past. While forces had been pre-assigned for Army close air support – both pre-planned and immediate – what the tapering of the counter-air campaign did was to set free a large quantum of additional air effort for augmenting the interdiction campaign.

Interdiction

Pakistan generally being a linear country, with its lines of communication running parallel to the international border with India, it was decided to interdict the railway system from Sukkur to Lahore and into the Sialkot-Shakargarh bulge. The aim was to prevent – to the extent possible – any reinforcements reaching the TBAs (Tactical Battle Areas), thus, reducing the effectiveness of Pakistan Army formations in war-fighting. For example, the Hunters from Pathankot, Su-7s from Halwara, Mysteres from Sirsa and Maruts (HF-24s) from Utterlai were used copiously to attack trains transporting military equipment, railway junctions and marshalling yards in their respective sectors bringing almost to a halt any day-time movement by rail in the Western Theatre. Canberra bombers and even An-12s were pressed into attacking selected targets by night to give as little respite as possible to the Pakistan railways.

Operating from Amritsar, the author's log book records two interdiction missions flown on December 6 and 8 on the rail stretches from Montgomery to Sialkot via Shekhupura (Lahore) in what came to be known as 'Search & Strike' missions. Generally flown in pairs of two aircraft, it was delightful to see a train chugging along on the tracks. The tactics followed were to first immobilise the train by attacking the engine with a salvo of rockets and then picking up juicy targets such as tanks, guns and other military equipment being ferried to the front in the next two to three attacks. Passenger trains were spared.

ACM Lal sums up the effect of the IAF's interdiction campaign in the Western Sector thus, "It was clear throughout the operation that the Air Force was effective in largely stopping Pak reinforcements from reaching the frontline and in reducing its movement of weapons and supplies all along the front.... Functioning in its classic role as interdictor, the Air Force was successful in isolating the battlefields where our ground forces repulsed Pak assaults ... and preserved the integrity of our western border with Pakistan."[10]

Close Air Support

Having had a ring-side view as the Vice Chief of the Air Staff (VCAS) of the less than optimum Army-Air Force cooperation mechanism in place during the 1965 Indo-Pak War, ACM Lal, after taking over as the CAS, had worked assiduously to make this very critical segment of war-fighting as efficient as possible. The revamping and restrengthening of the system were all embracing, starting from the apex level at Commands and TACs (Tactical Air Centres) at Corps level, right down to the 'last-mile' connectivity at the level of ACTs (Air Control Teams) and FACs (Forward Area Controllers). AVM Lazaro as the Air Officer Commanding (AOC) Advance Headquarters (HQ) with the Western Army Command had made sustained efforts in running training cadres as well as conducting Army-Air Force exercises to streamline procedures which enabled the reaction time for immediate close air support – from raising of the demand to aircraft on target – to less than two hours. Similarly, through repeated exercises, ground attack pilots were trained to pick up camouflaged Army targets for attack with the help of FACs. Exercises such as 'Summer Madness' in May 1970 and 'Lukewarm' and 'Golden Katar' during the 1971 summer months are well recorded in the author's log book; which incidentally, also included inter-squadron competitions to hone the pilots' skills.

Incidentally, all ground attack squadrons had Army cooperation as their primary or secondary roles, assigned to them in their respective sectors. For example, Nos 26 and 101 Sukhoi Squadrons at Adampur and No. 27 Squadron Hunters at Pathankot were given this as their primary role in the Chhamb sector while No. 32 Squadron, in which the author was serving at Amritsar, had Army cooperation only as its secondary role in support of XV Corps and I Corps formations. Similarly, Nos 3 and 31 Mystere Squadrons ex-Sirsa were earmarked for XI Corps while further south, Nos 10 and 220 Marut squadrons were available out of Utterlai for the Southern Army Command's exploits in the desert sector.

The pre-war meticulous planning/training paid off during the war, with judicious and timely air support being provided to the Army whenever asked for. The PAF had been restricted to generally staying away from the TBAs after the first four days of the war. Sukhoi squadrons from Adampur did a commendable job in the Chhamb sector which had come under pressure during the initial stages of the war. The air effort was further augmented by other squadrons whenever required or even perceived to be required, as it happened on December 6, when a false alarm was raised in Army HQ, prompting the Chief of the Army Staff (COAS) Gen Manekshaw to demand that every available aircraft be sent to the support of the Army in Chhamb.[11] The mistake was soon realised when it was revealed that the available effort was much more than the Army could utilise in close air support. Notwithstanding, the IAF started flying search and strike missions even in the close support role after the front stabilised in Chhamb with a clear-cut bomb line. In addition, bold and accurate night bombing by the Canberras and An-12s in the Poonch and Chhamb sectors put paid to any chances of a Pakistani offensive in these sectors.

The story was somewhat similar in the XI Corps sector in the Suleimanke area, where the older vintage Mysteres' belly launchers with 55 sneb rockets each proved to be potent weapons when fired in salvos. Lal quotes the IAF historian of repute, Pushpindar Singh, in his biography, paying a fitting tribute to the Mystere IVA:

> Providing close support to troops … more than 300 sorties were flown by day concentrating on Pak armour, dumps and lines of communication… Intelligence had reported about 300 tanks of

> the Pak Armoured Division concentrating between Suleimanke, Haveli and Amurka... Mysteres continuously attacked the wooded area around Haveli and succeeded in immobilising Pak armour and shooting up convoys and rail tankers.[12]

The IAF's incessant pounding of Pakistan Army positions also put to rest any Pakistani dreams of a breakthrough at Fazilka, with its armour pouring into Indian territory in the manner visualised in Tikka Khan's grandiose strike force plan for the ultimate 'Mother of all Offensives' to reach Delhi.

Battle of Longewala

Perhaps the most glorious chapter of the IAF's action against Pakistani armour came in the Jaisalmer sector on the desert sands of Longewala, and that needs a special mention. This was the sector where the Indian Army's No. 12 Division under Maj Gen Khambatta had been tasked for an offensive push into Pakistani territory with the aim of securing Rahim Yar Khan (RYK). Its success would not only have destabilised the Pakistani defences in Punjab, but also in the J&K sectors, allowing the planned Indian offensive in the Shakargarh sector to sweep the Pakistani forces trapped there. The advance on RYK was to commence on D+1 i.e., on December 4 but was delayed by a day by Khambatta as he felt his forces were not fully ready for the offensive.

The Pakistan Army, on the other hand, decided to launch a brigade-sized attack on the night of December 4-5, spearheaded by an armour regiment of T-59 tanks to cross the border towards the Indian post of Longewala and race towards Ramgarh. Knowing that the bulk of the Indian 12 Division was on a different axis, the aim was to invest Jaisalmer the same night if no resistance was found at Ramgarh, and run over the IAF base at Jaisalmer. It was a bold plan indeed and had it succeeded, it would have changed the very outcome of the war. It failed on many counts which have been chronicled along with other details of the episode by this writer in "Pages from History", *India Strategic*, October 2013 edition.[13] But the main reason was turning back of the leading tank columns from close to Ramgarh, when they found that other elements of the force were not keeping pace with them, and then failing to attack the Indian post at Longewala and, in the process, daylighting themselves. Also, the Pakistani plan had not catered for PAF support, nor had the attackers visualised the swiftness of the IAF's response.

In the event, the enemy force lay exposed to the IAF and were annihilated after two days of repeated and relentless attacks by just a handful of Hunters from Jaisalmer in what can described as a classic example of 'armour vs. air' battle.

To redux, during the night, General Officer Commanding (GOC) 12 Division, citing his helplessness to defend Jaisalmer had given the option to Wg Cdr MS Bawa to vacate the base with his men in the same manner as he had done with the Coy Cdr, Maj Chandpuri for the Longewala post. However, both decided not to quit their respective locations. While Chandpuri felt he and his 100-odd men had a better chance of survival by quietly staying put at the post, Bawa, on the other hand, activated the ground defences with his own men to protect the airfield, while waiting for daylight to come to take on the enemy with just four single-seat Hunters at his disposal.

The dawn did break and, along with it, all hell broke loose for the Pakistani forces when the first pair of Hunters spotted the enemy tanks advancing towards Longewala – with the help of Air Officer-in-charge Personnel (AOP) pilot Maj Atma Singh who was airborne in his Krishak aircraft – and lost no time in engaging them. This started a dance of death and destruction meted out to the enemy on the sand dunes opposite Longewala post, being watched by Chandpuri and his men from the trenches where they had taken cover. It was like an unending relay where soon after the first pair left the target area, the second pair was came swooping over the enemy. The sheer panic and frustration of the enemy force can be gauged from a message intercepted on December 5 evening, that says it all:

> *Dushman ki hawai fauj ne nak me dum kar diya hai. Ek hawai jahaz jata hai aur doosra auta hai aur bees-bees minute ooper nachta hai. Chaalis*

> *fisadi fauj aur samaan halak aur tabah ho chuka hai. Aage jaana to kya peechhe murna bhi mushkil ho gaya hai. Jaldi hawai fauj madad ke liye bhejo warna waapis murna namumkin hai.*
>
> – Wg Cdr Bawa's Personal War Dairy signal intercept during the war. Once again, quoted ad nauseam in different publications.

Roughly translated, it revealed the desperate situation of the enemy, indicating 40 per cent casualties in men and material and SOS call for close air support without which even withdrawal was considered impossible.

The PAF, of course, was nowhere in sight with the Hunters having a field day on December 6, as well. By the evening of that fateful day, the four Hunters had expended 300 T-10 rockets and 7,000 rounds of 30 mm cannons, destroying 37 enemy tanks and damaging the rest plus a plethora of vehicles, which also resulted in a devastating number of troop casualties. Incidentally, all this was done without a single shot being fired either from an RCL anti-tank gun or, even a rifle shot. Wg Cdr Bawa (later Air Marshal) wrote in his diary, "... The battle of Longewala will be remembered not only by our people for the victory achieved by our Air Force but also by Pakistan for the defeat of its armour in this Thar Desert Outpost."

Years later, in 1996, Mr JP Datta visited Air HQ with a request for a few Hunter sorties from Jaisalmer for his film "Border", that he was making on the Battle of Longewala. He was directed to the office of the Assistant Chief of the Air Staff (ACAS) (Ops), then occupied by this writer. He was given all assistance including ferrying a few Hunters from KKD to Jaisalmer for the film shoot, but with a firm commitment from him that he would stay true to the historical facts of the battle as it had happened. "Border" was released on June 13, 1997. The story had been totally fictionalised – but, at whose behest?

Lal observes in his autobiography, "Though 12 Infantry Division had nothing to do with the stopping of the Pak tank force at Longewala, it nevertheless observes a Longewala Day in celebration of its victory. Do we?"[14]

Targeting Pakistan's Energy Sector

Interestingly and perhaps for the first time, Air HQ's comprehensive air offensive plan also included economic targets with special emphasis on Pakistan's energy sector. As the war progressed, the oil refinery at Attock, the Mangla hydroelectric power complex and the Sui gas plant were attacked during daylight hours by Hunters from No. 20 Squadron and No. 44 Squadron's An-12s. But it was the OCU Hunter pilots from Jamnagar who were the first to light the fires in Karachi by attacking the huge oil tanks farm at Kiamari near the harbour area in an extempore mission allowed by the Stn Cdr, Gp Capt Pete Wilson, on the very first morning of the war on December 4.[15] Led by the CO, Wg Cdr Don Conquest, the mission was flown ultra-low level to evade the enemy radars. Conquest recalls, "As we neared Karachi, the large oil tanks loomed out of the sky, their silver paint shining in the morning sunlight. We made two runs ... and after the first; there were huge balls of fire and volumes of smoke coming out of the storage."

It turned out to be a highly successful raid as the oil tanks kept burning for days after the attack. However, as it was not a pre-planned mission and not known to many people; it also created a lot of controversy with the Indian Navy taking the credit for having set Karachi ablaze – a claim that has crept into every history book and archives on the 1971 Naval War. Fortunately for the IAF, the myth surrounding the 'Karachi' episode was exploded by none other than retired Cmde Ranjit Rai, a Naval Historian of repute who made a categorical mention in his book, *Warring Navies,*[16] that it was the IAF which had attacked the Kiamari oil tanks on December 4, 1971, not the Indian Navy.

History repeated itself on the night of December 9, when Wg Cdr Badhwar-led four Canberra bombers of No. 35 Squadron in the attack on the oil tanks at Kiamari with six 1,000 lb bombs and set them on fire again. Was it a coincidence that the Navy's missile-boat attack against Karachi harbour, code-named 'Op Python' came soon after, with the Navy claiming that it had set Karachi harbour on fire? The fact according to ACM Lal is that neither Service knew of each other's plans of attacking Karachi harbour that night. However, notwithstanding the confusion, Lal believes that "... the loss of millions of litres of oil was undoubtedly a major factor in the growing realisation among military commanders in West Pakistan that they could not fight a war of any duration against India. It gave them justification for ending the war when that opportunity was offered by the Indian Unilateral Declaration of Ceasefire on 17 December."[17]

Among the earlier mentioned pre-planned energy targets in Pakistan, brief details of the attack on the Sui gas plant by An-12s are covered later under the IAF's 'Innovative Special Operations' section. However, the daring raid on Pakistan's Attock oil refinery, which was led by No. 20 Squadron CO, Wg Cdr Cecil Parker, merits a mention here. The Lightnings had researched and rehearsed well, trying out different belting options for penetrating steel structures like oil tanks and allowing the resulting fires to do the real damage. Parker recalls how they disrupted AD guns protecting the target by carrying out a diversionary attack on the PAF base, Chaklala, "This diversionary attack paid off and our first West-East attack on the refinery, drew no ground fire.... We had the unusual sight of a refinery on fire! The blaze was still visible to our Canberra crews on their night bombing raids."[18] Parker repeated the attack two days later but found mainly charred remains and debris. "Along with the IAF attack on the Karachi oil refinery on December 4, Pakistan was now running short on fuel which intelligence told us was being trucked into the country over land", he concludes.[19]

In another daring attack by the Lightnings, this time led by the Flt Cdr, Sqn Ldr RN Bhardwaj, the Hunter formation bombed and damaged the Mangla Dam and its hydroelectric power house which was heavily defended by ack-ack guns. Though suffering hits by ground fire, they managed to return to base without any loss. It is interesting to note that the Lightnings went on to become the most decorated fighter squadron of the war, earning awards that included two MVCs and five VrCs.

Photo Reconnaissance

Some readers may wonder as to how photo reconnaissance can form a part of a chapter devoted to offensive operations but could it be denied that the two are inexorably linked. Photo Reconnaissance (PR) of enemy targets/dispositions gives vital clues to the planners in shaping operations and is of immense value prior to and during operations. PR can also aid in carrying out Battle Damage Assessment (BDA).

There is also a belief amongst some war historians that even though the Army had spelt out its requirement for PR, this was not possible before the commencement of hostilities for obvious reasons. These statements at best can be considered only partially true as, even though there were constraints in crossing the borders before the war commenced, some vital missions did get to be flown against targets of importance, albeit clandestinely, in the months preceding the war in December 1971. The author has five such PR missions recorded in his log book during the period October 31 to November 30, 1971, covering diverse enemy targets in different sectors from Domeil bridge and the surrounding areas in Muzzafrabad in Pakistan Occupied Kashmir (POK), Mirpur opposite Jammu, right down to Rahim Yar Khan in the desert sector, etc. Incidentally, No. 32 Squadron had been given four Su-7s, capable of carrying an internal belly-mounted, single AFA-39 camera each, and had been allotted the PR role as well. These specially modified aircraft were used for the PR missions including the one to capture Chaklala airfield on lens[20] on December 7 and subsequently, while searching for a PAF radar in Lahore area.

Later, living up to the IAF tradition of *jugaad* (or innovative capability), our engineers had also modified a couple of UB-16 rocket pods with the tubes removed to carry two Vinten F-95 cameras each, angled in such a way that a pair of pods could take a panoramic horizon-to-horizon view of the target area during the photo run. This combination was used by me to photograph Murid airfield on December 10. A great advantage of the Vinten set-up was that one had to climb to only 1.5 km compared with 5 km height for the AFA-39 camera to capture an airfield widthwise in a single frame, thus, drastically reducing the exposure time over target.

For strategic reconnaissance, there was always the PR Canberra-equipped No. 106 Squadron based at Agra, which was tasked to carry out a large number of Special Reconnaissance (SR) missions during the war. Writing in *Bharat Rakshak*, Air Mshl GCS Rajwar (then a young Flight Lieutenant) lists out three missions he flew with his CO, the indomitable Wg Cdr RS Benegal (later Air Commodore) in the Western Sector.[21] These included photographing the Karakoram Highway from Khunjerab Pass up to about one-third the distance to Gilgit in POK to check whether the highway was indeed open at that time of the year for the Chinese to be able to send huge quantities of military supplies to Pakistan over the land route – as claimed by one of the Delhi-based envoys from a neutral country. It was a treacherous sortie weather-wise and almost came to be abandoned but for a lucky break in the clouds, permitting a steep nosedive over the pass for the long photo run towards Gilgit. Apart from providing very valuable data and photographic inputs from deep inside enemy territory, the mission finally dispelled all fears that Karakoram Highway was operational in the month of December – much to the relief of the Air Chief and the Government of India.

The other two memorable missions described by Rajwar include photographing the Longewala area after the classic battle of 'armour vs. air' on the sand dunes of Thar, capturing the burnt-out enemy tanks and their feverish manoeuvring to escape the relentless rocket and front-gun attacks by the IAF Hunters. Then, there was a long and gruelling sortie flown to the distant Pakistani base at Gwadar along the Arabian Sea coast, close to the Pak-Iran border, to determine whether Pakistani naval ships had taken refuge there. The photo recce proved the absence of Pakistani warships in Gwadar – vital information much needed by the Navy. It also proved Iran's collusion with Pakistan with the sightings of an Iranian oil tanker heading towards Karachi and a transport aircraft of the Iranian Air Force offloading supplies at the nearby airstrip. For their feats, Benegal and Rajwar were awarded the MVC and VrC, respectively.

IAF's Innovative Special Operations

Role of TACDE in Night Bombing Operations

The saga of night offensives in the Western Sector would be incomplete without detailing the accounts of the TACDE pilots who flew daring single-aircraft night bombing missions against enemy airfields. Incidentally, the TACDE came into being less than two months before the Pakistan Army went on a genocidal rampage against its Bengali population in the then East Pakistan. In its initial *avatar*, it was raised on February 1, 1971, as the Tactics and Combat Development Squadron (TACDTS) at Adampur. As the name suggested, its charter was to develop new methods of combat and attack with fighter and fighter-bomber aircraft to make the Air Force more effective.[22] A little later, the name of the unit was changed to TACDE i.e., Tactical Air Combat Development Establishment, and it was relocated at Ambala.

The unit was set up under the command of Wg Cdr AK Mukherji, who had recently returned from the UK after having done the Day Fighter Leaders' Course with the Royal Air Force (RAF). The unit was provided with two types of frontline aircraft of the time in two flights with Sqn Ldr DK 'Dice' Dhiman and Sqn Ldr OP Sharma as flight commanders of the Sukhoi Su-7 (S-22) and MiG-21 (Type 77), respectively. The unit started with eight pilots (especially selected senior and experienced flyers), four each from different S-22/Type77 units to form a core team for the task.

Within months of its formation, however, as the unit was getting down to the task at hand, war clouds started gathering in the sub-continent. In July 1971, the unit was asked to start training for live armament operations at night. Hitherto, while night live armament was part of the Pilot Attack Instructors' Course, offensive operations were not being practised by the frontline squadrons, mainly because of lack of advanced navigational aids and computer-aiming gunsights for weapon delivery, as they are available on the more modern aircraft today. Notwithstanding, the experienced aircrew of TACDE started to hone their skills in night navigation under near blackout conditions by selecting navigator routes over sparsely populated areas and carrying out simulated medium/steep dive attacks over airfields such as Sarsawa, etc. Co-located in No. 32 Squadron at Ambala, this writer recalls emulating TACDE pilots with a ghost night syllabus of our own to achieve similar skills for night operations – just in case.

ACM PC Lal recalls in his biography *My Years with the IAF:* "At night, especially when there is no moon, landmarks are difficult to make out – they simply get obliterated in the darkness. So, the straighter the route, the fewer the turns, the better is the chance of reaching the correct destination."[23] The art of using rice paper with a pencil-drawn track, superimposed on a million map and then following it through in the dim pencil-thin cockpit light in what came to be known as 'moving thumb display' was perfected. Night aerobatics were practised purely on instruments, thanks to the Russian 'AGD' (artificial horizon) which, unlike their Western counterparts would not topple even in manoeuvres like loops and rolls of the top and which helped immensely in building confidence for pull-up attacks over target. It may be remembered that unlike multi-crew cockpits like the Canberra light bombers and An-12s which were used for night bombing operations during the war, fighter aircraft like the Su-7s or MiG-21s had but one single 'Jock' who mans the cockpit as the pilot, the navigator and, the bombardier, et al.

In the event, when war broke out, the TACDE was prepared to take on the task. For the next three to four nights, TACDE pilots flew night bombing missions against a number of PAF Tier I and Tier II airfields such as Sargodha, Chander, Risalewala, etc., in dim moonlight conditions. They lacked the range to attack the PAF's in-depth airfields such as Peshawar and Mianwali as the limited number of long-range tanks for the Su-7s, as mentioned earlier, had been earmarked for No. 32 Squadron for the strikes against Shorkot Road. After having flown two day time sorties against Shorkot Road on December 4, the author distinctly remembers seeing Dice Dhiman huddled in a corner of a room in the Amritsar Base Ops Complex – earmarked with a solitary red-light bulb for night adaptation – trying to coax the 'rods' in his eyes to get themselves activated for better night vision before walking to his aircraft for a mission with Sargodha as the target. The TACDE operated from both Adampur and Amritsar during this period.

A question asked often is how effective were these missions? It needs to be understood that there cannot be two opinions on the limited efficacy of these single aircraft missions as far as destruction of targets was concerned, flown randomly as they were with just 2 × 500 kg bombs per aircraft. But, overall, they did achieve the aim of causing harassment and giving sleepless nights to the personnel of the airfields attacked, and generally demoralising them. These raids also helped in tying up PAF air defence resources to a considerable extent, for the entire length of the war, even though the TACDE had stopped night counter-air operations after the first few days of the war. In addition, in most of these missions, the targets were reached with such accuracy that made PAF planners and their Western mentors (including Brig Chuck Yeager) believe strongly that these were being assisted by Russian 'Moss' Airborne Warning and Control System (AWACS) aircraft. In reality, there was no such thing except that a MiG-21, call-sign 'Sparrow' (a brainchild of Air Mshl MM Engineer, AOC-in-C WAC) used to get airborne to act as a relay station to pass any important information, including presence of enemy aircraft in the area of operations that were picked up by our radar stations. The Indian government's official history of the Indo-Pak War of 1971 recounts: "Analysing the reasons for the failure of the PAF, H.P. Willimont writes" (War in Peace – An Analysis of Warfare since 1945),

> The IAF was assisted by Soviet Moss aircraft. These were AWACS aircraft and this war seems to have been first conventional war when such aircraft were used to fulfil their detection, control and communications functions. Every move that the PAF made was immediately known to the IAF and the AWACS aircraft in conjunction with active electronic counter-measures, threw a blanket over Pakistani radar and communications. The IAF was able to operate between 320 and 480 km (200 to 300 miles) behind the front line with impunity.

This analysis is totally incorrect, as no Russian Air Force AWACS aircraft operated from Indian soil or over the Indian skies. It is, in fact, a signal tribute and acknowledgement of the skill and effectiveness of the IAF men and material. (Applicable not only for TACDE pilots but the entire lot of air warriors who successfully tackled enemy targets far from the Indo-Pak border, by both day and night.)

An-12s in their Bombing Avatar

But all the innovative exploits of the TACDE would pale in comparison to what one of the An-12 squadrons pulled off by converting the lumbering four-engined turbo-prop cargo transporter aircraft into a formidable bomber. No. 44 Squadron, the 'Himalayan Geese', under the dynamic command of Wg Cdr VB Vashisht, covered itself with glory in the Western Sector during the 1971 War. The idea of converting An-12s for area bombing was first mooted by none other than then ACM Arjan Singh who, overriding the initial apprehension of An-12 crews, asked them to give it a fair trial. Initial trials began in 1967 and continued sporadically. Then, during the monsoon period in 1971, there was a tragic fatal accident when the squadron lost its commanding officer and an entire crew while practising a live bombing mission at the KK ranges in Central India. Wg Cdr Vashisht who took over the squadron in August 1971, under these trying circumstances, had his task cut out – that of restoring morale and making the squadron battle-ready in the shortest possible time. With an able and proactive Flight Commander, it was not long before the squadron was ready for battle.

Honing its bombing skills and modifying the delivery platform with an iron bomb cradle for each 500 lb bomb, which was designed by an Army Officer, the squadron moved to Bareilly in Central Air Command a few days before the war commenced. With a maximum bomb load of 40 such bombs, a six-aircraft mission packed quite a punch of TNT.

Vashisht led the opening shot of night bombing missions with six An-12s, carrying a mix of 500 lb High Explosive (HE) bombs and napalms over the Changa Manga forest on the night of December 3, 1971, and followed it up again on December 4 night. Intelligence reports had indicated that the area had a large ammunition dump and large troop concentrations. The devastating fires that started after the bomb explosions had a debilitating effect on the Pakistan Army.

Over the next two weeks, the squadron flew around 45 missions against a variety of targets that included a Pakistani artillery brigade at Haji Pir Pass that was harassing Indian operations, a divisional headquarters at Fort Abbas, the Sulaimanke bridge, a railway yard at

Hyderabad and the Sui gas plant. The icing on the cake was a cheeky day raid on Skardu airfield on December 17 – the last day of the conflict – with Vashisht leading a force of Canberra bombers, dropping his bombs from as low as 180 ft agl and peppering the Skardu runway with a large number of craters.

The Changa Manga forest raids by An-12s along with Canberras had put effective brakes on Pakistan Army's 1 Armoured Division that was waiting for orders to cross over for an offensive thrust into India. On the other hand, the night raid over Haji Pir and the day raid over the Sui gas plant reportedly proved to be even more effective. While the gas plant was seen to be burning for several days after the raid, the Air and Army Chiefs personally rang up to congratulate the squadron for the successful Haji Pir raid.

The use of An-12s as potent bombers is a classic example of the innovative spirit (or *jugaad* as it's called in local language) for which the IAF is well known. Combine it with astute and determined leadership and the effects can surpass all expectations. Little wonder, it had many military aviation experts around the world shaking their heads in disbelief. Trestled bombs neatly placed on rollers in the fashion of normal logistics supplies and, with no bombing sights on board, bombs being rolled out of the aircraft on a signal from the navigator. A stop watch was used to regulate the release of the bombs to make sure that the entire target area was fully covered. Vashisht went to the extent of tasking the squadron tail gunners to open up with a full burst of ammunition as a parting gift for the enemy, as the aircraft pitched up in supply-drop style to roll out the bombs through the rear ramp doors.

Assessing IAF's Offensive in the West

Was the IAF's all-round offensive able to achieve its objectives in the Western Theatre? The answer to that question should be an emphatic yes. Undoubtedly, the IAF's well-orchestrated counter-air campaign in the opening days (and nights) of the war succeeded in putting the PAF very considerably on the defensive. According to Jasjit Singh, the PAF was forced to employ as much as 57.8 per cent of its total air effort for air defence.[24] The consequences of this process were spelt out by a Pakistani Major General soon after the war. Jasjit quotes him saying, "The defensive strategy of the PAF, in fact, gave the IAF a free hand to interdict Pakistan's communications and other strategic targets and to keep pressure on the Pakistan troops in the forward areas.... IAF could operate without hindrance in the forward areas and over Pakistani vital communications along her borders."[25]

After achieving its counter-air objectives, quickly shifting its focus onto CSFO, with large scale interdiction of Pakistani communication systems and the Pakistan Army's logistics areas, as also providing the required amount of close air support to the Army, the IAF not only pinned down the Pakistan Army in different locations but also succeeded in providing the requisite counter-force to Tikka Khan's strike force, immobilising it before it could even get off to a start.

In the end, while the IAF acted as a spearhead in the Indian military's *blitzkrieg* to Dacca in the East; in the West, it stood as a wall to thwart any offensive design of the Pakistan Army to violate India's territorial integrity.

Perhaps it would be best to quote ACM Lal who summed it up by asking a question, "How did we perform in December 1971?" and also provided the answer, "Well, we can generally say we did not do too badly. In fact, we did rather well: we won the war."[26]

Mission Accomplished!

Notes

1. Air Cmde Jasjit Singh, *Defence from the Skies* (New Delhi: KW Publishers, 2007), p. 139.
2. History Division, Ministry of Defence, Government of India, *Official History of the 1971 India Pakistan War*, chapter-X, The IAF in the West, p. 418.
3. Ibid., p. 414.
4. Ibid., p. 423.
5. Air Mshl V K Bhatia, "Shorkot Road Attack," *Bharat Rakshak*, April 2, 2015, http://www.bharat-rakshak.com/IAF/history/1971war/1280-vinod-bhatia.html#gsc.tab=0. Accessed on June 1, 2021.
6. Adm Arun Prakash, "A Sailor's Memoir of the 1971 Air War", *India Strategic*, Vol 14, Issue 12, pp. 68-70.
7. Arjun Subramaniam, *India's Wars 1947-1971* (Noida: HarperCollins, 2016), p. 395.

8. Singh, n. 1, p. 142.
9. n. 2, p. 423.
10. ACM PC Lal, *My Years with the IAF* (New Delhi: Lancer International, 1986), p. 268.
11. Ibid., p. 231.
12. Ibid., p. 264.
13. Air Mshl VK Bhatia, "Battle of Longewala", *India Strategic*, Vol 8, Issue 10, pp. 60-63.
14. Lal, n. 10, p. 284.
15. Air Mshl VK Bhatia, "Indo-Pak War 1971, IAF First to Light the Karachi Fires", *India Strategic*, Vol 8, Issue 11, pp. 64-66.
16. Cmde Ranjit Rai, *The War Diaries 1971, Warring Navies* (Mumbai: India Publications Company, 2014), p. 110.
17. Lal, n. 10, p. 268.
18. AVM Cecil Parker, "Flying Tales, Indo-Pak War 1971", *India Strategic*, Vol 14, Issue 10, pp. 78-79.
19. Ibid.
20. Air Mshl VK Bhatia, "Indo-Pak War 1971, Capturing Chaklala (On Lens)", *India Strategic*, Vol 15, Issue 2, pp. 68-70.
21. Air Mshl GCS Rajwar, "1971 Bangladesh War, Flying with the Legend", *Bharat Rakshak*.
22. Lal, n. 10, p. 243.
23. Ibid., p. 244.
24. Singh, n. 1, p. 142. The MoD's official history ups this figure by a couple of notches by suggesting estimates of the PAF AD effort as high as 70 per cent.
25. Ibid., p. 142.
26. Lal, n. 10, p. 319.

4. Offensive Air Operations in the Eastern Theatre: The Coercive Impact and Some Lessons

Harish Masand

Introduction

The 1971 War, with particular reference to the war in East Pakistan, has been described as the finest moment in Indian military history after independence. It has also been described as 'a true *blitzkrieg*, following the lines of Liddel Hart's theory of "the expanding torrent" derived from the tactics that the German military followed in the offensive of 1918[1] that were further refined in the German invasion of Poland in September 1939 and the low countries of Europe later in 1940, making this a 'lightning campaign'.[2] Most certainly, the campaign, with the fall of Dacca and the birth of a new nation in just 13 days after hostilities formally commenced with the preemptive air attacks by Pakistan Air Force (PAF) on Indian airfields in the Western Theatre on the evening of December 3, 1971, lends itself to be compared to the German *blitzkrieg*. However, it needs to be pointed out that the capture of Dacca was neither planned nor truly expected. The Indian aim and the Army's plan were limited to liberation of large tracts of territory where an independent Government of Bangladesh could be formed and the millions of Bengali refugees, having fled to India, could be resettled.[3] While a number of reasons could be assigned to this limited aim, it was quite obviously due to the cautious approach of the Army since, even as late as December 13, Gen Manekshaw, then Chief of the Army Staff

(COAS) issued a signal asking the Army formations in the East to capture the Pakistani strongholds and towns that had been contained and bypassed earlier without a mention of Dacca at all.[4]

The chapter argues that the key element or the essential foundation of this lightning campaign of 1971 in the Eastern Theatre was complete air supremacy or dominance of the skies over erstwhile East Pakistan. It was this dominance that made all other air operations as well as surface operations, on both land and at sea, possible and on which this victory was built. Unfortunately, even the Indian Air Force (IAF) has tended to underplay this foundation of the victory while also overlooking some of the important lessons to be drawn from this war. The chapter would also cover all Offensive Air Operations (OAS) in the Eastern Theatre, with particular reference to their coercive impact and how that led to the surrender of Pakistani forces in East Pakistan on December 16, 1971. While a lot has been written on this campaign, for warriors as well as students of military history, it is important to critically re-examine even such outright successes to separate the nuggets of golden lessons that may have been lost in all the din, dirt and euphoria of this glorious chapter in Indian military history, particularly in this year when we celebrate its Golden Jubilee. With this objective in mind, the chapter aims to generate greater thought and debate on this well-chronicled history.

Order of Battle and Numerical Superiority

Undeniably, the Indian Air Force had overwhelming numerical superiority in the Eastern Theatre with 11 fighter squadrons by the time hostilities formally commenced. These included four Hunter squadrons, No. 7 Squadron from Bagdogra, Nos 17 and 37 from Hasimara and 14 in Kalaikunda. Out of these, only No. 14 Squadron operated the advanced version, Mk 56A, which could carry 230-gallon drop-tanks on the inner stations, giving it a much better radius of action. The other three squadrons operated the older version Mk 56, capable of carrying only 100-gallon tanks on all four stations which limited the radius of action. Apart from this, with four drop-tanks, the aircraft could not carry rocket launchers or any other external armament load and had to depend on just the four internal 30 mm Aden cannons with 135 rounds each.

The three MiG-21 squadrons, Nos 4 and 28 from Guwahati, and No. 30 from Kalaikunda, operated the FL or Type 77 version with a total of three external stations. These could be armed with two K-13 Air-to-Air Missiles (AAMs) or UB-16 57 mm rocket pods or 500 kg bombs on the two wing stations. Both their air interception radar and AAMs were not very effective at lower altitudes due to clutter and spurious heat sources. At the same time, the MiG-21FL could either carry a 490-litre external drop-tank on the ventral station or a gun pack/gondola with a 23 mm cannon. However, with the gondola, the endurance and radius of action of the aircraft were severely restricted, particularly at low-levels. All these were severe limitations on the air combat potential of the aircraft.

The three Gnat squadrons, No. 15 from Bagdogra, No. 22 from Kalaikunda/Dum Dum in Calcutta and No. 24 from Tezpur, while extremely capable in air combat against the F-86E Sabres, were again limited by their radius of action and could not effectively operate against Dacca at low-levels. Thus, in the initial phase in the battle for air superiority, the Gnats largely performed air defence or Combat Air Patrol (CAP) duties close to their operating bases.

The lone Su-7/22 squadron, No. 221 Squadron, originally from Central Air Command (CAC), was moved to Panagarh just before commencement of hostilities on December 3, 1971. The Su-7 had four wing stations with twin 600-litre ventral tanks apart from two internal 30 mm cannons. While the Su-7 had excellent ground attack capabilities, and even matched the MiG-21 in air combat, as was later realised and would have useful in combat against the F-86 Sabre,[5] it also suffered from a limited radius of action and, thus, limited combat time over targets like Dacca from Panagarh, when operating at low-levels. In addition, No. 16 Squadron, operating the Canberra light bombers from Gorakhpur, under the CAC, was also assigned and utilised for some missions under the Eastern Air Command (EAC).[6] However, some of these squadrons were under strength. For example, No. 37 Squadron only had 14 fighters against an establishment of 16.[7] In all, the total fighter strength was about 160 between these 11 squadrons.[8]

Against these 160 fighter/fighter-bombers was a single No. 14 Squadron of the PAF, operating from Tejgaon airfield at Dacca with 16 upgraded F-86 Sabre aircraft initially[9] till it lost two aircraft to Gnats over Boyra/Garibpur in the now famous air Battle of Boyra on November 22, 1971, even before formal commencement of hostilities.[10] On December 4, this lone squadron at a single airfield of Tejgaon had 14 Sabres facing the much larger IAF from almost eight different bases.[11] In all fairness though, the IAF also had to cater for the Chinese threat, particularly after the debacle of 1962, and had to keep a number of aircraft at various bases in readiness to counter any Chinese moves in support of Pakistan, at least for the first few days. As an example, both Nos 4 and 28 Squadrons had to leave behind six aircraft each at Tezpur to meet any such contingency.[12] In addition, eight aircraft of No. 30 Squadron were moved to the Western Theatre on December 5 itself, with the remaining four serviceable aircraft following on December 8. Similarly, No. 7 Squadron was moved West on December 7 while No. 221 Squadron moved to Ambala later on December 14.[13] The three Gnat squadrons were also not initially utilised against Dacca due to the low-level profiles specified by the EAC. Considering all this, it could be surmised that out of the 11 fighter squadrons, only six squadrons were initially utilised against East Pakistan for OAS, dropping to five squadrons by the fourth day and then building up to about eight squadrons when the three Gnat squadrons started operating at medium to high levels and were also switched over to Close Air Support (CAS) and interdiction missions.

Pakistan's Strategy

Pakistan denuded its military and particularly its Air Force in East Pakistan based on its strategy of "defence of East Pakistan lies in West Pakistan".[14] Kaiser Tufail justifies this Pakistani military strategy due to the military situation being seen as hopeless and "the PAF's air element not expected to last beyond two-odd days at best", as it actually happened.[15] Taking a contrarian view, it could be argued that, considering the manner in which the battle was fought, had the PAF assets in the East been beefed up by another two to three fighter squadrons at different bases with some radar cover and Anti-Aircraft Artillery (AAA), air superiority of the type achieved, the liberation of Bangladesh could have been delayed to an extent or, perhaps, even denied due to international political and diplomatic pressure on India.[16] Even the blockade of the Bay of Bengal with the carrier fleet, led by the INS *Vikrant*, that became a force-multiplier in this war,[17] may have become far more difficult.

Reconnaissance and Intelligence

It is undeniable that good and timely intelligence is the basis for any successful operational plan and its execution, military or otherwise. The fog of war invariably degrades available intelligence, making it even more important to collect good intelligence before commencement of hostilities and to update it regularly during the war through all available means. It is also just as important to pass on all filtered intelligence, instead of mere raw data, to the field units and the actual war-fighters.

In mid-1971, in a timely move to meet the reconnaissance needs in this theatre, the EAC decided to equip around seven Hunters, six fighters and a trainer of No. 37 Squadron based in Hasimara with three Vinten cameras each for Fighter Reconnaissance (FR). Earlier, Vampire T-55 trainer aircraft of Nos 101 and 108 Squadrons met the reconnaissance needs. After conversion of these two units to Su-7/MiG-21s, these assets were lost though the Su-7s, as of No. 221 Squadron, came with an in-built AFA-39 camera, which was good for vertical photography. In any event, the Vampire had become highly vulnerable to enemy air defences even in the early 1960s due to its vintage and performance. The Strategic Reconnaissance (SR) asset with the IAF in 1971 was the Photo Reconnaissance (PR) version of the Canberra, which too was similarly vulnerable over hostile air space, particularly by day. By the time hostilities commenced, No. 37 Squadron had done nine FR missions but No. 221 Squadron had not been utilised in this role till December 2/3.[18]

FR missions by No. 37 Squadron commenced in October with the last one as late as December 2 over Comilla and Lalmai Hills when IV Corps in that area had already started offensive operations.[19] Viewed from any angle, this was too late for any meaningful planning for the planned offensive. Additionally, none of these missions was over Tejgaon or Kurmitola airfields in Dacca, that were reported to be the bases for the PAF's Sabre squadron, because Dacca was perhaps considered "too deep in East Pakistani territory for the IAF to have carried out reconnaissance missions before operations".[20] The Su-7's standard reconnaissance profile was a run at 10,000 ft at very high speeds, generally 1.1 Mach, at which speeds the Sabre could never hope to catch the Su-7. However, even No. 221 Squadron was also under-utilised by the Army as well as the Air Force, for reasons that are difficult to fathom even today.[21] As a result, no target photographs of Tejgaon or Kurmitola, indicating their layout, key installations, blast pens and likely parking areas of the Sabres were available to the squadrons at the commencement of hostilities.[22] Even on the first day, December 4, such reconnaissance was not immediately carried out to make such target photographs and intelligence available to the operators for the missions next day.[23] While Jagan mentions that No. 221 Squadron flew a Su-7 reconnaissance mission over Tejgaon on December 5,[24] its results and photographs, if any, were not passed down to the operating squadrons. The Canberras of No. 106 Squadron carried out damage assessment reconnaissance missions on December 8 by which time most of the airfields including Tejgaon and Kurmitola had been rendered unusable[25] and were visited for limited repeat bombing just to keep them in that state. It is obvious from this that initially, even the Navy did not have any photographs of their likely targets in Chittagong and Cox's Bazaar, which they probably got only after the above missions.[26]

Some information was also collected from PAF defectors who came across to India and joined the Mukti Bahini in the fight for the liberation of Bangladesh.[27] Inexplicably, even this limited information and rudimentary sketches of the airfield layout, including parking areas of aircraft, were not disseminated to the operating squadrons to assist the attacking formations in picking the right targets in the first pass itself.[28] Due to lack of such vital intelligence, attacking formations, in the specified lo-lo profiles, had to pull up and then look for suitable targets while the heavy Anti-Aircraft Artillery (AAA) picked on the unlucky ones amongst them or, with their attention focussed on identifying the targets on the ground, lay themselves open to attacks by the Sabres on Combat Air Patrol (CAP). On December 4 itself, the IAF lost four Hunters and one Su-7 over Dacca, out of which two were confirmed lost to AAA: Flt Lt SG Khonde in a Hunter from No. 37 Squadron and Sqn Ldr SV Bhutani in a Su-7 from No. 221 Squadron. Two Hunters of No. 14 Squadron, Sqn Ldr KD Mehra and Flt Lt K Tremenheere, were lost to Sabres while there are differing accounts on Sqn Ldr AB Samanta of No. 37 Squadron.[29] Be that as it may, the fact remains that five aircraft were lost over Dacca itself without destroying a single F-86 on the ground or causing any notable disruption in their operations at Tejgaon while two Hunters of No. 7 Squadron were lost to AAA at Lalmunirhat,[30] lack of adequate intelligence on the targets certainly being a contributory factor in such losses.

Achievement of Air Supremacy

While the battle for air superiority can be said to have truly commenced with the Boyra engagement and shooting down of two Sabres on November 22, as mentioned earlier,[31] the opening shots from the Indian side after declaration of hostilities were appropriately fired by the daring attacks by night on December 3 by 'Kilo Flight', the air arm of the Mukti Bahini formed with the support of the IAF, with their single Otter aircraft and Alouette helicopter.[32] The same night, eight Canberra aircraft with 8 × 1000 lb bombs each attacked the two airfields, Tejgaon and Kurmitola, at Dacca. However, the runways, installations and the Sabres on the ground remained unscathed by these attacks and PAF operations the next day were unhindered. The results were no better even the next night.[33]

Earnest efforts to destroy the Sabres on the ground or shoot them down in the air were launched the next morning, on December 4, by wave after wave of Hunters, MiG-21s and Su-7s, with the first Time on Target (ToT) of 0705 h Indian Standard Time (IST). Inexplicably, despite the huge numerical asymmetry in the IAF's favour, the missions were planned in a lo-lo profile, which did not permit carriage of effective munitions for airfield attacks and had little or no combat fuel reserves. The Hunters carried all four 100-gallon tanks with just internal cannons, while the MiG-21s in the strike role carried the 490-litre ventral drop-tank, thus, without the gun pack, and two UB-16 57 mm rocket pods. Even with all four drop-tanks, the Hunters from Hasimara were operating beyond their calculated lo-lo radius of action, which gave them no combat reserves and also cut into their diversionary fuel. Due to this reason, the EAC had tasked MiG-21s from Guwahati to rendezvous with the Hunter strike formations over the target and cover them against the threat from the Sabres during the pull up and attack phases.[34] Unfortunately, many of these raids were intercepted short of the target when the MiG-21s had not established contact with the strike formations. Due to this reason, a majority of the strike formations had to disengage and return home or engage the Sabres with low fuel states and little perseverance in combat, returning home at medium to higher levels without any diversionary fuel.[35]

A summary of the first wave of attacks against Tejgaon airfield indicated that out of the 17 Hunters, 14 MiG-21s (out of which six were on escort role) and two Su-7s, only four MiG-21s of No. 28 Squadron, two Su-7s of No. 221 Squadron and two Hunters of No. 14 Squadron got through to the target but caused little damage. Only one Mi-8 of the Pakistan Army was damaged and several personnel injured, with three of them later succumbing to injuries.[36] By the end of the first day, three Sabres were shot down in air combat, as also admitted and confirmed by Kaiser Tufail, while two to three Hunters were lost in air combat,[37] and one Hunter and one Su-7 were lost to AAA over Dacca, with some other aircraft also damaged.[38]

More importantly, with a realistic assessment of the day's achievements and losses, it was realised that the day's raids, a total of 112 counter air sorties, were not yielding the desired results. The MiG-21s, armed only with the primitive K-13 AAMs without a gun, were not effective in shooting down Sabres in the air because of the poor performance of the K-13 in dogfights and at low-levels while the Hunters and Su-7s with internal cannons, which could have effectively engaged the Sabres in air combat, were not intended to be used in this role and, in any case, did not have the fuel reserves to do so due to incorrect selection of the lo-lo profiles. The losses, particularly to the heavy AAA, were not commensurate with the results achieved since the PAF was still capable of mustering at least eleven Sabres for operations. It was also realised that the lone squadron of Sabres, forced on the defensive with such massive numerical asymmetry, would not pose a threat to Indian airfields or surface forces. While "the heavy presence of aircraft over the skies of Dacca did have a psychological impact",[39] the coercive impact would have been far greater if the offensive had been planned better at medium/high levels right from the start[40] with a lesser focus on air defence of own airfields wherein 111 sorties of CAP, amounting to almost 40 per cent of the total effort,[41] were mounted.

Based on this review of the first day, the EAC ordered fighter sweeps the next morning to try and lure the PAF Sabres into air combat. Accordingly, a mission of eight Hunters, four each from Nos 17 and 37 Squadrons, was first launched with some more to follow through the day. The PAF, perhaps warned by their AR-1 radar about the numbers, wisely declined such unequal battle.[42] Unfortunately, once again, these missions were largely at low-levels with little time to loiter over Dacca or the fuel to engage in meaningful combat if the Sabres had actually decided to engage when the formations turned home at their extreme range. A four-aircraft Gnat armed patrol, launched later in the day from Dum Dum, at 25,000 ft also returned without being challenged, despite having descended to 8,000 ft over Dacca to loiter and invite air combat for some time.[43] The Sabres did not respond, perhaps wisely against superior numbers obviously trying to lure them into combat, unless their airfield or survival was under threat.

The EAC finally came around to bombing of runways by the evening of December 5, with the first trial mission over Kurmitola based on the suggestion of Wg Cdr 'Bhoop' Bishnoi, Commanding Officer (CO),

No. 28 Squadron and Gp Capt 'Mally' Wollen.[44] Based on the success of this mission, that Headquarters (HQ) EAC was anxious to confirm in a hurry,[45] four MiG-21s with 500 kg M-62 bombs were launched the next morning, with another four as escorts, against Tejgaon airfield to great effect. This was followed by another raid of eight MiGs just after mid-day and a similar attack on Kurmitola airfield in the early evening.[46] Concurrent with these strikes against airfields in Dacca, other satellite airfields in East Pakistan like Jessore and Barisal, had also been attacked to prevent their use. Extensive damage was done to the runways at Tejgaon and Kurmitola, keeping the PAF busy during the night of December 6 to repair and recover at least a 5,000 ft strip of runway at Tejgaon to permit fighter operations the next day. However, a lone MiG-21 strike before sunrise at 0430 h IST on December 7 put paid to the efforts to get the runway operational, making the Flight Commander of the Pakistani No. 14 Squadron, Sqn Ldr Dilawar Hussein, say that when he went to the runway to inspect the state of damage, tears rolled down his cheeks. "The fate of East Pakistan has been decided, he muttered to himself, sentimentally".[47] Seeing the writing on the wall, the PAF pilots were evacuated and escaped through Burma in two batches in a twin Otter in the wee hours of December 9 and 10, leaving behind 11 Sabres out of the initial 16.[48]

Air supremacy, resulting in complete dominance of the skies over East Pakistan, was thus, won in less than 72 hours, though at some cost. Considering all the aspects, it is felt that if the IAF had adopted medium or high level strikes with bombs from the very first wave, given the numerical superiority, it could have grounded the lone Sabre squadron in Dacca in the first couple of hours itself, perhaps with fewer losses and expedited the surrender of the Pakistani forces.[49] Further, even after the experience of 1965, the IAF had also not devised suitable air combat tactics for the jet age despite many IAF pilots having trained on F-86 Sabres in the US between 1962-65,[50] and at the Day Fighter Leaders School in the UK till 1957,[51] which could have improved the air combat kill ratio. Operational squadrons, and individual pilots, were thus left to their own devices to formulate tactics, with many wingmen just sticking to their leader without being of any help during manoeuvres and, sometimes, being shot down. Such a state was to continue even into the 1971 Indo-Pak War till the formation of the Tactics and Combat Development and Training Establishment (TACDE), which started development and dissemination of combat tactics to operational squadrons only after the 1971 War.[52]

Nonetheless, it is indisputable that it was this dominance in the air, achieved with great effort, bravery and sacrifice, that paved the way for unrestricted freedom for other operations, including the bold heliborne move across the Meghna river, by Sagat's IV Corps from December 9 and the drop of 2 Para at Tangail on December 11, 1971.[53] As practitioners of aerospace power, air warriors need to adequately emphasise this aspect as the foundation of such manoeuvre operations while drawing the right lessons in future analyses and discussions on this war.

Naturally, the Army focusses more on its own contribution to this great victory. For example, JFR Jacob, then a Major General and Chief of Staff of Eastern Command of the Army, does not even mention that air supremacy was to be a prerequisite while discussing the evolution of plans and strategy.[54] While joint planning and operations are not being analysed in this paper in any detail, except to the extent of the air support provided to the Army and the Navy, the inadequacy of joint planning is reconfirmed by such land-centric evolution of plans and strategy wherein the Air Force and the Navy are considered as merely supporting arms/ Services and not as the major players in the planned offensive due to lack of understanding of air power.[55] Even the 'official history' of the 1971 War puts little emphasis on this aspect with just a bland statement that "the IAF and the Navy, on the one hand, *contributed* to the rapid advance of the Army and, on the other hand, thwarted the attempt of Pak troops to escape".[56] Just ponder over the outcome if the IAF, and the Navy, had not been able to *contribute* to the extent they actually did. It is only when discussing the failure of Gen Niazi's strategy to defend East Pakistan that the official history mentions Indian air supremacy as the first amongst many factors.[57] Jacob also laments the lack of the promised two squadrons of Mi-8s, when Mi-8s were only just about arriving in crates at Bombay in December 1971 as per the contract schedule, while relegating

Sagat's effort as "a token crossing",[58] ignoring the herculean effort made by the tiny Mi-4 fleet in helping get almost a division-sized force across the Meghna. This is contrary to all other accounts; particularly by Sagat himself saying that "he made preparations to that end with wholehearted cooperation of Gp Capt Chandan Singh".[59] In the same vein, Jacob also erroneously claims the credit for the now-famous interception over Boyra when Gnats of No. 22 Squadron downed two Sabres on November 22, 1971.[60] Typically, the Army only misses the Air Force when not available as flying artillery or when subjected to enemy air strikes, as exemplified by Boyra from November 19-22,[61] without realising that the best way the Air Force can contribute to their operations is when they neither see enemy aircraft over them nor their own fighters which should be busy keeping the enemy pinned down elsewhere.

The above accounts need to be contrasted with the enemy's perception and assessment. Dilawar's sentiments on the morning of December 7 have already been quoted earlier. The overall impact and coercive effect of the Indian air supremacy truly come out in Niazi's reply at the surrender ceremony to Air Mshl Dewan, Air Officer Commending-in-Chief (AOC-in-C) EAC, when asked why he surrendered though he had the troops to hold out much longer. Niazi pointing to the wings on Gp Capt Chandan Singh's chest, said, "This had hastened the surrender. I and my people have had no rest during day or night, thanks to your Air Force. We have changed our quarters ever so often, trying to find a safe place for a little rest and sleep so that we could carry on the fight, but we have been unable to do that".[62] While Niazi does not mention the above statement in his account of the war, focussing essentially on how he was betrayed by the political and military leadership in West Pakistan, he does mention Indian air supremacy in many places as the first factor which hampered his operations while also rejecting the Indian Army's claims of a "lightning' campaign".[63]

CAS and Interdiction

A significant improvement in the organisation for providing air support to the Army in 1971, as compared to 1965, was the establishment of an Advance HQ at Fort Williams and a Tactical Air Centre (TAC) at every Corps/sector, with a clear demarcation of the bases and affiliated squadrons providing such support. Having learned from the performance in 1965, the Chief of the Air Staff, ACM PC Lal, also ensured that each Corps also had a number of well-trained Forward Air Controllers (FACs) seconded to them by the IAF well before commencement of hostilities.[64] Fortunately, at that time, the IAF also had surplus pilots in the squadrons,[65] particularly fighter pilots, who were familiar with their particular area of operations and the pilots of the squadrons providing the support, making communications and control easier, with fewer possibilities of jamming or misdirection.

Close Air Support (CAS) and interdiction missions started in earnest from December 4, since the IAF was not allowed to carry out any offensive missions before hostilities had formally commenced.[66] Even with the focus of the IAF on counter-air missions, on that day itself, the IAF flew 55 sorties in support of the Army. However, Jagan does cite Maj Gen AK Verma on the failure of the IAF to provide a promised CAS mission against Akhaura that day, due to its preoccupation with counter-air missions[67] even though IV Corps received the maximum support through the war amounting to over 500 sorties out of a total of about 1,350 sorties.[68] This was essentially due to Sagat's understanding of what air power could do for him in his bold and imaginative use of his forces.[69] However, as mentioned previously, the EAC flew 111 CAP sorties on the first day[70] due to air defence being the first laid-down objective for the IAF[71] perhaps based on its experience of losing a large number of aircraft on the ground in 1965, with 36 aircraft destroyed and another 17 damaged, to enemy air raids.[72] While this priority of objectives may have been suitable for initial operations in the Western Theatre, the EAC should have realised that a single Sabre squadron, which did not launch any preemptive strikes on December 3 concurrently with the strikes in the West, would have its limited capacity overwhelmed by the planned counter-air missions on December 4. Such timely realisation could have saved a lot of effort from such CAPs that could have been better utilised in CAS and interdiction missions whereby, perhaps, even this lone promised mission against Akhaura may not have been missed.

By the end of the day, such a realisation did dawn on the EAC and more effort was switched towards support of the Army. The next day, December 5, the CAS effort doubled and amounted to 111 sorties. However, some effort towards CAPs continued to be wasted as exemplified from the focus of No. 22 Squadron in Dum Dum whereby some pilots even did three sorties of CAP that day out of the five to six sorties each, perhaps to prove a point on "the orange juice Air Force".[73] By December 8, the CAS effort had increased to 121 sorties though, thereafter, the demands from the Army were progressively reducing as they encountered lesser resistance and, on many occasions, there was surplus effort available, with aircraft either just sitting on the ground waiting for an immediate demand or launched on interdiction missions beyond the known Forward Line of Own Troops (FLOT), particularly against riverine traffic.[74] In the East, the IAF flew over 2,000 combat sorties out of which around 68 per cent of the effort of over 1,350 sorties was devoted to CAS missions[75] with some more on reconnaissance for the Army.

In addition, once air supremacy was achieved, from the night of December 7/8, Caribous of No. 33 Squadron based in Guwahati were pressed into night bombing of Tejgaon and Kurmitola airfields in an innovative and bold move to harass the PAF and obstruct their efforts to repair the operating surfaces while denying the Pakistanis any rest, till the fighters took over by day.[76] While these area-bombing missions were more of nuisance value due to inaccuracies in bombing, their overall psychological and coercive impact cannot be underestimated as indicated by Niazi's statement of December 16 quoted earlier. In addition, in another innovative application suggested by Gen Sagat, Caribous also attacked and harassed the Pakistan Army garrisons holed up in fortresses like Maulvi Bazar, Bhairab Bazar, Lalmai and Comilla to add to the psychological impact on the enemy.[77]

The Indian Navy's Eastern Fleet, led by its flagship, the aircraft carrier INS *Vikrant* also contributed notable effort in the air campaign while carrying out its main task of blockading East Pakistan from the Bay of Bengal despite serious boiler problems that restricted its speed to just 14 knots.[78] With its full complement of 18 Sea Hawks and five Alize aircraft, the *Vikrant* was in position by the night of December 3/4 and launched eight Sea Hawks with rockets and guns against Cox's Bazaar airfield on the morning of December 4.[79] After an eight-aircraft strike by Hunters of No. 14 Squadron on Chittagong airfield earlier in the morning and a confirmation by the EAC that there were no PAF Sabres in that area, to which the Sea Hawks would have been vulnerable, the *Vikrant* launched another eight Sea Hawks against Chittagong airfield and harbour in the afternoon.[80] In addition to such attacks against shore installations and sea craft by Sea Hawks and Alizes, the Navy also provided some CAS effort in the southern portions of Chittagong hill tracts, an area which was not easily within reach of IAF fighters till the Gnats of No. 24 Squadron were moved to Agartala on December 12. Unfortunately, many of these naval CAS missions failed to establish contact with the FACs or targets and were, therefore, ineffective.[81] The Navy flew a total of 123 sorties on Sea Hawks and 70 on Alizes. Out of these, 23 Sea Hawk sorties were flown in support of the Army.[82]

Special Targets and Coercive Operations

Apart from the psychological and coercive impact of total dominance in the air, as mentioned earlier and also evident from Niazi and Governor Malik's frantic signals on December 8/9,[83] the EAC began attacks on targets of strategic significance as the demands for counter-air and CAS missions started decreasing and more air effort became available. This commenced with an attack on Joydebpur Ordnance Factory on December 8 and one mission by An-12s on December 12/13.[84] However, the most significant of such coercive operations was the attack on the Governor's House on December 14. The quick reaction of the EAC, and the units under it, was evident from a chance interception of a wireless message about a planned meeting of top Pakistani officials and others at noon at the Governor's House. Four MiG-21s from Guwahati and four Hunters from Hasimara were immediately launched to carry out the attack while the meeting was in progress. The attack resulted in the immediate resignation of Governor Malik and fleeing of his Cabinet to the Intercontinental Hotel. As per Jagan, this attack was an act of spectacular intimidation and the last psychological blow to a crumbling regime that prevented street-by-street fighting.[85]

As per Arjun Subramaniam, "Niazi's will to resist was broken by a combination of 'feeling enveloped' from all directions" with Sagat's aerial manoeuvres in tandem with the paradrop at Tangail "combined with the precision strike by the IAF's MiG-21s and Hunters on the Government House" which ensured complete psychological disintegration of Niazi's forces.[86] This attack has also been described as "the proverbial last straw on the camel's back".[87] The above *coup de grace* was followed by attacks on Dacca University campus where Pakistani troops for the defence of Dacca were reportedly holed up. This was the last nail in the coffin of the East Pakistan Army conveying the message that the IAF would relentlessly continue to hunt them down, meaning that "you can run but you can't hide".[88]

Conclusions

While describing offensive air operations in the Eastern Theatre, this chapter has argued that the essential foundation to this victory in 1971 was laid by the air supremacy in the skies over East Pakistan. Without such dominance in the air, it would not have been possible for the Army to move forward at the pace it did, without suffering unacceptable losses to enemy air action. Nor would it have been possible for Gen Sagat Singh to carry out the heliborne outflanking manoeuvres across the Meghna river and make Dacca his objective. The paradrop of a battalion group at Tangail on December 11 would also not have been possible without such dominance in the air. Keeping the skies over East Pakistan and the Bay of Bengal clear of enemy Air Forces is what gave the Army and the Navy the freedom to operate with impunity and move at the time and place of their choosing in pursuit of their objectives without fear of an attack by enemy Air Forces.

Without the forces of Sagat's IV Corps and Gen Nagra's 101 Communication Zone at the gates of Dacca from almost all sides by December 14/15, it may have been impossible for Gen Jacob to convince Gen Niazi of East Pakistan to lay down arms and surrender. The *coup de grace* was also delivered from the air by the timely and precision attacks on the Governor's House on December 14, leading to Malik's resignation and obvious effect on Niazi, evident from his statement quoted earlier. This was followed by air attacks on the Pakistani troops hiding within Dacca University campus. Such demoralising blows and the consequent psychological disintegration of the Pakistani forces were instrumental in the collapse of their resistance, leading to the surrender, thus, avoiding street-by-street fighting in Dacca that could have delayed their defeat with needless loss of lives on both sides.

This chapter has also argued that the Pakistani strategy of 'defence of the East lies in the West', which led them to denude their forces, particularly Air Forces, in East Pakistan, was flawed and actually worked in India's favour. Had the Pakistanis invested a little more in their Air Force in the East, the conflict could have been prolonged and may well have brought international pressure to halt military operations before the capture of Dacca and the final surrender. Gen Manekshaw's signal of December 13, which ordered occupation of the fortress towns that had been earlier bypassed without mentioning Dacca, is also indicative of this possibility. Such an end state may have resulted in unforeseen consequences for the future of Bangladesh.

Considering all this, it is unfortunate that the importance of such air supremacy has not been adequately acknowledged in later analyses and discussions on this glorious victory. Admittedly, the air battles were fought against a vastly inferior enemy and the desired air supremacy could have been achieved in the first few hours, instead of the two days that it actually took, but that does not truly detract from the achievement except to drive home the lesson that operational plans need to built based on a correct assessment of the prevailing environment and accurate intelligence, with offensive and innovative application of air power.

Despite hitherto unprecedented levels of cooperation among the three Services and provision of over 1,350 sorties, or more than 68 per cent of the total combat effort, devoted to CAS, apart from helicopter and transport support, the need for better joint planning based on a better understanding of each other's capabilities and limitations still emerges from this war. If this had been done in the months of preparation preceding the war, the military objectives and the timeframes may well have been completely different, with Dacca identified as the centre of gravity and the most important objective. With such air supremacy, greater emphasis on manoeuvre warfare could have emerged and the requisite air and surface assets to make that possible for all three Corps in the Eastern Theatre could have been planned. As it happened, only Sagat's IV Corps grabbed the opportunity with the available air assets and cooperation of Gp Capt Chandan Singh, while the other two Corps, II and XXXII, essentially fought a frontal attrition war notwithstanding Jacob's later claim of manoeuvre warfare.

The Indo-Pak War of 1971, and particularly the air operations in the Eastern Theatre, comprise a glorious chapter in the history of the Indian military that has many lessons, some of which are still to be learnt and appropriately adapted through better education and cross training for all three Services.

Notes

1 Peter Paret, Gordon A Craig, Felix Gilbert, eds., *Makers of Modern Strategy: From Machiavelli to the Nuclear Age* (Princeton NJ: Princeton University Press, 1986), p. 803.

2. Jasjit Singh, *Defence from the Skies* (New Delhi: KW Publishers, 2007), p. 143.

3. Randhir Singh, *A Talent for War: A Military Biography of Lt Gen Sagat Singh* (New Delhi: Vij Books India Pvt Ltd, 2013), pp. 115-118; PC Lal, *My Years with the IAF* (New Delhi: Lancer International, 1986), pp. 171-172; SN Prasad and UP Thapliyal, eds., *The India-Pakistan War of 1971: A History* (New Delhi: Natraj Publishers, 2014), pp. 447-449.

4. JFR Jacob, *Surrender at Dacca: Birth of a Nation* (New Delhi: Manohar Publishers, 1997), p. 129.

5. Author's personal experience on Su-7s in No. 101 Squadron in 1973 and particularly when on the staff of TACDE, AF, in 1978-79; PVS Jagan Mohan and Samir Chopra, *Eagles over Bangladesh: The Indian Air Force in the 1971 Liberation War* (New Delhi: HarperCollins Publishers India, 2013), p. 168.

6. Mohan and Chopra, ibid., pp. 59-60; and the Orbat shown with 'Airfields and IAF units in the Eastern Sector' before Contents.
7. Ibid., p. 67.
8. Ibid., pp. 378-79; Arjun Subramaniam, *India's Wars: A Military History 1947-1971*, (Noida: HarperCollins, 2016), p. 352.
9. Ibid., p. 352; M Kaiser Tufail, *In the Ring and on its Feet: Pakistan Air Force in the 1971 Indo-Pak War* (Lahore: Ferozsons Pvt. Ltd, 2017), p. 177.
10. Mohan and Chopra, n. 5, pp. 81-91; Tufail, n. 9, pp. 140-141; Subramaniam, n. 8, pp. 367-370. While Arjun Subramaniam mentions that there were four Sabres out of which three were shot down, both Jagan Mohan and Kaiser Tufail bring out that there were only three Sabres in that engagement out of which two were lost to the Gnats with the leader, Wg Cdr Afzal Chaudhry getting back. Wg Cdr SF Soares, the No. 2 in the Gnat formation, also recalled that there were only three Sabres and confirmed seeing Chaudhry's damaged aircraft during his visit to Dacca just after the war, in a telephonic conversation with the author.
11. Tufail, n. 9, p. 135.
12. Mohan and Chopra, n. 5, pp. 100-101.
13. Ibid., p. 381.
14. Singh, n. 2, p. 123.
15. Tufail, n. 9, p. 135.
16. Mohan and Chopra, n. 5, p. 371. While this book suggests an additional squadron in Kurmitola airfield in Dacca, it may have been more appropriate for the additional squadron to be based at Chittagong, which was out of range for most IAF aircraft at low-levels, as also mentioned at p. 160, except the Hunters of No. 14 Squadron from Dum Dum or Kalaikunda. Additional squadrons would have also given the PAF the ability to go on the offensive against IAF airfields that may have made the battle for air supremacy bloodier and longer, considering the manner in which it was initially fought.
17. Subramaniam, n. 8, pp. 350-351.
18. Mohan and Chopra, n. 5, pp. 67-70, 92-94 and 97.
19. Ibid., pp. 92-96. Mohan and Chopra erroneously mention the date of this reconnaissance as December 1 as also the timing. On that day, Wg Cdr 'Suppi' Kaul was called to HQ EAC. The author personally led two aircraft to Guwahati the next morning, prepared the maps and then undertook the mission as Suppi Kaul's wingman in the forenoon of December 2. For some more details on FR by No. 37 Squadron and this mission, see Harish Masand, "My Experiences and Some Lessons of the 1971 War", *The Blue Skies Podcast,* April 18, 2021, https://blueskiespodcast.com/blog/f/my-experiences-and-some-lessons-of-the-1971-war. Accessed on May 17, 2021.
20. Mohan and Chopra, n. 5, p. 108.
21. Telephonic conversation with Air Cmde Sridharan, then commanding No. 221 Squadron in 1971, April 8, 2021; and Mohan and Chopra, n. 5, p. 97.
22. Email exchange and telephonic conversation with AVM BK Bishnoi, then commanding No. 28 Squadron, April 3-6, 2021. Also see Mohan and Chopra, n. 5, pp. 151-152 and 236.
23. Ibid.

24. Ibid., p. 169.
25. Ibid., pp. 237-38.
26. Ibid; personal conversations with VAdm Vinod Pasricha on June 4, 2021 and RAdm PD Sharma on June 3, 2021, who flew the Sea Hawks from the INS *Vikrant* during the war and confirmed that they had no target photographs for the initial attacks.
27. Mohan and Chopra, n. 5, pp. 34-42 and 67-68.
28. n. 21 and n. 22.
29. Mohan and Chopra, n. 5, p. 385; Tufail, n. 9, p. 189. While Jagan Mohan lists Sqn Ldr Samanta as lost to AAA over Dacca based on the account by his wingman Flt Lt SKJ Nair in the mission report, Kaiser Tufail's account at p. 146 and explanation at n. 12, p. 153 -appears more plausible.
30. Mohan and Chopra, n. 5, p. 385.
31. Please see details on two Sabres, n.10.
32. Mohan and Chopra, n. 5, pp. 94-95 and 106-108.
33. Ibid., pp. 108-109, 168; Tufail, n. 9, pp. 147-148.
34. Mohan and Chopra, n. 5, pp. 109-119. For some inaccuracies in this account, please see Harish Masand, "Eagles over Bangladesh: Getting the Facts Right," VAYU III/2014, pp. 110-114, https://www.vayuaerospace.in/Issue/202005312051329266.pdf. Accessed on May 10, 2021.
35. For an example of such a strike, please see Harish Masand, "The 4th of December 1971," *The Blue Skies Podcast,* April 18, 2021, https://blueskiespodcast.com/blog/f/4th-december-1971. Accessed on May 17, 2021.
36. Mohan and Chopra, n. 5, pp. 119-131. While the summary on p. 131 counts 18 Hunter sorties, it was actually 17 sorties since the very first formation from No. 37 Squadron comprised of three aircraft.
37. Ibid; and Tufail, n. 9, pp. 188-189.
38. Mohan and Chopra, n. 5, pp. 150-153.
39. Ibid.
40. Masand, n. 19.
41. Mohan and Chopra, n. 5, p. 152.
42. Ibid., pp. 168-169.
43. Ibid., p. 169; and conversation with Wg Cdr Sunith Soares on April 7, 2021.
44. Mohan and Chopra, n. 5, pp. 168-174; and conversation with now AVM BK Bishnoi between April 3-6, 2021.
45. Mohan and Chopra, n. 5, p. 174.
46. Ibid., pp. 185-192 and 194-197.
47. Tufail, n. 9, p. 148.
48. Ibid., pp. 149-51.
49. Masand, n. 34.
50. Subramaniam, n. 8, p. 317.
51. Gp Capt Kapil Bhargava, "TACDE," *Bharat Rakshak,* November 10, 2012, http://www.bharat-rakshak.com/IAF/units/squadrons/13-tacde.html. Accessed on March 17, 2021.
52. Author's personal dairy.

53. Singh, n. 2, p. 143; Subramaniam, n. 8, p. 383; Mohan and Chopra, n. 5, pp. 294-295.
54. Jacob, n. 4, pp. 55-77. Please also see the lessons from pp. 157-163, particularly on p. 158 where credit is given only to the Army.
55. Masand, n. 19; Jacob, n. 4, pp. 169-175 with particular reference to Questions 1(b) and 5. This portion also confirms that air intelligence was not given any importance by the Army.
56. Prasad and Thapliyal, n. 3, p. 401, emphasis added.
57. Ibid., p. 446.
58. Jacob, n. 4, pp. 76, 173.
59. Prasad and Thapliyal, n. 3, p. 448.
60. Jacob, n. 4, p. 72.
61. Mohan and Chopra, n. 5, p. 83.
62. Ibid., p. 355.
63. AAK Niazi, *The Betrayal of East Pakistan* (New Delhi: Manohar Publishers, 1998), pp. 130-131, 200, 217-219 and 275.
64. Mohan and Chopra, n. 5, p. 159; Subramaniam, n. 8, pp. 375-376.
65. Masand, n. 19.
66. Subramaniam, n. 8, pp. 367-368.
67. Mohan and Chopra, n. 5, pp. 167-168.
68. Ibid., p. 177; Subramaniam, n. 8, p. 389.
69. Lal, n. 3, pp. 214-215.
70. Mohan and Chopra, n. 5, p. 152.
71. Singh, n. 2, p. 125; Mohan and Chopra, n. 5, p. 59.
72. Subramaniam, n. 8, p. 332; Jasjit Singh, *The Icon: Marshal of the Indian Air Force Arjan Singh* (New Delhi: KW Publishers, 2009), p. 208; Jagan Mohan and Samir Chopra, *The India-Pakistan Air War of 1965* (New Delhi: Manohar Publishers, 2005), Appendix A-C for claims and actual losses.
73. Mohan and Chopra, n. 5, pp. 152, 182-183.
74. Ibid., pp. 244-245, 371.
75. Ibid., pp. 382-383; Singh, n. 2, p. 144.
76. Ibid., pp. 228-233, 245-248, 265-266, 303, 370. It, however, may be noted that even MiG-21s and Su-7s could have carried out such harassment bombing by night by single aircraft at random timings from medium and high levels.
77. Ibid., p. 340; PVS Jagan Mohan, "Remembering Sagat Singh (1918-2001)," *Bharat Rakshak,* October 12, 2006, http://www.bharat-rakshak.com/ARMY/personnel/martyrs/175-Sagat-Singh.html. Accessed on June 3, 2021. Also see PC Lal, n. 3, p. 231.
78. Subramaniam, n. 8, pp. 348, 360.
79. Prasad and Thapliyal, n. 3, pp. 380-381.
80. Mohan and Chopra, n. 5, pp. 150, 160.
81. Ibid., pp. 160, 163, 254, 318.
82. Prasad and Thapliyal, n. 3, pp. 395-397.
83. Mohan and Chopra, n. 5, pp. 263-264.
84. Ibid., pp. 238-39, 318.

85. Ibid., pp. 326-336, Masand, n. 34; Harish Masand, "The Attack on Governor's House," *The Blue Skies Podcast,* April 18, 2021, https://blueskiespodcast.com/blog/f/the-attack-on-governors-house. Accessed on May 17, 2021.
86. Subramaniam, n. 8, pp. 433-434.
87. Prasad and Thapliyal, n. 3, pp. 403, 410-11.
88. Mohan and Chopra, n. 5, pp. 342-243; Masand, n. 85.

5. Air-Land Operations in the East: The Game Changer

Arjun Subramaniam

Introduction

A distinct feature of most narratives of India's spectacular military victory in East Pakistan in December 1971 is the underplaying of joint operations to accommodate single-Service achievements. It is only in recent times that some amount of study is being done into the fine print of how operations on the ground, in the air and on the waterways, were intrinsically linked with one another to create a joint operational effect that led to the psychological collapse of the Pakistan Army with much of its fighting potential intact. This chapter will offer a nuanced perspective of some of the widely-acclaimed air-land operations and maritime air operations, along with a few lesser-written-about ones, where the Indian Air Force (IAF) added significant value in driving operational outcomes. The chapter will also showcase the importance of informed and decisive leadership in the planning process, particularly when it came to the ability of the IAF leadership to impress on the Indian Army that several other enabling roles of air power other than offensive air power could make a difference to the tempo of operations on the ground.

Planning for Battle

ACM PC Lal, the IAF chief, was, without doubt, the principal orchestrator of the IAF's aerial campaign, in both the Eastern and Western Theatres. Unlike in 1947, 1962 or 1965, where the IAF Chiefs were dwarfed in age and personality by their Army counterparts, no such situation existed in 1971. Despite the larger-than-life presence of Gen (later Field Mshl) Manekshaw, the Army Chief, both Lal and Adm Nanda, the Naval Chief, held their own during operational discussions in the planning and preparatory phase that spanned almost eight months from March-November 1971.

India's military force structure strategy vis-à-vis Pakistan prior to the 1971 War was simple: build asymmetry by widening the quantitative gap and narrowing the technical gap between the two armed forces. From an IAF perspective, this was achieved by adopting a multi-pronged strategy that involved upgrading existing platforms like the Hunter and MiG-21 fighter aircraft; complementing old but reliable platforms like the Canberra bomber-cum-reconnaissance aircraft with new ones such as the Sukhoi-7 fighter-bomber aircraft, and, lastly, by galvanising the indigenous military industrial complex to support capability building. Organisations like Hindustan Aeronautics Limited (HAL) pitched in to accelerate India's defence preparedness. Aiding this indigenous drive was the growing Indo-Soviet strategic bonhomie, which resulted in an accelerated licensed production programme that was further cemented by the Indo-Soviet Friendship Treaty of September 1971.

Much has been written over the years about the overwhelming advantage enjoyed by the Indian Army in the Eastern Theatre. A closer look at numbers reveals that the asymmetry conformed to more or less a ratio of 3:1, which was generally a globally accepted norm for victory during offensive operations in the plains. The Indian Army's Eastern Command under Lt Gen JS Aurora deployed a little over three Corps around East Pakistan comprising around nine infantry/ mountain divisions and three regiments of armour. Added to this were approximately two divisions of 'fighting fit' Mukti Bahini regulars in dispersed locations, both within Bangladesh and on the borders. Ranged against this force were a little over three and a half divisions and almost two regiments of armour of the Pakistan Army, albeit hastily organised and reinforced from the West.[1]

The IAF, on the other hand, built up overwhelming superiority in the East in every domain be it aircraft, airfields or air defence radars. It could call on almost 10 fighter squadrons and a bomber squadron for the entire range of offensive air operations. The three Mi-4 helicopter units in the East were well-trained to execute the never-attempted-before heliborne operations at the brigade and divisional levels; and it was in a position to muster almost 50 transport aircraft to execute the Indian Army's first two-battalion airborne operation What was significant in the steady build-up of IAF capability was the fact that its Chief, PC Lal had a ring side view of all the mistakes made during the 1965 War – he was the Vice Chief during the period. In his quiet and unassuming way, Lal went about addressing the major deficiencies using a systems approach. Building of blast pens to disperse and protect aircraft; procuring and locating air defence radars and modern communication systems to prop up the air defence network; locating Mobile Observation Posts (MOPs) along the border to provide early warning to airfields of incoming air strikes through radio communication; ensuring adequate armament stocks and moving squadrons from their peace-time locations to the forward locations were among the measures initiated to ensure that the IAF was ready in all respects to fight a two-front war.[2] As against a Pakistan Air Force (PAF) air defence network, which comprised only one high level radar in the East,[3] the IAF had a better organised radar network.[4] This would play a critical role in directing IAF interceptor aircraft against the lone PAF Sabre squadron as it attempted to carry out ground attack missions against advancing Indian Forces.

The IAF had concentrated its forces in the East with four main objectives. First was to achieve air superiority over the East Pakistan skies by overwhelming the single Sabre squadron, either in aerial combat, or by destroying it on the ground. This, the IAF argued, would enable the Indian Army to progress its operations unhampered by aerial interference. Surprisingly, cratering of Tejgaon airfield at Dacca, the home base of the Sabre squadron, was not initially considered as a means to achieve the first objective. This would result in a lot of unnecessary air effort being wasted on the first two days of the war before the IAF struck on the right weapon to render Dacca airfield unusable. Second was to preserve own air assets against aerial attack with robust all round air defence. Third was to support ground operations with responsive Close Air Support (CAS), effective interdiction of rear echelons and supply lines that connected the various East Pakistani fortresses and enclaves. And last to aid in vertical envelopment of enemy positions by Special Heliborne Operations (SHBO) and air-borne operations.

Reflecting the improved synergy between the Indian Army and the IAF, most airfields in the Eastern Sector had adequate offensive punch, and were carefully chosen to support the ground offensive.[5] While the fighter squadrons at the airfields of Panagarh, Dum Dum and Kalaikunda were allocated forces to support II Corps operations, the north Bengal airfields of Bagdogra and Hashimara had a good mix of air defence and ground attack capability in the form of Gnats and Hunters to support XXXIII and 101 Communication Zone operations. Similarly, air assets at Gauhati, Kumbhigram and Agartala in the form of fighter squadrons and helicopter units were to prove invaluable in providing support to Sagat Singh's IV Corps and operations by 101 Communication Zone. Though the forces allocated during the actual conflict were not specifically meant for a particular Corps, keeping in mind the flexibility of air power and its ability to influence far-flung battles in multiple Corps zones, great thought was given to basing forces to remain synchronous with the ground battle.[6]

Shaping the Battlefield

Prior to December 3, and much to the frustration of some of the Indian field commanders, even as several Indian Army formations made inroads into East Pakistan, the IAF was not pressed into action as New Delhi did not want to seem to be the initiator of the conflict. After much provocation and some losses suffered by the ground forces to strafing and rocket attacks by Sabres from No. 14 Squadron PAF operating out of Tejgaon (Dacca), the IAF first provided air defence cover during the Battle of Boyra. On November 21, as the Pakistanis called upon the lone armoured squadron of approximately 14 Chaffee tanks along with repeated air strikes to throw back the numerically superior Indian Forces in a counter-attack, the IAF was finally called into action, much to the relief of the Indian brigades under attack.

Controlled by a radar unit located at Barrackpore, a few miles out of Calcutta, four Gnat fighters of No. 22 Squadron were 'scrambled' on two occasions – once in the morning and then in the evening – to try and intercept the Sabres that were attacking the Indian brigades. Much to the frustration of the Gnats and the Indian brigades, the Sabres had vanished from the area by the time the IAF fighters arrived over Boyra. After another unsuccessful attempt on the morning of November 22, the Indians finally drew blood in the afternoon thanks to some aggressive flying by a bunch of four 'young guns'.[7] In a classic aerial dogfight between two comparable machines, the IAF Gnats pounced on a careless bit of tactical flying on the part of the experienced PAF Squadron Commander who was leading his formation of three Sabres on a ground attack mission. While Wg Cdr Chaudhry, the Commanding Officer of the squadron managed to get back unscathed, his two young formation members were shot down by Ft Lt Roy Massey and Fg Offrs Lazarus, Ganapathy and Soares. Massey, Lazarus and Ganapathy were the IAF's first Vir Chakra awardees of the conflict. This tactical engagement has been one of the most dissected aerial engagements of the 1971 War and numerous lessons were drawn from it.

Soon after he took over command of No. 37 Squadron (Black Panthers) at Hasimara (an air base in North Bengal) in April 1971, Wg Cdr Swaroop Krishna 'Suppi' Kaul (later the Chief of the Air Staff – CAS) was asked by the Senior Air Staff Officer (SASO) in Eastern Air Command, AVM Devasher to explore the possibility of modifying the Hunter Mk 56s to carry photo-recce pods.[8] This was considered a key operational requirement to create a mosaic of ground deployments of the Pakistan Army in East Pakistan. Accordingly, from May-June 1971, around six fighter aircraft and a trainer of the squadron were modified with Vinten cameras, two side-looking F-95s and a forward-looking F-135 in the nose. By October 1971, the Black Panthers were doing Fighter Reconnaissance (FR) missions inside East Pakistan, photographing areas/targets of interest that helped improve the situational awareness of the Indian Army. Kaul did some nine photo reconnaissance missions before the war, the last one being as late as December 2 over Comilla and Lalmai Hills for IV Corps.

Early Battles

While significant gains were made in the northwest sector of operations towards Thakurgaon and Dinajpur, the border defences at Hilli were a tough nut to crack and a Pakistan Army battalion, 4 Frontier Force (FF), and a company of 13 FF along with some armour and artillery fought a valiant defensive battle against 202 Brigade of the Indian Army from well-fortified defences. This prolonged battle of attrition from November 22 to December 7 ended when the defences at Hilli were bypassed by another Indian brigade as the defenders withdrew to their depth defences at Boyra. Air Mshl B.N. 'Bingo' Gokhale was amongst the youngest IAF pilots to take part in the 1971 operations. He recollects that his first mission on December 4 as part of a four aircraft Hunter formation from No. 7 Squadron was an interdiction mission against a railway station near Hilli. No. 7 Squadron in particular flew several missions in support of 202 Brigade in what turned out to be among the fiercest battles in the East. This was part of the operational plan to isolate Hilli and prevent any reinforcements from coming in, or enabling the defenders to withdraw towards their depth defences at Boyra.[9] After incurring some losses during the initial days of the war, the Indian Army rightly looked at bypassing fortified forward defences, rather than taking them on headlong.[10]

The effective neutralisation of the lone Sabre squadron in East Pakistan by repeatedly attacking Tejgaon airfield outside Dacca till it was unusable contributed significantly to the progress of the ground battles thereafter. Without belittling the effort of the Hunter and Sukhoi strikes over Tejgaon (Dacca) airfield, it was without doubt the innovative steep dive bombing attacks by MiG-21s of No. 28 Squadron and No. 4 Squadron that created unrepairable craters and made the runway unusable. Planned and orchestrated by the enterprising duo of

Gp Capt Mally Wollen (station commander at Tezpur) and Wg Cdr Bishnoi (Squadron Commander of No. 28 Squadron, also at Tezpur), Flt Lt Manbir Singh of No. 28 Squadron, now a sprightly and adventurous octagenarian, recollects that he was amongst the first to carry out live trials of steep dive attacks with 250 kg Russian bombs on December 5, at Kurmitola, an unused airfield close to Dacca, before peppering Tejgaon airfield for the next two days and three nights with similar attacks.[11] Though the IAF suffered a fair bit of attrition during the first few days of the air campaign, both to Sabres and ground fire, it achieved almost total air superiority by December 7, thus, paving the way for unrestricted CAS and interdiction, heliborne and airborne operations thereafter.

The systematic degradation of Tejgaon airfield forced the Sabre squadron pilots to abandon 11 out of the 16 aircraft by December 6, and flee to West Pakistan via Burma in a Twin Otter light aircraft. To be fair to the adversary, despite the poor leadership of their Squadron Commander, No. 14 Squadron PAF and the rest of the pilots led by its Flight Commander, Sqn Ldr Dilawar took on a much superior IAF with courage and bravery.[12] In hindsight, had the PAF based two more fighter squadrons in the Eastern Sector, the trajectory of the ground battles would have been different. From a joint perspective, this was the biggest operational mistake that East Pakistan's Martial Law Administrator and Commander of all Pakistani forces in the East, Lt Gen AAK Niazi, made.

Effective Close Air Support: IAF's Unsung Forward Air Controllers

Even while striving to achieve complete air superiority, the IAF provided effective Close Air Support (CAS), now called Battlefield Air Strikes (BAS) over some of the tough peripheral battles being fought at Hilli, Kamalpur, Akhaura and the Belonia bulge. One of the reasons for the relatively better performance of the PAF in CAS missions as compared to the IAF in 1965 was because of better integration of the Forward Air Controllers (FACs). This time around every Indian Army Corps had a Tactical Air Centre (TAC) with trained FACs, who orchestrated the CAS in response to the requirements of field commanders.[13]

An FAC provides the last mile connectivity between attacking airborne platforms (fixed wing aircraft or attack/armed helicopters) and their designated targets on the ground. The FAC could either be ground based or direct fire from a light/scout helicopter. The FAC concept became an integral part of air-land operations in World War II where it was used effectively by Montgomery's 8th Army and Tedder's Royal Desert Air Force as also by the Allies during their operations in Italy and the Normandy landings. The concept was further refined during the Vietnam conflict and adapted well by the Pakistan Army during the 1965 India-Pakistan War.

ACM Lal took cognisance of this and ensured that all Indian Army Corps in 1971 had well trained FACs seconded to them well before the outbreak of hostilities. Two such FACs in the Eastern Sector were Flt Lts Savur and S.C. Sharma, both Dakota pilots from No. 49 Squadron. While the former was attached to II Corps and was involved in operations from November onwards, the latter was on attachment to 8 Mountain Division commanded by Maj Gen K.V. Krishna Rao, which was part of Sagat Singh's rampaging IV Corps. After a spell of intensive training at Tejpur to familiarise himself with fighter operations and controlling fighter aircraft during CAS, little did Sharma realise that he would be part of the first heliborne operation conducted by India's armed forces against an external adversary on December 7, as the entire 4/5 Gorkha Rifles (4/5 GR) would be landed close to Sylhet Garrison by 105 Helicopter Unit led by Sqn Ldr C. S. Sandhu and supported by a couple of armed Chetak helicopters led by Flt Lt Singla.[14] Recounting his version of the action packed eight days that he spent with the Gorkhas in the thick of battle, directing CAS missions and coordinating aerial resupply and Casualty Evacuation Missions (CASEVAC) with a callsign of *Hellcat Control*, Sharma recollected over the phone from Jaipur, Rajasthan:

> After a helicopter recce of the proposed landing zone to the south of the road railway bridge south of Sylhet on the morning of 7th by Gp Capt Chandan Singh, Brig Quinn, the brigade commander and Lt Col Harolikar, the CO of 4/5 GR, it was decided that the

> whole battalion would be landed between 1600 hrs and sunset in about four waves. I was in the first wave with the CO and two other officers and about 75-80 troops of 'C' Company. To our surprise, the Pakistanis were waiting for us at the Landing Zone (LZ) with at least a company of well dispersed troops. As soon as the helicopters started hovering for landing, the firing commenced – drowned by the noise of the helicopters we were unaware of the reception waiting for us until the helicopter crew asked us to get off quickly by asking us to jump off from the hovering choppers from about five feet. It was only when we had jumped off with all our equipment dispersed here and there that we realised we were under fire. Quickly assuming control after asking all the troops to lie still in the fading light, Harolikar took stock of the situation and realised that the subsequent waves were not going to come in until he radioed that the Landing Zone was clear. Having ascertained the position of the defenders as they shouted "Allah-o-Akbar" to intimidate the pinned down Gorkhas, he and his company crawled stealthily across the Landing Zone and when they had closed in to less than 40 metres, the Gorkhas sprang up in unison shouting "Jai Kali Maa, Ayo Gorkhali" and closed in with Pakistani troops of 31 Punjab Regiment, mowing down many with their khukris. The defenders retreated to a village 400 metres away and when all was clear, Sharma radioed via his LUP-734 portable radio set that all was clear and the remaining waves could come in. Lighting up the LZ with a mere two lights, the rest of the battalion was heli-landed through the night as 'C' company ensured no interference from the Punjabis and a Baluchi company, which had reinforced the Pakistani defences around midnight. The stage was set for a fierce battle the next morning.[15]

The Indians had not anticipated such fierce resistance at Sylhet and as Harolikar and his men fought the Sylhet brigade in a series of skirmishes, Sharma was right there at the forefront of the battle with Harolikar as part of his 'Rover Group'. For the next six days, Sharma directed air strikes by Hunters and Gnats against targets in and around Sylhet and ensured a steady stream of dropped supplies and regular CASEVAC by Mi-4 helicopters of 105 Helicopter Unit (HU). Harolikar is effusive in his praise for Sharma as he repeatedly directed IAF fighters onto targets in the Sylhet garrison.[16] The young IAF officer was awarded a Vir Chakra for his courage and willingness to stay with forward elements of the battalion as they closed in on Sylhet. Sharma recollects that he even ventured out on a few night ambushes as the Gorkhas harassed the Pakistani troops as they attempted to retreat towards the Sylhet Garrison. Sharma also recalls the events leading to the surrender of the entire Sylhet Garrison of over a brigade to a mere battalion of the Indian Army on December 16. After spending another 10 odd days in the area, Sharma returned to his Dakota squadron by early January 1972. He had no idea that he would be put up for a gallantry award and it was only in March 1972 that he came to know from the papers that he had been awarded a Vir Chakra. His experience with 4/5 Gorkhas is what 'jointmanship' is all about!

The overwhelming superiority of numbers meant that the IAF could not only provide air support to the forward battles being fought, but also carried out interdiction of trains, ammunition dumps and defences around the fortresses of Dacca, Narayanganj and Sylhet. This was done primarily by the rocket-firing Hunters and Sukhoi-7s as they blasted logistics reinforcements and defences around the beleaguered garrisons.

Classic Joint Operations : IV Corps in Action

As 57 Mountain Division, 23 Division and 8 Mountain Division under Maj Gens Ben Gonsalves, R.D. Hira and K.V. Krishna Rao respectively (the three divisions from IV Corps) found themselves on the East banks of the rivers Meghna and Surma respectively, their Corps Commander, Lt Gen Sagat Singh was searching for innovative solutions to seriously threaten Dacca by the end of the first week of operations in his Corps Zone. Turning to his IAF Task Force Commander, Gp Capt Chandan Singh (later AVM), he remarked, "Chandan, do what you have to but get me across the Meghna river to put pressure on the Dacca Garrison. If there is a window of opportunity, I want to be the first into Dacca." If there was anyone in the IAF who could match up to Sagat's energy and his ability to convert operational ideas into outcomes, it was his fellow Rajput, Gp Capt (later AVM) Chandan Singh, the quasi-official Helicopter Task Force Commander in the theatre.[17]

If Sagat Singh's heliborne operation at Sylhet comprised a heavyweight boxer's right hook, he followed up like any good boxer with a solid punch to Niazi's gut between December 9 and 11, when he helilifted more than a brigade worth of troops from Ben Gonsalves' battle-hardened 57 Division across the mighty Meghna river to two landing zones at Raipura and Narsingdi, which were barely 60 km from Dacca. Not satisfied with that, he pressed-on with a left hook on December 12 by helilifting another brigade to Narayanganj, around 40 km Southeast of Dacca. Between December 6 and 12, a 14-helicopter task force from three units (105,110 and 111 Helicopter Units of the IAF) had landed over 4,000 troops and most of their supporting equipment, including ammunition and light artillery guns, in three locations by flying around 350 sorties, including over 100 by night.[18] The operation was summed-up by Chandan Singh, who wrote:

> The success of the heliborne operations was mainly due to the guts, determination, perseverance and courage of the pilots. However, it must be said that without the air supremacy achieved by our fighters and fighter-bombers, this colossal task could not have been carried out.[19]

IV Corps' operations during the Bangladesh campaign comprise an ideal case study for the conduct of aggressive joint operations driven by operational commanders. Gp Capt Chandan Singh, the Station Commander at Jorhat and an accomplished and aggressive transport pilot with extensive operational experience and a gallantry award under his belt for his exploits during the 1962 conflict with China, was the single point contact with Sagat Singh. Between them, they juggled with the fairly large complement of helicopter resources at their disposal.

With almost two squadrons worth of Mi-4s put together from 105, 110 and 111 Helicopter Units, and a few IAF and Army Aviation Alouette helicopters, Sagat and Chandan worked tirelessly to plan multiple heliborne operations and helilift operations to outflank and surprise the enemy.

Over 350 sorties were flown by the Mi-4 and Alouettes of the IAF and the 659 Army's Air Observation Post (AOP) unit in the Sylhet and Ashuganj sectors, lifting almost three brigades with their logistics and artillery requirements in what came to be known as the 'Meghna Air Bridge Operation'.[20] This operation also marked the baptism by fire of the Indian Army's small helicopter arm as pilots flew risky communication and reconnaissance sorties with their daring Corps Commander Sagat Singh and one of his equally enterprising Divisional Commander, Maj Gen Ben Gonsalves, as they put the pieces of their innovative helilift operation across the Meghna river together.[21] Two bold commanders with tremendous 'out of the box' risk-taking ability, Sagat Singh and a much junior Chandan Singh, changed the contours of the 'Race to Dacca'.

Even in the case of CAS, IV Corps exploited the IAF's fighter assets to the maximum. Out of a total of approximately 1,350 CAS missions flown in the Eastern Theatre, over 500 of them were flown in support of IV Corps.[22] Sagat Singh understood the importance of additional firepower and psychological impact of CAS and pushed both the TACs to their limits as they struggled to cope with the pouring requests from Sagat's formation commanders for continuous air support. To its credit, Eastern Air Command responded brilliantly and supported Sagat's rapid advance by even sending Gnats of No. 24 Squadron to operate in the ground attack role from Agartala runway on December 12. The runway was extended by a few thousand feet so that the fighters could operate from there and strike targets at Sylhet, Maulvi Bazaar, Ashuganj, Bhairab Bazar and Brahmanbaria within minutes.[23]

INS *Vikrant* in Action

After an initial flurry of attacks by IAF Hunters of No. 14 Squadron on Chittagong airfield on the morning of December 4, the *INS*

Vikrant, commanded by Capt Swaraj Prakash, took over the task of carrying out airfield attacks on Cox's Bazaar airfield[24] and interdiction missions against shipping with their Sea Hawks. By doing so, they indirectly supported 83 Brigade of IV Corps as it headed south to capture Chittagong. From December 5 to 14, not only did the inland riverine ports of Khulna and Chalna face heavy air attacks from the *Vikrant*,[25] there was also extensive destruction of port infrastructure, runway installations at Cox's Bazaar and Chittagong and significant destruction of the Pakistan Navy's residual naval potential in the East in the form of patrol boats and landing craft.[26] Sea Hawks and Alizes of INAS 300 and INAS 310 with their guns, rockets and bombs sank almost eight patrol boats and an equal number of merchant ships with the *INS Brahmaputra* too joining the lop-sided naval battle by sinking a few patrol boats off the coast of Chittagong.[27] The effective blockading of Chittagong and Cox's Bazaar not only sealed off any escape routes for the Pakistani forces, but also choked the seaborne supply routes into East Pakistan. VAdm Pasricha recalls the operations from the flight deck of the *Vikrant* during those exciting early days of combat:

> I flew about 15 sorties on the Sea Hawk in those seven days of operations and we mainly used 4" rockets and 250/500 lb bombs to attack surface targets. The entire complement of 18 Sea Hawks and 5 Alizes were on board. With the limitations of the *Vikrant's* max speed due to technical problems, launch used to be quite a tricky proposition with full weapon load. We would achieve sustainable speed after the catapult launch only by either flying level or even having to lose about 10-15 feet of height as soon as we cleared the carrier. It demanded flying skill of the highest order and was highly risky to say the least.[28]

When asked about the synergy in air-naval and ground operations while he was operating from the *Vikrant*, VAdm Pasricha was candid enough to admit that there was none and that the Indian Navy had no intelligence at all about PAF activity in Chittagong and Cox's Bazaar.

"We also did not know that IAF Hunters had visited the area before us on December 4."[29] Despite these minor snafus (snafu is a military acronym from World War II which means *situation normal, all f---d up)*, the result of the various successful operations by the three Services was that it precipitated the collapse of Pakistani resistance across sectors and gave hope to aggressive generals like Sagat Singh to revise their initial operational objectives and go for the big prize, Dacca. The lack of inter-Service coordination in the Chittagong sector was not a widespread malaise, however, as the Indian Army and Indian Air Force demonstrated great synergy in many sectors. The Sylhet battle was one such example.

Floating Down from the Skies

Adding to Niazi's woes was the Tangail para-drop operation by 2 Para on December 11, in the area to the north of Dacca. This was in an area that was under the operational control of 101 Communication Zone, the division sized force under Maj Gen G. C. Nagra. Initially planned as a brigade-sized drop by 50 Para Brigade in three separate operations of a battalion each, with objectives that ranged from the capture of a bridge, an airfield, and at Tangail to secure a bridge, it was reduced to a battalion drop due to various tactical reasons. Suffice to say, it was a cautious decision that looked at leveraging the surprise of a small force and making it look like a large force, rather than risk a large force without much strategic pay-off. Even then, the successful operation involved over 50 transport aircraft of different types along with Gnat and MiG-21 fighter escorts, which got airborne from two airfields, Dum Dum and Kalaikunda. While the bulk of the heavy drop equipment and a small complement of troops emplaned at Dum Dum, primarily on Packet aircraft, the majority of the paratroopers got onboard Dakotas at Kalaikunda.

Supporting this ambitious operation was a covert operation led by a young Corps of Signals officer, Capt P.K. Ghosh, who had linked up with the Mukti Bahini in mid-November in the area between Mymensingh and Tangail. His role in identifying the Dropping Zones (DZs), keeping them under surveillance and directing harassing raids on convoys played a critical role in shaping the battlefield.[30] The operation was reminiscent of the many covert operations conducted by the Allies prior to Operation Market Garden, as the airborne operation to capture the areas around the bridge at Arnhem in Belgium came to be known. The operation fulfilled its objectives as it caused panic in Dacca as news trickled in that a brigade had been dropped and that it was only a matter of time before forces converged onto Dacca.

Coercion and Capitulation

The psychological impact of innovative operations generally gets underplayed in any post-war analysis as it seemingly takes away some sheen from the hard-core contact and aerial battles that occupy pride of place in conventional warfare. One operation that caused a disproportionate impact on the psyche of East Pakistan's leadership as they huddled in Dacca during the closing stages of the war was the strike by IAF fighters on the Governor's House in Dacca on December 14. In an operation driven by hard intelligence based on wireless intercepts, four MiG-21s and four Hunters attacked the palatial house in the vicinity of the Dacca Cricket Stadium in quick succession while Governor Malik himself was chairing a meeting, with UN officials in attendance. MiG-21s from No. 28 Squadron followed up this attack with rocket attacks on specific buildings in Dacca University where suspected Pakistani troops and collaborators were taking shelter. Lt Gen Shamsher 'Shammi' Mehta, a major in 1971 and a Squadron Commander from 63 Cavalry, and part of the leading element of PT-76 tanks that got to Dacca, called the bombing "a game changer in the fall of Dacca." He considered the IAF's bombing campaign around Dacca a "victory of the mind over matter." Flt Lt Manbir Singh, one of the stalwarts of No. 28 Squadron, would find himself on the steps of the Governor's House a few days after the strike, examining the damage his squadron had done. More importantly, he would walk away with two small brass cannons as war booty – they now occupy pride of place in No. 28 Squadron and No. 4 Squadron of the IAF, the two MiG-21 squadrons that participated in the air strikes on the Governor's House.

Final Thoughts

Was the capitulation of Dacca so simple, or was it a result of joint orchestration of forces in multiple operations that caused a psychological disintegration, rather than a physical destruction of combat capability? Gp Capt Manna Murdeshwar (Retd), one of the key members of the operational planning staff at Eastern Air Command had a ringside view of operations in the Eastern Theatre and recollects vividly that it needed a little over six months of continuous effort by way of visits, discussions, conferences and persuasion to build a rapport with the Indian Army formations, singling out 101 Communication Zone and IV Corps as particularly enthusiastic about the use of air power.[31] In a glowing tribute to IV Corps, ACM Lal writes:

> By bold and imaginative use of the Air Force available to it, 4 Corps presented a most convincing demonstration of how well the two Services could work together. This was possible due, in large measure, to the fact that the GOC of the Corps himself (Sagat Singh) was a paratrooper, who had lived and worked in close proximity with the Air Force for many years. 4 Corps never asked the Air Force to do what it could not and whatever the Air Force was called upon to do, it did most effectively.[32]

Considering that the Indian armed forces had never undertaken an airborne operation before, the 2 Para drop at Tangail on December 11 to capture the bridge on the Poongli river merits attention as a timely manifestation of this newly found cooperative operational spirit between the Indian Army and the IAF that Lal refers to.[33] The pressure exerted by the Indian Navy with its persistent attacks on Chittagong and Cox's Bazaar, sustained interdiction of Pakistani shipping, and a small but rather ill-fated amphibious assault by a company of Gorkhas, played a part in piling on 'joint pressure' on Niazi to surrender.[34]

Never had all three Services of India's armed forces operated with such simultaneity before, although much of the joint effort in the Chittagong sector was unplanned. Without doubt it comprised joint operations, which played a pivotal role in the Bangladesh campaign. On display also was the quality of operational art exercised by Indian Commanders like Sagat Singh, Mally Wollen, Chandan Singh and Swaraj Prakash as the battle progressed. At the tactical level, Shammi Mehta fondly recollects that informal camaraderie, pre-launch bonding and free-flowing operational communication where rank and protocol did not matter were the hallmarks of operations in the IV Corps sector. However, also clear was that this synergy was 'personality driven' and not institutionally driven joint operations that was on display. This particular trait of Indian operational art continues even today and merits serious examination in the ongoing restructuring and transformation of India's armed forces.

Notes

1. For an Indian perspective of the force levels in the east, see Maj K. C. Praval, *Indian Army After Independence* (New Delhi: Lancer, 1988), pp. 401-411.
2. ACM PC Lal's comparative analysis of the IAF's Order of Battle (ORBAT) and all the measures initiated to strengthen the IAF is succinctly described in a narrative form in his book, *My Years with the IAF* (New Delhi: Lancer, 1986), pp. 187-189, 223.
3. S Sajad Haidar, *Flight of the Falcon* (Lahore: Vanguard Publishers, 2009), p. 227.
4. S.N. Prasad and U. Thapliyal, *The India-Pakistan War of 1971* (Dehradun: Natraj Publishers, 2014), p. 210.
5. See map depicting airfields and IAF units in the Eastern Sector in P.V.S Jaganmohan and Samir Chopra, *Eagles over Bangladesh* (New Delhi: Harper Collins, 2013), p. v.
6. Also see, Lal, n. 2, pp. 187-188.
7. The four Indian pilots were Flt Lts Massey and Ganapathy and Fg Offrs Lazarus and Soares.
8. Telephonic interview with ACM S.K. Kaul on April 5, 2021.
9. Interview with Air Mshl Gokhale on September 18, 2014, at Pune.
10. For an excellent tactical narrative of the Battle for Hilli, albeit from an Indian perspective, see Maj Gen Sukhwant Singh (Retd), *India's Wars Since Independence* (New Delhi: Lancer, 2009), pp. 146-147. A Pakistan version of the battle has been narrated by the brigade commander of 205 Brigade under whose command the defences at Hilli were placed. See interview with Maj Gen (Retd) Tajjamul Hussain Malik by Maj Agha Amin, one of Pakistan's best modern military historians in "The Battle of Hilli – A Narration by Pakistan Brigade Commander,"

http://defence.pk/threads/the-battle-of-hilli-a-narration-by-pakistani-bde-commander.143866/. Accessed on March 9, 2014.

11. Interview with Air Cmde Manbir Singh, VrC (Retd) on January 5, 2014, at Pune. Also see Lal, n. 2, p. 203.
12. The dogfight between Dilawar's formation and Wg Cdr Sundaresan's formation of Hunters, ironically from No. 14 Squadron, IAF, comes to life in Jaganmohan and Chopra, n. 5, pp. 147-149. For a PAF perspective, see Haider, n. 3, pp. 238-239.
13. Jaganmohan and Chopra, n. 5, p. 159.
14. Sandhu, Singla and another young pilot, P.K. Vaid, from 105 HU would go on to win Vir Chakras for their exploits during the numerous heliborne missions they would fly during the war.
15. Telephonic interview with Wg Cdr S.C. Sharma, VrC (Retd) on January 11 and 12, 2015.
16. Brig Harolikar, "Inside a Chakravyuh in Sylhet," http://bravestofthebrave.com/?p=14. Accessed on October 25, 2014.
17. Arjun Subramaniam, "Brilliant, Unconventional and Fearless", *The Tribune*, May 9, 2021.
18. For a personal narrative of the operation from the man who orchestrated it as the IAF commander alongside Sagat Singh, see, AVM Chandan Singh, "The Meghna Crossing," in, Maj Gen Dhruv Katoch and Lt Col Quazi Sajjad Ali Zahir, eds., *Liberation: Bangladesh 1971* (New Delhi: Bloomsbury, 2015), pp. 218-222.
19. Ibid.
20. For a detailed narrative of the Meghna Air Bridge Operation, see Jaganmohan and Chopra, n. 5, pp. 215-221. For a recent analysis of the helibridge and heliborne operations by an IAF helicopter pilot, see Air Cmdr Rajesh Isser, *The Purple Legacy: Indian Air Force Helicopters in Service of the Nation* (New Delhi: KW Publishers, 2012), pp. 63-79.
21. Mandeep Singh Bajwa, "Flying to Victory: An Air OP Pilot's Story," *Hindustan Times* (Chandigarh), January 12, 2014, http://www.hindustantimes.com/punjab/chandigarh/ flying-to-victory-an-air-op-pilot-s-story/article1.aspx. Accessed on October 18, 2014.
22. Jaganmohan and Chopra, n. 5, p. 383 (summary of sector-wise CAS missions).
23. Lal, n. 2, p. 212.
24. Jaganmohan and Chopra, n. 5, pp. 130-150. Also see Prasad and Thapliyal, n. 4, p. 380.
25. For a crisp narration of naval action during the first week of the war, see VAdm Mihir Roy, *War in the Indian Ocean* (New Delhi: Lancer Publishers, 1995), pp. 202-212.
26. Prasad and Thapliyal, n. 4, pp. 381-385.
27. B. Harry, "Damage Assessment – 1971 Indo-Pak Naval War," http://www.ordersofbattle.darkscape.net/site/cimh/Navy/kills%281971%29-2.pdf. Accessed on February 8, 2015.
28. Interview with VAdm Vinod Pasricha on October 4, 2014.
29. Ibid.
30. "The Saga of Captain P.K. Ghosh, VrC," from *Veekays History Book*, a blog maintained by Maj Genl V.K. Singh, one of India's prolific military writers. At

veekay-militaryhistory.blogspot.in/2013/4/the-saga-of-captain-pk-ghosh-vrc-html. Accessed on January 26, 2014.

31. Email exchange between the author and Gp Capt Murdeshwar in February 2014 on his perceptions of what was right and what went wrong during the 1971 War.
32. Lal, n. 2, pp. 214-215.
33. Jaganmohan and Chopra, n. 5, pp. 291-295.
34. For a detailed overview of "Operation Beaver," see Ministry of Defence Publication, *Official History of the India-Pakistan 1971 War*, pp. 649-652, http://www.bharat-rakshak.com/LAND-FORCES/Army/History/1971War/PDF/. Accessed on January 2, 2014.

6. The Battle of Longewala: The Quick Response and Decisive Impact of Air Power

Bharat Kumar

Some of the most significant and decisive events of the Indo-Pakistan War of 1971 were the Battle of Boyra on November 22, (when the intruding Sabres were promptly shot down by the midget Gnats airborne from Dum Dum); the bombing of Dacca and the attack on the Governor's House in particular, and the establishment of air supremacy over the then East Pakistan; the Meghna helibridge, the Tangail paradrop, the sinking of the PNS *Ghazi*, the aerial attack on the Karachi oil farms, the attack on Karachi harbour by the Indian Navy missile boats; and the Battle of Longewala. It would not be wrong to say that amongst these events, what brought victory and laurels to India in the shortest possible time was the Battle of Longewala and which, perhaps, put paid to the Pakistani plan of launching a Corps-level offensive supported by the entire Pakistan Air Force (PAF) in the central sector. It would, therefore, be worth examining the background and the actual conduct of the battle.

The Battle of Longewala was between the Indian Hunter aircraft operating from the newly constructed airfield at Jaisalmer and a Pakistani thrust comprising two armoured regiments supported by two infantry brigades. This historic battle lasted just over two days during which the enemy was decimated.

One of the lessons learnt during the Indo-Pak conflict of 1965, was the paucity of airfields in the Punjab and Rajasthan sectors. Accordingly,

Utterlai, Jaisalmer, and Nal airfields were constructed, and Care and Maintenance Units (C&MU) established there with very limited manpower at each of these bases. At Jaisalmer, it was 14 C&MU with one officer and 17 airmen. With the probability of a conflict between India and Pakistan increasing, it was decided to activate these bases in September 1971. At that time, Jaisalmer had just the runway, taxi tracks, and hardened aircraft shelters besides a make-shift Air Traffic Control (ATC) building. It did not have the other basic infrastructure to support air operations – no bulk petrol installation for storage of fuel, no electrical runway and taxiway lighting, etc. Wg Cdr MS Bawa, who was nominated as base commander in September 1971, had to motivate the men and supervise the work with the augmented manpower that was inducted from numerous units as part of Air Heaquarters' (HQ's) Manpower Augmentation Plan. He ensured that the base became operational within a short time. For its air and ground defence, Jaisalmer was given a P-30 radar, a troop of six L-60 anti-aircraft Bofor guns and a company of the Territorial Army. Six Hunter aircraft of No. 122 Squadron (Hunter Operational Training Unit or OTU had been rechristened for the duration of the war) were inducted from Jamnagar, with allotted tasks of air defence of the airfield and close air support to 12 Infantry Division. In addition, No. 12 (Independent) Air Observation Post (AOP) Flight was deployed at the airfield initially but moved near HQ 12 Infantry Division when hostilities became imminent. The base was fully operational by the third week of October, 1971.

The Thar desert, of which Rajasthan is a part, extends into Pakistan. The surface lines of communication, especially West of Jaisalmer, were scanty and consisted of a few tracks, with a metalled road from Jaisalmer to Longewala via Ramgarh. Pakistan's only railway link between its lone port of Karachi and Lahore and beyond ran opposite the Jaisalmer sector. Rahim Yar Khan was the most prominent place in the sector. Pakistan had also not built any roads East of this railway line and just a few tracks existed up to the international border. The area was full of sand dunes – their height and frequency increasing as one moved West from Jaisalmer.

Pakistan's 18 Infantry Division deployed in Rahim Yar Khan sector consisted of two cavalry regiments (22 Cavalry was equipped with the Chinese T-55 tanks and 38 Cavalry had antiquated World War II era and somewhat unreliable Sherman tanks), three infantry brigades and the usual other elements. The Indian 12 Infantry Division's appreciation was that 18 Division would be deployed in a defensive role mainly to protect Pakistan's vital lines of communication, with little possibility of any offensive tasks. 12 Infantry Division had been tasked to capture Rahim Yar Khan and then exploit the situation further. It planned to achieve this objective by launching an offensive through Kishangarh. Hunters from Jaisalmer were to support this offensive. The division had been allotted 12 Hunter sorties per day with an assurance that, if required, the air effort would be stepped up from D+2 onwards.

The Pakistan General Headquarters (GHQ) had a different plan for its 18 Infantry Division. Besides safeguarding the vital lines of communication in the sector, it was ordered to undertake an offensive with both its armour regiments along with two infantry brigades on the night of D-day with the objective of capturing Jaisalmer airfield the following morning. The entire offensive was planned by the GHQ. The order stated that D-day would be conveyed subsequently. The distance from the international border to Jaisalmer is nearly 140 km. It was an ambitious target as the Pakistani force would have to stick to the desert track till Longewala, followed by metalled road onwards to Ramgarh and Jaisalmer. The division had also not been trained in desert warfare and did not have specialised 4 × 4 wheeled vehicles to traverse the sandy desert terrain.

On receipt of these orders, the General Officer Commanding (GOC) 18 Division discussed the plan with the commanding officers of his two cavalry regiments who agreed on the viability of the plan and the high probability of its success. This was subject to availability of air support during at least the first three days of the operation. This requirement was conveyed to the GHQ which seemed to have been assured by Pak Air HQ of this support, provided a warning of a fortnight was given to them to activate Jacobabad airfield.

While officers of 38 Cavalry did carry out a recce of their axis of advance up to the international border, 22 Cavalry did not initiate any such step.

The GOC 18 Division received a hand-written order on the morning of December 2, 1971, to launch the offensive the following evening to capture Jaisalmer by December 4 morning – hostilities between India and Pakistan had not commenced at that time. During the briefing for the operations, the PAF representative in the meeting dropped a virtual bombshell when he stated that air support would not be available as a fortnight's notice to Pak Air HQ for activation of Jacobabad had not been given. The brigade commanders pointed out the inherent dangers in launching the land offensive without air support and suggested that the operation be either postponed or cancelled. The GOC referred the matter to the Chief of the General Staff (CGS) at the GHQ who ruled that since very little air action was expected from the Indian Air Force (IAF), the operation must go through in 'the national interest' even without air support. The GOC did not agree to the brigade commanders' suggestion to refuse to undertake the operation as he feared that he would be marked a coward and that would be the end of his career. However, commander 51 Brigade was able to convince the GOC to change his objective from Jaisalmer to Ramgarh. The GOC ordered that the operation would go ahead as planned even without assistance from the Pakistan Air Force. Pak 51 Infantry Brigade and 22 Cavalry were to be in the lead and 206 Infantry Brigade with 38 Cavalry were to follow. H-Hour was set as 2130 hrs on December 3, when the force was to cross the international border.

Pakistan launched Operation Chengiz Khan on the evening of December 3, when the PAF attacked numerous IAF airfields and radars – Jaisalmer was, however, not targeted. The Pakistani ground offensive, however, faced various organisational and logistics problems and could not kick-off. The GOC revised the H-hour to 0200 h on December 5, and later ordered that the force was to cross the border at last light.

Pre-planned air operations from Jaisalmer were launched on December 4, and supported the Indian Army offensive through Kishangarh.

The Pakistani column commenced its move from its launch pad around midnight of December 4. The noise of the tanks and vehicles was picked up by an Indian patrol at around midnight. This information was conveyed to 'A' Company of 23 Punjab that was located at Longewala post. The patrol was instructed to get back as soon as the tank column was sighted. However, when the patrol did sight the tanks, it could not pass the message due to communication problems. The information finally reached the Divisional Headquarters at 0230 h on December 4. The GOC was taken aback by this sudden and totally unexpected move as it had been appreciated that the desert terrain would not allow Pakistan to intrude along that axis. There were just no reserves to counter this intrusion. Unable to think of any solution, he rang up the base commander, Jaisalmer, and informed him about the Pakistan thrust, with Jaisalmer as its likely objective. The GOC also informed him that he was trying to send a small contingent of tanks to Longewala to intercept the Pakistanis and beef up the Longewala post, as required. He requested the base commander to launch aircraft to locate and engage the enemy armour and infantry. While the base commander accepted the commitment, he stated that the aircraft could be launched only at first light as the Hunters did not have the wherewithal for night operations. Then onwards, there was a frenzy of activity at Jaisalmer to reconfigure the aircraft to carry T-10 rockets – the ideal weapon for the task. Two pilots were detailed to get airborne at first light, reconnoitre the road Jaisalmer-Ramgarh-Longewla and then the track therefrom to the border and engage enemy tanks wherever they were sighted.

The first pair of aircraft taxied out when it was still dark and took off even before first light, flew low along the Jaisalmer-Ramgarh-Longewala road, trying to spot any movement but there was none. All this changed when they approached Longewala. By this time, there was greater light and what they saw ahead of them made their heartbeat faster and their adrenaline shoot up. What looked like lots of matchboxes from a distance, now clearly stood out as a body of tanks! The enemy tank column had arrived at Longewala a little earlier. The lead Hunter pilot counted 32 of them and then stopped any further count. They did not see any enemy aircraft in the area. The leader observed one of the tanks moving towards the Longewala post apparently to attack it. He immediately went in for an attack and blasted it with his rockets. His wingman, in turn, knocked out the second tank. By this time, the pilots developed doubts about whether the tanks they had attacked were, in fact, Pakistani – the doubt arose as they had been briefed that some Indian tanks would be sent to the area to intercept the Pakistani column. Fratricide is the worst thing that can happen. Fortunately, for them, one AOP aircraft that was to perform the role of airborne Forward Area Controller (FAC) arrived and confirmed the identity of the tanks. With their fears allayed, the Hunter pair resumed their hunt by carrying out as many as 13 more passes between them (instead of the normal 1-2 passes and then getting back to base), destroying five tanks and damaging another ten. During these attacks, they came under intense anti-aircraft fire from the tanks. The lead aircraft was hit, its hydraulics and radio were knocked out, but it managed to land back safely. The Pakistani tanks carried two 100 gallon barrels full of diesel just behind the cupola of each tank. The fuel caught fire when hit by the 30 mm rounds of the Hunters, engulfing the tank in flames. This made the pilots' job that much easier, giving them greater opportunity for more kills. The Pakistani tanks played every trick in the book to protect themselves. They fired with their machine guns at the attacking aircraft and also tried to create additional problems for them by moving around in circles and raising a lot of dust. These tactics did not appreciably deter or distract the attackers and they kept scoring hits. Not a single pass went without getting a victim.

The second Hunter pair soon appeared on the scene and continued the unfinished task of the first pair of aircraft. During one of the attacks, the tank gunner became so desperate that he opened up at the diving aircraft with his main 100 mm gun. Fortunately, the round failed to score a direct hit but whizzed past so close to the aircraft as to disturb its aerodynamics. Consequently, the aircraft continued to mush in during the pullout manoeuvre and scraped the sand dune during its recovery from the dive. The pilot was lucky to pull out though his aircraft was badly damaged and could not build up speed beyond 250 knots. The skilful pilot managed to land the aircraft safely.

The base commander now faced the dilemma of whether to wait for the damaged aircraft to be repaired or send out the other aircraft singly, a practice not recommended for tactical reasons. Any delay would have given breathing space to the intruders and time to regroup and may be withdraw – a totally unacceptable situation. The base commander took a calculated risk and approved single aircraft missions, if the aircraft in pairs were not available. Thus, the Pakistani tanks remained under attack till sunset. The pilots continued to be directed by the AOP pilots. One of them had to force-land at Jaisalmer helipad but continued his direction by using the aircraft radio on the ground. The Auster was temporarily repaired that night and flown out early the next morning. In the meanwhile, the Hunter pilots extended their 'area of interest' right up to the international border and accounted for many vehicles. By the end of the day, 17 sorties had been flown, with some of the aircraft flying as many as five sorties, while a few pilots flew three sorties. The claimed enemy losses were 22 tanks destroyed, another 30 damaged, besides accounting for vehicles and trains. An intercept that evening summed up the havoc caused by the Hunters. The translation of the communication intercept was as follows: "The enemy Air Force is playing hell with us. As one aircraft goes away, another comes and dances, remaining overhead for twenty minutes. Forty per cent of our Army (personnel) and equipment have been destroyed. What to speak of going forward, turning back has become very difficult. Send the Air Force for help quickly; otherwise, it is impossible to return." It certainly boosted the morale of all the personnel at Jaisalmer.

Jaisalmer came under an aerial attack by a Pakistani C-130 transport aircraft but did not suffer any damage as the entire bomb load was dropped just outside the airfield. To add to the base's problem, the GOC warned that night that he feared that some elements of the armour and infantry column might be headed towards Jaisalmer and Bawa should try and protect his assets as the Army was in no position to augment Jaisalmer's resources. Bawa was entirely on his own. The Hunters were, once again airborne at first light and recced all possible approaches to Jaisalmer but did not find a single enemy vehicle. It was a false alarm. The aircrew got back to their task of massacring and decimating whatever was left of the attackers. During the day, additional Hunters had flown in from Jamnagar and had joined the fray. The squadron flew 18 sorties and the wreckage of 37 tanks could be seen around Longewala that evening. The Battle of Longewala was practically over! The Pakistanis had been mauled by the relentless attacks by the Hunters, their morale was shattered and they were in no position psychologically to offer any resistance. But this was not the end of the IAF's exploits as the Pakistanis were to get more bashing during their retreat and the IAF's mopping up operation.

Air operations continued against the retreating forces. In addition, Hunters from Jaisalmer provided support to both 11 and 12 Infantry Divisions, and carried out interdiction against the Pakistani lines of communication besides delivering a knockout punch to the Sui gas plant which took over a year thereafter to get back into action.

No. 122 Squadron flew 222 operational sorties during the entire war, averaging 16 sorties per day. It could have flown many more but for lack of close air support demands and paucity of targets. The squadron had decimated a massive armour and infantry thrust entirely on its own, without the loss of a single aircraft. It also goes to the credit of the squadron that it maintained nearly 100 per cent serviceability thanks to round-the-clock voluntary toiling by the ground crew who exhibited very high technical skill.

It must be conceded that Pakistan's plan for the capture of Jaisalmer was just brilliant, with a high probability of success if it had been executed properly as also if the timeframe of its attainment of the assigned objective had been more realistic. The pitfalls in the plan would have been evident to enable their rectification and modification if the plan had gone through the normal staff scrutiny and been war-gamed. The timing of the launch of the offensive and the axis of advance had not been anticipated by the Indians and caught the Indian 12 Infantry Division absolutely unprepared, leaving it with no option but to call the IAF to its rescue. It is to the credit of the IAF that it did not let its sister Service down.

Imagine the scenario wherein Pakistani armour under the PAF's cover had advanced along its axis, unopposed by Indian 12 Infantry Division and had captured either Ramgarh or, more importantly, Jaisalmer within a day or so. It would have been reminiscent of the German *blitzkrieg* of World War II. But this was not to be. While Pakistan had an ace up its sleeve, it had not anticipated the Indian hand and their ace got trumped by the Indian Air Force and, thus, they lost the battle. The Pakistan Army brass did not realise the impact of air power in modern warfare. They had apparently either forgotten, or decided to ignore, the lessons of history. It so happens that it was in India that the role of air power in future conflicts was first propounded way back in 1920. After the Third Afghan War and the Waziristan Campaign, it had become an accepted doctrine in the British Indian Army that no major operation could sensibly take place without the availability of air support. "Air power would not guarantee success, but it would hopefully prevent defeat."[1] Over a period of time, this dictum has altered somewhat to "Air power may or may not ensure your victory, but its lack will certainly bring you to defeat." This doctrine has stood the test of time and remains valid even more today, especially when one considers the increasing lethality of air power. The other characteristics of air power viz quick response, flexibility and ability to strike at vast distances add to the cost that air power can impose on an adversary. The IAF exhibited all these characteristics except for the vast distance, as the flying time from Jaisalmer to Longewala was a mere ten minutes.

Since the quality of the leadership plays a significant part in any operation, it would be only right to have a look at the quality of leadership at Jaisalmer vis-à-vis that of the invading force. Wg Cdr MS Bawa had successfully commanded a fighter squadron and was the chief instructor at the Armament Training Wing. He was reputed to be a 'go-getter' and he displayed this trait by the speed with which Jaisalmer became operational, with the personnel drawn from a plethora of units and gathered at Jaisalmer temporarily. He motivated them and they delivered the goods in an environment that was anything but conducive. He was totally involved with the aircrew, shared their feelings and paid great heed to their suggestions. When the aircraft were damaged by the enemy ground fire on the first day of the battle, he did not refer the matter to the higher authorities and decided to launch single-aircraft missions – it was a calculated risk and if things had gone wrong, he would have been held responsible for a decision which was tactically speaking wrong. He did not leave this decision to the detachment commander and told him that he would answer to the authorities if so required. The aircrew were motivated and experienced, and exhibited a high quality of leadership, flying skills and initiative, resulting in extremely good results. On the opposite side, the Pakistani commanders were not motivated, and their morale took a further beating once they were told to launch the offensive without air support. They also had not motivated their personnel as was evident from a large number of desertions that took place once the force crossed into India.

The second characteristic of air power that needs to be looked into is rapid response. Aircraft on air defence missions are normally ordered to be either on two or five-minute readiness and get airborne well within this period. If the situation so warrants, aircraft on ground attack missions can also be ordered to standby on 15 or 30-minute readiness by housing the aircraft and the aircrew not far from the take-off point. In this case, it was night time and no aircraft was on standby. The base commander, Jaisalmer, was informed of the Pakistani intrusion at about 0230 hours. It was not possible to launch the aircraft immediately as the aircraft did not have the wherewithal for night vision and had to wait for daylight. Besides, the two aircraft that were earmarked for air defence operational readiness, the other aircraft had been configured the previous evening according to the missions that had been assigned by the Army. It was realised that T-10 rockets were the most suitable weapon for engaging the tanks. The ground crew – their number was extremely limited as the majority of the squadron's assets were at Jamnagar – had to now fit the rocket rails and load the rockets which is a time-consuming task. Every person pitched in and the aircraft were ready well before first light. The aircrew proceeded to the aircraft when it was still dark and taxied out, groping their way, as the Hunters did not have any landing lights and Jaisalmer did not have an electrical runway and taxiway lighting system installed. It was just about first light when the aircraft got airborne. Could one have responded any faster?! Obviously not. Almost the same scenario played out the next day except for the fact that the aircraft were already configured for the carriage of T-10 rockets. The aircraft were turned round quickly and repairs were carried out wherever required. The ground crew were working at the aircraft almost round the clock to ensure that the allotted tasks could be executed. Had it not been so, it would not have been possible to launch 17 sorties on the first day.

The biggest impact of air power lies in its lethality. It is based on weaponry (sophistication and payload) and the accuracy of its delivery. When the doctrine of the inevitability of air support was propounded in 1920, an aircraft normally had just a few 20lb, and still fewer 120lb bombs, besides .303 machine guns. Delay fuzes were in use and the heavier bombs came into use a decade or so later. Even though the lethality of such aircraft was rather low and totally non-effective against houses and other structures made of mud, they still had an impact on the morale of the tribesmen. Now compare this to the armament of the Hunter aircraft that entered service in the early 1950s – four 30mm cannon and 12 T-10 rockets – a quantum jump indeed. Of course, the Hunters could also carry 2 × 500lb bombs or two napalm containers, but these were not the ideal weapon for the task. The gyro gunsight permitted armament delivery with a fair amount of accuracy. The lethality of the Hunters becomes evident when one notices the ease with which Pakistani tanks succumbed to the T-10 rockets and 30mm rounds. The sophistication in aircraft weaponry has since then increased manifold and there is just no target that cannot be engaged and neutralised with a suitable aerial weapon. Today is the age of precision-guided munitions using various devices like lasers, inertial navigation systems, Global Positioning System (GPS), etc. besides various types of seekers to ensure pinpoint accuracy. Rockets and cannons are fired at fairly close ranges and the attacking aircraft are vulnerable to the anti-aircraft guns and shoulder-fired surface-to-air missiles. However, modern weapons can be launched from greater distances, providing the requisite safety to the aircraft. The decision of the CGS of the Pakistan Army to brush aside the likely impact of a small force at Jaisalmer air base proved fatal. This lapse was not something new but in the absence of joint planning and lack of full understanding on the lethality of air power, such mistakes are bound to be made. It is unfortunate that in most cases of planning by the ground forces' commander, the role of the Air Force figures in the end and as an adjunct, not as the decisive, contributory element. Ideally, he should initiate his planning by asking his Air Force counterpart about how the Air Force can make the surface forces' task easier.

No. 122 Squadron's performance must be gauged from the fact that with just five aircraft for the task and quite a few becoming unserviceable, as many as 17 sorties were flown on December 5, with some aircraft flying six sorties in a little over ten hours of daylight. This was possible due to factors that are normally not fully appreciated. Firstly, the dedication and the technical skill of the ground crew in turning round and rectifying the aircraft in the shortest possible time. The few personnel of the R&SU (Repair and Salvage Unit) who were at Jaisalmer ensured that the aircraft that had suffered battle damage was restored to flying status at the earliest. These ground crew were highly motivated and their morale went really sky high once they came to know that their efforts had borne fruit and the invaders had been dealt a mortal blow. The efficacy of this small force was enhanced by these factors and resulted in the decimation of the invaders.

The lethality of air power in the modern age can be gauged by the happenings in Operation Desert Storm (January 17, 1991 – February 28, 1991) in which the coalition Air Forces pounded the Iraqis for 42 days after which the ground forces had a practically free run to a quick victory. It was again evident during Operation Iraqi Freedom in which the "*shock and awe*" bombing campaign in 2003 helped overthrow Saddam Hussain. However, in both these operations, though the main destruction was caused by the aerial campaigns, the mopping up operations were carried out by the land forces. Similarly, in Kosovo during March-June

1999, the Serbs were bombed day in and day out; it is different that they succumbed only under the threat of a ground invasion and a ceasefire came into being.

However, there are at least two land battles in which victory was won by air power alone, without any role played by the ground forces. It so happens that both these battles took place in India. The first of these was the Pink's War of 1925. It was a 54-day aerial campaign (March 9-May 1, 1925) in Waziristan in which five Royal Air Force (RAF) squadrons forced the Waziris to accept the British terms. Normally, a ground-based campaign would have involved at least two brigades and around one to two years, with lots of casualties. In this case, the war lasted just 54 days in which the British lost just one aircraft and two pilots and that too in an accident. The ensuing peace lasted much longer. The Pink's War should have been a trend-setter and the RAF should have been given a free hand from then onwards but glory to another Service was not acceptable to the British Indian Army brass and they never permitted the RAF to undertake the operations again. While the Pink's War lasted 54 days, the Battle of Longewala, which was the showpiece of the responsiveness of air power and its lethality, lasted just two days – strictly speaking, the back of the Pakistani offensive was broken by the evening of the first day. Not a single aircraft was lost despite some desperate but intense ground fire by the Pakistani tank crews. One can speculate about the duration of the battle and its outcome if the Pakistani intruders had been engaged by the Indian 12 Infantry Division on its own. It must be brought out that there was no major engagement between the Pakistani and Indian forces except for a few artillery attacks on the Pakistani gun positions after the intruders had retreated into their own territory. It was solely the effort put in by the Hunters from Jaisalmer that brought about this resounding victory.

The Battle of Longewala thus, remains a unique one in the annals of aerial warfare where the intruding armour forces were decimated by air power alone. It will always be remembered as one of the proudest moments in the history of the Indian Air Force.

Disclaimer: The chapter has previously been published in author's book, Bharat Kumar, *The Epic Battle of Longewala* (Natraj Publishers, 2020).

Note

1. Brian Robson, *Crisis on the Frontier: The Third Afghan War and the Campaign in Waziristan 1919-1920* (UK: Spellmount, Staplehurst, 2007), p. xiv.

7. The Bombing Saga: Canberra and Antonov-12 Operations in the 1971 War

PVS Jagan Mohan

The Evolution of the Heavy Bomber Force in the IAF

As an Air Force that evolved out of the Royal Air Force's (RAF's) doctrine and training, it was but natural that the Indian Air Force (IAF) emerged out of World War II with a philosophy on the employment of heavy bombers.

After Independence, the IAF had set up three "heavy bomber" squadrons operating the B-24 Liberators in the early 1950s. In the massive re-equipment effort of the 1950s, the English Electric Canberra was an obvious choice to replace the obsolete Liberators. Originally designed to be flown as a high-altitude bomber, using "beam riding" techniques, the aircraft could deliver massive bomb loads across hundreds of miles. The introduction of extensive radar coverage and interceptors like the Sabres and Starfighters meant that the Canberra would have to transform its role into a low-level intruder utilising a hi-lo-hi profile and operate mostly by night for protection.

The English Electric Canberra featured round and wide fuselage, straight tapered wings, with a dihedral tailplane and elevators. First flown in 1949, a mere four years after the end of World War II, it entered RAF service in 1951. In 1956, the IAF, looking for a replacement for the B-24 Liberators as the main component of its bomber strike force, chose the Canberra. The Indian Air Force's first order for 65 B (I) Mk 58 bomberinterdictors, 7 T Mk 54s and 8 PR Mk 57s (photo-recce) was placed in 1957. Later, another 6 B (I) 58s (bomber (interdictor), 2 T 54s (trainer) and 2 PR 57s were acquired to take total acquisitions to 90. The first unit to equip with the Canberra was the 106 SPR Unit (Lynx) followed by No. 5 Squadron (Tuskers) with the B(I)58s at Agra. The T Mk 54s equipped the Jet Bomber Conversion Unit (JBCU). By September 1958, Nos 16 (Rattlers) and 35 (Rapiers) Squadrons had re-equipped with the Canberra, taking it to a total of five units that flew this aircraft. The three units, Nos 5, 16 and 35 were considered the primary combat element.

The aircraft was powered by two Rolls-Royce Avon engines, and could fly across the sky at 580 mph at 33,000 ft altitude. It was only marginally slower than the F-86 Sabre. The Canberra was extremely agile for its size and could even give a Starfighter a run for its money at altitudes less than 5,000 ft. The Canberra carried a crew of two – sometimes three – consisting of a pilot and navigator/bomb-aimer. It could carry a bomb-load of 8,000 lb, which gave it the capability to carry in one sortie what would take four Mysteres, or four MiG-21s could deliver, and it could do so at a range that was four to five times what a MiG could haul its load to. The ability to haul massive bomb loads over extensive distances was what kept the Canberra units still relevant in the 1971 War.

The B(I)58 variant, where the "I" stood for "Intruder" could be armed with rockets and a four-gun external Aden gun pack. It could step into a ground attack role provided air superiority had been achieved. All variants carried an 'Orange Putter' tail warning radar, which notified the pilot of interceptors vectoring it from the rear and enabled evasive action.

While the three bomber squadrons trained for the battle to come, the JBCU – led by a squadron leader – fulfilled a dual role. It trained pilots and navigators designated for induction into regular bomber squadrons and also contributed its nine T.Mk 54 bomber trainers to operational duty.

Prior to the 1971 War, the Canberras saw brief action in Congo as part of the UN force, and extensive action in the 1965 India-Pakistan

War. During the 1965 War, the Canberras flew 196 sorties, attacked almost all major Pakistan Air Force (PAF) airfields (with the exception of Mauripur) and over 600,000 lb of bombs were dropped. One Canberra was lost to aerial action, when towards the tail end of the war, a F-104 Starfighter managed to shoot down a B(I)58 on its return leg. The pilot survived but the navigator was lost with the aircraft. No Canberras were lost to Pakistani anti-aircraft fire. Overall, it was a successful record for the aircraft. Their dramatic contributions included attacking Peshawar, Kohat and the Badin radar station. When hostilities came to a close, the Canberra aircrew took a large chunk of the honours.

Between the wars, attrition losses were replaced by the purchase of 10 B.66 variant from the United Kingdom in 1969 and 8 B(I)12 variant from New Zealand in 1970. Additionally, two PR 66 aircraft and two trainers were acquired. Most of the B66 variants went to No. 5 Squadron operating from Agra.[1]

In the run up to the 1971 War, the bomber force was augmented by the introduction of the Antonov-12 (An-12) transport aircraft in a bomber role. The An-12 was powered by four turbo-prop engines and could carry a load of up to 20,000 lb in the transport role. The first attempt to use these as bombers was envisaged during the 1965 conflict but the war ended before the aircrew could train for the role. Subsequently the squadrons undertook training and refined tactics to drop bombs loaded on pallets that were unloaded via the conveyer belt over the target. It must be said that the Antonov-12 in the bomber role was not a precision instrument, but the IAF invested in using the aircraft as a strategic bomber for large area targets.

The Bombing Campaign in the 1971 War

The bomber campaign of the 1971 War entirely driven by Headquarters (HQ) Central Air Command (CAC), under the leadership of AVM Maurice Barker. The CAC controlled all the Canberra assets at Agra, Gorakhpur and Pune, as well as transport squadrons, maritime squadrons and the strategic photo-reconnaissance unit.

The Canberra strike force of the IAF prior to the declaration of hostilities was concentrated in three stations. Agra (No. 5 Squadron, JBCU, No. 106 SR Squadron[2]), Gorakhpur (No. 16 Squadron) and Pune (No. 35 Squadron). Additionally, the CAC also controlled No. 44 Squadron, flying the Antonov-12 transport aircraft. These aircraft were positioned at Bareilly.

A look at the bombing campaign undertaken by the Canberras in the Bangladesh War has to be studied in three distinct operational areas.

- The Eastern Sector, consisting of targets all over Bangladesh, covered mostly by No. 16 Squadron operating from Gorakhpur.
- The Western Sector, which consisted of the major Counter-Air Strike (CAS) targets: PAF bases of Sargodha, Mianwali, Peshawar, Kohat, Rafiqui and Chaklala. These targets were covered mostly by No. 5 Squadron at Agra, with support from No. 16 Squadron, JBCU, and a detachment of No. 35 Squadron.
- The Southwestern Sector, with targets in the Karachi area, as well as the southeastern portion of Pakistan. These were under the purview of No. 35 Squadron operating from Pune.

Additionally, the strategic bombing effort undertaken by No. 44 Squadron flying the An-12 transport aircraft will also be examined separately.

The list of bombing targets was planned at Air HQ in consultation with the Air Chief P C Lal.[3] The CAC further reviewed the list of targets and passed these on to squadrons for implementation. Each squadron would then individually prioritise their strategic bombing effort based on this list. Occasionally, they would also address tactical bombing requests on the frontline which were routed from Western Air Command to the Air HQ with final communication to the Central Air Command.

The first priority for bombing were mostly the major PAF air bases. Sargodha, Mianwali, Rafiqui, Masroor, Tejgaon and Kurmitola.

Between the 1965 and 1971 Wars, some squadrons had changed their tactics. In No. 16 Squadron for example, the unit ditched the concept of exact Time Over Target (TOT) for their bomber streams, keeping the unpredictability of the aircraft's TOT as the attacker's advantage. They also formed fixed "pilot-navigator" teams for better crew resource management. Finally, more emphasis was laid on planning sorties in line with tactical and strategic requirements – unlike the 1965 operations, where the IAF, seemingly by force of habit, sent its Canberra squadrons against Sargodha night after night with no pre-determined objectives.

A typical Canberra bomb load would be 8 × 1,000 lb bombs. In this configuration, the Canberras would carry two bombs on their under-wing pylons and six bombs in their internal bomb bay. Additionally, some World War II era vintage 4,000 lb bombs – dubbed "block busters" were also available, though their reliability was unknown. But that was not all – also available in the bag of tricks was the oddly named "Y" bomb.[4]

The Y bomb was an indigenously designed bomb consisting of thousands of small spiked tripods that would fall out and spread themselves over an airfield. These would stick to the tarmac with the help of a special adhesive. It had been developed by Wg Cdr Kushlani in collaboration with the National Chemical Laboratory, based on an idea of[5] the then Air Officer Maintenance Air Mshl Y V Malse.

The CAC allocated four airfields against which thc new bomb would be used. The plan was to fly two-aircraft missions, with one aircraft dropping flares to light up the target airfield, while the second aircraft would fly in at low level to drop the bomb on the runway. In the end, the idea to use an aircraft to drop flares was abandoned and it was to be delivered by a solitary aircraft.

Canberra Operations in the East

No. 16 Squadron, based at Gorakhpur, provided the primary component for the Canberra employment in the Eastern Sector. The squadron's attention was divided across both the Eastern and Western Fronts.

After the failed preemptive strike by Pakistan Air Force (PAF) aircraft at various Indian airfields on the evening of December 3, the plan to strike back at the enemy airfields was activated almost immediately. The station commanders with Eastern Air Command were called in for a meeting that evening to finalise the plans for attacking the PAF at Dacca the next day. One point was made very clear – the first strikes against the airfields would be done by the Canberras of Central Air Command, which were the only force equipped to operate by night.

Thus, the first offensive strike against Tejgaon was flown by eight Canberra B(I)58s of No. 16 Squadron from Gorakhpur – four aircraft each against the airfields of Tejgaon and Kurmitola. Each aircraft carried 8 × 1,000lb bombs and navigation was done by the full moon. On the very first night, the Canberras arrived over Dacca at 2.10 a.m. (Indian Standard Time – IST) to find no blackout enforced. The aircrew faced the surprising challenge of identifying the location of the airfield in a sea of lights. They received unexpected help as they were greeted by a barrage of Anti-Aircraft (AA) fire from Tejgaon's defences. The raid and the AA barrage lasted for over an hour. The Canberras arrived in a stream, each aircraft braving the AA fire to drop their payloads and make way for the next to launch its attack. But Tejgaon's vital installations and runway were undamaged and though its Sabres were parked in blast pens with no sheltered covering, they remained unscathed. One of the Canberras may have strayed ten miles Southeast of the intended target and dropped its bombs on the Adamjee Jute Mills in Narayanganj, causing civilian casualties in the workers' housing areas.[6]

The Eastern Air Command continued the pressure on the PAF by dozens of daily strikes against Tejgaon the next day. The strength of the defending squadron of the PAF was slowly whittled away by losses in air combat and on the ground. The pressure was continued by another night strike against the Tejgaon-Kurmitola complex. Once again, four Canberras of No. 16 Squadron struck the airfield on the early hours of December 5, to keep the pressure up. But, as on the previous day, the high-level bombing by the Canberras was ineffective and no damage was done either to the runway or the airfield installations at either of these bases.

The realisation that the PAF squadron was limited only to the Dacca area opened up the possibility of using the Canberras more boldly. The first daylight employment was on the afternoon of December 5, when four Canberras of No. 16 Squadron were used against Pakistan Army fortifications in Jessore. The Canberras staged from Gorakhpur to Dum Dum, before taking off to drop nearly 28,000 lb of bombs on Jessore. They were escorted by Gnats (of No. 22 Squadron) operating from Dum Dum, just in case the PAF decided to show up.

The next day, December 6, was the day the PAF was grounded for good, due to the highly effective precision strike on the Tejgaon runway by the MiG-21s from Guwahati. With no PAF fighter taking to the air after that in the Eastern Sector, the IAF had a field day for the rest of the war, picking targets of its choosing. The offensive in the Jessore sector continued with No. 16 Squadron contributing another 7 sorties and 33,000 lb of bombs used against enemy fortifications. Most of the subsequent missions were interdiction. The fortress of Khulna was attacked on December 7, with the road and rail approaches being targeted.

On December 9, two Canberras were fitted with the dorsal gun pack and rocket pods and were effectively used against boats and riverine traffic at Naryanganj. One of the Canberras, flown by Sqn Ldr S D Karnik was hit and damaged by small arms fire and he had to recover to Dum Dum. Two days later, the refinery at Chittagong was attacked in the evening hours by three aircraft. Sqn Ldr S D Karnik, the Flight Commmander was at the forefront of these missions.

The squadron returned to Tejgaon on the night of December 11/12. Eight Canberras struck the Tejgaon/Kurmitola complex again – this time armed with the 4,000 lb "block buster" bombs. This was the heaviest ordnance available with the IAF at that time. Arriving over Tejgaon at 3.15 am, six of the eight aircraft dropped their bombs. One direct hit was scored on a building which turned out to be the PAF Officers' Mess, causing numerous casualties. Another bomb fell near the Pakistan International Airlines (PIA) hangar but turned out to be a dud! The damage it could have caused had it exploded can be only be left to the imagination. The fate of the other four bombs is unknown, some of them probably swallowed up by the marshy lands surrounding the airfield.

Air Cmde Inam-ul-Haq, the Air Officer Commanding (AOC) of the PAF, Dacca, confirmed the after effects of this raid:[7]

> Indian Canberra bombers also kept on raiding frequently at night. Their bombing was hopeless, doing little damage to any important installation. A bomb fell not too far from my house and close to the bungalow where Begum Khalida Zia was detained. A stray bomb, however, did land on our Officers' Mess, the debris from which fell on many of the personnel in trenches. Squadron Leader Rabbani, the only Bengali officer loyal to Pakistan till the very end, died immediately. He was one of my last students at Risalpur in 1953. He later became a navigator.
>
> The following morning, I had gone to see an injured general officer at CMH. The place was cluttered with dead and injured, the air putrid all over. By chance I entered a room in which dead bodies were stacked and I was shocked to see our senior air traffic officer lying among the dead but breathing very feebly. His lungs were in a mess, being the result of previous night's bombing on the Officers' Mess. On my pointing out, the medical staff worked on him and brought him back to life, literally.

As the Indian Army's noose tightened around Dacca, the Indian Air Force was on an all out offensive to support the advancing troops of IV Corps under Lt Gen Sagat Singh. With Dacca's fall imminent, the squadron was ordered to concentrate its efforts on the Eastern Front. This made for a welcome change for the Commanding Officer (CO), Wg Cdr P Gautam and his navigation leader, Sqn Ldr K.K. Dutta, who till then were flying solely on the Western Front.

On December 14, the CO led four aircraft to strike Pakistan Army positions East of Dacca near the Meghna river, to help the helicopter effort to airlift troops across the Meghna from Chandpur to Daudkandi in the environs of Narayanganj. The aircraft staged through Dum Dum, flying low level to the Sita-Lakshya river. Nearing the target, the Canberras popped up to 6,000 ft, made a dog-leg left turn and flying from East to West to avoid overshooting into Indian Army positions, attacked the Pakistan Army positions in a westerly direction, overflying Tejgaon and Kurmitola again in the receding light.

On December 15, Gen Sam Manekshaw announced a cessation of aerial bombardment starting at 4.30 pm, to allow the Pakistanis to come to terms with their surrender terms. Prior to the cessation coming into effect, several offensive sorties were flown which included the last Canberra operations over East Pakistan.

No. 16 Squadron put up three aircraft to attack Kurmitola Cantonment, the formation led by Wg Cdr Gautam, with Sqn Ldr P M Takle and Fg Offr B R E Wilson flying the other two aircraft. While circling around to attack the target, the No. 3 aircraft in the formation, Fg Offr Wilson overflew Tejgaon airfield and was hit by the Pakistani AA guns. The aircraft went straight down – no distress call was given. This was the only loss of a Canberra on the Eastern Front. The ceasefire came into effect minutes later, and the next day, just after noon, the Pakistan Army in East Pakistan surrendered.

The Canberras in the Eastern Sector undertook 53 sorties. A total of 300,000 lb of bombs were dropped against multiple targets throughout the front. Their efforts were augmented by Caribou and Antonov-12 raids which dropped another 150,000 lb of bombs on their night missions. The night time attacks by the Canberras, Caribous and An-12s were largely ineffective and their sole value, if any, consisted in mere harassment of the night time defences. However, the day-time employment of the Canberras against Pakistani strongholds, road and riverine traffic did fetch encouraging results and contributed to the overall demoralisation of the Pakistan Army.

Canberras in the Western Sector

The bombing campaign in the Western Sector was fought by a mix of units operating from Agra as a home base. While No. 5 Squadron under Wg Cdr M B S Talwar was fully invested in the operations, it was augmented by a detachment of four Canberras of No. 35 Squadron and the aircraft of JBCU under Sqn Ldr S Thakar located at Agra as well.

Additionally, half of No. 16 Squadron participated in the operations as well, led by their CO Wg Cdr P Gautam.

On December 3, the balloon went up at 1700 h at Agra when all the aircrew of the various squadrons and detachments were recalled to the Ops Room for briefing. Just a few minutes earlier, the PAF had done multiple dusk raids against various Indian airfields close to the border. Agra was untouched at that point.

Various targets were earmarked for the first offensive sorties of the night – the main PAF airfield at Sargodha was accompanied by targets at Mianwali, Murid, Shorkot, Risalawala and Chander. Of these, with the exception of Chander, all other airfields were actively used by the PAF. The most treacherous of these targets would be Mianwali, located the farthest away from the Indian border, and home to the PAF's bomber force of Martin B-57 Canberras. Any attacking bomber would be in easy range of intercepting fighters from Sargodha, Risalawala and within easy detection range of the radar at Sakesar.

The first offensive missions of the Canberras, however, were interrupted by the PAF attacking Agra in the middle of the night at around 9 pm. One lone B-57 of the PAF made a 450 mile incursion into Indian territory to drop a stick of bombs on the Agra runway. Most of the bombs missed the runway, or did not explode, however, one did find its mark on an intersection causing all the aircraft to use half the width of the available runway for take-off. Some of the Canberras staged through Ambala for refuelling. Agra would put up 19 sorties that night attacking Sargodha, Mianwali, Murid, Chander, Risalawala and Shorkot. Most of these were by No. 5 Squadron.

The first offensive bomber sortie was done by a relatively junior crew belonging to No. 5 Squadron – Fg Offr V Pratap and Fg Offr S C Mahajan, who flew the mission to Shorkot airfield (Rafiqui), which unknown to the IAF was the same airfield that the PAF B-57s that attacked Agra were staging from! Just as they were making their bombing run on the airfield, the runway was fully lit. The crew had the satisfaction of watching their bombs explode in the centre of the lit runway before a barrage of AA fire came up to greet them. What they didn't know at that time was that Rafiqui airfield was preparing to receive a PAF B-57 which was just about to land from its long trip to Agra. This B-57 was the second aircraft returning from a raid on Agra and it was fired upon by the AA gunners as well!.[8] This PAF aircraft then landed on the damaged runway, suffered a tyre burst , and ran off the runway into the dirt, damaging itself.

No. 5 Squadron mounted two raids on Shorkot that night, and another two raids on Sargodha. All the four aircraft of No. 35 Squadron's detachment had participated in these strikes as well, with a strike against Mianwali by three aircraft.[9]

The quick retaliation by the Canberras not only kept the PAF up but also bought in some quick results. The PAF admits that a secondary runway at Sargodha was hit and the debris kicked onto the main runway rendered it unusable for a few hours. All the aircraft returned unscathed on the very first day of operations.

On the second night of bomber operations (December 4/5), 19 sorties were flown against the Pakistani air bases. Sargodha and Mianwali were the main targets. One Canberra belonging to the JBCU, tasked with attacking Mianwali with a TOT of 2000 h failed to return. It fell victim to an air-to-air missile launched by a Mirage III scrambled from Mianwali. Both the crew members, Flt Lt L M Sassoon and Flt Lt R M Advani were killed when the aircraft crashed near the village of Nara, about 18 miles from Khushab.[10]

The aircraft from Agra were supplemented by four of the Canberras by No. 16 Squadron from Gorakhpur, which also staged via Ambala for fuel before going on to attack Mianwali. The full moon prevalent in the early December nights made navigation much easier. All the four aircraft flying in a stream found their targets and dropped their bomb load from an altitude of 6,000 ft. On the return leg, they got down to 1,000 ft above ground altitude and successfully made it back. This formation was led by the CO Wg Cdr Gautam.

On the night of December 5, No. 5 Squadron put in eight aircraft against airfields in Pakistan: four against Sargodha, two against Mianwali and two against Shorkot.

The raid on Sargodha was quite successful. The PAF admits that the main runway was successfully cratered making it unusable for several hours.[11] An engineering facility received a direct hit, killing two PAF officers who were at work. However, a price was paid, when one of the four aircraft was hit by AA fire over Sargodha. Canberra IF960 flown by Flt Lt S K Goswami and Fg Offr S C Mahajan went down after a few minutes at the village of Bhalwal.

No. 5 Squadron also recorded success against Shorkot airfield. Two direct hits were recorded against the runway, making it unusable over the next three and a half days.

This was also the night that the "Y" bomb was used in anger. This sortie was flown by Wg Cdr P Gautam of No. 16 Squadron, and can be categorised as one of the most dangerous sorties flown by a Canberra crew during this war. On a predetermined course set by his navigator Sqn Ldr K K Dutta, Gautam flew his Canberra northwest of the Sakesar radar station till they spotted the Namal lake reflecting the moonlight over its vast surface. He then turned the aircraft on a heading of 240 degrees and slowly came down to deck level. That path bought him straight down the main runway of Mianwali. As Gp Capt K K Dutta explains:

> Right from the runway, we were getting lower and lower and lower. And then we found our position … a little to one side. My estimate is that we were at our max speed which is 360 kt.. and at 50 feet over the runway very fast. We dropped the bomb …they were expecting … AA fire started, all around like Diwali. I still remember (saying) 'sir, let's run' … he also knew … full throttle. And right in front, one gun was coming in, pop pop pop. And he (Gautam) gave a little bank and went down (the middle and over) the village, at the other end, I could see thatch roofs, looked muddy to me, … he turned up, avoided, gave a bank sort of thing and flew at full speed. We were close to 450 kts or so.[12]

The delivery of the Y bomb was spot on – just along the length of the runway. The Pakistanis were initially puzzled about the lack of an explosion. But subsequently, they discovered the steel tripods on the runway and were able to organise manpower to clear them off the runway before the adhesive could fully set in. While the Y bomb was novel and ingenious, the results it fetched were inadequate. A delayed fuse bomb would have put the runway out of action for much longer than what actually transpired.[13]

Starting December 6, for the next couple of nights, the Canberra missions against the airfields petered down as the IAF started focussing on supporting the ground operations. Added to this was the fact that the moon was in the waning phase, cutting down on the ground visibility. The Canberras now started flying interdiction missions supporting the ground battles. Over the subsequent days, support was provided in the Chamb, Zafarwal and Raiwind marshalling yards.

On the night of December 9-10, six aircraft were sent to Nawabshah, Chamb and Lodhran railway junction, four of these being part of a formation from No. 5 Squadron. The raid was supposed to be a milk run, with no opposition, either in the air or on the ground, encountered. However, one aircraft was lost. The Canberra B66 IF1024 flew into the ground in the desert on the return leg. The diminishing moonlight, coupled with the relatively unmarked terrain of the desert, completely devoid of vegetation probably caused spatial disorientation, with fatal results. The crew of three, Flt Lt R D Naithani (pilot) and his two navigators Flt Lt G Theophilus and Flt Lt Manohar Purohit were killed.

Over the subsequent days, till the night of December 16, another 60 odd sorties were flown in support of the ground troops over various battle areas, Suliemanke, Chamb, Changa Manga and Bhawalpur being some of the areas. The rate of the sorties were curtailed by the poor visibility during the night. Most of the missions were limited to hitting rail junctions.

The PAF airfields were not visited again, with one exception.

On December 16, the Pakistani forces surrendered in the East, and operations in the West were to wind down on the evening of December 17. Most of the offensive operations were stood down for December 17, however, a couple of hours before the ceasefire was to become effective, Central Air Command sent in the last bomber mission of the war – an Antonov-12 transport aircraft, flown by No. 44 Squadron CO, Wg Cdr V B Vashisht, was sent to the northern airfield of Skardu in the Gilgit area. This aircraft was followed by three Canberras. The An-12 dropped 38 × 500 lb bombs on the airfield, followed by the Canberras. All the aircraft returned safely.

The value of attacking Skardu at such a late moment in the war was questionable. And it was fortuitous that the raid was accomplished without any losses. But it did convey a message that the Indian Air Force was out there in full force.

The Southwestern Sector

The last sector that can be geographically studied in isolation is the Southwestern Sector of the India-Pakistan border, comprising the Sind, Nayachor, Karachi and Kutch areas. While most of the frontline battles were being fought from the air bases of Uttarlai, Jaisalmer and Jamnagar, the bombing effort was all entirely provided by the main component of No. 35 Squadron operating from Pune.

No. 35 Squadron was under the command of Wg Cdr K K Badhwar. Ahead of the operations, one small detachment of four aircraft was sent to Agra to augment the counter-air offensive in the Western Sector. The remaining aircraft mostly operated from Pune, setting up four aircraft missions to attack targets in the Karachi complex that staged via Jamnagar for fuel.

The very first night that the IAF Canberras retaliated in the north, Wg Cdr Badhwar led four aircraft to attack PAF Masroor, which at that time was hosting a mixed force of B-57s, Sabres and T-33s (later augmented by F-104 Starfighters). The Canberras staged via Jamnagar and had a staggered TOT starting around 4 am. Each aircraft dropped 8 × 1,000 lb over the airfield, but no significant damage was recorded on the ground. During the return leg, the aircraft recovered directly to Pune.

The second night, December 4, the squadron put up two missions of four aircraft each, the first mission striking Masroor around 8.30 pm. When the first mission arrived, PAF Masroor was still recovering from the devastating after effects of a dusk raid carried out by four Hunters from the Operational Conversion Unit (OCU) at Jamnagar, which had put out of action several PAF aircraft on the ground. The bombs from the first wave put Masroor's secondary runway out of action.[14] The second mission, led by the CO arrived over Masroor at approximately 4.00 am. Their bombing was accurate enough – the main runway was hit, and a taxiway culvert was blown away. The latter prevented retaliatory offensive missions from being launched from Masroor for a period of time. The third aircraft from the second mission, the Canberra B(I)58 IF923, flown by Flt Lt S C Sandal and Flt Lt K S Nanda failed to return. While egressing out of the target area for Jamnagar, the No. 4 aircraft observed a flash ahead, at about 40 miles out of Karachi, and it was speculated that the aircraft may have hit the sea trying to get down to low level.

Later, on the night of December 5, three aircraft were sent again from Poona, staging through Jamnagar. The specific target given to them was the Bulk Petroleum Installation (BPI). This raid bought in excellent results again – a direct hit destroyed a PAF RB-57 Canberra stored in a hangar, and badly damaged a T-33 trainer aircraft. The secondary runway received damage as well.[15]

Some 24 h later, on the night of December 6, another mission of four aircraft damaged the secondary runway and taxi track at Masroor.[16] The pressure was kept on by a second mission that was sent in the early hours of December 7 to PAF Drigh Road[17] for the first time. Drigh Road was revisited on the night of December 7.

During this time, the CO had been asking for permission from the Central Command to attack a new target of opportunity that had been seen multiple times while egressing from the attacks from Masroor: these were the oil tanks at Keamari in Karachi harbour. These oil tanks were not in the list of targets prioritised by the Central Command and multiple requests to hit them were not approved.[18]

On the night of December 8, No. 35 Squadron was to put up another raid on Drigh Road to coincide with the Indian Navy's missile boat attack. Badhwar asked for permission to mount an eight aircraft strike to hit Drigh Road, but faced opposition as the Command was reluctant to have more than four Canberras staging through Jamnagar at any stage. Badhwar suggested that only four aircraft would stage through Jamnagar, while the other four would fly direct to target from Pune.[19] Keeping in view the runway limitations at Pune, and the full fuel load required to travel the distance, the bomb load was decreased to 6,000 lb per aircraft for the four aircraft. The 1,200-mile round trip journey would mark the longest that the IAF aircraft had flown on any offensive sortie.

Once near Karachi, Badhwar never had the intention of attacking Drigh Road with the second formation. He was always set on attacking the oil tanks from the very start. They scored direct hits on the tank complex and the oil kept burning for several nights after that. Badhwar's navigator on this flight, Flt Lt Y P Singh, would recall the vivid sight:[20]

> Flying at 8,000 feet at minimum speed due to the bombing run, aircraft buffeting because of the open bomb doors, we must have painted every air defence radar within 250 km. Not to mention the Pak night interceptors based at Karachi, and the fireworks of the heavy ack-ack guns!
>
> We were over the oil tanks. I pressed the bomb release switch, watched as the bombs hit the tanks. The devastation below on impact was spectacular. Our bombs had turned those fuel storage tanks into a huge, nay, an enormously huge ball of fire. It was a sight worth taking all the risks in the world! We did an orbit over the target. We could see that as the tanks exploded and caught fire, the fiery debris flew in all directions and hit other tanks nearby, creating a chain reaction. The fireball on the ground was seen by the rest of the bombers which were now over Drigh Road runway and dropping their bombs there.

The subsequent oil blaze that was not put out for days caused demoralisation all around. Air Cmde Rais Rafi, PAF, who had moved part of his bomber force from Mauripur to Mianwali would later note:[21]

> Most of our families were at Mauripur. The base had received a hard pounding from the Indian Air Force that night and suffered quite a bit of damage. The huge oil storage fire at Karachi harbour due to

> enemy air action was quite demoralising to the families at Mauripur. They thought the IAF must have wreaked such havoc everywhere else which is not so. There was a barrage of telephone calls (to Mianwali)... lady after lady spoke to me requesting to talk to their husband...by the fourth call. I was fed up!

Contrary to what one would think, this attack on the oil tanks was not received well by the Central Air Command and would cause some friction thereafter.

The squadron diverted its attention away from the Karachi area after that last strike and focussed on other targets. Nawabshah airfield was attacked on the night of December 9 by seven Canberras staging via Jodhpur (This included two Canberras from the Agra detachment). Subsequent nights were spent on railway yards at Rahim Yar Khan and other areas in the southwestern desert.

As the war was winding down in the East, the squadron returned to Karachi for one farewell visit to the harbour on the night of December 15. Once again, the oil tanks in Karachi were the target, as well the naval installations. The squadron put up five aircraft, with Badhwar acting as a pathfinder, dropping target indication bombs (employed for the first time in the war), with a formation of four Canberras which dropped 8,000 lb of bombs each in his wake, hitting the harbour facilities and also causing some civilian casualties.[22]

This was the Rapier's parting gift in the December War.

The 'Other' Bombers : An-12s

The saga of bomber operations is not complete without mentioning the contribution of No. 44 Squadron, "Himalayan Geese", under the command of Wg Cdr V B Vashisht. The squadron trained on the aircraft using conventional bombs, loading as many as 24 × 500 lbs, as well as a napalm load that consisted of 9 × 1,000 lb containers. Delivering these involved flying at very low levels to avoid AA fire as well as radar detection, at tree-top heights and in blackout conditions. Vashistht selected only about 8 out of the 30 odd pilots available with him for the task. The bomber detachment moved to Bareilly in Central Air Command at the beginning of December.

The An-12s used the same streaming tactic as the Canberras, arriving over the target at set intervals. The very first mission was on the night of December 3/4 when two aircraft led by Vashisht attacked the Changa Manga forest area where the Pakistan Army's Armoured Division was held in reserve. The target was attacked using 500 lb bombs the first night, and using napalm the second night by six aircraft that dropped 66 × 500 lb bombs and 55 × 1000 lb napalm containers.

On December 5/6, six An-12s flew against the Pakistan Army positions in the valley near Haji Pir. Some 140 × 500 lb were dropped where a Pakistan Army Brigade was concentrated. The Integrated Logistics System (ILS) system at Poonch airfield was ingeniously used as a direction aid for the An-12s for their bombing run. This raid was considered one of the more successful attacks – the Pakistani artillery guns that had been targeting Indian positions fell silent after the attack and the Pakistan Army's threat to Poonch was considered neutralised.

On subsequent nights, with moonlight being the sole navigational aid, Ford Abbas and the approaches to Suleimanke Headworks were attacked with napalm. Suleimanke was attacked the second night by four An-12s but the bombs missed the target.

With the diminishing moonlight, the An-12s had to move the time over target for their raids closer to dusk or dawn. On December 11/12, the first attack in daylight hours was carried out over the Rohri railway junction by two aircraft led by Vashist. They had some success tracking the railway line and dropping the bombs along the way.

Two aircraft were sent to the Eastern Sector to target the Jaydebpur ordnance factory, to the north of Dacca. The air superiority that the IAF enjoyed over there meant the sorties could be carried out in broad daylight with very little AA opposition. Though both bombs and napalm were used, a post war assessment concluded that the An-12s missed the target.

On December 15, three An-12s were sent to attack the Sui gas plant, which was previously hit by Hunters operating from Jaisalmer. The attack was unsuccessful, with official sources noting that "though 80 × 500 lb bombs were dropped, they failed to hit the target in the failing light".[23] Aerial photos of the gas plant did show considerable damage to the cooling plant, and it is assumed that the damage was done by the Hunters.

The last raid by the An-12s was conducted on December 17, just minutes before the ceasefire came into effect. The single An-12, flown by Wg Cdr Vashisht, led a formation of three other Canberras in broad daylight and dropped its bombs on Skardu airfield. The daylight raid was successful, with good photographic evidence gathered of the bombs striking the runway. Though on the return leg, the An-12 apparently went through a period of uncertainty under the belief that a PAF Mirage III was pursuing it. In reality, none of the PAF fighters was known to have flown so further north as to interfere with the Indian air effort.

Conclusion

In the 14-day war, 245 offensive sorties were flown by the Canberra bomber squadrons of the IAF across both fronts. Five aircraft and eleven aircrew were lost due to various causes. One loss to enemy aerial action, two to AA fire, and two to undetermined causes. The average strength of the Canberra force during the war was 38 aircraft over the duration, and the losses amounted to a tenth of that force. In hindsight, these were heavy losses for the force, but a necessary price to pay for what the Canberras achieved – which was suppression of the Pakistan Air Force assets and a general reduction on the strategic and tactical supplies and logistics chain supporting the Pakistani war effort.

It may be debatable whether the counter-air missions against the PAF's airfields achieved good results or not, but what cannot be denied is that the nightly raids on the PAF airfields kept the PAF on the edge. Occasionally, luck favoured the Canberras via the direct hits achieved on some of the runways or in the case of Masroor, the destruction of the RB-57 and the damage to the facilities. Also undeniable was the mass demoralisation caused among the Pakistani population that the Canberra strikes on Karachi had achieved, though it imposed collateral damage in terms of civilian lives.

While remaining less glamorous, the disruption carried out along the Pakistani transportation and logistical chains by the specific targeting of railway junctions, riverine traffic and Army formations also contributed to the swift outcome of the war.

The Canberra bomber force was recognised by the award of two Maha Vir Chakra (MVC) awards (one each to Wg Cdr M B S Talwar and P Gautam) and 11 Vir Chakra (VrC) awards. Six of the eleven VrCs were awarded to navigators. Separately, the sole Canberra PR squadron also received one MVC and four VrCs. It has been stated that the VrC award for Wg Cdr K K Badhwar was originally slated to be a Maha Vir Chakra, but the friction with Command HQ and other officials over the targeting of the Keamari oil tanks played a part in that recommendation not going through. This did cause some discontent among the aircrew at Pune and after much wrangling, Badhwar was given an Ati Vishist Seva Medal as well[24] – one of the few cases of 'double awards' made for the same war effort. All these awards, however, were one-tenth of the total awards given to IAF personnel.

The Antonov-12s contributed another 40 sorties to the war effort. The results achieved by these aircraft comprised a mixed bag. The size and vulnerability of the aircraft to ground fire meant that its exposure over hostile terrain had to be kept to the minimum. Most of the targets allotted to the An-12s had to be close to the border, and at a considerable distance away from active PAF bases to avoid the possibility of interception. Of course, the conditions were made favourable only by the IAF's counter-air offensive against the Pakistani airfields that kept the PAF either cooped up or busy defending its bases, so that they could not extend themselves more to protect the rest of the country.

ACM Lal states that the 500 lb bombs used by the An-12s were of World War II vintage.[25] They were so old that 40 per cent turned out to be duds. The usual bomb-load was to 24 or 25 × 500 lb fitted with bigger tail cones. But after December 10/11, the bomb-load was increased to 36 × 500 lb fitted with smaller tail cones. The aircraft suffered minor damage from ground fire but there were no casualties, and no aircraft loss. With no precision bombing aids, and operating by the use of visual sighting or timed bombing runs, the exact results of the Antonov-12 bombing effort is difficult to determine. Very little damage assessment can be made based on Pakistani sources. However, it may be pertinent to quote Air Cmde Kaiser Tufail of the PAF here:

> While the accuracy of these heavy bombers was never a factor, the explosion of bombs in the near vicinity of ground troops was certainly unnerving.[26]

One cannot deny the raw courage and determination shown by the aircrew of No. 44 Squadron. Led by Vashisht, the squadron flew these lumbering transports at 100 ft altitude for their bombing missions, and by night, and they did so night after night and suffered no losses. Rightfully, the CO, Wg Cdr V B Vashisht earned a Maha Vir Chakra. Additionally, the squadron also earned two Vir Chakras and five Vayusena Medals.[27]

Table 1: Key Units and Players

Canberra Bomber Units

Unit	CO	Flt Cdrs	Nav Leader
5 Squadron (Agra)	Wg Cdr M B S Talwar (MVC)	Sqn Ldr R C Kohli Sqn Ldr S C Jain	Sqn Ldr D C Bhandari (VrC)
16 Squadron (Gorakhpur)	Wg Cdr P Gautam (Bar to MVC)	Sqn Ldr P M Takle (VM[28]) Sqn Ldr S D Karnik (VrC)	Sqn Ldr K K Dutta (VrC)
35 Squadron (Pune)	Wg Cdr K K Badhwar (VrC)	Sqn Ldr A K Bhadra (VrC) Sqn Ldr K Chandrasekhar	Sqn Ldr G S Thapa (VrC)
JBCU (Agra)	Sqn Ldr S Thakar	Flt Lt Kepu Sengupta	Flt Lt C A W Robert

Antonov-12 Bomber Units

Unit	CO	Flt Cdrs
44 Squadron (Agra)	Wg Cdr V B Vashisht (MVC)	Sqn Ldr G S Ahluwalia (VrC) Sqn Ldr A K Bhide (VM)

Acknowledgements: The author acknowledges the help received from the Canberra India Association, Gp Capt Conrad Dalton, Gp Capt K K Dutta, Gp Capt S D Karnik, Wg Cdr Anil Ghosh, Air Mshl Bharat Kumar and Air Mshl Vikram Singh.

Notes

1. It is estimated that 15 Canberras were lost to peace-time and war-time operations till 1971.
2. No. 106 SR Squadron consisted of one flight of photo reconnaissance Canberras with no offensive capability, and a flight of Dakotas for aerial survey work.
3. P.C. Lal, *My Years with the IAF* (New Delhi: Lancer, 2009).
4. Apparently named after Air Mshl Y V Malse's first name "Yeshwant". Air Cmde K Sanjeevan, *Memoirs of a Spanner : My Story* (New Delhi: Notion Press).
5. Y V Malse, Interview with the author, 2003.
6. No reliable assessment of civilian casualties caused by aerial operations in East Pakistan is available. The West Pakistanis periodically released casualty figures during the war and also conducted press briefings on site at bombed-out areas; their numbers for the Adamjee casualties were 275 killed and 150 wounded. No independent verification for this figure is available; no post-war survey was carried out by the Bangladesh government that arrived at correct figures.
7. Inamul Haq Khan, "Saga of PAF in East Pakistan -1971", Planet Earth Blog, November 17, 2009, https://imranhkhan.com/2009/11/17/saga-of-paf-in-east-pakistan-1971
8. Rais Ahmed Rafi, *PAF Bomber Operations 1965 and 1971 Wars* (Karachi: PAF Book Club, 2001), p. 106.
9. Anil Ghosh, *Mission 307 Alpha: The Epic Journey* (New Delhi: No. 35 Squadron, IAF, 2018).
10. Kaiser Tufail, "Air Defence in Northern Sector – 1971 War," *Aeronaut Blog*, February 21, 2011, http://kaiser-aeronaut.blogspot.com/2011/02/air-defence-in-northern-sector-1971-war.html. Accessed on June 2, 2021.
11. Ibid.
12. Gp Capt K K Dutta, VrC, interview with the author.
13. John Fricker, "Post-Mortem of an Air War," *Air Enthusiast Magazine*, May 1972; refers to a Mirage III that had burst its tyre landing at Mianwali after Gautam's Y bomb attack.
14. Kaiser Tufail, *In the Ring and on its Feet* (Lahore: Ferozesons, 2018), p. 93.
15. Ibid. *Dawn* newspaper reported 50 civilian casualties in the neighbouring colony near Masroor.
16. This raid also resulted in civilian deaths in the residential areas southeast of Masroor. *Dawn* newspaper reported as many as 74 fatalities for this raid.
17. PAF Drigh Road, in its pre-independence days, was home to the Aircraft Depot of the RAF – and was the birthplace of the IAF – when on April 1, 1933, the first flight of No. 1 Squadron was raised there. Drigh Road still had an active airfield and was being used by the PAF.

18. While it may be easy to find fault with Command HQ for not approving the oil tanks as a target, their proximity to civilian residential areas in Karachi may have been a factor. Especially, the densely populated village of Bhutta which was right next to this facility.
19. Air Cmde K K Badhwar's interview with Gp Capt Conrad Dalton, *Youtube,* November 5, 2019, https://www.youtube.com/watch?v=ejDTmFof7Qs. Accessed June 2, 2021.
20. Y P Singh, *One Night Over Karachi. – The Epic Journey – The Saga of 35 Squadron Air Force* (New Delhi: No. 35 Squadron, IAF, 2018).
21. Rafi, n. 8.
22. "Wednesdays Air Raid Death Toll Now 71," *Dawn* (Karachi) December 17, 1971.
23. Official History of the Indian Armed Forces – 1971 Bangladesh War.
24. Dilbagh Singh, *On the Wings of Destiny* (New Delhi: KW Publishers, 2013).
25. Lal, n. 3, p. 303.
26. Tufail, n. 14, p. 85.
27. A unique fact about An-12 bomber operations is that officers of the technical branch, as well as warrant officers and Non-Commissioned Officers (NCOs) of flight gunner trade took part on these sorties—one of the few opportunities given to those outside of the flying branch to take part directly in offensive flying missions. Four of the five VMs went to these technical officers or flight gunners.
28. The VM award to Sqn Ldr P M Takle was made posthumously in 1973 as he died shortly after the 1971 War in an air accident.

8. Game-Changing Helicopter Employment

Rajesh Isser

If there is any home-grown campaign in India that truly boosts the concept of jointness, it is the war for liberating Bangladesh. The multiplying effect of synergy among the three Services created magic on the Eastern Front while containing damage in the West. The whole gamut of joint support structures such as Advance Headquarters (HQ), Tactical Air Centres (TACs), Forward Air Controllers (FACs), Ground Liaison Officers (GLOS) and others worked in a coherent manner to achieve air superiority in the East and effective Offensive Air Support (OAS) in the West. The *blitzkrieg* on the ground in East Pakistan, ably supported by a well coordinated air campaign demonstrated the air-land battle concept well before it came into common parlance in the 1980s and 1990s.

Wars, it is said, are fought in the minds of the Generals, Air Marshals and Admirals. Nothing could be truer than what was demonstrated in the lightning moves of the Indian Army/Indian Air Force (IAF) combine in the East. Learning from the Vietnam campaign, the IAF top brass, in collusion with Lt Gen Sagat Singh, General Officer Commanding (GOC) IV Corps, conceived a series of Special Heliborne Operations (SHBOs) that leap-frogged the Indian infantry into the centre of gravity of Gen Niazi's forces. The early surrender was due to the speed of advance that even took the Indian Army HQ by surprise! This was surely the best example of what mutual respect and faith in each other's capabilities could bring about among the Indian Armed Forces.

While the historical focus remains on the pioneering SHBO missions that redefined tactics, commanders at all levels displayed remarkable ingenuity and creativity to grab every opportunity for denting the enemy's might – special armed operations by helicopters along with the Mukti Bahini comprise one such story. Though a drop in the ocean in the overall scheme of things, the effect this had on the morale of the local fighters and populace was immeasurable. Recent campaigns of the North Atlantic Treaty Organisation (NATO) underline support as the lynchpin for success; the Indian armed forces demonstrated it well in 1971. The successful large scale airborne assault at Tangail was the icing on the cake of what true jointness could bring about. Rarely in history has a more coordinated and successful airborne assault been recorded than done by the IAF-Indian Army combine in 1971.

Innovative Employment of Helicopters

While helicopters as war machines, vital suppliers and gunships were first employed in France's Algerian Campaign in 1950, it was the Vietnam War that brought them to the fore as game-changers in such dirty wars. Helicopter employment was only limited by a commander's creativity and risk-taking limits. The whole world sat up and took notice – and so did a few Indian commanders during the war for the liberation of East Pakistan in 1971. The first, Lt Gen Sagat Singh, was the maverick corps commander of IV Corps, one of the formations which was tasked with offensive operations towards Dacca from the East. He had seen what the Mi-4s could do in terms of SHBOs and vertical envelopment in Mizoram. Supporting him in leveraging the potential of the Mi-4s was one of the IAF's most audacious middle-level commanders, Gp Capt Chandan Singh, who he designated as his Air Force task-force commander, an appointment that never really existed at the time. Together, they orchestrated the most audacious series of operations over one week with just over a squadron worth (11-15) of Mi-4 helicopters from Nos 110 and 105 Helicopter Units (HU). Gen Sagat was not very well liked by peers and superiors for his maverick attitude. But he had seen what Mi-4s could do during the

1966 Mizo campaign by Indian joint forces. During the 1971 War, he commanded IV Corps that was to do a secondary (feint) attack from the East (Tripura). But in his hands fell the eleven Mi-4s of No. 110 HU in Kumbhigram. Together, they did the unthinkable and produced a miracle that only a fog of war throws up.

Using Mi-4s to launch whole battalions and brigades across innumerable waterways that included the mighty river Meghna and its tributary, the Surma, Sagat and Chandan first bypassed and bottled-up the Sylhet garrison with merely a battalion, and then helilifted two brigades to the doorsteps of Dacca. This left Dacca vulnerable and forced its garrison to surrender.[1] Though Sagat was made to wait for other formations to catch up, the series of heliborne operations that he executed could well be considered to be game-changers that accelerated the collapse of the Pakistan Army in East Pakistan and the creation of Bangladesh.[2]

The Air-Land Battle Concept in the East

Concept of Operations: Indian Army[3]

The Army Commander had reminded his formation commanders that the battle in East Pakistan would be a fluid one and that his operational instructions should be used as a basis for general guidance. Though final objectives would remain unaltered, formation commanders should be prepared to constantly review thrust lines and intermediate objectives as per changed situations. These modifications involved by passing sizeable enemy strongholds, which not only indicated a significant change in concept, but also expressed a growing confidence and realisation by Eastern Command that a swift advance into the vitals of East Pakistan would threaten Dacca and bring about a total collapse and defeat of the Pakistani forces. Initial plans catered for securing the line of the Brahmaputra and Meghna rivers. Further detailed planning could only be done taking into consideration the progress of various thrusts. It was envisaged that IV Corps would cross the Meghna between Daudkhandi and Bhairab Bazaar and advance towards Dacca.

101 Communication Zone Area with 95 Mountain Brigade Group of four battalions, 2 Para Group, followed by 167 Mountain Brigade would advance towards Dacca from the North. It was felt that these forces would be supported in their advance to Dacca by the Siddiqi Force, a large group of freedom fighters which had been operating with good effect in Tangail district.

Contingency plans were also made for elements of II Corps to cross the Padma at Goalundo for which purpose suitable inland water transport craft were placed at Dhubri to assist 95 Mountain Brigade or move elements of 20 Mountain Division, if required. Army Headquarters Reserve of 50 Independent Para Brigade was to provide one complete battalion drop and two-company drops. It was appreciated that the most important area for the main drop was Tangail in order to ensure early pressure on Dacca. Second priority was given for two company drops to assist in securing Magura if necessary. Due to the limited availability of Mi-4 helicopters, all these helicopters were allocated to IV Corps to enable them to ferry troops as required. The air effort allotted to the Army was sufficient to cater for an average of 120 sorties per day. Naval forces were to blockade Chalna and Chittagong and the naval air arm was to be used in the area Chittagong-Cox's Bazaar.

Mi-4 units had seen continuous operational service in India's northeast, supporting the Army's counter-insurgency operations in Nagaland and Mizoram, lifting commando teams into action and helping to preempt hostile infiltration to and from China. They had often suffered hits from small arms fire; on one occasion, a Mi-4 even returned to base with a poison-tipped arrow sticking in its undercarriage! The operational climax for the Mi-4s in IAF service came during the 1971 War when this helicopter played a key role in the Indian Army's *blitzkrieg*-style advance to Dacca.

Whilst the Indian II Corps battled its way from the western side, the IV Corps thrust came from three directions in the East, across 155 miles (250 km) of border between then East Pakistan and Meghalaya to the north, through to the Feni salient in the extreme south of Tripura. One column moved in from the Silchar-Karimganj area towards Sylhet, another along the Akhura-Asjuganj axis and the third in the South, with the objective of containing Comilla and cutting off Chittagong. Whilst battling against the two Pakistani divisions ranged against them, IV Corps had to contend with the most formidable riverine terrain, criss-crossed by rivers and streams that make the area a logistic nightmare for any offensive action.

Supporting the advance was No. 110 HU, with 10 Mi-4s on strength and another two Mi-4s attached from No. 105 HU.[4] Mi-4s were intimately involved in the spectacular progress made by the Army, particularly by 8 Mountain Division. No. 110 HU transported troops, guns, ammunition and equipment, evacuated casualties and conducted reconnaissance for the field formations in the sector. On December 7, 254 troops were airlifted from Kailashahar to the Sylhet Sector in the face of heavy ground fire. Next day, another 279 troops and 97 tonnes of equipment were airlifted from Kalaura, mostly at night. An additional 584 troops and 125 tonnes of supplies and nine field guns were lifted between December 9 and 10, to reinforce the build-up against Sylhet, which was held by the Pakistani 313 Brigade. No. 110 HU then moved to Agartala for the heliborne operations from Brahmanbaria to Raipura.

Mi-4s could be said to have forced the pace of the Army's relentless drive, which now saw heliborne infantry leap-frogging past natural obstacles and enemy defences, with MiG-21s and Gnats strafing and rocketing strongholds, in a text book display of coordinated air power. The biggest operational task yet undertaken by the IAF's helicopter force was between December 11 and 15. On December 11, 1,350 troops and 192 tonnes of equipment were airlifted from Brahmanbaria to Narsingdi, including in particular the lead battalion 4th/5th Gorkha Rifles of 59 Mountain Brigade, spearheading 8 Mountain Division's intrusion in Sylhet. The Gorkhas and their equipment were lifted across the Meghna river to the Southeast of Sylhet, forcing the much larger enemy force to abandon defences and, for fear of being cut off by the heliborne forces, pull back into the town.

Heliborne Operations

From December 7 onwards, helicopters began transporting troops, light guns, ammunition and fuel. In three days of operations, these helicopters had flown over 120 sorties to lift nearly 1,200 troops and 10 tons of load. Over 50 of these sorties were carried out by night. These operations facilitated the capture of Sylhet and certain other features in the same sector. Night movement of troops in large numbers must have caught the Pakistan Army by surprise. Besides fully armed troops in thousands, the load in hundreds of tonnes included recoilless (RCL) guns, gun shells and mortars, besides ration and small arms ammunition.

The IAF's small helicopter force could fairly claim credit for the speed of advance of the Indian Army in East Pakistan. As has been well recognised by the Indian Army, No. 110 HU was the key factor in the lightning campaign, where speed of advance was of the utmost importance. Other units that were given special mention were Nos 15 and 24 Squadrons whose Gnats provided escorts to the heliborne operations and close support over the entire Brahmanbaria-Sylhet axis. Other Mi-4 and Alouette III units, including No. 112 HU in the Jessore sector, conducted casualty evacuation, communication and reconnaissance flights. Some Mi-4s and Alouette IIIs were equipped as gunships and operated in this role both in the East and the Northwest of India, recalling their earlier role in 1965, when they hunted infiltrators with machine guns and anti-personnel bombs in Kashmir.

The Mukti Bahini Air Force

The birth of a *Bangladesh Air Force* took place as the Kilo Flight. On the night of December 3 and 4, Otter aircraft of this Air Force attacked fuel dumps at Chittagong, and an Alouette helicopter raided the fuel dumps at Narayanganj. Both the missions were successful. On December 4, this flight at Kailashahar airfield was placed at the disposal of GOC 8 Mountain Division, operating in the Maulvi Bazaar/Sylhet sector. The GOC demanded attacks by night on convoys, river barges and streamers on the Meghna, North of Bhairab Bazaar. The flight flew five sorties between December 4 and 7, hitting bunkers and troops concentrations at Maulvi Bazaar, and also destroyed two steamers and several 3-tonne trucks carrying troops.

Between December 7 and 12, the Alouette helicopter was constantly and effectively used as an armed escort during the special helicopter operations at Sylhet, Raipur, Narsingdi and Baidya Bazaar. It engaged targets as directed by the FAC at night also. After the first night raid on Chittagong fuel dumps, Otter aircraft were utilised for armed escort/ reconnaissance on a few missions only, in the same areas as the Alouette. The overall returns from this flight were not very encouraging, perhaps because it had no definite tasks. The contribution of this flight to the war effort was hardly significant. However, as far as raising the morale of the Mukti Bahini was concerned, it did serve the desired purpose. During the period of operations, the total flying effort of this flight was: Alouette 77 sorties/68 h and Otter 12 sorties/23 h.

A Herculean and Colourful Effort

The type-wise breakdown of the helicopter effort under the command of HQ, Eastern Air Command (EAC) for the conduct of air operations in the Eastern Theatre from December 3 to 17, 1971, was as follows:

Summary of Flying Effort: December 3-17, 1971

Some first-hand personal accounts of pilots who took part, as well as unit diaries of the time truly bring out the dynamic and fast-changing issues that exemplify true jointness. These are gleaned from unit war diaries and personal accounts (written debriefs available in units and Air HQ).[5]

Table 1: Summary of Helicopter Flying Effort in EAC

Type of aircraft	Sorties	Hours	Load (T)	Troops carried	Casualties carried
Mi-4	1,397	992:05	185.7	5,136	866
Alouette	894	726.35		809	282
Bell	113	84:00			31
Total	2,404	1,802:40	185.7	5,945	1,179

Source: Author's Compilation from War Diaries.

Extract from Unit Records of No. 110 HU:

Gp Capt Chandan Singh was the officer commanding of an Air Force Station in Assam. He was in the forefront of the air operations conducted for the liberation of Bangladesh, including planning and execution of the special helicopter operations. Prior to each mission, he personally carried out reconnaissance in the face of heavy enemy fire, and flew eight missions, deep into enemy territory, to supervise the progress of the helicopter airlift and to guide his pilots who were facing heavy opposition from ground fire.[6]

First-hand Account of Flt Lt Pushp K Vaid:

I got airborne approx. 1500 hours, and the other helicopters got airborne one after the other at an interval of 2 to 3 minutes, so by the time I had dropped my load and come back for the second load, the last helicopter was just getting airborne. We had enough fuel to do three trips each. But by the time I was going for my third trip, it was already dark. Also, the Pakistan Army had seen the helicopters and started surrounding the field we were landing in and were firing at us as we came into land. On my third flight, I must have seen as many as five hundred bullets or more coming towards me. I couldn't count of course but they looked like a lot of bullets along with tracer bullets. Amazingly not one bullet hit us. I warned all the other pilots to keep a look out and to reduce the time on the ground to minimum. We all finished our three trips and shut down for fuel at our bases. All of us checked our helicopters and not even one bullet had hit any helicopter.

While we were getting ready to start flying again, Gp Capt Chandan Singh, who was in charge of the Air Force side, said that we won't fly at night and that we will start flying next morning. That really upset the Army. They had not planned their soldiers or the ammunition or the food or the radio. They were not even sure of what or who had gone so far. All the helicopters had been filled up as the soldiers arrived with the idea that we will keep flying till everything had been moved. There was a big discussion between the Army and the Air Force. Eventually, after nearly three hours, it was decided that one helicopter will go, and if it came back the others will be sent.

Gp Capt Chandan Singh asked me to get a crew for the flight. I came to our rest room and asked for a volunteer to join me. Every one of my forty pilots wanted to come. I picked Flying Officer Kanth Reddy. We filled the helicopter with the radios and other equipment along with the soldiers. For our protection, we had a .38 revolver and a lungi. Lungi to pretend we were Bengalis. We always carried a flight engineer so that he could do all the handling on the ground, so that we won't stay on the ground too long. So off we went at about 2200 hours. Pitch dark. Our only navigational aid was the compass. We set course and as we got closer we heard our Air Force liaison officer, who had gone along with the Army, on his hand-held radio. He would not tell us what the situation was on the ground in case we turned back. He told us that it was all quiet and that he would light a fire for us so that we knew where to land. As the fire was lit, the entire Pakistan Army started firing at that fire. We could see the tracer bullets, hundreds of them. The poor soldier who lit the fire got hit on his thumb.

We landed and dumped everything we had as soon as we could, picked up the soldier who had been hit and got airborne in a second. After all the excitement of bullets, I asked my flight engineer to have a look at the helicopter and see if we had been hit. No, he said. Not one bullet, amazing. On my way back, I radioed the base to get all the helicopters ready so that we could continue flying right through the night. I landed back, picked up the next load and went dropped them. We then came back and picked the third load before the rest of the helicopters got ready. On the way back from our third trip, we noticed that our fuel gauge was showing zero fuel. We knew we had taken off with enough fuel, so either we had a leak or the gauge was not working. We had fingers crossed, legs crossed and were praying to whoever is up there to get us back to base. Well we got back to base, thanks to the LORD. At base we discovered that the cable to the fuel gauge had been hit. This was mended and then we continued flying with the rest of the helicopters right through the night till we had dropped the entire brigade at Slyhet.[7]

Account of War-time Activity by Air Cmde CM Singla (Retd):

... At Dimapur, I was asked to pick up an armed Chetak from Tezpur which had just been modified by and airlifted from BRD. It had one rocket pod on either side and each pod carried seven rockets. These could be fired in pairs or in salvo. In addition, on the helicopter floor, a twin barrel machine gun was mounted.

We were now required to learn to fire accurately by day and night. Practising on the machine gun was not a problem, but for the rockets we needed a gun-sight, harmonisation and above all, targets. It was decided that bundles of hay would be para-dropped over the thick jungles. The parachutes would form a canopy on tree-tops and these could be used as targets. However, the parachutes just went through the foliage. Ultimately, I hover dropped men on grassy hill slopes who hammered parachutes on the ground. These presented fair targets. We burnt several parachutes and became fairly proficient at firing rockets by day and night. Our first operational task came soon after. We moved to the vicinity of Kailashahar and launched the armed Chetak by night from the wilderness. To overcome recovery problem on a pitch black night, judicious use of concealed petromax was made. Enemy fuel dumps were successfully set afire by rockets that night.

Then onwards, we operated as a self-contained and mobile hitting outfit. We moved frequently to support troops as they advanced. I was ordered to fly in command on all armed missions. On one night, troops were to be inducted by Mi-4 helicopters. I was to give air cover. The Forward Air Controller told me on R/T that he was my pupil at Bidar. Our effective rocket firing over several missions that night was witnessed by a senior officer who flew as a passenger with us initially. Being an unstable platform, in our dive to aim and engage targets with rockets pairs, we had to come pretty low and close to the targets. We took some bullet hits that night. Subsequently, we hit and burnt ammunition trucks, boats ferrying troops by night and enemy concentrations. The helicopter had now got pierced by bullets all over. The engineers did a good job of repairs and despite vibrations, etc. we remained operational throughout the war.[8]

Extract from Unit Records of No. 110 HU:

... Squadron Leader Sanjay Kumar Choudhary (5863), Flying (Pilot), volunteered and landed with the first wave of troops to personally hold up and supervise the lighting of flares. During the process, the helicopter landing area came under heavy enemy gun fire. Regardless of own safety, and with the help of one jawan, he made daring efforts to light up the landing zone. Shortly thereafter, the jawan was killed by enemy fire. Undeterred Squadron Leader Choudhary single-handedly lit the flares and kept them lit throughout the night. This enabled the heliborne operation to continue the entire night till its successful completion.

Extract from No. 110 HU War Diary:

On 16th December 1971, Flight Lieutenant Ravindra Vikram Singh (9524) Flying (Pilot) was flying the C-in-C and Chief of Staff of Bangladesh with other passengers to Sylhet. At a height of 1 km, his aircraft was hit by enemy ground fire at 1720 hrs, where one bullet, after piercing the cabin injured the Chief of Staff of Bangladesh, hit an oil pipe, and resulted in leak of hot oil into the cabin. Pulling up immediately to 1.5 km. of height, he checked that the reductor oil pressure had started dropping to zero, giving limited time for action. It was by then dark and returning back to base or to any other airfield was impossible. He manoeuvred out of enemy area, selected a suitable field at Fenchuganj after approximately 15 minutes flying under trying circumstances in complete darkness and made a successful landing, saving the aircraft and the lives of the C-in-C and Chief of Staff of Bangladesh along with the other passengers and crew.[9]

No. 110 HU's Legacy

No. 110 HU was raised on February 19, 1962, with Mi-4 helicopters at Tezpur. During the 1971 War for the liberation of Bangladesh, within a brief period of 12 days, it was instrumental in demonstrating the flexibility of air power by successfully undertaking the first ever Special Heliborne Operation (SHBO) in war. It was utilised for 'vertical envelopment' extensively and carried out the famous helibridging operations in which the Indian Army was moved with creditable swiftness that finally brought a formidable enemy to his knees. The relentless operations changed the face of the Tactical Battle Area (TBA) in the theatre of operations (East of Dacca) in East Pakistan. SHBO missions contributed majorly to the most decisive liberation campaign ever in military history.

War Diary Extract:

> It had been assessed at higher formations that Sylhet town, a district and communication centre, was an important place from the military point of view and its fall would inflict a severe setback to the Pakistan Army. Thus, HQ IV Corps tasked 4/5 Gorkha Rifles of 59 Mountain Brigade to capture Sylhet and inducted Mi-4 helicopters of 110 HU to undertake SHBO missions to accomplish the ground plan. The main task was to helilift a battalion (4/5 GR) to Mirpara (outskirts of Sylhet) to secure the railway bridge over river Surma and occupy Sylhet airport/radio station to further operations. The challenges for the Unit helicopters did not end with Sylhet and the Unit was subsequently tasked to undertake extensive SHBO missions for furtherance of corps objectives as the battle progressed from different axes at Raipura, Narsingdi and Baidya Bazar. The following extracts

from the unit diary highlight the major missions flown during the 1971 operations:

03 to 06 Dec 1971 - Three 110 HU helicopters moved to Teliamura, while one was inducted at Aizwal and two at Imphal for communication and air logistics roles. Two more helicopters were subsequently inducted at Teliamura resulting in five helicopters operating there. All the helicopters were utilised for aerial reconnaissance and casualty evacuation and 57 casualties were evacuated on 4th Dec from the battlefield. These helicopters evacuated 42 casualties from the tactical battle area under enemy fire on December 5 and 36 casualties on December 6, 1971.

07 Dec 1971 - Battle of Sylhet (SHBO) - Five helicopters of 110 HU moved from Teliamura to Kailashahar for airlifting a battalion of troops to a point North of Surma River virtually in full view of Sylhet. On the same day, two of the Unit helicopters operating at Sylhet experienced heavy ground fire but were safely flown back to Kailashahar.

08 Dec 1971 - Battle of Sylhet (SHBO) - The air superiority gained was used to great advantage. Lt Gen Sagat Singh, Gp Capt Chandan Singh & Sqn Ldr CS Sandhu (CO 110 HU) worked out a contingency plan to operate at night to prevent being spotted by the enemy and reduce the possibility of enemy fire. Hand-held battery powered torches were fixed on the ground and used as landing aids for helicopters. At midnight, a helicopter airlifted vital equipment and more troops from Kalaura to Sylhet under heavy enemy ground fire. Flying three sorties each, all helicopters undertook night SHBO missions. During these missions, all the helicopters came under heavy ground fire and two of them were badly damaged, and though badly crippled managed to fly back to Kailashahar safely.

09 Dec 1971 - Sylhet & Raipura (SHBO) - This was the last day of Sylhet SHBO. All helicopters moved to Agartala by noon. A new task was given to lift troops and load from Brahmanbaria to Raipura.

Though ground fire was encountered enroute Raipura, no helicopters were damaged.

10 Dec 1971 - Raipura (SHBO) - The IV Corps Commander decided not to stop on the East bank of the Meghna River but to get across if possible to Dacca. The bridge across River Meghna was blown up and it was left to the helicopters to helibridge a sizeable force across the river. The operation to cross River Meghna began shortly before last light on 10 Dec 71 when about 100 troops were ferried to landing pads. By the time the second wave of helicopters arrived, it was quite dark but the helicopters landed safely. The movement of troops continued throughout the night and the next day. Though the normal capacity of Mi-4s was to carry 14 troops, the number of troops was increased to 23 men per trip.

11 Dec 1971 - Narsingdi (SHBO) - The Unit was given the biggest task of SHBO when eight helicopters of 110 HU were moved to Narsingdi from Brahmanbaria. By 0730 hrs, every helicopter had done three sorties each. After refuelling at Agartala, the second wave took off at 0900 hrs and carried out three sorties each. Two more details were flown. In all, a total of 834 troops and 58,600 kg of load were airlifted on 11 Dec 71 involving 99 sorties. More sorties could have been carried out but the Army could not cope up with the swiftness with which the SHBO was carried out.

12 Dec 1971 - 35 sorties were carried out at Narsingdi, airlifting 234 troops and 18,520 kg of load. Due to heavy ground fire, there were 30 casualties and one helicopter was sent to Sylhet for evacuation of these casualties. One helicopter met with an accident due to fire in air.

13 Dec 1971 - 282 troops and 14,850 kg of load were airlifted in 30 sorties on 13 Dec 1971. On 14th, 12 helicopters were positioned at Daudkandi early morning where they were employed to move a battalion of troops across the River Meghna to Baidya Bazar, barely seven miles from Narayanganj on the outskirts of Dacca. By evening 810 troops and 22,650 kg of load were airlifted in 79 sorties. From the time that the SHBO operations into Narsinghdi began on

10 Dec evening, till the landing of a battalion at Baidya Bazar, the pilots had already flown for 36 hours continuously, doing 409 sorties.

15 Dec 1971 - SHBO missions continued and 1,209 troops and 38,100 kg of load were airlifted to Baidya Bazar. One aircraft met with an accident but the morale of the Unit continued to be high. The next day, most helicopters were taken up for maintenance and inspection. One helicopter which was sent to Sylhet for casualty evacuation, airlifted 16 casualties while two other helicopters were utilised for Army communication sorties during the day. In the evening five helicopters took part in the Dacca Surrender Ceremony.

MI 4 Helicopters Disgorging Troops in Sylhet (East Pakistan) during 1971 ops

No. 110 HU Keeping the Jointmanship Alive during the 1971 ops East of Dhaka

Courtesy No. 110 HU War Record Room

SHBO and Casualty Evacuation Missions Flown by No. 110 HU in December 1971

As is evident, No. 110 Helicopter Unit was an integral part of the 1971 operations East of Dacca. Mi-4 helicopters undertook extensive helibridging operations in the riverine dominated terrain of East Pakistan where all the major bridges had been blown up by the enemy. These operations were led ably by the Commanding Officer (CO) of No. 110 HU, Sqn Ldr CS Sandhu. He was later awarded the Vir Chakra for leading these pioneer SHBO missions in the war. The enormity of the task undertaken can be judged from the fact that almost 500 sorties were flown in the direct face of enemy fire during these operations.

Table 2: SHBO and Casualty Evacuation Missions Flown by No. 110 HU

Sl No	Mission	Sorties	No of Troops	Total Load (kg)
1.	SHBO Sylhet	66	1,117	22,600
2.	SHBO Raipura	57	650	10,400
3.	SHBO Narsingdi	164	1,350	91,950
4.	SHBO Baidya Bazaar	200	2,019	60,750
5.	Cas Evac	-	269	-
6.	Total	487	5,136	1,85,700 (185.7 T)

Source: Extracted from No. 110 HU War Record.

Conclusion

Adapting in the 'Fog of War'

Adaptability in battle has two faces: the ability to sense a change in the situation, demanding a change in response; and the ability to commit to that requirement. What does complexity leadership entail in terms of fast-changing or asymmetric warfare? The Australian Army replaced the famous OODA (Orient, Observe, Decide and Act) loop with an Act, Sense, Decide and Adapt (ASDA) loop that deals better with non-linear, complex and unpredictable states. In the ASDA cycle, action is first because in uncertainty one needs to prod to elicit a requisite response for assessments to be made. Decisions are made based on these assessments, followed by deeper reflection and adaptation. However, the situation prevailing for decisions to be taken will dictate what to apply, that is, OODA, ASDA or something else.[10]

The 1971 War is illustrative. "Dacca was never an objective even in the final operational instruction by Army HQ to Eastern Command."[11] However, the famous probes by Mi-4s ordered by Gen Sagat Singh of Indian IV Corps, caused chaos and a fateful decision by Pakistani Gen Niazi to defend Sylhet by two brigades rather than defending the river Meghna crossings towards Dacca. It allowed IV Corps to reach the doorsteps of Dacca almost eight days earlier than thought to be possible. Deeper reflection allowed the Indian Army to quickly go for the jugular and reach the doorsteps of Dacca. This example of mental flexibility and agility is not unique; it is ever-present in battlefields with the victors.

Helicopters in general and Mi-4s in particular stood out as game-changers in the 1971 War. More importantly, it was open minds and the pervasive spirit of jointmanship that really achieved much more than just the additive totals of capabilities of the Services. Achieving air superiority over the entire East Pakistan enabled the Indian Army and IAF to do the unthinkable – help to liberate Bangladesh.

Notes

1. Ian Cardozo, "The Battle for Sylhet", *Scholar Warrior*, Spring 2020, pp. 98-105.
2. Rajesh Isser, "Asymmetric Competition Ahead for Indian Air Power," *Journal of Defence Studies*, Vol. 15, No. 1 (January–March 2021), pp. 1-24.
3. Rajesh Isser, *The Purple Legacy: IAF Helicopters in Service of the Nation* (New Delhi: Pentagon Press, 2012), pp. 63-64.
4. P.C. Lal, *My Years with the IAF* (New Delhi: Lancer Publishers, 1986), pp. 207-216.
5. Isser, n. 3, pp. 81-83.
6. No. 110 HU War Diary, extracted by the author, December 2012.
7. Debrief of Flt Lt P Vaid in War Diary, No. 110 HU extracted by the author, December 2012.
8. Personal account of Air Cmde CM Singhla, Files Air HQ, October 2012.
9. No. 110 HU War Diary, extracted by the author, December 2012.
10. Rajesh Isser, "Is Indian Airpower Preparing for Tomorrow's War?", *VIF Brief*, August 2019, p. 14, https://www.vifindia.org/sites/default/files/is-indian-airpower-preparing-for-tomorrow-s-war.pdf. Accessed on November 1, 2020.
11. Lal, n. 4, pp. 207-216.

9. Forward Air Controllers: Significant Operational Role

HK Bajaj

The Crucial 'Third Eye'!

Yes, those were the days, when a well-trained Forward Air Controller (FAC) could prove to be the crucial 'third eye' for the strike pilots and play a very significant role in any major ground battle by bringing to bear maximum weapon load from the third dimension (air) on to the enemy and thus be a major pawn in blunting even a most audacious enemy thrust/resolute resistance! The FAC's role started once the Close Air Support (CAS) mission (strike formation) reported over a preselected Contact Point (CP), approximately 20-25 km away from the target area. In a short span of time, the pilots were briefed on the type and number (concentration) of targets in the area, their type and amount of camouflage and likely appearance from the air. They were also briefed on the lead-in features to look for during the pull up, to quickly spot, select, align, aim, fire at the correct range and ensure destruction of the target in the first attack itself! The formation was then asked to fly at 900 kmph/420 ktph, on a specific course and time towards the target area. For the dive attack, the strike would pull up at the calculated time; and once in visual contact, the FAC, with the help of various prominent ground features, would visually direct and help each pilot to pick up the target at the earliest and execute a successful attack! Along with the pilots, the FAC was also required to look out for any enemy aircraft in the vicinity and warn them if there was any threat to any member of the formation; otherwise, give a 'tail clear' call. At the end of the attack, depending on the air situation, each strike formation would transmit the 'Flash Report'! Thus, the FAC was the last essential Air Force link with our forwardmost formations to demand and ensure successful delivery of additional armament on to the enemy and contribute towards success of the ground battle!

'The Life-Lines Don't Change!': The Leadership Counts!

In 1971, when the war clouds were building up, ours was the fortunate Pilots' Course (106th PC), with not even six months of service, which was available for this critical role; and some of us were further lucky to be positioned along with our frontline troops, participate in the ground battle and play this very vital role!! We were extensively trained in the FAC's role by then Wg Cdr MS (Minhi) Bawa [later Air Marshal and Commander-in-Chief (C-in-C)] at Operational Training Unit (OTU) Jamnagar. The excitement peaked in September 1971 when our course was attached to Air Headquarters (Air HQ) for two months. The next day, a few of us were issued a revolver and 24 live rounds each and flown to Udampur, 4 Tactical Air Centre Air Force (TAC AF), commanded by then Gp Capt (later Air Mshl, C-in-C) KIS Chhabra. After two weeks of extensive ground training and air exercises, we were attached to different brigades/formations of 15 Corps. On September 25, along with a GU 734 Radio/Telephony (R/T) set and a 'Satpal Light' (an aid to assist pilots to spot ground targets), I landed up in a bunker with 5 Sikh/191 Infantry Brigade at Chhamb. I was subsequently attached to 68 (I) Infantry Brigade, the corps reserve, meant for the offensive and located at Akhnur.

On December 3, 1971, when the balloon finally went up, a few of us (FACs) were at Udampur; and in an air exercise, we had checked all our equipment, radio sets, the frequencies, Contact Points (CPs), etc. In the evening, we were asked to report back to our operational units immediately. I, along with my FAC team of two R/T operators, one Naik Non-Commissioned Officer (NCO) i/c Air Support Signal Unit (ASSU) network/detachment) and a driver, reached 'our' Brigade Headquarters by late night (Fig. 1).[1]

Fig 1: Jammu-Akhnur-Palanwala-Chhamb Sector

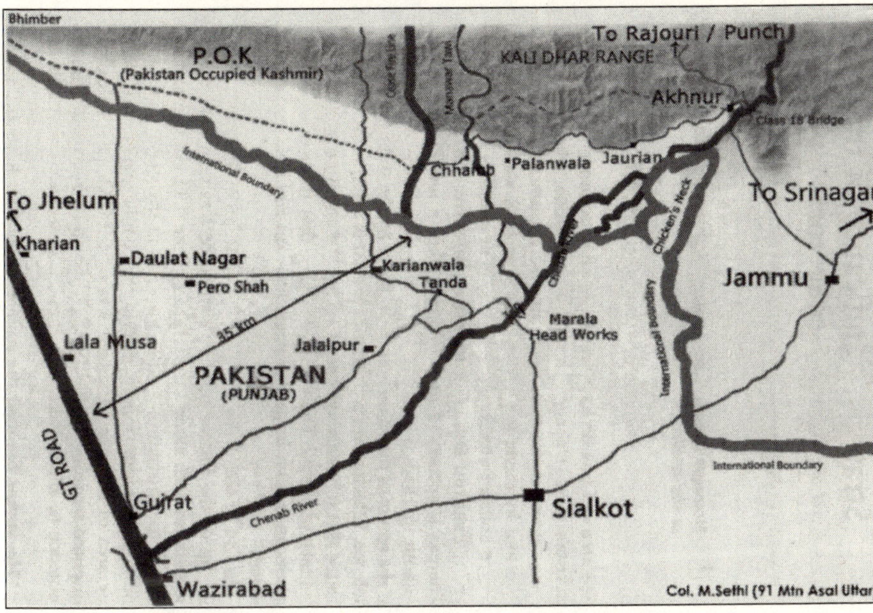

Source: Prasun K Sengupta 2017, n. 1. Figure modified by the author.

The Pakistan Army had launched a major offensive in the Chhamb salient with four infantry brigades, three armoured and eight artillery regiments. The attack in the 191 Bridge defended sector came through the intentional gaps left in defensive minefields through which the 68 (I) Infantry Brigade group was to have launched their offensive.[2] Yes, in Chhamb area, Pakistan had achieved surprise at both tactical and strategic levels. All forward posts along the Cease Fire Line (CFL) were subjected to intense artillery fire and a few of our Border Observation Posts (BOPs) were overrun. Looking at the build-up, December 3 night itself, 7 Kumaon was ordered to move up and occupy positions at Kachrial heights. However, they were surprised by the infiltrators who had already dug in there. They suffered major casualties, with their Commanding Officer (CO) and three other officers being wounded; and also, three tanks (T-55) of 72 Armoured Regiment (under Command 68 Infantry Brigade) were damaged.

On December 4, morning, our four Hunters, on a strike mission overflew Akhnur bridge at tree-top height. Although the Air Force markings were clearly visible, not only did our L-60 guns open up but also the small arms started firing; and a revolver round fell right in front of Brig Tom Morlin, commander, 68 Infantry Brigade, having breakfast under a tree! Later, the commander, along with his G3, Capt Chatterjee and self (on insistence and request) with my tentacle vehicle moved to 10 Infantry Division Advance HQ at Palanwala for further orders and reinforcement (Fig. 2).

Fig 2: Chhamb-Jurian-Akhnur Sector

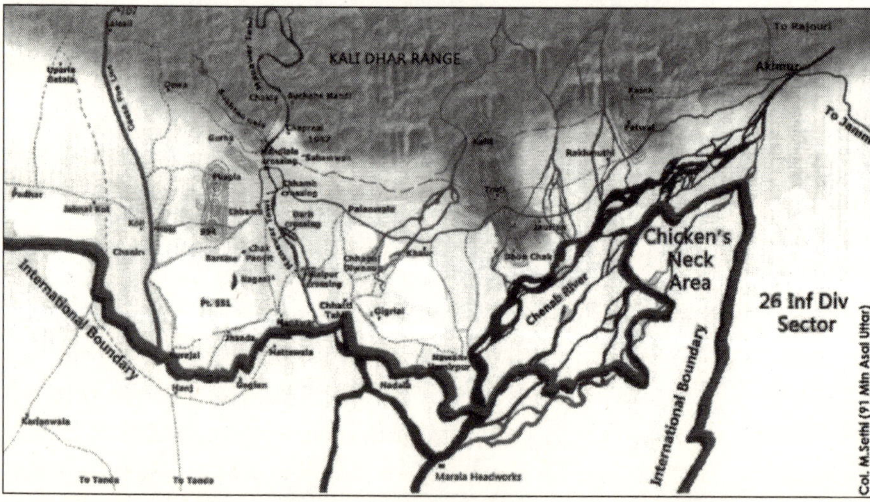

Source: Prasun K Sengupta 2017, n. 1. Figure modified by the author.

At the Divisional HQ, the commander took a reinforcement of one squadron of armour (T 55) and a company of 9 Jat. As we moved forward towards the second line of defence on the eastern bank of the Manawar Tawi, it was a pleasure to interact with Maj Guleria, Coy Cdr, 9 Jat who was bubbling with enthusiasm and the killer spirit. I, for the first time, saw a very seriously wounded battle casualty being taken on an open jeep; the reality of war was slowly sinking in!

About two km short of the eastern bank of the Manawar Tawi, we had an admin halt along with a troop of (three) tanks. The brigade commander then decided to take a tank and visit 7 Kumaon and also look up the armoured regiment at Manawar Tawi. The general area being that close to our likely area of deployment and with positive support of the troop commander (a major), I managed to argue my case and was permitted to follow them in another tank. Half way through our move, the commander summoned me to his tank. I jumped over and sat on the turret while the commander and troop commander stood in the two copulas. Soon, our tank was stopped by a Lieutenant who informed that there were infiltrators just 50 m on our left and were firing with automatic weapons. As soon as the officer and his team of ten men started firing at the hut in a cluster of trees, the bursts of fire started coming from the other side! As the bullets started whizzing past, the two copulas closed; and I found myself prominently sitting alone on top of the tank in my blue flying overall with a bright, orange toweled-collar and, of course, with NO WEAPON (I had deposited my revolver with our brigade armoury! Yes; it was a case of NO HOLSTER! I had not brought my webbing from Jamnagar; and from the brigade, I could not get a spare holster!)! The quick reaction was to jump down and run along the tank taking shelter from its hull. Then, the tank stopped, the turret moved and a tank shell was fired. The hut went up and came down; and then all was quiet!

The young, inquisitive pilot officer also followed the commander to see what was inside the hut! As I was moving through the shrubs, I noticed two bodies (dressed in turbans – yes, they were the infiltrators in disguise) lying in the approach path. I was about to cross over them, when I was stopped by a jawan following me! Yes, that was the second reality of war that I had seen on my first day of induction! In the meanwhile, the commander walked out with a walking stick in his hand and gestured, "*How do you like this as a souvenir of war?*" In the situation, my only response was, "*As long as we last the war, Sir!" In the cache, we found, two LMG, 6-7 semi-automatic rifles and a Chinese communication set!* The commander told me to pick any weapon for my self-defence which I politely declined!

- It now occurs to me that had we (Commander and myself) preferred to travel in our own light vehicles on this route, we would all have been easy targets for the infiltrators; and 'our war' might have been over then and there; or at least, very different from then on!

- Second, as would emerge later, in this story, had this enemy position (ambush) not been neutralised (with a tank shell) then, these infiltrators could have caused extensive damage to the subsequent build-up of our forces on this axis!

Once at the base of the hill (Kachrial heights), still approximately 7-8 km from the CFL and less than a km from eastern bank of the Tawi, we parked along with another 10-12 tanks which were already positioned under a large cluster of trees. It was these tanks which had been attacked by the infiltrators on December 3 night. The commander found that though no tank had been destroyed, the three tanks had been externally damaged by the infiltrators.

These tanks presented an ideal target for an air strike! The brigade commander called me to his tank and ordered a quick dispersion of all the tanks. However, the process had yet not started, when we heard Sabres (F-86) overhead and saw the first aircraft already in a dive attack on us! In a quick move from the top of the tank, the brigade commander went into a nearby, already overflowing trench; and I lay down in the open. The first aircraft released its bombs and it appeared as if they were only coming for us! The bombs overshot our position by just about 10 m and exploded. I was literally lifted off the ground. As the dust settled, I realised that it was the same dust that one looks for while firing and makes necessary corrections in the next pass! I looked around and found all our tank crew were engaging the aircraft with their ack-ack guns. There was a total of five aircraft and they were rolling in from different directions!

Realising that the targets for all five Sabres were just the tanks, I ran 50 odd yards away from this area and lay in the open. Subsequently, they strafed us with their six 20 mm guns (each). I along with another Army officer, who also did not find any shelter, kept a count of all five aircraft and lay clear of their strafing path every time! Yes, they had a free hand and attacked us for 20 minutes! Fortunately, there was no damage to any of our tanks or personnel! Just the outside slung beddings of two tanks caught fire, which was soon brought under control. I went back to my own tank for the return. But to my surprise, that tank moved to another position and stopped. I ran to board the brigade commander's tank which had already left. I then realised that I had lost my watch during the 'circus'; which I found on December 18, lying at the same place!

Yes, it was a 'jolting, lifetime experience' not only for the commander but even for the young 'Air Force lad' (each one of us) to be in the 'gun sights' of five fighter aircraft and yet get away! By sunset of December 4, then, Plt Offr HK Bajaj had got his first taste of the war; and was well inducted!! From then on, though it was just the beginning and there were many more surprises and close shaves yet to unfold, my belief in the 'Destined Life-Lines' had been further reinforced!

Progress of the Battle

We reached our pre-selected site and before last light, we were well established with our brigade operators room and a few bunkers which were to be our home for the next one month or so. Our location was approximately a kilometre short of Manawar Tawi and 1½ km southeast of Chhamb bridge. We (the FAC team) established our ground communications (ASSU network) with our one-ton vehicle; while, the GU 734 (ground-to-air commander set) and the 'Satpal Light' were kept in the FAC's jeep. I had NO GLO. However, I was in regular contact with our operations room, G3 and the brigade commander and thus received periodic updates and the requirement for Close Air Support (CAS). The officers' Field Mess was set up in a six feet-wide *nallah* covered with high *sarkanda* growth; and the Chinese radio set (captured from the infiltrators) provided the much needed entertainment and kept the morale high!

GOC 10 Infantry Division (Maj Gen Jaswant Singh) had four infantry brigades under his command. He deployed 28 Brigade in the hill sector, north and northeast of Chhamb from Sunderbani to Laleali down to Dewa; while 191 Brigade held firm base south of 28 Brigade in the plains West of Manawar Tawi, 68 (I) Infantry Brigade (meant for the offensive) with its three battalions, i.e. 5/8 Gorkha Rifles (GR),

7 Kumaon, 9 Jat occupied the northern half of the East bank of the Tawi; while, 52 Brigade (the fourth) was deployed on the southern half of the East bank (Fig. 3). 10 Infantry Division also had under its command 9 (Deccan) Horse (T54), 72 Armoured Regiment (T-55), 2 independent armoured squadrons ex-Central India Horse (AMX-13), two engineer battalions, six regiments of artillery (two medium, three field, one light), a company of 9 Para Commandos, a company of 12 Guards equipped with Anti-Tank Guided Missiles (ATGMs) and two Border Security Force (BSF) battalions manning the border.[3]

Fig 3: Deployment of 10 Infantry Division, December 3, 1971

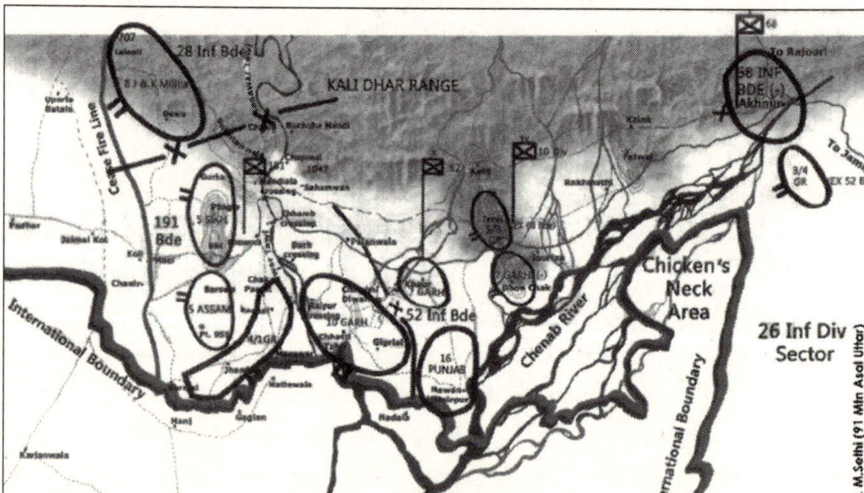

Source: Prasun K Sengupta 2017, n. 1. Figure modified by the author.

Commander 191 Brigade (Brig Jasbir Singh), out of the brigade's four infantry battalions (5 Sikh, 5 Assam, 4/1 GR and 10 Garhwal Rifles) had deployed three battalions which covered the CFL from the Manawar village-Jhanda area in the south to Mandiala in the north.

However, in the Barsala-Jhanda area, southwest of Chhamb, through which 68 (I) Infantry Brigade group was to have launched their offensive, a dummy minefield was left. 10 Garhwal Rifles, the fourth battalion of the brigade held positions East of Manawar Tawi[4] (Fig. 4).

Fig 4: Deployment of 191 Infantry Brigade, December 3, 1971

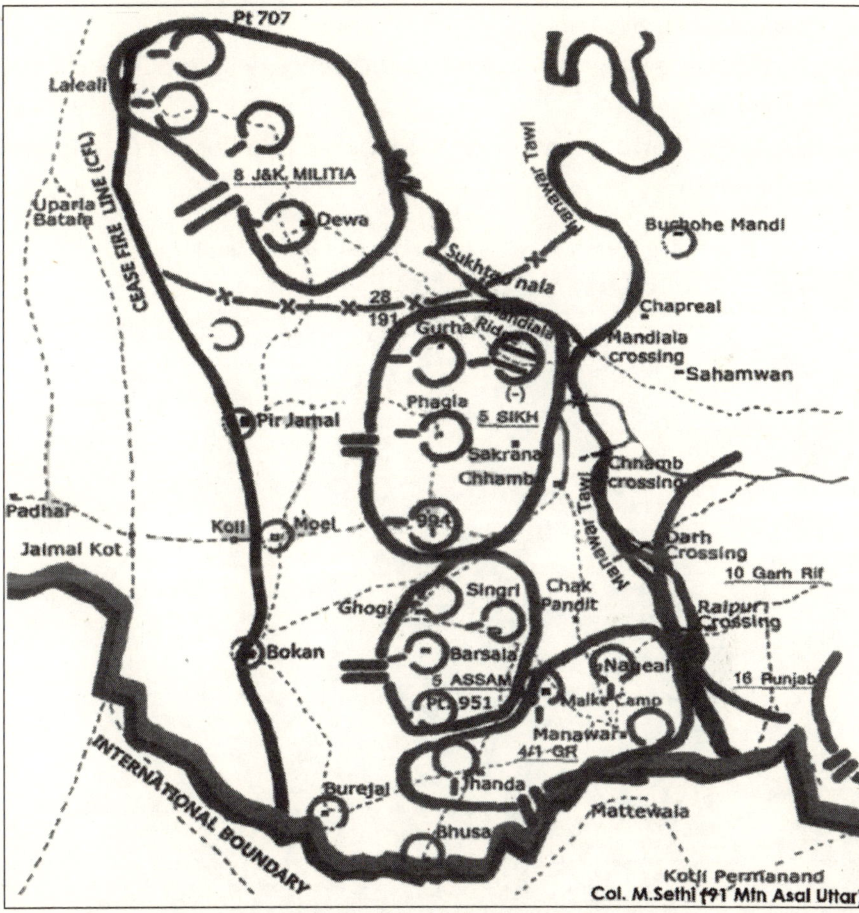

Source: Prasun K Sengupta 2017, n. 1. Figure modified by the author.

The Pakistani forces had a fair estimate of the Indian deployment in the Chhamb salient. Thus, with the aim to develop a major thrust in the north towards Mandiala where the opposition was negligible; and to secure a bridgehead near Mandiala crossing over the river as part of the first phase of their operation, the enemy grouped its resources and broadly employed them thus:

- One brigade group in the north to secure Mandiala crossing and establish a bridgehead up to the Kachrial heights.

- The second brigade group was employed to capture Chhamb and Mandiala heights.
- The third brigade group to contain the troops deployed from Barsala to Jhanda.
- While, the fourth Infantry Brigade attacked from Jhanda to Manawar in the south.[5]

Fig 5: Grouping of Enemy Resources and Broad Employment

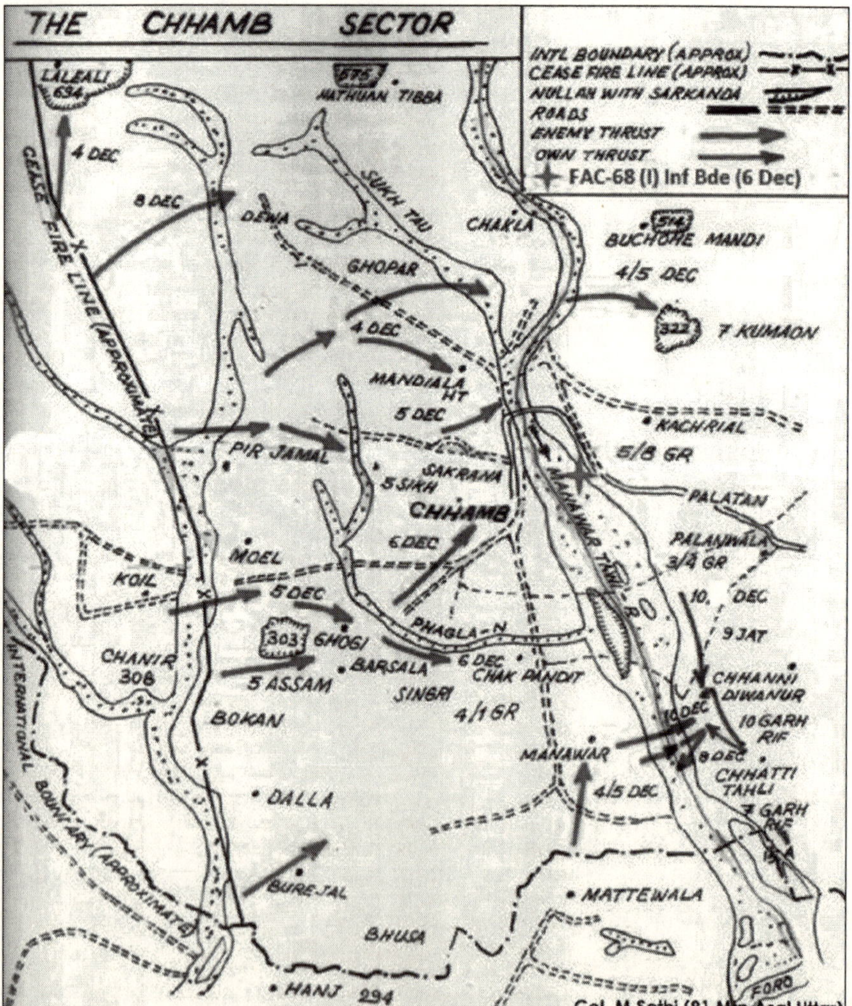

Source: Prasun K Sengupta 2017, n. 1. Figure modified by the author.

In spite of being heavily outnumbered and amid intense artillery fire on December 3 night, to start with, a few of the Forward Defended Localities (FDLs) in the 191 Infantry Brigade Sector had stood their ground stoutly. On December 4 morning, 9 (Deccan) Horse (T-54 tanks) and the recoilless (RCL) guns of 5 Sikh blunted a major armour thrust of the enemy towards the Mandiala crossing; and by mid-day, they had claimed 12 enemy tanks (M-36 Sherman/T-59) and two jeep mounted RCL guns in two different attacks. But the enemy pressed home the attack and by the afternoon, had captured Mandiala North.[6]

On December 4/5 night, a few infiltrators also attacked one of our (216) medium artillery batteries East of the Tawi and managed to destroy one gun and damage another three. In the ensuing encounter, 5-6 Pakistani soldiers were killed. Through the night, the infiltrators in their khaki uniform, mistaken for Defence Security Corps (DSC) personnel, in a surprise move, also managed to capture Chhamb bridge. Our troops realised it only once they had held a few vehicles and shot their occupants in the middle of the bridge. On December 5, early morning, our Gorkha troops of 5/8 GR gave the first morale booster by bringing 'three Paki heads' in revenge; cleared the bridge of enemy occupation and, thus, thwarted their attempt to establish a bridgehead.

Though 28 Brigade, north of the Chhamb bridge, along with elements of Deccan Horse, did launch a counter-attack, they did not succeed in dislodging the enemy from Mandiala North (just West of the bridge). During the afternoon, the enemy increased its pressure from the south and southwest of Chhamb; and after repeated attacks, by evening, Mandiala South had also fallen. Thus, on December 5 night, with the Pakistani thrust closing on to the crossing and endangering our troops West of the Tawi, it was decided to withdraw from Chhamb and stabilise defences along the eastern bank of the river.[7] The withdrawal of 191 Brigade was complete by midnight and Chhamb bridge was blown off by the last combat elements of the brigade (12 Field Artillery Regiment).[8] Thus, from midnight of December 5/6, 68 (I) Infantry Brigade, deployed East of the Manawar Tawi, came in contact with the enemy. However, the enemy artillery continued to shell the area West of the Tawi throughout the night.

On December 5/6 night, I met the then Flt Lt VG Kumar (FAC, 191 Brigade) at the caravan of Brig Jasbir Singh, Cdr 191 Brigade. RIP VG Sir. Though they all looked fatigued, it was a battle gallantly fought against a very heavily armed enemy. 5 Sikh and all other elements of the 191 Infantry Brigade Group took the brunt, fought valiantly but suffered heavy casualties. RIP Brave hearts. On December 12/13, they were conferred with many gallantry awards.

Limited Enemy Air Action, East of Manawar Tawi

On December 4 and 5, though one could hear our own formations in the air (on counter-air/air interdiction or on CAS missions West of Chhamb), apart from the four- aircraft strike (Hunters) that overflew us on December 4 morning, I did not see any of our aircraft over the area. On other hand, on the first day, at least four air strikes of 2/4/5 Pakistan Air Force (PAF) aircraft each were reported; while, on December 5 and 6, three enemy formations each struck our tanks, gun positions (216 and 39 medium), Division HQ and the troop concentrations at Palanwala with very little/no effect. However, from December 7 onwards, I did not see any PAF strike aircraft over our area nor was any enemy air action reported[9] (Appendix-A). On December 5 evening, when the commander 4 TAC called up to check enemy air activity over our area as also my safety, I did crib my heart out! However, he assured me that I would get a fair share of close air support, which we finally got.

Close Air Support by IAF on December 4 and 5

It's now well known and documented that the 'Falcons' (No. 101 Squadron) flew extensively in support of our land forces in the Chhamb sector during this war! Further, as it would also emerge and is a reasonable estimate, they carried out at least five CAS missions each under the control of Flt Lt VG Kumar (FAC, 191 Brigade) on the first two days. They (S-22s) attacked advancing armour, gun positions, convoys and troop concentrations with 64 × 57 mm rockets (R/Ps),

4 × 500 kg bombs and 30 mm guns; and caused extensive destruction. On December 4 morning, then Flt Lt J Bhattacharya and Flt Lt Gurdeep Singh, went in for a strike with 4 × 16 × 57 mm rockets each against a large concentration of tanks just south of Chhamb village. They planned to carry out four attacks each with 16 R/Ps to be fired per pass. However, in the first attack itself, as Flt Lt Gurdeep Singh fired his rockets, his aircraft was hit by enemy ground fire; his engine flamed out and with no successful relight, he survived a very low level ejection over the battlefield! He landed very close to his crashed (burning) aircraft near Burejal village (an Indian post, near the CFL), approximately 10 km south of Chhamb. It was Capt Appayya from Engineers (Indian Army) who first rescued the badly injured pilot from a highly active battle area.[10] A photo copy of a 'One Inch map' of Chhamb sector, as recovered by then Adjutant, 28 Pak Armoured Division, from an abandoned jeep, is attached (Appendix-B).[11] Even with the fate of their comrade unknown, the undaunted Falcons pressed home another four CAS mission on December 4, and five missions on December 5, all along the 191 Brigade Sector, with significant results!

Manawar Tawi: The Fresh Battle Line

Our 5/8 GR, commanded by then Lt Col (later, Lt Gen and Army commander) AS Kalkat, was deployed astride the Chhamb bridge along the eastern bank (*bandh*) of the Manawar Tawi. They were well dug in, in the trenches. Their positions along the *bandh* provided good natural cover against direct enemy fire as also unrestricted visibility across the river. The water level in the river was low and after our withdrawal from Chhamb, the distance between the opposing forces was just about 60-70 m. I picked up a position (approximately 700 m from the destroyed Chhamb bridge) next to one of the section commanders (a captain) of 5/8 GR. Right next to us, we had a troop of 12 Guards (2/Lt Prashant Kumar Gupta) manning an ATGM launcher with manual control (joystick). Further south, there was a troop of tanks of the 72 Armoured Regiment deployed. Just ahead of our position was an artillery Observation Post (OP). So at any one time, we had three observers looking through their binoculars and keeping an eye on even the slightest movement on the other side of the river. From this location, I had a comfortable R/T range with the strike aircraft up to most of my likely Contact Points (CPs). However, just to enhance the signal strength and distance, even against the objections of the section commander, I tried to install the thin tall aerial on my GU set with some camouflage of grass, etc. But sure, there was an immediate reaction with a good burst of small arms fire! Thereafter, I was fairly comfortable with the integral, three feet tall GU set aerial; and my reception strength automatically increased and appeared strength five! As on December 5/6 night, 7 Kumaon was deployed from Mandiala crossing to Buchohe Mandi, while 9 Jat secured the eastern banks of the Dhar and Raipur crossings.

December 6, my first morning, within visual contact of the enemy, was an eventful start to the day. The first target that appeared across the Tawi was a tank which rolled out of the thick cluster of trees just opposite our location. It was spotted by the ATGM operator (a naik); and it was heartening to see a well controlled missile (entac missile) launch and a direct hit! Our tank crew also took a pot shot on the same tank and ensured that it remained there as a permanent feature for the rest of the duration of the war; and sure, it also became a good reference point for me to guide the strike aircraft. Subsequently, as the sun rose, the tank commander observed two men (with some reflecting material, may be a map, in their hands) against the skyline on top of the Mandiala high ground. One tank round got both of them on the ground. Then, another four men appeared to take the injured away. Another round was loaded and fired. All four went up; and thereafter, no one came! Yes, that was the line of sight!

The Aerial Punch

As per the records available from my pocket diary, on December 6 and 7, 68 (I) Infantry Brigade was allotted three missions (Mission Nos 541, 544, 549). Mission No. 541 did not come on December 6; while on December 7, Mission Nos 544 and 549 attacked tanks concentrations, under the big cluster of trees opposite our site, one kilometre southwest of Chhamb bridge; and the tanks in hull down position across the Dhar and Raipur crossings (i.e. first and second crossings, approximately 2 and 4 km south of the destroyed Chhamb bridge, respectively). Further, as per my records, in addition to the strike missions directly allotted to 28 and 52 Brigades and 72 Armoured Regiment, another five missions (475 to 479) would have also struck enemy positions under the control of the FACs of these formations.

For the initial strikes, Satpal Light and that 'Destroyed Tank' parked close to the river bed proved to be good reference points for directing the strike pilots. Satpal Light was quite effective. The dug-in troops concentrations along the river bed were also attacked by the strike aircraft. Though, actual damage/casualties caused to dug-in troops were difficult to assess, it was a great morale booster for our own troops; and they would invariably come out and dance on the road below the *bandh*! Mostly, Sukhois from No. 101, Tactics and Air Combat Development Establishment (TACDE) and No. 26 Squadrons and Hunters from Nos 20 and 27 Squadrons carried out CAS missions in this sector. I felt very proud when I first heard my own flying instructor's name, then, Flt Lt (later Air Mshl and C-in-C) Michael (Mike) McMahon, on R/T. I used to record a brief target description, strike details, including names of the pilots, wherever I could pick up and the Flash Reports (if provided by the strike formation in the enforced limited R/T environment) in my pocket diary! *My call sign was 'Linda Control'.*

On December 8 and 9, three and four CAS missions of S-22s/ Hunters, respectively, successfully struck enemy positions opposite our brigade sector. The targets for all these missions were across the Dhar and Raipur level crossings; south, southeast and East of Chhamb village in the prominent cluster of trees; and also against troops concentration at Mandiala heights. Su-7s and Hunters attacked with bombs, rocket and 30 mm guns. A number of tanks, guns and vehicles were claimed; and enemy 'dug-in positions' along the West bank of the Tawi were pounded extensively. All mission leaders also reported (in their 'Flash/Ground Reports') very high intensity and volume of ground fire from enemy

Air Defence (AD) guns.[12] On December 8/9 night, the Pakistanis also tried to cross the Manawar Tawi at Raipur crossing but their attack was beaten back by 10 Garhwal Rifles (the holding battalion). In this attack, as we came to know later, the Pakistanis suffered very heavy casualties and we also got a few Prisoners of War (POW).[13]

Canberras and AN-12s Play Significant Role!

On three nights, from December 6/7 to 11, we also heard a Canberra (twice) and An-12 aircraft (once) overflying our location at tree-top heights, in a westerly direction, for targets West of the Manawar Tawi. The mission/target details of these aircraft were not known to us. In each mission, a Canberra aircraft could carry 8,000 lb of bomb load while the An-12 could drop 38 × 500 lb bombs against Army designated enemy-troops/tanks concentrations/gun areas. As is now known, the strike aircraft were directed to the targets either by the lighted arrows displayed on the ground by our forward troops or by the 'pathfinder fighter aircraft missions' which light the target areas with napalm and rockets; and the actual strike aircraft (Canberra/An-12) followed a few minutes later.[14]

In this sector, the enemy's offensive was well supported by intense artillery fire which continued till last the day of the war. On those pitch dark nights, the howling sound of a jackal was mostly followed by artillery shelling; and largely, it did not appear to be a coincidence! We also caught one Pakistani infiltrator from the top of a banyan tree. As a routine, I was at my operational site (trench) with 5/8 Gorkhas well before sunrise and returned to the Brigade HQ close to sunset. In the evening, I would have a detailed debrief, 'sitrep' (situation report) and briefing with the brigade commander, G3 and the operations room, identify likely targets and originate 'pre-planned demands' for the next day.

December 10: Pakistanis Get a Bloody Nose from Indian Army and Air Force!

December 10 was another hectic and 'close shave' day! From the early hours, the artillery fire was just non-stop. In the morning, I had two pre-planned missions. The first formation attacked enemy gun positions south of Chhamb; while, the second was a search and strike mission of two Hunters led by then Sqn Ldr (later, Air Mshl and C-in-C) RN (Mummy) Bhardwaj (No. 1) and then, Fg Offr BC (Lofty) Karambaya as his No. 2. The targets for them were troops and tanks concentrations in Chhamb village. As the formation set up an orbit over the area and was looking for the targets, I reported, 'two bogeys (2 Sabres), right one o'clock' to the formation. However, the No. 2 had already picked up the enemy aircraft. In the ensuing air battle, the No. 2 called out, "I am hit"; and a little later, Mummy Sir said, "I got one"! I remember last seeing No. 2 flying very low over the hills, streaming fuel (white smoke) and both aircraft pulled away to the East, just north of Kachrial heights. The formation returned to base safely. The news of the shooting down of one Sabre had the troops dancing with joy once again. The mission report, including details of the air battle, as submitted by then Fg Offr BC Karambaya, is now well recorded in Air Force history.[15] The PAF pilot killed in this aerial battle was Sqn Ldr Aslam Chaudhry.[16]

Subsequently, we came to know that the Pakistanis had launched a major offensive, with one infantry brigade supported by a regiment of armour, across the Dhar and Raipur crossings (Fig. 6). I had 'Immediate Demands' raised for the CAS. In this operation, 52 Infantry Brigade, 72 Armoured Regiment and Deccan Horse were also directly involved. I had a total of five CAS missions over the day against tanks, guns, vehicles and troops concentrations in this area; while, in addition to the air effort directly allotted to the above two formations, as per my records, another two missions of four S-22 aircraft each and one mission of two Hunters were also controlled by the FAC of 52 Brigade/72 Armoured Regiment (Plt Offr Y (Yuri) Suri, a course-mate); and struck enemy forces in this crucial land battle. With a well defined Forward Line of Own Troops (FLOT) along the Tawi, two prominent 'funnel' points, good reference of Dhar and Raipur crossings and a large concentration of enemy tanks and troops in the area (West of the Tawi) presented good targets for strike aircraft the whole day; and the Indian Air Force with Sukhois from the

Falcon (101) Squadron and Hunters from the Lightning (20) Squadron, loaded with 500 kg/1,000 pounder bombs, 64 × 57 mm rockets/68 mm SNEB rocket pods with 19 rockets in each pod and 30 mm guns[17] caused massive destruction and, thus, played a decisive role in not only blunting the thrust but also forced the enemy to retreat from East of Manawar Tawi.

Fig 6: 111 Infantry Brigade Attack and Indian Counter Attacks, December 10, 1971

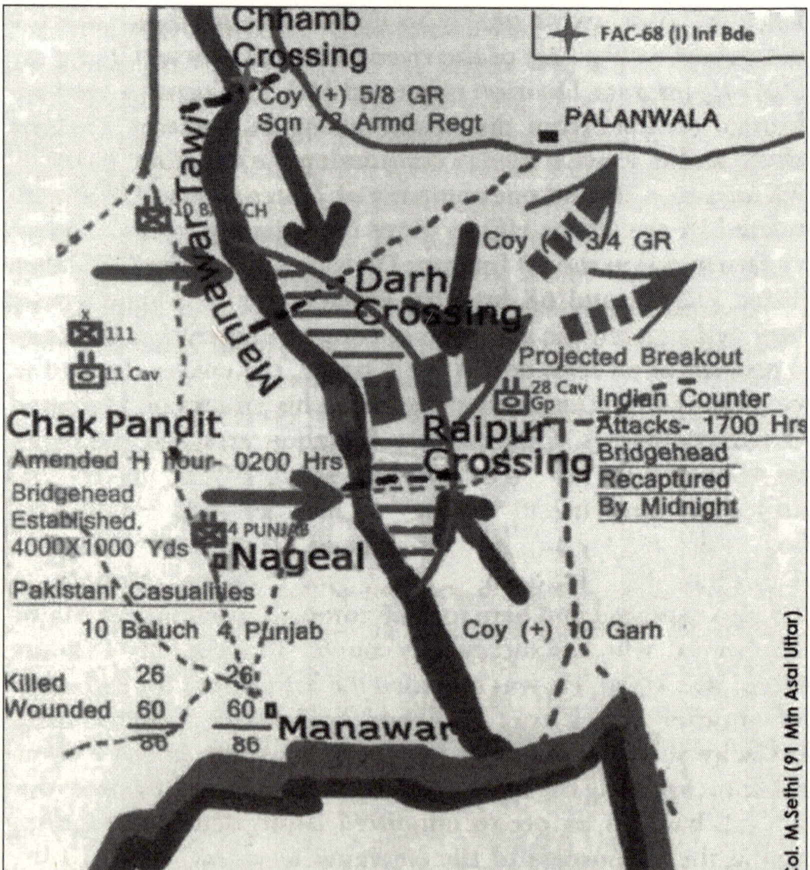

Source: Prasun K Sengupta 2017, n. 1. Figure modified by the author.

Note: Casualty figures taken from the book *Battle of Chhamb* (1971) by Lt. Col. Ahmad Saeed.

The defending 9 Jats troops were completely surprised with attacks developing in the night and through tall *sarkanda* grass across the river. It was later revealed that they did not have any surveillance element across the Tawi. 9 Jats fought valiantly at both the crossings and repulsed the initial offensives but were overrun in the subsequent attacks. *Maj Guleria, company commander (whom I had met on December 4) and his company subedar, at Dhar crossing, were captured, inhumanly tortured and brutally killed. RIP Brave hearts. The enemy managed to ingress and establish a bridgehead of approximately 3,000 × 900 m but their tanks got bogged down in marshy land opposite the crossing.* With timely reinforcement and a counter-attack with tanks and infantry, the enemy's advance was stalled and the bridgehead contained. However, in this counter-attack, some of our tanks (72 Armoured Regiment/Deccan Horse) also got bogged down.[18] *At both the Dhar and Raipur crossings, the quickly reinforced troops and the repeated air strikes by the IAF on the western bank, caused heavy casualties and destruction on the Pakistanis' subsequent build-up and stopped their momentum. Thus, before the last light, Pakistani troops were completely shaken, disorganised and were forced to pull back from East of Manawar Tawi.*[19] *Though, it was claimed to be a 'misreporting' by Maj Nazar Hussain, brigade major (BM) of the Pakistani 111 Brigade; but if he was to be believed, "by mid-afternoon, the attacking 28 Cavalry was down to FOUR tanks; and at 1400 hours, the new GOC 23 Pakistani Division ordered withdrawal of 111 Brigade from East of Manawar Tawi".*[20] However unknown to the Indian Army (GOC 10 Division), finally a two-pronged counter-attack by 5/8 GR, 7 Kumaon, 3/4 GR and 10 Garhwal Rifles supported by armour was launched from north and south, along the eastern bank of the Tawi. It was only by midnight that the Pakistani forces were completely pushed back to West of the Tawi. In this attack, they suffered very heavy casualties. In fact, the next morning, the whole area (east of Tawi) was found littered with bodies, indicating the intensity of the battle. Their six tanks were destroyed on the eastern side of the Tawi by our ground forces and one serviceable tank was also found abandoned.[21]

Back at D Company, 5/8 GR location, on December 10, during a short lull in the air activity, while we were having a packed lunch, one motor shell hit the *bandh*, just outside our trench and the tail unit fell inside. Yes, it was 'close'; but sure, our number was not up! We found that the jawan who had delivered us the lunch had been martyred; while, another three were wounded. Our FAC jeep also got a direct hit from an artillery shell, split into two and was on fire! My R/T operator and the driver too were lucky to be saved! Yes all, including the Satpal Light, went with the jeep!

Canberras Execute the Last Blow!

On December 11, five CAS missions of S-22s and Hunters attacked dug-in troops and tanks concentration opposite the Dhar and Raipur crossings, Chhamb village, Mandiala heights and Sukhtao *nallah* area The same day, the Lightning Squadron also flew a four aircraft dusk 'pathfinder' mission to mark and illuminate a target area infested with extensive, enemy dug-in positions, just West of the Tawi, for our Canberras to come and plaster a few minutes later. The Hunters carried out an accurate napalm drop followed by a rocket attack. The Canberras neutralised the target seven minutes later with 8,000 lb of bomb load each. Four extracts from the War Diary of Lightning Squadron are attached. The extracts also highlight strike details of eleven CAS missions (including a Canberra mission) flown by the squadron from December 8-11, 1971, in support of the Battle of Chhamb.[22]

After December 11, though the regular exchange of ground fire went on from either side, the enemy did not attempt any offensive; and nor did our ground forces take any major action to carry the war across the river.[23] On December 12, no air strike was carried out opposite our area; while on December 13, the last mission of four Hunters attacked dug in troops and a few bunkers at Mandiala heights (Sukhtao *nallah*); but did not spot any tank in the area. Thus, the FLOT, in this sector, stabilised along the Manawar Tawi!

On December 17, before the ceasefire came into effect in the Western Sector, there was a Diwali of sorts in 10 Division area and both sides kept all triggers pressed till 2000 h, the ceasefire time; may be, no one wanted to carry the load back and get into audit counting.

Memories to Linger!

The above short narration is just from one brigade (of 10 Infantry Division) from all along the Western Theatre! Sure, there would be many more untold stories of valour from the air as well as the ground operations! During the complete duration of the war, as per the brigade records, I had a total of 20 missions. Though, as of now, I would not be able to state the total number of claims by the CAS missions but a few points do emerge!

- Whenever our aircraft came in for a strike, it raised the morale of the troops sky high!
- Apart from one mission of two Sabres on December 10, which bounced our Hunter formation (and lost one Sabre in the air-to-air battle), after December 6, there was not a single PAF aircraft seen or reported along the Manawar Tawi/in this area. Thus, it could be said that the IAF had gained and maintained complete air superiority over the Tactical Battle Area (TBA) of 10 Division Sector till the end of the war! Towards this aim, as per the official history of the 1971 War, the IAF flew over 200 fighter/bomber sorties in support of our land forces in the Battle of Chhamb.[24] Close coordination with the Army, skilful execution of the task by all the air warriors, including, the operational, maintenance and administration staff; and professional handling and weapon delivery by the air crew contributed to the success achieved.
- Although the grit and gallant performance of our soldiers and air warriors who fought fearlessly, with many even laying down their lives; and the valiant display of raw courage and leadership at all levels of many participating formations and squadrons in the Battle of Chhamb have been widely documented, the performance of the Lightning and Falcon Squadrons needs a mention!

- When a tally was compiled for the Lightning Squadron (No. 20 Squadron) at the end of the war, the squadron turned out to be the highest scoring unit in the IAF during the 1971 conflict. Since its primary role was counter-air operations, the unit had a total of 13 enemy aircraft, including four C-130 Hercules, destroyed on the ground and two F-86 Sabres were shot down in air combat. In the eight days of operational flying during the war, the squadron flew a total of 121 sorties, fired about 15,000 × 30 mm rounds of cannon ammunition, dropped about 17,000 lb of HE bombs, 1,720 litres of napalm and 548 rockets at enemy targets. For this impressive performance, the Sqn Cdr, then Wg Cdr (later, AVM) CV Parker and Sqn Ldr (later Air Mshl and C-in-C) RN Bharadwaj were awarded the MahaVir Chakra (MVC). Five pilots, including, Sqn Ldr Jal Maneksha Mistry (posthumous) (RIP Air Warrior), then Lt (Indian Navy) (later, Adm, CNS) Arun Prakash and Fg Off BC Karambaya were honoured with the Vir Chakra (VrC). The squadron also earned two Vayu Sena Medals (VM) and two Mentioned-in-Dispatches (MnD)'.[25] The daring strike missions undertaken by all squadron pilots (as narrated in the referred article) speak volumes of their (IAF's) professionalism, grit and leadership!
- During the 1971 War, the Falcons (No. 101 Squadron) flew a total of 210 operational sorties on Sukhoi 7, striking airfields, ammunition dumps and supporting the Army. The major effort was in the Chhamb sector where 69 tanks, 20 heavy guns and 57 vehicles were destroyed. They emerged as the saviours of Chhamb and brought glory! Henceforth to be known as the "Falcons of Chhamb"! In recognition of their magnificent contributions, the Falcons were honoured as the highest decorated fighter bomber squadron during the 14-Day War with one MVC, one AVSM, eight VrCs, two VMs, one VSM and six MnDs'! The above quote is engraved on the 'Falcons of Chhamb' – Indo-Pak War Trophy – 1971' (Appendix-C). The rank, name, award conferred, number

of operational sorties flown/tanks destroyed and the role played by each officer during the war are also mentioned.

- The above extracts, from the records of just two squadrons of the IAF also highlight the rightful thrust given by the Indian Air Force to counter-air operations (i.e. against enemy airfields and aircraft on the ground/in the air) during the first three days of the war which paid rich dividends, initially in restricting and later severely limiting the war-waging potential of the PAF in this sector!
- The intensity of the enemy's ground fire from AD weapons in this sector was high but it lacked in accuracy; which was made up by very high volume. Thus, a number of our strike aircraft returned with bullet holes However, these aircraft were very expeditiously repaired and serviced by the skilled maintenance staff and again participated in the war.
- The IAF lost five aircraft (4 × S-22 and one Hunter) along with its three valiant pilots in the CAS role in the Chhamb sector.[26] RIP Air Warriors.
- In this war, India lost about 21,000 hectares of agricultural land and the Indian Army suffered maximum casualties in this battle. The total numbers of casualties were estimated at 1,353; which included, 440 killed, 723 wounded, and 190 missing and prisoners of war. The Pakistani losses were said to be about two to three times our number in both men and equipment.[27]

Once back at OTU Jamnagar, all of us officers from the 106th Pilots Course were very happy, proud and content; and knew that we were the lucky few who had carved their names in the history of the 1971 War; and each one of us had earned for himself 'his own personal video tape, permanently etched in his memory cells' that would start auto display, at any small trigger, any time, throughout our lives!

Forward Air Controllers: Relevance in 2020s and Beyond!

Forward air controllers belong to a bygone era and may not be relevant in today's milieu! Nevertheless, the requirement to quickly seek, detect, identify, select and designate ground targets, in close vicinity of own ground forces, to our airborne combat platform, so that the pilot/system can thereafter track and release lethal munitions at the correct range and achieve target destruction, would always remain critical; and play a crucial role in the success of any strike mission! However, in today's ever innovating, high-tech environment, the above tasks are most effectively and with much greater accuracy and efficiency performed with the available technologies, sensors, delivery platforms/systems and smart weapons, like the advanced Global Positioning System (GPS), Synthetic Aperture Radars (SARs), thermal imagery, attack drones, drone swarms, Unmanned Combat Aerial Vehicles (UCAVs), Remotely Piloted Aircraft (RPA), attack helicopters carrying pin-point accuracy laser guided bombs/missiles, directed energy weapons, Beyond Visual Range (BVR) fire and forget weapon systems, etc. Thus, in any future conflict, 'the young' Air Force officers might not be that fortunate to see war from close quarters; but would certainly perform much more demanding, challenging and satisfying roles and contribute decisively towards the success of any ground operation!

Disclaimer: The recount given above is more like my autobiography of those fourteen days of the 1971 Indo-Pak War. It includes only what I personally experienced, witnessed and now recall after nearly half a century! Yes, to maintain flow, I have included a few facts, figures and sketches (depicting deployment) taken from the write-ups of a few eminent defence experts, IAF history sheets ('Notes' below) and my pocket diary of the 1971 War which I still have; but in those too, the information included is to the extent I agree that might have happened at that time!

Parts of this chapter have previously been published in Gp Capt H.K. Bajaj, "Battle of Chhamb 71: Through the 6/5 Lenses of an FAC", *Bharat Rakshak*, December 13, 2020, https://www.bharat-rakshak.com/IAF/history/1971war/13399-h-k-bajaj.html#gsc.tab=0

APPENDICES

Appendix-A

Gp Capt (then Plt Offr) HK Bajaj (Retd), Pocket Diary of 71 War of then Plt Offr HK Bajaj

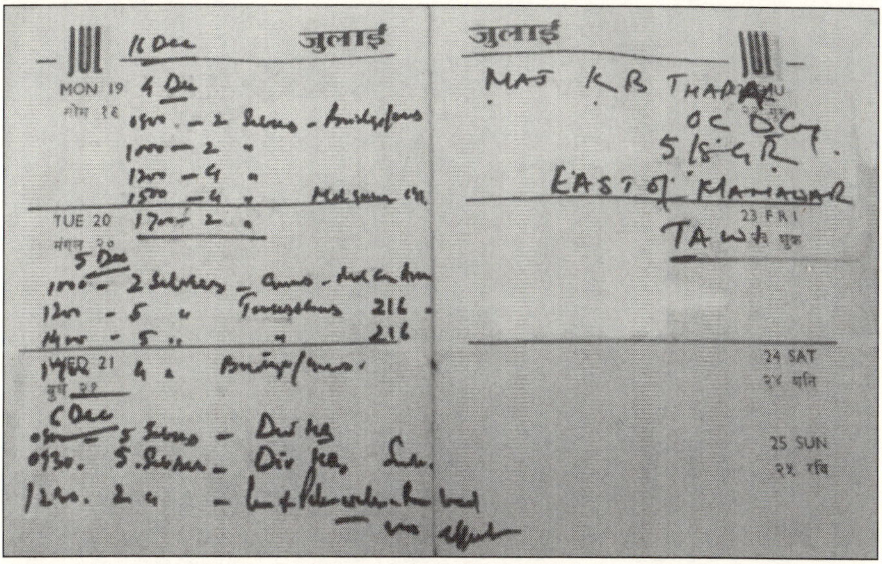

Source: Extract (16 Dec) from Pocket Diary of '71 War of then, Plt Offr HK Bajaj submitted by Gp Capt (then, Plt Offr) HK Bajaj (Retd)

Appendix-B

Gp Capt (then Flt Lt) Gurdeep Singh (Retd) of No. 101 Squadron, One Inch Map of 1971 of Chhamb Sector

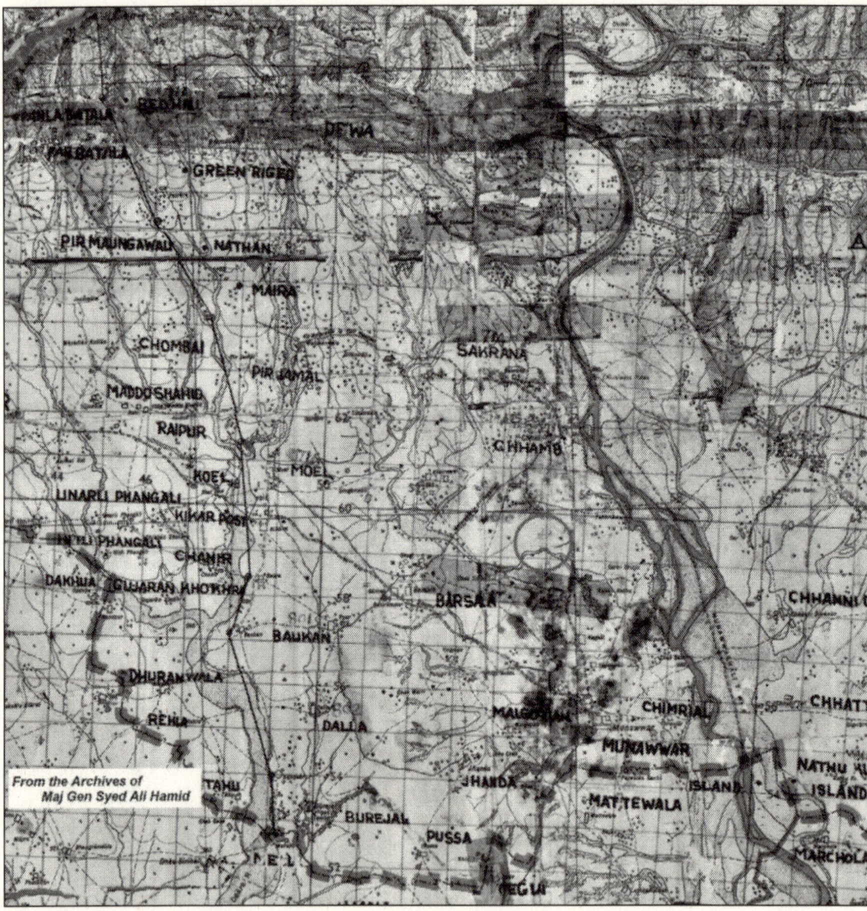

Source: One Inch Map of 1971 of Chhamb Sector
submitted by Gp Capt (then, Flt Lt) Gurdeep Singh (Retd) of 101 Sqn AF

Appendix-C

Gp Capt (then, Flt Lt) Gurdeep Singh (Retd) of Falcons of Chhamb (No. 101 Squadron), Falcons of Chhamb Indo-Pak War Trophy 1971

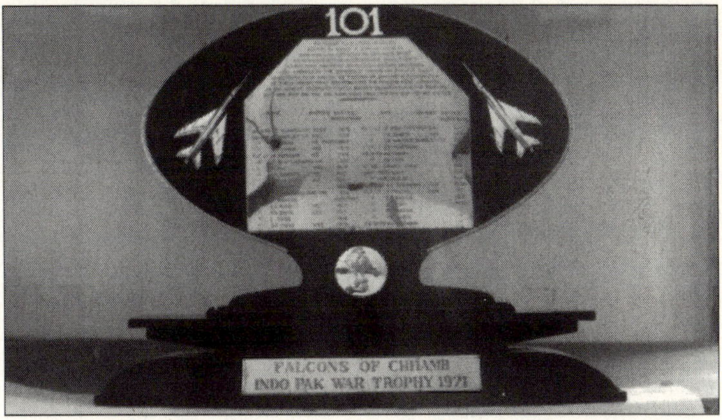

Source: Photograph of 'Falcons of Chhamb – Indo-Pak War Trophy 1971' submitted by Gp Capt (then Flt Lt) Gurdeep Singh (Retd) of Falcons of Chhamb (No. 101 Squadron AF)

Engraved on the Trophy

'The Falcons flew a total of approximately 210 Ops

Sorties on Sukhoi 7 striking airfields,

Ammo dumps and supporting the Army. Major effort was in Chhamb sector where sixty-nine tanks, twenty heavy guns and fifty-seven vehicles were destroyed.

They emerged as the saviours of Chhamb and brought glory.

Henceforth to be known as "Falcons of Chhamb". In recognition of their magnificent contributions the Falcons were honoured as the highest decorated fighter bomber squadron during the fourteen-day War with one MVC, one AVSM, eight VRCS, two VMS, one VSM and six MNDS.'

Gurdeep Singh
Group Captain+

Notes

1. Prasun K Sengupta, "Why CHHAMB Continues To Matter: A Historical Perspective," TRIS, October 2, 2017, http://trishul-trident.blogspot.com/2017/10/why-chhamb-continues-to-matter.html. Accessed on June 1, 2021. (The images have been suitably corrected, where the author was in disagreement with the contents; provided by Col M Sethi of 91 Mountain Regiment. In addition, a few other facts and figures, as brought out, have been collaborated with the referred article.)
2. Maj K.C. Praval, "1971 Operations – Case West – I," *Indian Defence Review*, March 14, 2011, http://www.indiandefencereview.com/spotlights/1971-operations-case-west-i/. Accessed on June 1, 2021.
3. Ibid.
4. Ibid.
5. Maj Gen Sukhwant Singh, "1971 War: Battle of Chhamb," *Indian Defence Review*, March 14, 2011, http://www.indiandefencereview.com/spotlights/1971-war-battle-of-chhamb/. Accessed on June 2, 2021.
6. Ibid.
7. Ibid.
8. Lt Gen Baljit Singh, "1971 War: Memories of the Chamb Battle," *Indian Defence Review*, September 11, 2018, http://www.indiandefencereview.com/spotlights/1971-war-memories-of-the-chamb-battle/. Accessed on June 2, 2021.
9. Gp Capt (then, Plt Offr) HK Bajaj (Retd), "Eight Extracts from his Pocket Diary of 1971 War" (Appendices – A, C & D), in Gp Capt H K Bajaj, "Battle of Chhamb 71: Through the 6/5 Lenses of an FAC," *Bharat Rakshak*, December 13, 2020, https://www.bharat-rakshak.com/IAF/history/1971war/1399-h-k-bajaj.html#gsc.tab=0. Accessed on June 3, 2021.
10. Gp Capt Gurdeep Singh (Retd), "Ejected Over No Man's Land!" *Bharat Rakshak*, December 22, 2018, https://www.bharat-rakshak.com/IAF/history/1971war/1375-ejection-over-no-mans-land.html#gsc.tab=0. Accessed on June 3, 2021.
11. Ibid.
12. Lt (IN) (later Adm, Chief of Naval Staff) Arun Prakash, "Four Extracts from the War Diary of Lightning Sqn - Close Air Support, Chhamb 71" in Bajaj, n. 9.
13. Singh, n. 5.
14. History Division, Ministry of Defence, Government of India, *Official History of the 1971 India Pakistan War*, Chapter X, IAF in the West, http://www.bharat-rakshak.com/archives/OfficialHistory/1971War/1971Chapter10.pdf, Accessed on July 2, 2021.
15. Wg Cdr B C Karumbaya VrC, "MSN 521 : Air Battle over Chhamb - 10 December 1971," *Bharat Rakshak*, December 13, 2020, https://www.bharat-rakshak.com/IAF/history/1971war/1401-lofty-karambaya.html. Accessed on June 3, 2021.
16. B. Harry, "IAF COMBAT KILLS - 1971 INDO-PAK AIR WAR," *Orbat.com*, September 6, 2006, http://orbat.info/cimh/iaf/IAF_1971_kills_rev1.pdf. Accessed on June 3, 2021.
17. Karumbaya, n. 15.
18. Singh, n. 5.
19. Sengupta, n. 1.

20. Maj (Retd) Agha Humayun Amin, "The Battle of Chamb-1971," *Defence Journal*, n.d. http://www.defencejournal.com/sept99/chamb.htm, Accessed on June 3, 2021.
21. Singh, n. 5.
22. Prakash, n. 12.
23. Singh, n. 5.
24. n. 14.
25. Jagan Pillarisetti, "When Lightning Strikes!," *Bharat Rakshak*, April 2, 2015, http://www.bharat-rakshak.com/IAF/history/1971war/1276-20-squadron.html#gsc.tab=0. Accessed on June 3, 2021.
26. Indian Air Force Accidents and Incidents, "IAF, IA and IN Aircraft Losses Database, 1971", http://www.bharat-rakshak.com/IAF/Database/Accidents/listing.php?qacid=50&qt=TY
27. Singh, n. 5.

10. Operational Approach and Psyche of Pakistan Air Force

Diptendu Choudhury

The Pakistan Fiza'Ya (Pakistan Air Force) plays a role in the psyche of its nation unmatched by any Air Force in the world except that by the Israeli Air Force. The PAF's motto, loosely translated from Persian is 'Lord of All I Survey'. It calls itself 'The Pride of the Nation', and is exactly that.

– Pushpindar Singh[1]

The Pakistan Air Force (PAF), the "pride possession of Pakistan",[2] has since its birth been inexorably entwined with the Indian Air Force (IAF). Twenty days after the imperial legacy of the decision on partition of the subcontinent, the Armed Forces Reconstitution Committee (AFRC) was set up under the chair of AVM Perry Keene, for the PAF "*to be created as such on the 15th August 1947.*"[3] The distribution of the eight fighter and two transport squadrons of the IAF between the two dominions, became a contentious issue. The Indian side insisted on the 80:20 ratio, eight squadrons to India and two squadrons to Pakistan, based on the manpower composition of the basis of partition. The AFRC Chairman, on the other hand, opined, that in view of the operational requirements of 'watch and ward' duties in the tribal areas of the North-West Frontier Province, Pakistan should be allotted five squadrons. With both sides entrenched on their stands, Lord Mountbatten intervened asking the Commander-in-Chief (C-in-C) of the IAF to look into the feasibility of raising an additional fighter squadrons from the reserves. On his confirmation of the feasibility, the final distribution agreed was of seven fighter and one transport squadrons to India, and two fighter and one transport squadrons to Pakistan.[4] The overarching vision of the Quaid-e-Azam Mohammed Ali Jinnah was to serve as a beacon light for the PAF, when in his address at the Flying Training School at Risalpur, he said, "There is no doubt that any country without a strong Air Force is at the mercy of any aggressor. Pakistan must build up her Air Force as quickly as possible. It must be an efficient Air Force, second to none and must take its place with the Army and the Navy in securing Pakistan's defence."[5]

Living in the Army's Shadow

Despite his words, the British leadership came in the way of a three Services concept which was "opted and enforced with variable results. Thus, were sown the seeds for lack of joint inter-Service planning from almost the start."[6] The division of the armed forces, set the stage for the selection of six heads of the Services. Both Prime Ministers (PMs) were happy to let Lord Mountbatten select them, except for the choice of Air Mshl Sir Thomas Elmhirst, who was the only exception having been specially chosen by Pandit Nehru – a choice which was to be fortuitous for the IAF as Air Mshl Elmhirst's first mandate with the PM was that "*the Indian Air Force would be an independent fighting service.*"[7] The IAF which was from its birth an independent Service due to the enactment of Clause 4 of the Annual Army and Air Force Bill[8] in 1932, was, therefore, able to continue as an independent service. The PAF was not so lucky, and due to the relatively low seniority profile of its original officers, was destined to remain under the shadow of the Pakistan Army.

The first PAF C-in-C was AVM Perry Keene, and the seniormost Pakistani officer was Wg Cdr MK Janjua, who had been a part of the AFRC, and went on to become the senior officer-in-charge administration as a Group Captain on August 15, 1947. The fifth PAF Chief and the first Pakistani officer to assume the mantle, Air Mshl Muhammad Asghar Khan, was a Wing Commander when the PAF was formed. The less seniority of the PAF's original officers defined its relations with the

Pakistan Army, which till today plays a dominant role, continuing to keep the PAF out of the loop in planning and decision-making on matters of national security. In Pakistan, the military has the final say in all matters of national security, and all security related decisions for all services rest with the Chief of the Army Staff (COAS).[9] Even today, PAF policy decisions are also determined by the COAS, with inputs from the Chief of the Air Staff (CAS). Therefore, the final decision-maker for air power policy is not the CAS, but the COAS.[10]

Post-Independence and after the first round of war in Kashmir, Pakistan sought to strengthen its military and especially its Air Force. Underpinned by the Cold War, the US geopolitics was driven by prevention of the perceived Communist expansionism in the region from the USSR and China. In May 1954, Pakistan signed a Mutual Defence Assistance Agreement with the US which provided significant economic and military aid, in return for the use of PAF bases for launching reconnaissance flights into the Soviet Union. Based on the Communist threat, the PAF's expansion plan was prepared by Gp Capt Asghar Khan, Gp Capt Nur Khan and Wg Cdr A. Qadir in March 1954. The plan called for a 768 aircraft and 44 squadron strong Air Force, comprising ten day-fighter squadrons, five night-fighter squadrons, six bomber squadron and one reconnaissance squadron, twelve fighter-bomber squadrons, six tactical light bomber squadrons, two twin-engine and one four-engine transport squadron and two maritime squadrons, over ten years from 1954-1964.[11]

By mid-1957, the US agreed to provide six fighter-bomber squadrons, one day-interceptor squadron, one light bomber squadron, one transport squadron, one jet conversion school, one air rescue flight and one recce flight, one flying training academy, radars and navigational aids, and various other maintenance, logistics and administrative aid.[12] In Pakistan's 'aid-era' between 1954 to 1965, the US provided military assistance worth $619 million, and cash or commercial basis purchases worth $55 million.[13] Air power expansion began in earnest almost immediately, with the first lot of the 120 F-86F Sabre fighters, followed by 26 B-57B Canberra bombers in 1959, and 12 F-104A in 1962. Though technologically these were the best aircraft available, their size always remained an area of serious concern to the PAF. This not only shaped its operational philosophy, but also became the overarching reason for it to 'preserve' its strength in its wars.

PAF Role: Perceptions and Differences

The consequences of being in the Army's shadow impacted the PAF's operational role. The second PAF C-in-C AVM Atcherley, was of the firm opinion that the PAF should first take on the enemy Air Force, then try to isolate the battlefield, and after that give direct support to the ground forces.[14] The seeds of discord were sown when Gen Sir Douglas Gracey, the C-in-C of the Pakistan Army, in a paper on "First Lessons From Korea", wrote: "The small Pakistan Air Force should be trained primarily for tactical support of the Pakistan Army and Navy, and be equipped to carry out this task with suitable aircraft."[15] Atcherley, wrote back: "I am not inferring that you don't know your job, I'm saying that you don't know mine. Air must be left to the airman; even Monty preaches that." And with regard to joint planning, he continued: "I feel we are only paying lip-service to Joint Service Planning, when you issue a paper on air strategy without even a formal reference to your colleagues."[16] This Army dominant approach continued through the 1965 War under President Ayub Khan, who according to Air Mshl Asghar Khan, "understood little of air operations" and "preferred to see the Air Force as an arm of the Army, an airborne form of artillery whose role should be to clear the way for the infantry and armour."[17]

Asghar Khan, groomed by the independent minded initial Royal Pakistan Air Force (RPAF) British C-in-C, was very clear on the role of the PAF. He emphasised that its main role was the air battle from which it could not be diverted, and till achievement of its primary aim, could only provide limited close support at any time, *"which should be treated by the Army as bonus"*. Gen Muhammad Musa Khan, the Pakistan Army C-in-C countered that consequently in the training and operational planning of the Army, it was assumed that air support might not be forthcoming, to the extent that "the Army's main counter-offensive was planned without air support."[18] He also goes on to state that after Air Mshl Nur Khan took over, he "altered Asghar's concept, and rightly decided that ground support was also an important function which the PAF could and should take on besides its main commitment."[19]

The differences in the perception of the role of the PAF and its divide with the Army showed itself in the 1965 War. Musa is scathingly critical of Asghar Khan, who he claims shocked the Army by contacting his IAF counterpart, in trying to keep the PAF out of the conflict in the Rann of Kutch. He writes that even the Supreme Commander was unaware of Asghar's actions while the Defence Secretary was,[20] indicating the divide in the senior leadership. Sajjad Haider, in defence of the action by Asghar Khan, writes: "Had the Indians committed their Air Force in support of their Army, our troops would have been attacked from the air and destroyed with impunity, bringing our land operation to a halt. The PAF would have been relatively ineffective as the battle area was too far from Mauripur, the only PAF base in the south."[21] In Operation Gibraltar, the second phase of the war involving infiltration in Kashmir, Asghar Khan was kept out of the loop by the General Headquarters (GHQ).[22] The PAF history also brings out that its government wanted to keep it out of war operations, and that in spite of desperate calls for air support in Poonch, it was not used.[23] When the third phase of the war finally kicked in with Operation Grand Slam, from the PAF's perspective, it was to have started with Asghar Khan's *coup de grace* – preemptive strikes.

Three facts emerge clearly: the *fait accompli* acceptance of the air battle as the main role of the PAF; the inter-service divide in the senior military leadership; and the absence of joint operational planning. It illustrates that gaining air superiority was considered fundamental by the PAF, and that close support to the Pakistan Army would be low key. The leaderships of the PAF and Pakistan Army were divided, taking decisions and acting independently of each other. And, finally, the absence of joint planning is underscored by the fact that the Pakistan Army plans neither included PAF participation, nor was any role assigned to it. This trend was to continue even in Kargil, in 1999, where, according to Nasim Zehra, the civilian leadership, and the air and naval chiefs were briefed on Operation Koh Paima for the first time on May 16, 1999,[24] after the operation, planned secretly by the clique of four generals, had already begun. It was only after the plan had started to unravel with the IAF getting engaged offensively, that the involvement of the PAF was sought, which the CAS opposed.[25]

Geography Decides Everything

Pakistan's security approach and military thinking which have led to four wars with India, are not easy to understand, but as Robert Kaplan explains, "Geography offers a way to make at least some sense of it all."[26] Pakistan's mountainous northern areas lie across the much-coveted Kashmir, and is a region through which the Indus flows into the country. The capital city Islamabad which lies on the Pothar plateau, is on the West of the Pir Panjal range that separates it from India's Kashmir Valley. Below it the five rivers – Indus, Jhelum, Chenab, Ravi and Sutlej – flow into the fertile Punjab, the heartland and power centre of Pakistan. Lahore, a historical and cultural epicentre is the capital of Punjab and lies just 50 km across Amritsar. On the West, Pakistan is bounded by the Suleiman and Kirthar ranges which border Afghanistan by the unsettled Durand Line. Between the mountains in the West and the Indian border on the East, in a Northeast to Southwest orientation, the Pakistan plains are neatly bisected by the mighty Indus. The plains are about 200 km across in the Punjab region in the north and Sindh region in the South, and in the middle, the Jaisalmer salient of the Indian Thar desert juts into Pakistan, squeezing it to less than 100 km. The Sindh region lies on the East of the Baluchistan region and is divided by the Kirthar range. At its base and on the Eastern tip of Pakistan's East-West coastline lies Karachi, its major port, the largest city and the capital of Sindh.

The turbulent Khyber-Pakhtunkhwa in the Northwest, the volatile Baluchistan in its Southwest and the relatively narrow plains, drive Pakistan's desire for strategic depth. The major road and railway lines of Pakistan, and, therefore, all its major communication and logistics networks, are also aligned with the river Indus, running in a Northeast-

Southwest direction. The major PAF air bases in 1971 of Peshawar, Murid, Mianwali, Sargodha, Risalewala, and Rafiqy were located in the Punjab region in the North, Jacobabad in the Central Sector, with Talhar and Mauripur in the South. Given the PAF's smaller size and orientation towards self-preservation, despite having a front tier of airfields, it chose to operate from its depth bases in an effort to keep its aircraft away from the easy reach of IAF bases. Pakistan's geography and the deployment pattern of the PAF defined its operational strategy and psyche.

Operational Approach: Myths and Realities of 1965

The 1965 War is important to assess the PAF's operational approach as it provides the necessary context of its mindset, and serves as a lead-in to the subsequent 1971 War. Both wars have, over the years, been built into a myth of Indian misadventures, defeated by the numerically inferior but professionally superior and aggressive PAF. The myth was perpetuated by the absence of official war records in the public domain and the partisan writings of John Fricker in his book *Battle for Pakistan*. It thrived due to the pro-PAF narratives built up amongst the Western strategic community, air power practitioners, academia and media in a Cold War milieu, where Pakistan was a member of the US driven Southeast Asia Treaty Organisation (SEATO), and India was not. Interestingly, the story goes that Fricker had offered to write for India initially and was turned down, which is a pity as it would have then won the war from the beginning! Thankfully, over the years, balanced and mature narratives have emerged from India and some from Pakistan, allowing for more objective assessments. So, what was the most likely PAF operational approach in 1965?

PAF Strategy and Execution

Pakistan planned to start the operations with preemptive dusk counter-air strikes against the major Indian air bases and key radars, with the aim of reducing the IAF's numerical superiority. Subsequently, night counter-air would continue with the bombers to keep the IAF under pressure, and inhibiting its air operations. The focus thereafter would be air superiority over Pakistani territory, while providing support to the ground battle. Haider avers that the PAF's preemptive was originally planned in the last week of June 1965, where Asghar Khan stressed that India's preponderance in numbers was cardinal in determining the PAF's tactically offensive strategy. It comprised the attacks on IAF bases to reduce its numerical superiority and create a more equitable balance of air power; prevent an enemy surprise attack as it could render the PAF ineffective and enable air superiority, leaving the Pakistan Army vulnerable. Preemption was, therefore, an imperative, and not a contingency. Six enemy forward airfields and three radars were to be struck 15 minutes before dusk.[27] Nur Khan, who took over the PAF just prior to the 1965 War, it appears, was initially more circumspect about the plan, but came around subsequently.[28]

In the final outcome, the PAF commenced with Combat Air Patrol (CAP) missions well before the air war actually commenced in the last light on September 1, when the IAF committed its Vampires and Mysteres in Chhamb. The PAF counter-air strikes, no longer preemptive, finally commenced five days later in the evening of September 6. It, however, capitalised on the opportunity provided by the absence of any Indian counter-air effort by carrying out the original plan, with mixed success. Asghar Khan writes:

> We were puzzled as to why the Indians, having started what amounted to a general war, had limited the offensive to the West only and why, having decided to start an offensive against West Pakistan alone, they had not used their Air Force against our vital installations, such as airfields and radar. By not doing so, they had given us a chance which we had never counted on – the chance to deliver the first aerial attack.[29]

The IAF paid dearly for its inadequacy of passive air defence measures, especially at Pathankot and Kalaikunda. But the failed strikes against Adampur, Halwara and Jamnagar were not launched as per the original plan, and Haider is critical of the leadership at Sargodha and Mauripur for the failure to do so. He writes: "The failure of the preemptive strategic offensive on 6th September was no less than a debacle, especially considering that the PAF operational readiness was at the optimum with missions fully rehearsed."[30] The PAF also carried out around 481 sorties of essentially pre-planned Close Air Support (CAS),[31] and given the limited expectations of the Pakistan Army, was considered effective. Its Canberras played an unsung and significant role in bombing operations, and "their performance was stunning".[32]

David and Goliath

Its smaller size has been used effectively to its advantage in the PAF's history and the accounts of some writers, to build the image of a heroic 'David' fighting against a much larger 'Goliath' and emerging victorious. The PAF's 1965 narrative is bolstered by somewhat over-enthusiastic claims: "The IAF planes came in waves, and with a numerical edge of 5:1, the Indians took a well calculated risk." There is no doubt the IAF was larger in size but 5:1 it was not. While there are minor differences depending upon the source, the reliably estimated figures are that the IAF had 290 aircraft (including 80 Mysteres and 48 Vampires) against the 187 of the PAF in the West.[33] The claim that *"the IAF planes came in waves"* while attempting to highlight its small size, actually indicates the persistence of IAF offensive missions and negates the PAF claims of air superiority. Also, while the phrase *"the Indians took a calculated risk"* is aimed to indicate the PAF's air combat prowess, it actually highlights the courage of the Indian pilots, who flew to the limits of the tactical Radius Of Action (ROA) and combat endurance, in a CAP intensive environment.

According to Hussain and Qureshi, "By the end of the fourth day of the war, the IAF had lost heavily in aircrafts and pilots, and the PAF had achieved the impossible – air supremacy all over Pakistan." Factually, out of its total 59 losses, the IAF lost 35 aircraft on the ground to the air raids.[34] Attrition is always measured in terms of the proportion of the quantum of air effort and the losses. Pakistan lost 43 aircraft in the 2,364 sorties flown, and, therefore, had an attrition rate of 1.82 per cent. India lost 59 aircraft in the 3,937 sorties flown and, therefore, had an attrition rate of 1.50 per cent. In his book, *Defence from the Skies*, Air Cmde Jasjit Singh cites that the PAF rate of loss was nearly three times in air-air engagements, losing 1.78 aircraft every 100 sorties, compared to .66 aircraft lost by the IAF. Therefore, despite the superior, technologically advanced inventory, and the claimed superiority of PAF pilots in training and motivation, the IAF pilots displayed better air combat performance.[35] Notwithstanding the same, the courage, commitment, professionalism and performance of the PAF pilots has never been in question from the IAF's perspective.

The issue of PAF air supremacy needs a closer look. According to Philip Mellinger, air superiority is defined as being able to conduct air operations "without prohibitive interference by the opposing force." Air supremacy goes further, wherein the opposing Air Force is incapable of effective interference.[36] As per the unpublished official history of the 1965 War, of a total of 3,937 sorties flown by the IAF, 1,568 were fighter-bomber and bomber sorties towards offensive missions; 1,352 CAP sorties were flown over IAF bases; and the balance 1,017 missions are simply recorded as fighter sorties.[37] These fighter sorties could not have all been CAP missions, and, therefore, if a conservative estimate of 400 sorties (roughly 40 per cent) were flown towards ground attack, the total offensive effort goes up to 1,968 sorties. A majority of these were multiple pass attacks, and in the case of counter-air missions, at the extremes of their Radius of Action (ROA). In both cases, it significantly increased their vulnerability to the 1,303 PAF CAP sorties, which amounts to 55 per cent of its total of 2,368 sorties flown.[38] Therefore, the nearly 2,000 IAF offensive missions executed with evident combat persistence, and a total of just 15 air combat losses,[39] would not have been possible if the PAF had actually gained air supremacy, as claimed. This is endorsed by Tony Mason who wrote, "In the war between India and Pakistan, air superiority was never contested."[40]

The *History of the PAF* which claims, "The PAF pilots were in a state of high morale bordering on ecstasy, its aircraft inventory was intact" and "a whimpering and prostrate enemy got a new lease for life",[41] is contrived rhetoric towards the myth of PAF superiority and victory. Haider gives a more sober perspective:

> In spite of the fact that more than four decades have elapsed since the 1965 war, the real truth is not common knowledge and hence the truth must remain the biggest casualty in the tragedy of errors played out by the leaders of that period. Like most wars, the 1965 war was an avoidable catastrophe. It was horrendously senseless and falsely contrived to appear as a victory. Only those martyred and their neglected, ravaged kin had to pay the terrible price for this farce. The legacy of the 1965 tragedy perpetrated 'a bigger watershed' in 1971.[42]

1971: 'A Bigger Watershed'

Drivers and Strategies

The Pakistan military high command held the belief that East Pakistan could not be threatened, as long as India was convinced that there would be major reverses on its Western border if its military were split up to engage both wings simultaneously.[43] Thus, the strategy of defence of East Pakistan lay in a reciprocal counter-attack by West Pakistan. Since Pakistan could not afford separate defence forces for the two wings and could not force its choice of time and place of war, the PAF was constrained to mould its plans accordingly.[44] The PAF examined all its war-fighting options, from launching an offensive on IAF bases, providing intensive ground support to the Pakistan Army, to a defensive battle to sort out the IAF over its own skies. It assessed that it could not go on the offensive due to its force levels, as counter-air meant higher attrition rates given the high-performance IAF Air Defence (AD) aircraft, SA-2 Surface-to-Air Missiles (SAMs) and AD guns, and radars. Intensive ground support was ruled out due to the need for air superiority. Therefore, the only viable option was to destroy the IAF in air battles over Pakistani skies a la 'Battle of Britain', and then, the situation permitting, launch an offensive.

The key drivers which governed the PAF's planning[45] were:

- Except for limited Mirage IIIs, it did not have aircraft capable of deep penetration.
- The removal of the Bengalis from the PAF led to some shortages in aircrew and ground crew.
- The MiG-19 were assigned for the AD and CAS roles. But not all were modified for air-to-air missiles, limiting their air combat capability. Also, the limited ROA restricted their employment in CAS.
- The concept of CAS had not received sufficient attention in the joint Air Force-Army planning level. The *History of the PAF* records it as "*only a vague option open to the PAF.*"
- The PAF had established satellite bases but did not have assets for their AD. The limited presence would dissipate their meagre resources.
- Their limited inventory obviated commitment to any major role without knowing the designs of the enemy, because once committed, losses were natural; this was considered too high a risk against an enemy with a big fleet.
- The enemy's ground moves were not known. Given the Indian Army's large size, it could open any number of fronts, thus, stretching the Pakistan Army. This made it difficult for the PAF to determine its CAS – offensive roles.
- The Pakistan government's war policy was not known, and its likely reaction was not communicated to the PAF. The likely duration of the war, its objectives and the extent of commitment not being defined, left PAF very little room to manoeuvre.

It was with these constraints and full knowledge of the IAF's strengths that the PAF prepared itself for the 1971 War. India's July 1971 Treaty of Friendship with the USSR played heavily on its mind, being acutely aware that it was taking on a much stronger, better prepared and trained IAF. Therefore, the broad strategy[46] of the PAF can be summarised as:

- It assumed a role of offensive-defence.

- Self-preservation to be a high priority consideration.
- It prepared for an elusive war the dimensions for which were not known.
- It adopted a defensive war strategy, with steady offensive probes.
- It adopted a policy of survival against all odds in a hostile air environment.
- The East Pakistan element of the PAF was pretty much left on its own, like in 1965, as it hoped to tilt the tables by the actions in the West.

Counter-Air Strategy

Since all the combat aircraft in IAF airfields would be in concrete pens, and camouflaged targets such as fuel tanks, ammunition dumps and command centres could not be readily identified or accurately attacked, like in 1965, the targeting choice once again was on runways and radars. The bombing of airfields was to deny their availability for certain periods, as this would reduce the availability of IAF assets against the Pakistan Army's campaign. Unlike the past, given the SAMs and AD guns at the airfields, multiple pass attacks would not be possible. The strikes on forward airfields were aimed at provoking retaliatory strikes, so that IAF fighters could be engaged over Pak territory like in the Battle of Britain. Meanwhile strikes to depth IAF airfields would be taken on by PAF bombers at night.

Offensive Strategy

Pakistan's grand strategy was to launch a massive offensive by II Corps under Lt Gen Tikka Khan, to capture large swathes of Indian territory. This would provide the vital leverage for Pakistan to not only save the East, but also put it in control of post war negotiations. The over-riding priority was to give maximum support to this offensive, and every other PAF objective was subordinated to it. The estimated 'cost' of this commitment was gamed by the planning staff at PAF HQ in July 1971, and a loss of 100-120 combat aircraft and pilots over the likely 7-10 days, was assessed. Air Mshl Rahim Khan was aware that this would amount to losing one-third of his Air Force. According to Haider, he had the full support of his senior commanders when he directed them to prepare their units accordingly in August, to ensure the success of the Pakistan Army's offensive.[47]

D-Day

For the first time, the PAF HQ had managed to convince the GHQ that any offensive would be coordinated with the PAF's opening strikes, and the mutually agreed D-Day was December 3, 1971.

Air Superiority

The pervasive primary mission meant air superiority would have to be achieved in the form of a moving umbrella over the Army's deep thrust. Beneath the AD umbrella, some direct offensive support by the PAF would be executed, to soften the Indian Army's resistance. The protective cover would continue until the Pakistani forces could dig in and secure their protection. Control of the air, even in the limited areas of Pakistan's counter-attack, involved not just the prevention of IAF interference, but attacks against its four to five bases around Gen Tikka Khan's offensive.

CAS Strategy

The PAF air staff decided that losing its limited resources and endangering multi-million-dollar aircraft for destroying tanks and other weapons was not acceptable, until the main offensive. Instead, the PAF was to maintain pressure with sustained strikes against some of the forward and rear Indian bases, in order to inhibit the IAF's offensive air support, interdiction and counter-air efforts. During this same period, the PAF was also to provide whatever air support was needed for the Pakistan Army's 'holding' actions along the entire 3,700-km border from Kashmir to Kutch. These relatively shallow-penetrating actions were meant to tie down as many of the enemy's resources as possible and to try to achieve a favourable tactical posture in the process. As the war progressed, the PAF was also to provide whatever air support it could to the Pakistan Navy within the limits of its maritime support capability which, in real terms, was near zero.[48]

The Final Outcome

The breakdown of the total PAF air effort of 3,027 sorties was: 1,748 AD sorties, 951CAS sorties, 290 counter-air (day/night) sorties, and 38 other missions. The daily average was 201 sorties.[49] The unpublished official Indian Ministry of Defence (MOD) history estimates 44 confirmed and six probable PAF losses in the West and 19 Sabres and three T-33s in the East (10 Sabre losses in combat, and balance 9 Sabres and 3 T-33s written off by the PAF to prevent capture).[50] Tufail claims that only 27 aircraft were lost (22 in the West and 5 in the East),[51] which definitely does not add up. In the absence of reliable assessment, this remains a grey area. According to the PAF, the outcome of the war in the East is referred to as a "heroic struggle" for a single squadron in a "no-win" situation,[52] which it definitely was. On the West, its history states that the IAF counter-air had no operational effect as it lost a large number of aircraft to the "hot reception" by the PAF CAP. It stuck to its aim: defence and preservation of its fighting capability.

In view of the large area of surface operations, the PAF could not be there all the time, and it was impossible for it to commit itself completely to ground support; it had to keep its guard up. Its history covers up the IAF strategic strikes on the oil and power facilities as bombardments on civilian areas of Lahore and Karachi. It, however, admits that the IAF attacks in support of the Indian Army and the Pakistan's lines of communication were well performed. It also says, "The Indian attack strategy was based on strong support from the air as a part of their concept of joint Army-Air operation."[53] As per Haider:

> Unlike the realistic planning and execution by the PAF, planning at the highest tiers of the national and Army leadership, including the President and the GHQ, was intrinsically flawed, to say the least. Not launching the punch of the Army, the No. 1 Armoured Corps, and the senseless assault by an unprepared force without air cover against

> Ramgarh in the south (hoping to capture Jaisalmer in a blitzkrieg) was an amazing blunder which caused incalculable loss of precious lives and equipment.[54]

The Psyche of the PAF Pilot

Since it is the man behind the machine who drives the ultimate outcome in war, the mindset and psyche of the PAF pilot need a mention. In a country where the military is held in high esteem and is considered a prestigious career, the PAF fighter pilot is perhaps the most privileged person – well paid, highly regarded and the subject of national adoration.[55] Kaiser Tufail writes that PAF pilots have flown in Algeria, Egypt, Iraq, Jordan, Kuwait, Libya, Qatar, Saudi Arabia, Sri Lanka, Syria, Turkey, UAE, UK, and Zimbabwe. Its pilots gained extensive experience on a wide range of fighters including the Gnat, Hunter, MiG-21FL/M, and Su-7. According to him, "First-hand knowledge about adversary aircraft, as well as well-honed flying skills of PAF's pilots were key factors in their remarkable performance during various conflicts."[56]

The PAF maintains skill-based posting to fighter types and younger age profile Squadron Commanders.[57] In the words of Asghar Khan, who had been the C-in-C for eight years:

> After Station Commanders, or perhaps even more important than them, is the selection of Squadron Commanders. They are the people who command the combat units of the Air Force. Their number in a small Air Force is necessarily small and their importance, therefore, all the greater. It is my belief that these few commanders must be above the average in their own spheres. I was prepared to overlook some human failings so long as they commanded respect in the air. They must be professionally sound and superior to those they are required to lead. No other quality, however great, can compensate for these essential requirements in the eyes of subordinates.[58]

The squadron commanders mandatorily undergo the Flight Leaders School which was instituted by Asghar Khan in 1958. This continues even today under its new avatar of Combat Commanders School, which is geared primarily towards the mid-career advanced air combat training of PAF fighter squadron commanders, air defence controllers, and instructors and for the development of advanced fighter weapons tactics.[59] In the PAF, the seniormost Air Marshal does not necessarily get to be the Chief. On the contrary, the exception has been the rule.[60]

A fairly clear picture of the pilot's psyche emerges when in addition to the above, the martial race stereotype and ascendancy as a superior combat pilot comprises a part of their regular grooming. Pushpindar Singh wrote in the concluding paragraph of his book:

> There is little doubt as to which of the prime air arms of the Indian subcontinent is more conscious of the importance of image building and intelligent public relations. The PAF has many friends and admirers amongst the world's aerospace media, not the least because of its sustained effort to 'put its best wing forward'. The PAF has had innumerable articles, features and books written about it, covered by international writers, journalists and photographers. This boosts morale.[61]

Essentially, most of the PAF narrative of victory has been built around its few successes in counter-air and air-air victories. This is probably because of the preponderance towards AD in its orientation. Its force composition, ethos and training are fundamentally focussed towards the air battle – air combat and fighting the enemy Air Force. It has a history of reticence towards support of the Army operations, which is reciprocated by the inadequate understanding of air power of its generals! It tends to dissociate itself from the legacy of the military defeats which it attributes to the Army, and has tried to perpetuate the myth that it won all the air wars and, thus, saved Pakistan. But since a military victory is not a bean count of inventory losses, but one of outcomes and achievement of national objectives, it is time to put some myths to rest. In the final outcome, the adversary is not ten feet tall, but a worthy foe.

Notes

1. Pushpindar Singh, Ravi Rikhye and Peter Steinmann, *FizaʼYa: Psyche of the Pakistan Air Force* (New Delhi: The Society of Aerospace Studies, 1991).
   Since the late Pushpindar Singh was originally planned to write this chapter, it is, therefore, only right that it begins with the opening lines of his seminal book. A book which served as an invaluable insight into the psyche of the adversary, for my generation of practitioners.
2. Syed Shabbir Hussain and Sqn Ldr M Tariq Qureshi, *History of Pakistan Air Force, 1947-1982* (Karachi: PAF Press Masroor, 1982), p. 1.
3. Ibid., p. 16.
4. Air Mshl Bharat Kumar, *An Incredible War* (Second Edition) (New Delhi: KW Publishers, 2014), pp. 15-21.
5. Ibid., p. 40.
6. Ibid., p. 114.
7. Ibid., p. 14.
8. "CLAUSE 4. - (Relations between Royal Air Force and Indian Air Force, and attachment of personnel.)," April 3, 1933, http://hansard.millbanksystems.com/commons/1933/apr/03/clause-4-relations-between-royal-air. Accessed on May 17, 2021.
9. Jonah Blank, Richard S. Girven, Arzan Tarapore, Julia A. Thompson, Arthur Chan, Vector Check, *Prospects of US and Pakistan Air Power Engagement* (Santa Monica: RAND, 2018), p. 6.
10. Shuja Nawaz, *Crossed Swords: Pakistan, Its Army, and the Wars Within* (New York: Oxford University Press, 2008).
11. Hussain and Qureshi, n. 2, pp. 95-96.
12. Ibid., p. 100.
13. Gp Capt Khalid Iqbal, Pakistan Air Force, "The United States-Pakistan Security Relationship," Research Report No. AU-AWC-86-115, Air War College, March 1986, https://apps.dtic.mil/dtic/tr/fulltext/u2/a177769.pdf. Accessed on May 17, 2021.
14. Ibid., p. 120.
15. Ibid., pp. 115-116.
16. Ibid., p. 117.
17. Air Mshl M Asghar Khan (Retd), *The First Round: Indo-Pakistan War 1965* (New Delhi: Vikas Publishing House, 1979), pp. 4-5.
18. Gen Muhammad Musa (Retd), *My Version: India Pakistan War 1965,* (New Delhi: ABC Publishing House, 1983), pp. 74-78.
19. Ibid., p. 79.
20. Musa, n. 18, pp. 74-79.
21. S Sajjad Haider, *Flight of the Falcon* (Lahore: Vanguard Books, 2009).
22. Khan, n. 17, p. viii.
23. Hussain and Qureshi, n. 2, p. 141.
24. Nasim Zehra, *From Kargil to the Coup: Events that Shook Pakistan* (Lahore: Sang-e-Meel Publications, 2018), p. 151.
25. Ibid., p. 213.

26. Robert D. Kaplan, *Revenge of Geography* (New York: Random House Inc., 2013), p. xxii.
27. Haider, n. 21, ch 7.
28. Khan, n. 17, p. 16.
29. Ibid., p. 15.
30. Haider, n. 21, ch 10.
31. AVM AK Tiwary, *Indian Air Force in Wars* (New Delhi: Lancer Publishers and Distributers, 2012), p. 134.
32. Haider, n. 21, ch 10.
33. Ibid., p. 119.
34. BC Chakravorty, D Phil, Chief Editor SN Prasad, D Phil, *History of the 1965 War,* (New Delhi: History Division, Ministry of Defence, Government of India, 1992), p. 170.
35. Air Cmde Jasjit Singh, *Defence from the Skies* (New Delhi: KW Publishers, 2013), pp. 250-260.
36. Phillip S. Mellinger, "Supremacy in the Skies", *Air Force Magazine*, February 2019, https://www.airforcemag.com/PDF/MagazineArchive/Magazine%20 Documents/2016/February%202016/0216supremacy.pdf. Accessed on May 23, 2021.
37. Chakravorty and Prasad, n. 34, p. 269.
38. Sobia Nissar, "PAF and Three Wars" *Defence Journal*, September 2001, http://www.defencejournal.com/2001/september/wars.htm. Accessed on May 22, 2021.
39. PVS Jagan Mohan and Samir Chopra, *The India-Pakistan Air War of 1965* (New Delhi: Manohar Publishers, 2009), Appendix B.
40. AVM Tony Mason, *Air Power: A Centennial Appraisal* (London: Brassey's, 1994), p. 64.
41. Hussain and Qureshi, n. 2, pp. 171-172.
42. Haider, n. 21, ch 10.
43. Ibid., ch 13.
44. Hussain and Qureshi, n. 2, p. 178.
45. Ibid., pp. 179-180.
46. Ibid., pp. 180-181.
47. Haider, n. 21, ch 13.
48. Ibid.
49. Nissar, n. 38.
50. SN Prasad, "Chapter X: IAF in the West," and "Chapter XIV; IAF in the Eastern Theatre" in S. N. Prasad et al. eds., *History of the 1971 India Pakistan War,* (New Delhi: History Division, Ministry of Defence, Government of India, 1992), pp. 455, 614.
51. The Print Team, "An Indian Admiral & Pakistani Air Commodore Debate the Finer Points of the 1971 War," *The Print,* February 23, 2018, https://theprint.in/opinion/kaiser-tufail-arun-prakash/37662/. Accessed on May 25, 2021.
52. Hussain and Qureshi, n. 2, pp. 188-189.
53. Ibid., pp. 190-193.
54. Haider, n. 21, ch 14.

55. Singh, et al., n. 1, p. 185.
56. Kaiser Tufail, "IAF's Balakot Disaster Two Years On," *Aeronaut,* February 26, 2021, http://kaiser-aeronaut.blogspot.com/. Accessed on May 25, 2021.
57. Singh, et al., n. 1, p. 185.
58. Khan, n. 17, p. 69.
59. Bilal Khan, "Pakistan Air Force: Combat Commanders School (CCS)," *QUWA,* October 16, 2016, https://quwa.org/2016/10/16/pakistan-air-force-combat-commanders-school-ccs/. Accessed on May 25, 2021.
60. Singh, et al., n. 1, p. 184.
61. Ibid., p. 186.

11. How did the 1971 War Alter Pakistan's Strategic Posture?

Shalini Chawla

The India-Pakistan relationship has gone through complex phases of dormant and intense hostility and tensions. The two nuclear armed neighbours have fought four conventional wars and have been dealing with the challenges of the threat of nuclear weapons (in their own respective ways!). While the bilateral relationship has been strained for most of the years, the terror attack on January 2, 2016, on the Pathankot Air Force Station was a big blow to the Modi government's peace initiatives towards Pakistan and led to complete suspension of the diplomatic dialogue between the two countries. On February 14, 2019, 40 Central Reserve Police Force jawans were killed in Pulwama, Jammu and Kashmir (J&K), in a gruesome terror attack claimed by the Pakistan sponsored Jaish-e-Muhammad (JeM). New Delhi reacted with punitive air strikes at Balakot in Khyber Pakhtunkhwa (KP) province of Pakistan, targeting the well acknowledged JeM training camp. Pakistan retaliated with offensive air strikes in J&K, which Islamabad claimed were demonstrative strikes indicating its capability and will to retaliate to India's military actions. The Indian government's decision to revoke Article 370 on August 5, 2019, which altered the special status granted to J&K, came as a surprise to Pakistan and since then, there has been a series of strong reactions/actions targeting India on the international front, attracting global attention and seeking mediation on Kashmir.

Pakistan's strategic posturing against India has revolved around the use of sub-conventional war, build-up of its conventional and nuclear capability, maintaining a projection of low nuclear threshold and intensifying the anti-India narrative at national and international fora. There have been alterations in the tactics and intensity of the posturing, but the underlying objectives and position have been consistent for the last fifty years. Pakistan, from the time of its birth has struggled with deep insecurity and an identity crisis, and this was reflected in its initial attempt to wage a war for Kashmir against India even while the partition was underway in 1947. Pakistan's India strategy evolved over the decades with the change in the power dynamics within Pakistan and the developments in geopolitics. The study of Pakistan's history suggests a significant shift in its thinking, actions, and strategy (vis-à-vis India) after its humiliating defeat in the 1971 War. Not only were the Pakistani leadership and populace disgraced and disgruntled with the division of the country but Pakistan was now convinced that it would not be possible to militarily defeat a conventionally superior India. Post 1971 War, two issues were critical for Pakistan: first, it was time for Pakistan to look for options to stay at par with India, if not defeat it; and second, at no cost allow further disintegration of Pakistan. Existing insurgency in Pakistan's tribal belt in Balochistan and restlessness in Khyber Pakhtunkhwa (then known as North-West Frontier Province – NWFP) posed a constant challenge to the ruling elites. It would be interesting to explore and analyse the shifts in Pakistan's strategic posture after the 1971 India-Pakistan War.

Determinants of Pakistan's Strategic Posture

Three critical factors, which are also interestingly interdependent, contribute in shaping Pakistan's strategic posture against New Delhi:

- **The Identity Crisis:** Pakistan has struggled with an identity crisis for over seven decades now. As a nation, Pakistan embraced and supported a complex set of contradictions in its beliefs, values and actions. Born as a Muslim state, it shared an ambiguous relationship with Islam: it aspired for the Western democratic ideas of modernity but supported an all-powerful military which never allowed democracy to flourish; it was proud to be an independent state but constantly struggled with insurgencies/opposition in its tribal areas and growing deep dissatisfaction in East Pakistan (before 1971). It claimed to be a democratic nation but remained hesitant to treat its citizens equally. The state suffered from an identity crisis, and religion has been used in Pakistan for reasons ranging from nation-building to strategic security.

- **Dominant Military Lobby:** Undoubtedly, the Army in Pakistan is a most organised and professional force whose power flows not only from the barrel of the gun but from its deep involvement in all important facets of the country. The military institution in Pakistan has managed to create, and sustain, an autonomous structure, financial freedom and flexibility for itself. The Army in Pakistan undertook the responsibility of not only guarding the nation's territories but also controlling the national policies, managing the economy, influencing the society, and, most importantly, guarding the ideological boundaries of the state. This self-built image of the Pakistan Army exceeds its effectiveness to manage the country and has progressively led the country into the mire of maladministration. The military never allowed the projected threat perception to scale down. Ambassador Hussain Haqqani very aptly stated:

  > Most nations raise an Army proportion to the size of the threat to their security. In Pakistan's case, the magnitude of security threats has been expanded to match the size of an Army inherited from the colonial era.[1]

- **Desire to Stay at Par with India's Defence Capability:** This has been a strong factor in shaping Pakistan's military doctrine, strategy and posture. Pakistan's desire to acquire high technology weapons, its alliance with the US (as early as in the 1950s), expanded strategic partnership with China, continued covert war against India and, very importantly, its ambiguous nuclear posture, with excessive reliance on a 'first use' doctrine reflect Islamabad's deep desire to neutralise India's conventional superiority.

Pakistan inherited certain complexities and the evolving power dynamics in the country which supported the build-up of the Army's powerful position, never allowed the complexities to settle down. From the time of its inception, Pakistan has writhed under perceived threat perceptions and is probably one of the most insecure nations, which diverts a major share of its national resources towards defence build-up.

The 1971 War: Assessing Shifts in Pakistan's Strategic Posture

Ideological Shift

The loss of East Pakistan not only altered the political and ethnic scenario in Pakistan but also the ideological dynamics of the country. More than the Indian or American response, what shocked the nation was the betrayal of Pakistan by East Pakistan itself. Pakistan justified the division by saying that the East Pakistanis – the Bengalis – were not true Pakistanis and, thus, not truly Islamic. This division of Pakistan created a fear of further segmentation, and the ruling elites increasingly believed that use of religious ideology would be the best option to unite people in the name of religion. Also, in the early 1970s, the disturbances in Balochistan created tremendous unrest and kept the leadership in Pakistan engaged. The Balochistan insurgency provided the military and the intelligence agencies in Pakistan an opportunity to project Afghanistan as an additional threat and to support the growing military expenditure, and maintain Pakistan's image as a garrison state.

The loss of East Pakistan and rise of insurgency in Balochistan created fear of further division and the leadership in Pakistan was inclined to adopt religious ideology as a counter to the perceived threat of 'division of Pakistan' and to motivate the nation for an aggressive anti-India posture (in the name of religion). The developments in Pakistan coincided with the global rise of Islamic ideology which facilitated Pakistan's journey into the radical ideology, pronounced by Zulfiqar Ali Bhutto and taken forward by General Zia-ul-Haq.

Global Rise of Islamic Ideology

The 1970s and 1980s witnessed the reemergence of Islam as a potent global force, starting with the spread of Saudi Wahhabi ideology. It was the Iranian revolution that shattered the secular basis of nationalist thinking and expectations of the modernisation and development theories. The revolution drew attention towards the significant changes that were taking place in many Muslim countries across the globe in the 1970s. Ironically, the revival of the Islamic ideology was most prominent in societies which were modern or in the process of modernisation, and having a well-trained, Western oriented, secular elite, for example, countries like Egypt, Lebanon, Tunisia, Turkey and Algeria.

In Egypt and Malaysia, the resurgence of Islam was manifested in the people's lives, the conventional religious beliefs and also the state politics. Religion came much more into practice and was reflected in the form of daily prayers, fasting and the way the people dressed. Muslim rulers emphasised on Islamic identity to gain legitimacy, and Islamic organisations and symbols assumed paramount importance for the state. Bhutto's turning towards Islam has to be studied taking into account the ideological developments worldwide.

Idea of an Islamic Pakistan

Pakistan was born as a result of the demand for a separate homeland for Muslims, as the All India Muslim League, led by Muhammad Ali Jinnah, strongly argued that Muslims had a special identity which would not be able to survive in a Hindu dominated society, thus, a separate homeland for Muslims was the only solution. But Jinnah's dream was quite different from what Pakistan eventually transformed into. There was lack of consensus over Pakistan's ideological and territorial contours, as Ayesha Jalal has pointed out:

> Jinnah's resort to religion was not on ideology to which he was ever committed or even a device to use against rival communities; it was simply a way of giving a semblance of unity and solidarity to his divided Muslim constituents. Jinnah needed a demand that was

> specifically ambiguous and imprecise to command general support, something specifically Muslim though unspecific in every other respect.[2]

Pakistan over the years drifted away from Jinnah's spirt, and the period post 1971 witnessed critical developments in Pakistan's ideological thinking and positioning. Bhutto turned towards Islam to counter his Islamic critics and to strengthen ties with the oil-rich nations of the Arabian Gulf. Islam in the 1970s and 1980s was used as a source of protest and opposition and to legitimise seizure of power. Ironically, it was the same Islamic ideology which was used by Gen Zia-ul-Haq to overthrow Bhutto.

Bhutto took forward the idea of *Islamic Socialism* and, thus, enforced Islam as a major factor in statecraft. Stephen Cohen rightly pointed out:

> If the Pakistan movement and the first twenty-five years of the history of Pakistan can be characterized as a struggle to turn Indian Muslims into Pakistanis, the years since 1972 have been an extension of the process; a struggle to turn Pakistanis into good Muslims.[3]

Bhutto's Islamic Socialism was considered insincere and it was seen more to establish the non-Indian identity of Pakistan.[4] Gen Zia put the state at the service of Islam and took steps to inculcate the Islamic practices within the state by banning alcohol and gambling, and declaring Friday as a non-working day (which was later revised by Nawaz Sharif).

General Zia-ul-Haq and Islamisation of the Pakistan Army

Gen Zia systematically reinforced the *Islamisation of Pakistan* which was propagated by his predecessor, Zulfiqar Ali Bhutto. Zia's vision was candidly pronounced in his own words:

> Pakistan, which was created in the name of Islam, will continue to survive only if it sticks to Islam. That is why I consider the introduction of the Islamic system as an essential prerequisite for the country.[5]

The General introduced mandatory 'Islamic Reforms' impacting the economy and Pakistani society. A number of banking and commercial practices based on Islam were introduced, a dress code in accordance with Islamic norms was stressed, new women's universities were proposed and strict regulations were imposed on the sale and consumption of alcoholic beverages.[6] The Pakistan Army in this period developed close links with the various Islamists groups, and religion was now used deeply in the strategic thinking. Zia, in the process of reinforcing the Islamisation of Pakistan and introducing Islamic reforms, allowed the Tablighi Jamaat (an Islamic missionary society) to operate freely within the Army. Zia was also the first Army Chief and the first politician in Pakistan to appear before the Tablighi's annual convention at Raiwind.[7]

It was during Zia's period that "Jihad" was included as the motto for the Pakistan Army apart from "Iman" and "Taqwa". Zia was entrusted with the task of Islamisation of the Pakistan Army when he took over as the Army Chief in 1976. Bhutto saw Zia as the right man to take the Pakistani military to the next stage of its evolution as the guarantor of an anti-India, Islamic ideology.[8] Zia, even as a Corps Commander, distributed books written by the Jamaat-e-Islami's founder, Maulana Sayyid Abdul Ala Maududi, as rewards for the officers who proved their calibre in various fields in his garrison. Adherence to the Islamic practices emerged as a major criterion for selection in the Army. According to Zia, a soldier had to be a true Muslim before he took on the responsibility of defending the Islamic Republic. In the armed forces, the status of the religious teachers was raised to the level of a commissioned officer. This became a major attraction for qualified individuals from universities and religious institutions.

Pakistan under Zia's regime, started to implement Islamic practices much more as compared to earlier political or military regimes in the country. The state was now being run on the values interpreted on the basis of religion. Perhaps the most critical part of this Islamisation was the impact on the education system of Pakistan, which shaped the young minds of the future generations. Islamic education during Zia's time gained the stature of a well-recognised and acceptable law governing the state structure, judiciary and also the military establishment to some extent. Very importantly, at the lower and middle levels of the military establishment, there was an emergence of radical military personnel who were *madrassa* graduates and were nurtured with the agenda of protecting Islam.

Islamic training and thought including lectures by Qayyum was introduced into the curriculum at the Command and Staff College. Qayyum, who resembles Iqbal in his writings, said that a Pakistani must not only be " a professional soldier, engineer, or doctor" but also "Muslim soldiers, Muslim engineers, Muslim doctors, Muslim officers and Muslim men".[9]

Although the students at the Staff College study Western strategy and doctrine, they are directed to intensify their core Islamic principles and values. Zia, in the process of reinforcing the Islamisation of Pakistan, encouraged the Tablighi Jamaat to operate freely within the Army. The Islamist parties and especially groups like the Tablighi Jamaat linked to the Deobandi tradition got much more access to the military officials. The 'Zia process' altered the culture of the military, and Islam became a critical factor in formulating military strategy and doctrine. *The soldiers of the state considered themselves soldiers of Islam.*

It was during this process of *Islamisation* that the major strategic development, the Afghan War, started and altered the dynamics of Pakistan's political, military and strategic policies. So, looking into history, one can say that in the 1980s, mainly two factors propagated the Islamic factor into the military: first was the 1971 War and the creation of Bangladesh: and, second, the Soviet invasion of Afghanistan which was viewed as an Islamic war against the Communist forces. Zia not only built an Army based on ideology but also fully supported the build-up of Pakistan's nuclear weapon capability (initiated by Bhutto!)

Making of a Bomb: Appeal for an Islamic Bomb

Pakistan's nuclear history can be traced back to as early as the 1950s when the US President made the "Atoms for Peace" proposal. The nuclear programme initially commenced with the objective of developing nuclear energy for civilian use, but Pakistan got serious about nuclear weapons after the 1971 War. After its third defeat against India, the Pakistani leadership was convinced that acquisition of nuclear weapons would neutralise India's conventional superiority. In the initial years from the early 1950s to 1971, Pakistan's official policy was build-up of the nuclear programme for the development of nuclear energy. Starting from the 1970s, under the leadership of Bhutto and, subsequently, in the coming decades, the development of the nuclear programme was shaped by increasing militarisation of Pakistan's state policies and its strategic alliances.

After the 1971 War, Prime Minister, Zulfiqar Ali Bhutto, who had been keen for Pakistan to acquire nuclear weapons even while he was in Ayub's Cabinet, made nuclear weapon capability a major public issue in spite of Ayub's antipathy to them. Bhutto was always inclined to have the nuclear capability as a deterrent. His conviction about nuclear deterrence strengthened after the 1971 War, when Pakistan did not receive the Chinese or US assistance. Also, Bhutto was not ready to accept any international norms and treaties restricting Pakistan's nuclear weapon development and insisted that acquisition of nuclear weapons was a *must* to match India's defence capability:

> All wars of our age have become total wars; all European strategy is based on the concept of total war; and it will have to be assumed that a war waged against Pakistan is capable of becoming a total war. It would be dangerous to plan for less and our plans should, therefore, include the nuclear deterrent. ... it is vital for Pakistan to give the greatest possible attention to nuclear technology, rather than allow herself to be deceived by an international treaty limiting this deterrent to the present nuclear powers.... If Pakistan restricts or suspends her nuclear programme, it would not only enable India to blackmail Pakistan with her nuclear advantage, but would impose a crippling limitation on the development of Pakistan's science and technology.[10]

1972: The Multan Meeting

Systematic efforts for building the nuclear weapon commenced after the 1971 War. Bhutto called for a secret meeting of top Pakistani scientists in Multan on January 20, 1972 and, curiously, the surreptitious meeting to discuss Pakistan's bomb was held under a *shamiana.* Khalid Hasan, the former press secretary to Bhutto, recollected and narrated Bhutto's words in the meeting. He told the authors of *The Islamic Bomb*, "Bhutto started slowly. He spoke of Pakistan's defeat and humiliation in the war with India, and vowed that he would vindicate the country's honour". He continued by saying that "he had always wanted Pakistan to take the nuclear road, but nobody had listened to him. Now fate had placed him in a position where he could make the decision, he had the people of Pakistan behind him, and he wanted to go ahead. Pakistan was going to have the bomb and the scientists sitting under the *shamiana* that day were going to make it for him."[11]

The meeting brought out the frustrations and complaints of the scientists regarding the bureaucratic hurdles and lack of leadership in the programme retarding the growth of the nuclear programme. Bhutto, as usual with his charismatic personality, was able to motivate the scientific community to get ready for building the bomb in three years instead of five years which the scientists had asked for. He received the enthusiastic response by the scientists "We can do it ... you will have the bomb!"[12]

The Islamic Bomb

After the Multan meeting, Bhutto made aggressive efforts to explore options to finance the nuclear weapon programme. He visited the Middle Eastern countries which included Iran, Saudi Arabia, Libya, Egypt, United Arab Emirates and Syria. The keenness of the Arab world to develop nuclear weapons did surface in a few reports in the past. In 1971, Col Gaddafi of Libya sent his Prime Minister to China to buy the nuclear bomb. He also approached France, Canada, West Germany, and even India, seeking assistance to build nuclear weapons in response to his offer of oil at low prices. The quest for nuclear weapons in the Arab world was because the Middle Eastern military balance had been predominantly in favour of Israel (suspected of testing a nuclear device in 1969) and the United States had made sure that the Israeli dominance in terms of conventional weapons would continue. This had led the Arab world, which had enough resources, to turn towards the nuclear option.[13] Thus, Bhutto's request for assistance received an enthusiastic response. He was looked upon as the champion of the Islamic cause. He was able to convince Saudi Arabia and Libya about the strong possibility of Pakistan being able to build a nuclear bomb as Pakistan's civilian nuclear programme had reached a level of erudition.[14] Though there is no direct evidence of the Libyan and Saudi support to Pakistan, it is believed that secret meetings were held in Paris to work out the modalities with representatives from Pakistan, Libya, Saudi Arabia and Iran. Bhutto did not have to wait too long for financial support from the Arab world. The prices of oil went up extensively following the international oil crisis in 1973. The moment was appropriate for Bhutto's appeal for financial assistance to support the 'Islamic Bomb'. In February 1974, he hosted an Islamic summit in Lahore, which was attended by the leaders of 37 Muslim countries. The forum laid the ground for an alliance between the wealthy Muslim nations and the poor Islamic countries, to fight the Zionists and their Western supporters.[15] According to some unidentified sources, as cited by Steve Weissman and Herbert Krosney (*The Islamic Bomb),* huge sums of money, close to a billion dollars, were raised for Pakistan. It is believed that Gaddafi and Bhutto came to a formal agreement in February 1974 during the Islamic summit hosted by Bhutto in Lahore, and Libya agreed to finance the entire Pakistani nuclear programme in return for the first bomb that was to be made. According to Mohammad Beg, a former Pakistani diplomat and journalist:

> Mr. Bhutto told me that during the Islamic summit in Lahore, he had several discussions with Colonel Gaddhafi about the manufacture of an atomic bomb by Pakistan … [Gaddhafi] promised Mr. Bhutto that he would provide however much money was needed. And, in return, he asked Mr. Bhutto if Libya could have the first bomb.[16]

Reportedly, in a few months two couriers from Libya reached Pakistan, each carrying $100 million in cash. The King of Saudi Arabia also offered financial support for the bomb and in return expected Pakistan to provide a security umbrella for the kingdom.[17] Libya, in return, desired complete access to nuclear technology and also wanted the Pakistani scientists to train Libyan technicians in the operation of hot cells, neutronics and the handling of nuclear waste.[18]

Continued Projection of a Low Nuclear Threshold and Uncertainty

Pakistan acquired nuclear weapons capability in 1987, although the overt nuclearisation happened much later in 1998. In the pre-nuclear test period, Pakistan's doctrine was that of ambiguity. Although, Pakistan even today does not have an officially announced doctrine, statements made by responsible policy-makers in Pakistan outline basic elements of its nuclear doctrine. There is an unofficial code adopted by the Pakistani leadership, based on *Indo-centricity, credible minimum deterrence, strategic restraint* and *first use.* Very interestingly and rather ironically, the code asserts on the principles of a peaceful programme revolving more around maintaining a balance against the Indian force build-up, but it includes making a first strike in response to not only a conventional attack by India but also a posed threat from India.

To deter India from using conventional force, Pakistan holds the position of first use, in case it "feels" the need. Pakistan did send a message to India as soon as it was ready with the bomb, regarding its willingness to use the nuclear weapon in the case of India's conventional move. A Q Khan in an interview to Kuldip Nayar said:

> If you ever drive us to the wall, we will use the bomb. You did it to us in East Bengal. We won't waste time with conventional weapons. We will come straight out with it.[19]

Nuclear weapons remain integral to Pakistan's overall strategic positioning against India. While New Delhi's nuclear objectives have been primarily political objective for deterrence, Islamabad acquired the nuclear weapons for *war prevention* and to conduct the policy of sub-conventional warfare through terrorism, without fear of Indian military retaliation. This explicitly explains Pakistan's nuclear positioning which relies on a *first use doctrine* projecting a low nuclear threshold and an element of uncertainty.[20]

The Quranic Concept of War

Post 1971 War, a strong tide of Islamisation dominated the strategic thinking of the Pakistani leadership. Zia's active plan for the Islamisation of the Pakistan Army derived support from the interpretation of the teachings of the Holy Quran. The Holy Quran has been interpreted (to facilitate the strategic objectives) to develop Pakistan's doctrine and strategy of war.

The most comprehensive and precise study on war doctrine and strategy in the context of the Holy Quran has been by Brig S.K. Malik in his book, *The Quranic Concept of War*. According to Brig Malik's interpretation, the Holy Quran places war doctrine, its theory, and practice as very different from the Western thinking on the subject. Brig Malik interprets that "the Holy Quran has given a comprehensive treatment to its concept of war" and "determines all aspects of the use of 'force' in inter-state relations."[21] Brig Malik in his work regards the Quranic philosophy of war as supreme which provides directions for the initiation, planning and control of war. According to his interpretation, the very "initiation of war is for the cause of God" and *jihad* is the "most glorious word in the vocabulary of Islam". Gen Zia enthusiastically sponsored and supported the Brigadier's work and in his foreword for the book, he suggested:

> The professional soldier in a Muslim Army, pursuing the goals of a Muslim state, CANNOT become 'professional' if in all his activities he does not take on the colour of Allah.[22]

Terror, according to the author and the majority of the Pakistani military officers, is central to the war strategy. Use of terror as an instrument to impose your will and decisions on the enemy has been legitimised citing examples from the Holy Quran and arriving at the conclusion that, "When God wishes to impose His will upon his enemies, He chooses to do so by casting terror in their hearts".[23]

The Islamic concept as derived from the Holy Quran by Brig Malik relies on the use of terror in the preparation stages of war itself in order to assure victory and achieve direct results.[24] Thus, terror has been legitimised in the Islamic ideology which has till today shaped the military strategy of Pakistan. Brig Malik asserts, "Terror struck into the hearts of the enemies is not only a means, it is the end in itself."[25] War strategy, according to the Holy Quran, might have different forms depending on various factors but it must be effective and capable of striking terror into the hearts of enemies. It is emphasised that *fear* has to be an important part of the preparation of war and it determines that "the test of utmost preparation lies in our capability to instil terror into the hearts of the enemies"[26]

The Quranic 'misinterpretation' of the conduct of modern war legitimises *jihad* and the use of terror. One of the most effective modes of generating terror is through the projection of a *low nuclear threshold* and *covert warfare* and, thus, creating physical and mental unrest and fear in the enemy territory. Pakistan's strategic thinking and posture reflect its belief in using terror as an effective instrument of war.

Pakistan's Grand Strategy

The grand strategy has been formulated and evolved on the perceived Indian threat and Pakistan's Kashmir agenda. This has allowed the rise of the military in the country's power structure and facilitated its image as a 'nation-builder' and sole guardian of the sovereignty and survival of Pakistan. The 1971 War was critical in shaping Pakistan's strategic choices and alliances. Pakistan's grand strategy after 1971 incorporated two important objectives which decided the future course of action for the Pakistani leadership:

First, to expand territory eastward (take Kashmir). This implied a rise in covert activities in J&K and added emphasis on radical Islam in the name of *jihad*. Thus, terrorism was to be adopted as a foreign policy tool.

Second, to expand control westward (to gain leverage in Kabul). This implied creating strategic depth in Afghanistan and also facilitating a Pakistan friendly government.

Pakistan's Covert War: Terrorism as a Foreign Policy Tool

Pakistan opted for the covert route in its first aggression in 1947, which had the concurrence of the Pakistani leadership. The Pakistan Army, with the approval of the political leadership, decided to exploit a local uprising which had broken out in Poonch, hence, taking the initial step in covert warfare. Pakistan accelerated its infiltration activities and in order to carry out guerrilla warfare operations, sent a large number of Pathan tribesmen, Punjabis and other Pakistani nationals to defeat the J&K State Forces.

The aggression of 1947-48, formed the basic guidelines for Pakistan's future military strategy against India. The war established the pattern of Pakistan's covert war strategy as an important component of its grand strategy. The Pakistan Army leadership learnt many lessons to improve its strategy. The ceasefire agreement of 1949 failed to stop Pakistan in its covert actions in the Kashmir Valley. During the 1965 War, Operation Gibraltar was the covert component and again, in 1999, the Kargil War started under the guise of infiltration by the militants.

In the late 1960s and 1970s, there was a significant shift in Pakistan's posture. Religion had started to gain momentum in Pakistan due to the ideological orientation, and the leadership saw religion as a binding force for the nation that would potentially prevent further disintegration of the country. In the 1970s, the religious ideology flourished with Bhutto's Islamic state policy and *jihad* became the tool for Kashmir. *Jihad* was also used to legitimise the diversion of national resources towards the build-up of conventional military force and the nuclear weapons programme.

Pakistan's covert war became more organised in the 1970s with a clear objective of not only conducting terrorism in the Kashmir Valley but also, now motivating people in the name of *jihad* and garnering popular support. It is also interesting to note that in pursuit of the covert strategy, Pakistan did not limit itself to Islam. It was willing to promote terrorism and create terrorists from even other religions. For example, in the 1970s, it started to fund, encourage and support the Sikh separatist organisation, the Khalistan movement. Gen Yahya Khan invited Dr. Jagjit Singh Chauhan, who took over the leadership of the Khalistan movement, to Pakistan, and welcomed him as a leader of the Indian Sikh community.[27]

Starting in the 1970s, Pakistan moved towards increasing Islamisation which shaped the military's mindset and also intensified the covert war. In the 1970s and 1980s, Pakistan's strategy in Kashmir relied mainly on two factors: their own Islamisation – Kashmir became important from the ideological point of view; and secondly, efforts to garner the support of the people in Kashmir. Pakistan adopted a two-pronged approach to garner the people's support: it encouraged alienation of the people through propaganda on the basis of the Islamic factor and by propagating the idea that Kashmir was illegally occupied by India. While Pakistan was preparing itself for a more aggressive approach in the 1970s, the Soviet occupation of Afghanistan in 1979 altered the strategic dynamics in Pakistan's favour. Pakistan became the frontline state for the United States, received generous military assistance from the US, and Gen Zia's military regime undertook the responsibility of training the Mujahideen to conduct covert operations to fight the Soviets. The operations directed by the US comprised one of the largest planned by the US and shaped a relationship between the Central Intelligence Agency (CIA) and the Pakistani intelligence agency, the Inter-Services Intelligence (ISI) as the two worked and coordinated for about a decade. The US' war in Afghanistan in the 1980s led to structural and organisational development of the factor of religion in war. The declaration of *jihad* in Afghanistan led to the legitimised institutional development, preparing young fighters to fight the Russians.

In the 1980s, religious resurgence, coupled with increasing alienation of the youth for diverse reasons, started to grow in Kashmir, and Pakistan's strategy began to concretise. The insurgency in Kashmir became much more organised after 1988. The militants gained experience in Afghanistan and were more professional in conducting sub-conventional warfare. Highly trained Mujahideen, many of them professional Special Forces, and terrorists, joined the fighting in Kashmir. The ISI nurtured and trained the anti-India groups which have continued to be the military's assets and have been used successfully as proxies against India till date. In the 1990s and 2000s, Pakistan's covert war expanded to other parts of India with much more intensity.

Desire for Strategic Depth and Control over Afghanistan

One can presume that the desire for strategic depth would have started to be nurtured after Pakistan's defeat in the 1971 War, in which it lost a significant portion of its military assets also. It was after 1971 that Bhutto propagated the concept that Pakistan is not just a South Asian state but also a West Asian one. The Army under Gen Zia-ul-Haq (since 1976) projected itself as the defender of not only the territorial boundaries of the state but also the 'ideological boundaries'. Strategic depth in this respect was interpreted to include the Muslim nations in order to gain support on varied fronts, including funding of Pakistan's nuclear programme which commenced in 1971.

Without going into the details of Pakistan's Afghanistan policy, it will not be incorrect to say that Pakistan has been overly obsessed with the desire to gain strategic depth in Afghanistan. The all-powerful military and the intelligence agency, ISI, which authored and executed the policy of strategic depth since the late 1980s through the 1990s when they strongly backed the Taliban, till today believe in having strong control over Afghanistan. At no stage was the policy of "strategic depth" logical or viable for Pakistan and its adoption of the doctrine of strategic depth and, thus, control over Afghanistan has been considered a strategic blunder which facilitated Pakistan's drift into extremism.

Revocation of Article 370: Pakistan's Strategic Posture Today

Pakistan's strategic posturing evolved post 1971 War and has revolved around the *projection of (perceived) threat perceptions, projection of victimhood and nuclear brinkmanship.* Its threat perceptions and desire to stay at par with India inclined it to join and sustain alliances with the major powers – the United States and China – and seek support from the Muslim world. Pakistan judiciously managed a rather unique set of alliances (with the US and China) at the same time.

Revocation of Article 370 by India challenged the centrality of the military's positioning and actions. Pakistan's position on Kashmir – which it claimed for decades as an *unfinished agenda of the partition* – was questioned. There has been frustration, anger and helplessness in the regime and varied reactions were seen targeting the Indian leadership. There has also been an effort to garner support from the international community in support of Pakistan's position on Kashmir.

Pakistan's strategic posture post revocation of Article 370 can be described as follows.

Highlighting Threat Perceptions

Pakistan has long held the narrative of its (perceived) threat perceptions. From the time of its creation, Pakistan has suffered a deep sense of insecurity owing to its geography, small size, having a (perceived) hegemonic neighbour India and insurgencies within. The narrative of threat perceptions have been sustained to allow the dominance of the military, justify the covert war against India and diversion of substantial national resources towards defence spending. This narrative of threat perceptions is likely to further strengthen in Pakistan which is apparent from the statements coming from the Pakistani leadership. Imran Khan has claimed, "The Hindu supremacist Modi government poses a threat to Pakistan as well as the minorities in India". The effort to highlight the threat posed to Pakistan's existence is likely to continue at the domestic as well as international front.

While highlighting the threat perceptions is not new in Pakistan, the difference that one sees now is that there is an effort to drive a revised narrative of India's image. The revised narrative is based on India being run on a Nazi ideology. The effort is also to project that "India is a threat to the existence of Pakistan and to the Muslims of the world."

Prime Minister Imran Khan made multiple statements on social media describing the current Indian posturing as a threat to the minorities of the world.

Projection of Victimhood

Projection of victimhood has been a strong factor in Pakistan's positioning. Portrayal of victimhood (in the past and now) allowed Pakistan to attract enormous financial, military and diplomatic support from the Western world and China. The projection has been used to legitimise Pakistan's sub-conventional war for the last five decades in the Kashmir Valley and other parts of India (and in Afghanistan). The narrative has been maintained gradually and strongly after 9/11 when its counter-terrorism willingness and capability were repeatedly questioned by the United States. Post 9/11, Pakistan did manage to receive over $30 billion of US aid on the pretext of being the frontline state in the war on terror and also to fight insurgency and terrorism within Pakistan. Its alliance with the United States post 9/11 helped the recovery of Pakistan's ailing economy and opened the long-desired supplies of defence equipment from Washington. According to the US Department of State, the US overt security related aid and assistance to Pakistan stood at approximately $16.9 billion during 2002-2012.[28] It is interesting to note that the arms deliveries to Pakistan in the period 1999-2006 amounted to $4.6 billion[29] at an average of $575 million per annum. The US military sales were substantially reduced by the Trump Administration owing to the US' displeasure over Pakistan's sustained support to the Afghan Taliban and the Haqqani network in Afghanistan.

This narrative of victimhood has continued with the insistence that Pakistan has been compelled to act and behave aggressively owing to India's actions and positioning in Kashmir. Pakistan has often taken the position that the US has been responsible for radicalisation in Pakistan. At the Council on Foreign Relations, New York, Imran Khan said:

> Pakistan, by joining the US after 9/11, committed one of the biggest blunders. Seventy thousand Pakistanis died in this. We had, some say, over a hundred and fifty billion, say two hundred billion ... some economists, Pakistanis ... two hundred billion lost to the economy. And on top of it, we were blamed for the US not winning in Afghanistan. I thought it was the worst period for Pakistan.[30]

With the Biden Administration coming in, Pakistan has been keen to revive its relationship with the United States. After Biden's announcement of withdrawal from Afghanistan by September 11, 2021, the situation in Afghanistan has worsened and the Taliban has intensified fighting and is increasingly taking control of the Afghan territory (at the time of writing this chapter). Pakistan has supported the Taliban throughout and has a sense of victory in Kabul with the US withdrawal but the positioning once again, as we see lately, is of victimhood! There have been frequent statements claiming that Pakistan is very concerned about the severe security implications of the rising instability in Afghanistan.

Highlighting Islamophobia

Islamophobia has been a crucial factor in Pakistan's positioning in the recent times. Imran Khan's speech at the 74th session of the United National General Assembly had several references to Islamophobia:

> There are 1.3 billion Muslims in the world. Muslims living across all continents. Islamophobia has grown since 9/11 and it is alarming. It is creating divisions.... We failed as the Muslim world to explain that there is no such thing as radical Islam. In Pakistan, we were the eye of the storm and our government coined the term "enlightened moderation"... the West could not understand what was the problem. They don't look at religion the way we do. And so, in their eyes, Islam was an intolerant religion. It became a watershed.[31]

Talking of Islamophobia does complement Pakistan's projected victimhood and also strengthens its position amongst the Muslim nations. Pakistan did manage to get robust support from Turkey and Malaysia on the Kashmir narrative.

Nuclear Brinkmanship

Imran Khan has repeatedly flagged the possibility of a 'nuclear war' post revocation of Article 370. Highlighting the nuclear factor by Pakistan displays its immaturity and desperation to attract global attention towards Kashmir. Prime Minister Imran Khan, in his unrelenting tweets has repeatedly highlighted various aspects of the nuclear threat, for example, both India and Pakistan possess nuclear weapons and, thus, any crisis in the region is alarming; Pakistan has nuclear weapons and, thus, the probability of a nuclear war is high; India's nuclear weapons are a threat to global and regional security, etc.

Pakistan has used the nuclear card in the past spasmodically and this stems from its basic insecurity as a state and its failure to develop its strengths. Islamabad has long tried to balance its domestic vulnerabilities with the nuclear weapons which it treats as the ultimate guarantor of its survivability and security. Its nuclear history and thinking explicitly explain its nuclear behaviour and brinkmanship that we see today.

Pakistan's nuclear posturing did suffer a blow to some extent with India's air strikes in Balakot on February 26, 2019. But, it seems that Pakistan's reliance on nuclear weapons to serve its strategic objectives has not been altered. Its reliance on nuclear deterrence has intensified with the constantly growing asymmetries between India and Pakistan over the last two decades. Pakistan's repeatedly flagging of the nuclear threat could be attributed to mainly two factors:

- First, Pakistan has spent an enormous amount of national resources in the build-up of the nuclear arsenal on the pretext that nuclear weapons are the ultimate weapons for the state's survival and security. Pakistan has always prioritised its defence expenditure even though it has been at the cost of the socioeconomic development of the country. The leadership at this point wants to justify the enormous nuclear build-up to its own population and assure them that nuclear weapons will ultimately guard Pakistan's fortune.

- Second, Imran Khan wants to remind India and the international community about the presence of nuclear weapons in the region and the dangers emanating from a potential nuclear war. Pakistan is certainly trying hard to get the international attention on Kashmir by flagging the nuclear threat.

Growing Reliance on China

China's assistance to Pakistan over the last six decades has expanded from a purely military relationship to economic and diplomatic levels. Beijing's all-out support to Pakistan provided it room to shrink its reliance on the West (especially the US). Importantly, Pakistan's military build-up has continued with Chinese defence imports despite severe economic challenges. In the last two decades, the focus of Pakistan's arms procurement has been modernisation of the Air Force and build-up of the maritime aerial strike capabilities of the Navy. In this regard, technology transfer from China has been a key feature. Pakistan has been very proud of the Chinese fourth generation fighter aircraft JF-17s (earlier called the FC-1). Although the initial announcement by the Pakistan Air Force (PAF) indicated acquiring 150 JF-17s, the current execution of the procurement/production plans indicates that the PAF intends having a higher number of JF-17s in its inventory. The JF-17 is co-developed by Pakistan and China and is being built by China's Chengdu Aircraft Industry Corporation (CAC) and the Pakistan Aeronautical Complex (PAC). Regarding the co-production of the aircraft, reports suggest that PAC has been producing 58 per cent of the JF-17s' airframe, and the CAC 42 per cent.[32] Pakistan has received the JF-17 Block I and II, and Block III is awaited.

Post revocation of Article 370, China's unflinching support to Pakistan has been discernible. Beijing used its position in the United Nations to call for a closed door meeting at the Security Council to discuss Kashmir after the revocation of Article 370, guarded Islamabad's case at the Financial Action Task Force (FATF) to restrain blacklisting of Pakistan, and, very importantly, has offered to extend military support to strengthen Pakistan's position in the wake of rising tensions between India and Pakistan. China has reportedly offered to deploy a certain number of the upgraded version of JH-7A II fighters on the Sino-Pak border.

An "official Chinese-language media report" dated September 28, 2019 (translation done by the Centre for China Analysis and Strategy, New Delhi) stated:

> In the face of the strong Indian Air Force, Pakistan's efforts are clearly not enough. China, on the other hand, could help Pakistan turn the tables by providing a fighter which will have remarkable "strength multiplication" combat efficiency.

According to the report, against the backdrop of India-Pak confrontation, the Chinese aircraft (JH-7AII variant) "can not only effectively suppress air defense system of Indian troops; all the more can let Pakistani fighters hold superiority in the air confrontation."

Beijing feels that Pakistan's economy is not in a position to deal with the "urgent needs of war" and, thus, China's offer would leverage the powerful air combat effectiveness of the JH-7 AII for strength multiplication and achieve victory for Pakistan. The JH-7AII variant is reportedly equipped with a more advanced radar and avionics system, enhancing its flight performance. While the details of this move by Beijing are not fully known, the fact is that this indicates that China is clearly thinking in terms of offering direct military support to Pakistan to deal with any scenario of a probable India-Pak conflict.

Conclusions

Pakistan's strategic posture against New Delhi is likely to focus on the following fronts:

- Pakistan will continue with its aggressive diplomatic campaign against India and the revised narrative of India will continue to evolve.

- On the domestic front, Pakistan will continue its assertion on *Kashmir Banega Pakistan.* Efforts to internationalise Kashmir and attract global attention towards it will continue. Imran Khan, in his article in *The New York Times*, stated, "If the world does nothing to stop the Indian assault on Kashmir and its people, two nuclear-armed states will get ever closer to a direct military confrontation."[33]
- Projection of victimhood is likely to be strengthened. The leadership will continue to shift the blame for radicalisation and terrorism on the US and India.
- Nuclear brinkmanship is critical for Pakistan's strategic posturing and the central assumption on which Pakistan has progressed and built up its nuclear arsenal is that a credible nuclear deterrent would compensate for the inferiority of its defence forces and their small size. Pakistan has conducted covert war against India under the nuclear umbrella for over four decades now. Although its low threshold projection has been challenged by New Delhi, Pakistan's reliance on nuclear deterrence will intensify with the growing asymmetries between India and Pakistan.
- Pakistan's reliance on sub-conventional war is unlikely to alter any time soon. The covert war is likely to intensify with the Taliban being in a strong position in Afghanistan.
- Pakistan is likely to highlight Islamophobia at the international level to facilitate extended support from the Muslim nations for its Kashmir agenda.
- The momentum of the growing Sino-Pak alliance is unlikely to slowdown any time soon. With the US pullout from Afghanistan, China is aiming to play an active role in Afghanistan and will accept Pakistan's assistance in this regard. There have been reports of a few challenges in the China-Pakistan Economic Corridor (CPEC) projects. But will these challenges impact the Sino-Pak alliance? The answer is NO. Beijing's continued strong support for Pakistan's strategic posture is not unpredictable. Defence imports from China are likely to continue, reducing Pakistan's reliance on the Western military equipment.

- Pakistan's partnership with Turkey is likely to grow as the two have common strategic interests. Both Pakistan and Turkey need friends at this moment and the evolving partnership is mutually welcomed.

Disclaimer: Parts of the chapter have previously been published as Dr Shalini Chawla, "Abrogation of Article 370 and Pakistan's Strategic Posture", in Vijay Sakhuja ed., *Pentagon Yearbook South Asia Defence and Strategic Perspective 2020* (New Delhi: Pentagon Press, 2020), pp. 11-22.

Notes

1. Hussain Haqqani, *Reimagining Pakistan: Transforming A Dysfunctional Nuclear State* (Noida: HarperCollins, 2018), p. 161.
2. Ayesha Jalal, *The State of Martial Rule* (Cambridge: Cambridge University Press, 1990), p. 16.
3. Stephen Cohen, *The Pakistan Army* (Karachi: Oxford University Press, 1998), p. 89.
4. See Stephen Cohen, *The Idea of Pakistan* (New York: Oxford University Press, 2005), p. 170.
5. "General Zia ul-Haq's Address to the Nation on July 5, 1977", quoted in Hasan Askari Rizvi, *The Military and Politics in Pakistan 1947-1986* (Lahore: Progressive Publishers, 1986), pp. 289-293.
6. Cohen, n. 3, p. 91.
7. Cohen, n. 4, p. 113.
8. Husain Haqqani, *Pakistan: Between Mosque and Military* (Lahore: Vanguard Books, 2005), p. 112.
9. *On Striving to be a Muslim* (Lahore: Islamic Book Centre, 1978) as cited by Cohen, n. 3, pp. 95-96.
10. Zulfiqar Ali Bhutto, *The Myth of Independence* (London: Oxford University Press, 1969), p. 153.
11. Steve Weissman and Herbert Krosney, *The Islamic Bomb* (New York: Times Books, 1981), pp. 17-18.
12. An account of the Multan meeting can be found in Shahid ur Rehman, *Long Road to Chagai: Untold Story of Pakistan's Nuclear Quest* (Islamabad: Printwise Publication, 1999), pp. 16-19. Also see Zahid Malik, *Dr A.Q Khan and The Islamic Bomb* (Islamabad: Hurmat Publication, 1992), p. 128, as cited in Owen Benett Jones, *Pakistan Eye of the Storm* (New Delhi: Penguin Books, 2001), p. 196.
13. Major Gen D K Palit and PKS Namboodiri, *Pakistan's Islamic Bomb* (New Delhi: Vikas Publishing House, 1979). p. 6.
14. Ibid., pp. 6-7.
15. Douglas Frantz and Catherine Collins, *The Man From Pakistan: The True Story of the World's Most Dangerous Smuggler* (New York: Twelve, 2007), p. 22.
16. Ibid., p. 22.
17. Ibid.
18. Weissman and Krosney, n. 11, p. 67.

19. "'If you drive us to the wall, we will use the bomb' – In December 1986, India launched the largest war game ever. Pakistan responded with a message of its own". *The Telegraph*, November 4, 2007, https://www.telegraphindia.com/7-days/if-you-drive-us-to-the-wall-we-will-use-the-bomb-in-december-1986-india-launched-the-largest-war-game-ever-pakistan-responded-with-a-message-of-its-own/cid/1534921. Accessed on June 20, 2021.
20. For details, see "Pakistan's Nuclear Brinkmanship", in Tilak Devasher, ed., *Pakistan Insights 2020* (New Delhi: Pentagon, 2021), pp. 103-111.
21. Brig S.K. Malik, *The Quaranic Concept of War* (New Delhi: Himalayan Books, 1986), p. 1.
22. Ibid., Foreword by Zia-ul-Haq.
23. Ibid., p. 57.
24. Ibid.
25. Ibid., p. 59.
26. Ibid., p. 144.
27. See B. Raman, *The Kaoboys of R&W: Down Memory Lane* (New Delhi: Lancer, 2007).
28. Susan B. Epstein and K. Alan Kronstadt, "Pakistan: U.S. Foreign Assistance", *Congressional Research Service Report for Congress*, October 4, 2012, https://www.refword.org/pdfid/508911b72.pdf, p. 20. Assessed on June 20, 2015.
29. Richard F. Grimmett, *CRS Report for Congress; Conventional Arms Transfers to Developing Nations, 1999-2006,* September 26, 2007, p. 67, https://fas.org/sgp/crs/weapons/RL34187.pdf. Accessed on June 30, 2021.
30. "A Conversation with Prime Minister Imran Khan of Pakistan", Council on Foreign Relations, September 23, 2019, https://www.cfr.org/event/conversation-prime-minister-imran-khan-pakistan-0. Accessed on October 10, 2019.
31. Full Transcript of Prime Minister Imran Khan's Speech at the UNGA, *Business Recorder*, September 27, 2019, https://www.brecorder.com/2019/09/27/524851/full-transcript-of-prime-minister-imran-khans-speech-at-the-unga/. Accessed on September 30, 2019.
32. Franz-Stefan Gady, "China Overhauls Pakistan Air Force JF-17 Fighter Jet", *The Diplomat*, May 22, 2019, https://thediplomat.com/2019/05/china-overhauls-pakistan-air-force-jf-17-fighter-jet/. Accessed on June1, 2019. Also, see "JF-17 Thunder Aircraft", Pakistan Aeronautical Complex, Kamra, https://www.pac.org.pk/jf-17. Accessed on May 1, 2021.
33. "Imran Khan: The World Can't Ignore. We are all in Danger", *The New York Times,* August 30, 2019, https://www.nytimes.com/2019/08/30/opinion/imran-khan-kashmir-pakistan.html. Accessed on September 2, 2019.

12. Fifty Years after the 1971 War: Revisiting India's National Strategy

Kapil Kak

The crisis that erupted in Pakistan towards end-1970 was not a political or ideological one. Its roots lay in Pakistan's inability or unwillingness, or both, to substantially address the issue of its pronounced ethnic fault lines. Even five decades later, Pakistan is unable to resolve this key national security imperative. Back then, the Bengali population, which comprised 60 per cent of Pakistan, and had suffered as second-class citizens since Pakistan's very inception, saw a rare opportunity in the 1970 elections. They believed they could at last establish themselves as equals with the Western part.

The announcement of elections was made by President Yahya Khan in the hope that the results would be inconclusive, leaving the political initiative and the balance of power within the country in the hands of the martial law administrator. But "whatever hope there may have been of an inconclusive result were dashed by the effect of the East Pakistani flood and cyclone disasters at the last stages of the election campaign. The incompetence of the administrative response and the apparent lack of West Pakistani interest gave powerful support to Sheikh Mujib's complaints about the impact of rule from Islamabad."[1]

In the elections, Sheikh Mujib's Awami League obtained a clear and convincing majority. According to the law, Constitution and convention, he should have been called by Yahya Khan to form the democratically-elected Government of Pakistan, as its Prime Minister. But, Zulfiqar Ali Bhutto, the ambitious West Pakistani political leader would have none of that. He misled and beguiled Yahya "not to follow up the result of the elections by allowing Sheikh Mujibur Rahman to become the prime minister of the whole of Pakistan."[2] "Because of West Pakistanis' hatred of Bengalis and fear of losing power, Bhutto and the Army formed a temporary alliance to check Rahman and stall the democratic process. In these circumstances, Rahman and his party despaired of gaining power by constitutional means".[3]

Bhutto's obsessive ambition to become the undisputed Pakistani leader; if not that, then, at least of West Pakistan, no matter at what cost, thus, became the nub of Pakistan's severest crisis since its creation. As TN Kaul avers, "The military leadership of Pakistan fell into Bhutto's trap and started an unprecedented campaign of atrocities, suppression of Bengalis, oppression of intellectuals and minorities with such ruthlessness and cruelty as had not been seen since Hitler's days".[4] This, indeed, was the second trigger for the commencement of the war of liberation in Bangladesh into which India got embroiled, the first unquestionably being the denial of democratic rights to the people of East Bengal following the 1970 elections.

Through his policy aimed at violently crushing the autonomy movement in East Bengal, arresting Mujib, dubbing him a traitor and outlawing the Awami League, Yahya Khan had taken a stand which left him (and Pakistan) with little room for retreat. An Army climb-down or compromise with Sheikh Mujib or the Awami League might have discredited him. But the ruling coterie in West Pakistan, which had been thriving so far by exploiting the resources of East Bengal would not have allowed him to do so even if he might have decided to go in for a compromise. The ambitious Army hawks, on whom Yahya Khan depended much for his support within the establishment, might have overthrown him had he decided to soften his stand.[5]

An important development was Pakistan's mischief in the middle of its preoccupations relating to the election results. An Indian Airlines Fokker Friendship aircraft was hijacked to Lahore and destroyed by Pakistani agents and militants from Jammu and Kashmir (J&K) on January 30, 1971. India played a strategic master stroke by suspending over-flights of all Pakistani aircraft, civil and military. This key decision was to impose severe constraints on the ability of Pakistan later, at the height of the crisis in October-November 1971, to build up its forces in East Bengal. Ten months after the Indian ban on Pakistani over-flights, US Secretary of State Rogers in a meeting with President Nixon on November 24, 1971, told him, "It is a 2,500 mile flight to resupply the troops in East Pakistan ... the logistics, you know are impossible ... my own judgment is that probably it will get worse".[6]

Refugee Influx: Security Compulsions

The gravest threat to India's security, stability and well-being arose from the massive and unending influx of millions of refugees driven out of their homes by the holocaust against them by the Pakistan Army from March 25, 1971, onwards. This was perhaps the sole reason for the conflict that followed. The number of refugees swelled from a quarter of a million on April 21, to 1.48 million by May 6, mostly into the states of West Bengal, Assam, Meghalaya and Tripura.

The threat perception arising from the refugee influx acquired grave proportions when the number progressively increased to reach 6 million in July, to eventually peak at 9 million by November. Pakistan had successfully pushed out 8-10 per cent of East Bengal's population into India! Articulating Pakistan's export of its internal security threat to India as constituting a challenge to our national interests, Indira Gandhi, in a speech on May 24, rightly commented, "What was claimed as an internal problem of Pakistan has also become an internal problem of India".

As to the unbearable pressures on the fledgling Indian infrastructure to assist the refugees, AP Venkateswaran, then Joint Secretary, Soviet and East Europe Division, Ministry of External Affairs (MEA) and later Foreign Secretary, recalled to this writer, "I visited many refugee camps, located in public offices and government schools in flood and cyclone-ravaged areas, where food and shelter were being provided. The situation could be described as a human catastrophe. It was common to have 30-40 children accommodated in a tiny room. The stench of human excreta was unbearable. In my assessment, war appeared inevitable. How long could this go on?"[7]

The presence and continued influx of refugees justifiably generated security apprehensions in the minds of the public and the political and military leadership alike. There was apprehension in the Parliament about whether forcing millions of refugees into another country should not be included in the definition of aggression. Jayaprakash Narayan, the avowed Gandhian, demanded a military attack on Pakistan. The impact of the refugee crisis on national interests had multiple dimensions.

First, the Pakistan Army's hot pursuit of Bangladeshi rebels created insecurities along and around the border. A large number of Pakistani intelligence agents, posing as refugees, reportedly entered India and tried to cause communal strife and indulge in sabotage. By the end of August 1971, at least four hundred trained Pakistani agents had been rounded up in Assam and Meghalaya.

Second, the negative impact on socio-economic development, specifically of the relatively more poverty-stricken West-East Bengal border region was evident. Third, the concentration of refugees in a small area of West Bengal had the potential to generate tensions in a state where conditions were already unsettled. On the other hand, dispersal to other parts of the country would have only tempted Pakistan to push out even more Bengali people. Fourth, large numbers of refugees were concentrated on the border, and with the continued inflow, especially of Hindu minorities, there were apprehensions of major communal violence in West Bengal and Assam, the states most affected. In hindsight, it is a tribute to the people of India that they demonstrated an innate commitment to the cherished core value of secularism throughout the refugee influx. But would it have been wise to bet on this scenario should the crisis have prolonged?[8]

India's National Interest Protection

Indian armed forces and the intelligence services were watching the development of the constitutional crisis in Pakistan and the grave problem of refugee influx with close attention. But as a foreign chronicler stated, "Their advice to the Cabinet at the end of March '71 appears to have been that India was not ready for immediate intervention in East Bengal and that any military action to help the Bengalis would have to wait"[9] In that sense, the Pakistan Army's increasingly hardening stand on non-acceptance of the legitimate political demands of the Awami League and the persistent crackdown were perhaps encouraged by the realisation in early summer that India was unlikely to react militarily.

Unsurprisingly, in her speech at Ranikhet as well as in Parliament in the first week of June, Indira Gandhi ominously warned that if the international community did not act early, India would be compelled to consider "other solutions to this problem". To be sure, international concern for the plight of the refugees led, in almost every country, including the US and Europe, to the build-up of sympathy of the general public, civil society and media towards India, and hostility towards Pakistan. The question is: how did India plug-in this sympathy factor into the East Bengal crisis and the related policy calculus? As JN Dixit states, "The Government of India decided on a two-track approach to resolve the East Bengal crisis. Firstly, to support the liberation struggle to exert pressure on the Pakistan government to respect the electoral verdict of '71. Secondly, mobilise international public opinion through bilateral contacts and the UN. While India successfully followed the first track, the second track was beset with several hurdles, particularly because of US support to the Pakistani regime."[10] China's espousal of the Pakistani position, and, more significantly, the China-US collusion exacerbated India's external challenges. This aspect is addressed in more detail subsequently.

India's consistent stance during the security crisis of March-November, 1971 was based on the assessment that its interests would be best served by bringing diplomatic pressure to bear on Pakistan through the influence of international opinion. It was believed that this approach – logical and well-reasoned, as the Pakistanis should have perceived – would lead to a negotiated settlement to create space for the Mukti Bahini, the liberation force, and accommodate East Bengali aspirations within Pakistan. But the short-sighted and mulish attitude of the Pakistani rulers – strongly supported by the US and China – matched by the equally determined resolve of the East Bengali population to go their own way, in the face of the reign of terror unleashed against them, rendered this policy option a *non sequitur*.

In line with the above-mentioned thinking, External Affairs Minister Swaran Singh told the UN General Assembly in September, "A political settlement acceptable to the people of East Bengal was the only way to resolve the conflict and help the refugees to return to their homes."[11] Indira Gandhi, during her six-nation tour in November, made it clear at various places that India only desired the early return of the refugees under conditions acceptable to them. She only emphasised a settlement between the people of East Bengal and the Pakistan government. Even at that late stage, "she did not stipulate whether such a settlement could be within the framework of a 'United' Pakistan or outside it".[12] India's options to secure its national interests were, thus, fast running out. Fortuitously, the long monsoons provided some time and space, just as public opinion in favour of an effective action was building up.

Military Retaliation Imperatives

Due to the gravity of the problems faced and the likelihood of their highly adverse consequences, opinion clearly veered towards a commitment to the creation of an independent Bangladesh. The die appeared to have been cast, but how was this to be achieved? The resolution in the Indian Parliament, resolutions in a number of state legislative assemblies, military and intelligence assistance to the Mukti Bahini, setting up of a provisional Bangladesh government, sanctuary given to a large number of members of the Pakistan National Assembly and support to a high number of diplomats who had defected, were clear signs of the Indian security objectives.

Providing a flavour of those times, MK Rasgotra, then India's Deputy Chief of mission in Washington, later Foreign Secretary, vividly recalled in a conversation with this writer:

> We could anticipate forebodings of trouble, especially after the demand for autonomy was not conceded. The severity of the crackdown came as a surprise and shock, and that is about the time, we saw the White House further firm up its support for Yahya. The State Department perspective was more favourable to India than the White House. Pakistani missions were also getting split. Bengalis were separating. We had to provide assistance to them, including financial support, to enable them to maintain themselves.[13]

India was confronted by a binary choice: either support Pakistan to firmly put down the massive East Bengal rebellion against the West Pakistani military junta, which was out to crush them or support Bangladesh, in whichever way possible, to emerge as an independent nation. When it was evident by about May-June that the government was unlikely to take military action, powerful pressures got generated for India to accord diplomatic recognition to the Bangladesh provisional government. Tajuddin's émigré government was also pressing for recognition. But Indira Gandhi was firm, that "unless Bangladeshis established effective control in some areas and proved to the world through their own struggle that the people were with them, recognition by India would only create the impression that India was trying to divide Pakistan by setting up a puppet regime in Bangladesh", further adding "when the time comes we will do it."[14]

There were sharp variations in the perceptions of the Indian elites. A strong lobby projected the thought in the media that the break-up of Pakistan was not in India's national interest. Another perspective was that any actions to snatch away East Bengal from Pakistan would only strengthen the latter, by taking away "its economic and military liability." Yet another view articulated was, "While the most powerful consideration influencing Indian public opinion was the conviction that India must necessarily be on the side of a people 'struggling to be free', it was also argued that it was in India's national interest that Pakistan should break up; and the failure of the government to act decisively against Pakistan was attributed by some to a combination of softness and an excess of moralism inherited from a bankrupt philosophy of international relations."[15] Jayaprakash Narayan, External Affairs Minister Swaran Singh, Union Minister KC Pant, and later Indira Gandhi herself, projected India's security predicament to world leaders but all of them returned empty-handed.

Some believed that the Bangladesh crisis deepened and extended the radical premises of Nehru's foreign policy that had been going on in India since the Sino-Indian War of 1962. Because in the first phase of the crisis, as stated earlier, pending stepped up military readiness levels, it was perceived that the national interest would be best served by bringing diplomatic pressure to bear on Pakistan through the influence of international opinion. But as K Subrahmanyam perceptively argued at that time, "One must be clear when diplomacy of persuasion must end and diplomacy of threat of force and force itself should be considered".[16] One more issue of national interest concerned the proposition put forth in some quarters about whether it would not be more prudent to absorb the pressure of the refugees, obtain international aid for this purpose and reconcile to the domination of the West Pakistani military over East Bengal than to react militarily. This view is said to have got traction in some quarters in the Union Cabinet itself, to be expectedly ruled out as an option by Indira Gandhi.

Many others believed that the prospects of greater India-Pakistan tension would have enhanced if the military option had not been exercised. In addition, the economic burden of recurring expenditure on the refugees, the fear of communal tension in West Bengal and elsewhere in the country and erosion in the credibility of the government in West Bengal and among the East Bengal rebels, were other factors that shaped India's politico-military-diplomatic strategy.

As the government's history of the war argues, "War was forced on India. Though the possibility of war between India and Pakistan could not be ruled out after March 1971, India had first tried all other means to solve the problem, although her leadership had the prudence to prepare for the worst, if the worst came. A close look at the Indian response from March 25 to December 3, 1971, reveals that diplomatic efforts and military preparations were undertaken simultaneously and in tandem." It goes on to add, "Interrogation reports of the Pakistani officers, who surrendered later, revealed that, initially, Pakistan did not expect a major war with India just then. It was estimated that the East Bengal crisis would be short-lived and it would be easily dealt with by force."[17]

Having run out of all diplomatic options, Indira Gandhi and her key advisors assessed that India was faced with security compulsions wherein it would be unable to protect its national interests without resorting to a possible war. In the public domain, K Subrahmanyam convincingly projected the argument – subsequently to resonate in important world capitals – that it would be more economical to fight a war to solve the problem of Bangladesh than to feed millions of refugees indefinitely. This calculation was not based on economic considerations alone but took into account the political, social, diplomatic and strategic cost-benefits for India. He provided numerous instances in contemporary history of the threat of the use of military force or its application by countries to safeguard their national interests.

Around early October 1971, Yahya Khan stepped up his activities to increase the probabilities of war through war preparations. Troops were concentrated along the border and the civilian population along the western border towns, and villages was evacuated. Yahya's famous declaration of November 25, 1971, "I may not be here in Rawalpindi during the next ten days, I may be fighting a war" need hardly be recalled to underscore Pakistan's strategy of bringing the crisis to a stage where the military option became a Hobson's choice for India.

Significantly, in the hugely challenging security environment that prevailed, the determination of the leadership to pursue the military option was made in the face of daunting odds. First, the contrarian input that the dangers of escalation into a war would have a serious impact on India's economy. Second, the likelihood of intervention by the United States or China would skew the cost-benefits against military retaliation. Nonetheless, Indira Gandhi took the decision she believed would serve India's overall national interest best. The objective was to undertake military force application for liberating East Bengal to eventually create the geopolitical space for an independent state of Bangladesh.

It is important to recall that there was no Indian intention to garner territory for permanent occupation either in East Bengal or West Pakistan. As TN Kaul later noted,

> India has never gone to war against another country for the acquisition of that country's territory. India does not believe in acquiring territory through war and keeping it as a fruit of victory ... India has always advocated the peaceful solution of international problems and denounced the use of force or threat of force for their settlement. It was in this spirit and against this background, that India's Prime Minister had declared before, during and after the 1971 War with Pakistan that India had no design on the territory of Pakistan or Bangladesh.[18]

As we shall soon see, Indira Gandhi's oft-articulated policy objective did not have any resonance in the India-baiting US White House. The US initiated coercive military actions in the Bay of Bengal, which were totally uncalled for, and only went to further erode American credibility in that war.

Great Power Responses

This section seeks to evaluate the role played by the Soviet Union, the United States and China, the three major powers of that time, in informing India's strategic calculus for military force application to attain the politico-strategic outcome of an independent Bangladesh.

The Soviet Union

It would be useful to recall that in the run up to the Tashkent Agreement (1966) and after it, the Soviets attempted to befriend Pakistan and provide it military supplies, although Indira Gandhi left them in no doubt about what its repercussions would be. During her visit to Moscow later that year, a blunt message was conveyed to the Brezhnev-

Kosygin duo "that if the Soviet Union gave military hardware to Pakistan, they would not only fail to wean it away from China or the US, but might lose the friendship of India."[19]

"But from 1968 onwards it was evident", as Ronen Sen opined in a conversation with this writer, "that the Soviets adopted a position which would, in their view, provide them leverage with both India and Pakistan; links only with India would not enable them to attain their objective. They supplied tanks, guns and other type of equipment until after the 1971 Indo-Soviet Treaty. Fighter aircraft were also on offer, but there was a problem from the Pakistani side."[20] Consequently, the Soviet position in the initial stages appeared balanced, nuanced somewhat by the differential perspectives articulated by President Podgorny and Prime Minister Kosygin. But the Pakistani crackdown in East Bengal in end-March and the Chinese commitment to Pakistan changed the situation.

To the Soviet Union, countries friendly to it in the subcontinent, even when not allies, were important to check US designs that could point a dagger at the soft underbelly of the Russian bear. India became a natural choice due to its dominating position. In addition, a friendly India could help the USSR in checking the Chinese designs against it. India also had become worried due to the threatening activities of Pakistan and China. Hence, to protect their mutual interests, the Soviet Union and India began to move closer.[21] A defining strategic highpoint was the government taking the initiative of getting the Soviet promises plugged into the Indo-Soviet Friendship Treaty of August 9, 1971, tentative variants of which were under consideration for over a year.

The treaty, described by some as the "most momentous decision in 24 years of independence", was acclaimed countrywide in view of the grave threat to the nation's security and the coordinated hostile attitude of the US and China. Contrarians described it as "a second Tashkent imposed", and a "departure from non-alignment". Completely oblivious of this seminal strategic development, the American reaction could be best described as 'shock and awe.' Kissinger described it as 'bombshell' saying, "We learned first from the newspapers … its bland provisions could not obscure its strategic significance."[22] The Americans clearly saw it as a counter to the Sino-US pincer against India, and to create a strategic stand-off between China and the US supporting Pakistan, and the Soviet Union being on the side of India. It thus deterred the Chinese and the US from actively intervening in the December 1971 Indo-Pak conflict.[23]

In the critical stages leading to the treaty, there was no typing of documents; only handwritten letters and notes were exchanged among Indira Gandhi, PN Haksar (her Principal Secretary), DP Dhar (Chairman, Policy Planning Division of the Ministry of External Affairs, and her key trouble-shooter, who sagaciously helped orchestrate multiple strands of India's national strategy) and PN Dhar (her Private Secretary). But, there were credible reports that the Soviets were having second thoughts. This was indeed worrisome, for without the Indo-Soviet Treaty in place, there was no way a military campaign by India could have been thought feasible. To allay last-minute Soviet misgivings, Indira Gandhi rushed DP Dhar to Moscow for a top secret meeting with Kosygin and Gromyko. The top secret record of the discussion (since declassified) provides a rare insight into the manner DP Dhar underscored the gravity of the security challenges facing both India and the Soviet Union in the subcontinent, and the critical need for the latter's obligations to be spelt out in "black and white."[24]

It is to the credit of the Soviets that during the war they remained resolute in their support for India in the face of multiple American diplomatic pressures, threats of cross-sectoral retaliation and even direct warnings. The Nixon-Kissinger duo was focussed upon the Soviets as key to the settlement of the war-crisis. They threatened that Soviet policy towards India would jeopardise the upcoming strategic arms limitation talks, a Middle East settlement, the European security conference, trade with the US and the proposed May 1972 summit meeting, for all of which the Soviets were pressing. The Americans also threatened to 'leak' a memorandum (of November 5, 1962) in which John F Kennedy had made a commitment to Pakistan against aggression from India.[25]

The Soviets had possibly assessed that the Americans were overplaying the limited cards they had, a perspective the Indian leadership shared.

For, on December 10, 1971, Kissinger told Nixon that if the US pressure on China to put its forces on the India border worked, the danger of a corresponding move by the Soviet Union to support India would be real. Kissinger said, "I must warn you, Mr. President, if our bluff is called, we'll be in trouble."[26] There was one key dimension on which the Soviets seemingly 'yielded'. Nixon and Kissinger were both possessed by America's worst-case visceral and mortal fear of Indian plans (?) to annex West Pakistan or at least retake Pakistan-Occupied Kashmir. Kissinger asserted that he had ample documentary proof. The Soviet top leadership was repeatedly threatened to dissuade India against such a move, an aspect that is being addressed subsequently.

The Soviet support, particularly the Indo-Soviet Treaty, seemed to provide the Indian Air Force (IAF) a direct operational benefit. On December 8, 1971, the Americans pressed the Shah of Iran to wet-lease two squadrons of F 104s to "the hard-pressed" Pakistan Air Force (PAF). Even a swap deal in which Jordanian F 104s would be sent, with the Shah dispatching an equal number to Jordan, was in the offing. But the Shah conveyed that in the light of the Indo-Soviet Treaty, he was not prepared to risk a confrontation with the Soviet Union. As Kissinger confirmed to Nixon on December 10, "Four Jordanian planes have already moved to Pakistan, twenty-two more are coming. We're talking to the Saudis, the Turks, we've now found, are willing to give five."[27]

United States

In the run-up to the Indo-Pak War, the Cold War dynamics tended to generate even stronger negative impulses in Indo-US relations. Given the US-Soviet enmity with China, both had a *modus vivendi* in South Asia to contract its influence in the region. This was reflected in the US support for Soviet mediation post-1965 War at Tashkent. But 1971 witnessed a discontinuous strategic change in that the US, under Nixon and Kissinger, decided for a 'tilt' towards China in an attempt to curb Soviet ambitions in different parts of the world.

The main concern of the White House was that the political turbulence within East Bengal should not result in a war that could threaten the balance of power. And during a period when Nixon's 'path-breaking' initiative towards China was being made, a regional war was perceived as jeopardising such a strategic leap of self-interest. The cause of democracy in Pakistan's eastern half was seen to be of no consequence. With Pakistan playing the role of a key intermediary, US willingness to compel Pakistan to create conditions necessary for the refugees to return was, thus, limited, further reducing India's security policy options.

The Americans seem to have understood quite early that West Pakistan's domination of East Bengal could not be maintained indefinitely. As Kissinger said, "There was no likelihood that a small military force owing loyalty to one wing of the country could indefinitely hold down a population of 75 million of the other...an independent Bengali state was certain to emerge...[28] The Soviets and the Chinese were also reconciled to this inevitability. Yet, India was compelled to undertake military retaliation against Pakistan for the safe return of nearly nine million refugees, and, for this outcome, Bangladesh to emerge as an independent nation was a security imperative.

India also witnessed how during the height of the crisis, the Nixon Administration completely overlooked the reports and assessments of their consul generals in Dhaka and Kolkatta, particularly the former, Archer K Blood. "These reports portrayed the situation objectively and urged the US Government to pressurize Yahya Khan to come to terms with Mujibur Rahman."[29] The State Department's South Asia specialists were, in Nixon's view, pro-Indian. But the Nixon-Kissinger anti-India obsession continued and they strengthened Yahya in every way, including with military supplies. During Swaran Singh's visit in mid-June, it was revealed that the Americans were continuing arms supplies despite their persistent denials. Not unexpectedly, the indifference of the US Administration to the perilous plight of the refugees and its uninterrupted US military supplies to the Pakistan Army, while publicly denying the same, shifted American public opinion to restrict the scope for support to Pakistan. As MK Rasgotra recalled in a discussion with this writer:

> We, at the Indian Embassy in Washington, started propagating factual information on refugees to universities, members of the Senate and House of Representatives, the Senators' Assistants and the media, which was particularly hostile to Nixon. We took dozens of Senators to India, including the influential Ted Kennedy, to see the situation themselves. In June '71 we published a Black Book on atrocities in East Bengal, followed by an update three months later in the form of a Red Book. These had a dramatic effect.[30]

As mentioned earlier, the Americans were deeply concerned about the implications of the Indo-Soviet Treaty. The issue came up during the imperturbable Swaran Singh's Washington visit in June. Secretary William Rogers made noises about 'non-aligned' India going the other way, and strengthening the Soviet Union. MK Rasgotra recalls that meeting, with Swaran Singh replying, "Your Excellency, what is your problem? The treaty is not against the US. I have the authority of the Prime Minister to sign an identical treaty with the US."

It would be useful to recall here a completely baffling Indian request of May 13, 1971, to the US government for making available four C 130 transport aircraft, and the crews to fly them, to help ferry East Bengal refugees from the over-burdened state of Tripura to Assam. At the time, when India was in the American cross-hairs and their national interests were at cross-purposes, it is inconceivable who made such a request and why? This initiative appears particularly naïve, when the IAF then had more than adequate airlift capacity, with about 10 operational transport squadrons, comprising An-12, Packet, Avro and Dakota aircraft, being available. The US State Department announced on June 12 that the US would participate in the airlift. The airlift exercise, code-named Bonny Jack, was terminated on July 14.[31] Ironically, exactly four months later, the Americans were back in the Indian region, but this time with the Seventh Fleet!

The Indian leadership was aware of the US limitations to seek to influence India. In fact, William Rogers told Kissinger on November 24, "The leverage we have is very minimal ... any action against them would be symbolic rather than substantial."[32] At the daily Nixon-Kissinger meetings on the South Asia crisis from December 6 onwards, the predominant apprehension expressed was on India moving its forces from East Bengal to West Pakistan, and annexing it. Hopes were expressed that West Pakistan "would make offsetting gains up in there (Kashmir)." Kissinger's understanding was obviously imaginary scenario building which had nothing to do with facts.

As the first set of politico-military options for a coordinated US-China interventionist approach, Kissinger's idea of backing up the warnings with a show of force was moving a carrier force into the Bay of Bengal; the other arrow in the quiver being pressure on the Chinese to move troops to the border, with the Soviets, in Nixon's words, "being told to get the hell out of West Pakistan."With the Chinese not walking the talk on their moving troops until the end, that caused utmost frustration to Nixon and Kissinger, the Indian leadership was hardly deterred by the attempted US coercion. As PN Dhar, then Secretary to the Prime Minister noted, "Indira Gandhi and her advisers were convinced it was a symbolic gesture, meant for consumption by Pakistan, China and the Muslim states of the Middle East. In any case, Dhaka was expected to fall before the fleet could do anything about it."[33] Interestingly, Kissinger at his meeting with Nixon on December 15, two days before India announced a unilateral ceasefire, made his fanciful claim. He said, "I have this whole file of intelligence reports which makes it unmistakably clear that the Indian strategy was to knock over West Pakistan".[34]

The American decision to send a nuclear aircraft carrier task force to the Bay of Bengal did, however, have an impact on Indian policy-makers. It led to an acceleration of the Indian nuclear programme and eventually to the testing of a nuclear device two and a half years later, in May 1974.[35]

China's Role

The first official response to the Pakistani military oppression in East Bengal was Chou Enlai's bombastic letter to Yahya of April 13, "Should the Indian expansionists dare to launch aggression against Pakistan, the Chinese government and people will fully support the

Pakistan government and people in their just struggle to safeguard state sovereignty and national independence."[36] This was of a piece with similar propagandist statements made by the Chinese leadership during the Indo-Pak War of 1965. But in 1971, the flow of Chinese military and economic assistance to Pakistan continued after their April statement.

Was there a fear of the possibility of Chinese intervention and an assessment of the effect of the same on India's national interests? The Indian assessment was perhaps shaped by three aspects. First, the mistaken belief of the Pakistani leadership that they would win the war in the East Bengal with Chinese help, "which Bhutto claimed had been promised when he had visited that country in early November."[37] On July 28, at his meeting with Nixon and Kissinger, US Ambassador in Pakistan Joseph Farland, also "anticipated that conflict between India and Pakistan would draw in China as well."[38] In actual fact, unknown to the US and Pakistan, the Chinese position appeared to have shifted from that in April to the Bhutto visit in November, when the promise turned to providing 'resolute support'. Because, in the Chinese assessment, the determination of the East Bengalis to cast off the West Pakistani yoke, and that of the Indian leadership to find a permanent solution to the refugee influx, made an independent Bangladesh inevitable. The question of 'resolute support' (read military intervention) would only have arisen if the very existence of Pakistan – in the West – was at stake.

The second aspect was India's extremely friendly relations with the Himalayan kingdoms of Nepal, Bhutan and Sikkim, of which the last had not acceded to India then. This meant a strategic buffer was in place should China have opened a military front to deflect Indian military pressure against Pakistan. The third dimension comprised a purely military consideration: weather-terrain-closure of the Himalayan passes precluding any Chinese effective military actions. Interestingly, such was the ignorance of the terrain factor in American thinking that when Kissinger alluded to it in his meeting with Nixon on December 6, the latter rejoined "that it had not prevented the Chinese Army from crossing the Yalu river in the dead of winter during the Korean War."[39]

The Indian government's Interdepartmental Group, assessing Chinese intentions seems to have also drawn the aforementioned conclusions, based on "little or no increased military along the Northern borders and a less negative public stance toward India than during the 1965 War."[40] The Indian political and military leadership was right in its assumption that the Chinese support to Pakistan even in its most challenging and grave moments, would be confined to verbal and moral encouragement. This was quite unlike Nixon and Kissinger, who reached the opposite conclusion. They incorrectly expected the Chinese to intervene militarily, clearly based on a misinterpretation of Chinese perspectives and communications, and more on their pronounced anti-India obsession.

National Crisis Management and Decision-Making

For the political leadership, the challenge to safeguard and project India's national interests in a security crisis of grave proportions – with no international help, barring the Soviet Union – was an enormous one. It is to the credit of Indira Gandhi, her key ministerial colleagues and political-military advisory team that they handled the crisis with statesmanship, sagacity and resolute determination. On Indira Gandhi it was said, "She is at her best in a crisis. In normal times, she is apt to be hesitant and indecisive, vacillating and wavering. In a crisis, she seems suddenly to take courage, and strike at the right moment and place."[41]

Articulating the decision-making of that period, Principal Secretary to the Prime Minister, PN Haksar, wrote 18 years later, "It was in the year 1971 to 1973 that we once again became possessed of a promise of restoration of national will for a brief period. The periods of successfully coping with the problems of foreign (security) policy in the Nehru period and in the period of Smt Indira Gandhi's Prime Ministership, are thus relatable to one dominating factor, namely the existence of a widespread belief in national purpose, a national will and credibility."[42]

Clearly, during the 1971 crisis, there was a deep consciousness of national interests and objectives, and the ability and commitment to choose long-term interests over narrow short-term parochial considerations. Unquestionably, Indira Gandhi demonstrated the single-minded courage and disposition to see the military option decision through. Having tested the diplomatic waters and evaluated public opinion, the key political trio, Prime Minister Indira Gandhi, Defence Minister Jagjivan Ram and Foreign Minister Swaran Singh, are said to have weighed the likely consequences of different and complex courses of action and adopted a solution which minimised the adverse impact of the East Bengal crisis on India's national interests.

The Prime Minister was very ably assisted by the three Service Chiefs, Gen 'Sam' Maneckshaw, ACM Pratap Lal and Adm SM Nanda, Defence Secretary KB Lall, Foreign Secretary TN Kaul, External Intelligence Chief RN Kao, Director Intelligence Bureau RN Banerjee and most of all Chairman, Policy Planning Committee DP Dhar and Principal Secretary PN Haksar. DP Dhar was doubtless the strategic mastermind, who single-handedly helped orchestrate the multi-layered and complex strands of India's grand strategy. He was ably assisted by PN Haksar. The critical need for the Mukti Bahini to stay the course with courage, determination and commitment was resolutely tied up by RN Kao of the Research and Analysis Wing (R&AW). All three were trusted confidants of the prime minister. Satinder Lambah, then a young undersecretary in the Ministry of External Affairs (MEA), recollects "PN Haksar's 'mastery over things' and how even the Foreign Secretary knew when the former said anything, it was at the behest of the PM. A Bangladesh Cell, with liberal financial powers was set up; the External Publicity Division under Joint Secretary SK Singh (later Foreign Secretary) coordinated international public relations very efficaciously."[43]

Reviewing the national crisis management with the benefit of a five-decade-long hindsight, some aspects stand out. First, a courageous political leadership that was willing to take risks to safeguard long-term national interests in the face of extremely daunting odds. Second, build-up of a national consensus to the extent pragmatism dictated. Third, orchestration of a diplomatic campaign to seek legitimacy for a war considered inevitable. And, lastly, provision of the fullest support and freedom to the armed forces to plan the timing, military objectives, as also the actual conduct of operations. It was the unparalleled synergy among the political, military and diplomatic dimensions of national crisis management and decision making that enabled India to successfully undertake military force application, in centuries of its history, to achieve the politico-strategic outcome of militarily creating an independent country, Bangladesh.

Disclaimer: Parts of the paper have previously been published as Kapil Kak, "Revisiting 1971 War and the IAF's Role: India's Interests and Compulsions", in Air Commodore Jasjit Singh ed., *Role of Indian Air Force in 1971 War* (New Delhi: KW Publishers, 2013), pp. 39-59.

Notes

1. Robert Jackson, *South Asian Crisis: India, Pakistan, Bangladesh* (New Delhi: Vikas, 1978), p. 21.
2. TN Kaul, *Diplomacy in Peace and War: Recollections and Reflections* (New Delhi: Vikas, 1979), p. 179.
3. Ashok Kapur and A Jeyaratnam Wilson, *Foreign Policies of India and her Neighbours* (London: Macmillan Press, 1996), p. 104.
4. Kaul, n. 2, p. 179.
5. *History of Indo-Pak War 1971, Part II,* History Division, Ministry of Defence, New Delhi,1992, p. 229.
6. US Department of State, *Foreign Relations of the United States, 1969-1976,* Vol XI, South Asia Crisis, 1971, Document 199.
7. Discussions with AP Venkateswaran, former foreign secretary, at Bangalore on November 4, 2011.
8. Writing for a syndicated column published in various newspapers, K Subrahmanyam, then director of the New Delhi based Institute for Defence Studies and Analyses, analytically put forth the deeper security implications of the developments in Bangladesh, including the problems posed by the refugee influx. See his *Bangladesh and India's Security,* compiled and published by Maj Gen DK Palit (Dehradun: Palit and Dutt, 1972), p. 99.
9. Jackson, n. 1, p. 37.
10. JN Dixit, *Across Borders: Fifty Years of India's Foreign Policy* (New Delhi: Picus, 1998), p. 105.
11. n. 5, p. 262.
12. Ibid., p. 275.
13. Discussions with MK Rasgotra, on November 16, 2011.
14. Kaul, n. 2, p. 181.
15. Jackson, n. 1, p. 37.
16. Palit, n. 8, p. 72.

17. n. 5, p. 276 and p. 287.
18. TN Kaul, *Ambassadors Need Not Lie: Some Aspects of India's Foreign Policy* (New Delhi: Lancers International, 1988), p. 107.
19. Kaul, n. 2, p. 175.
20. Discussions with Ronen Sen (special assistant to DP Dhar, India's ambassador to Moscow, during the East Bengal crisis, and later ambassador to Germany, the UK, Russia and the US) on November 23, 2011.
21. n. 6, p. 268.
22. Henry Kissinger, *The White House Years* (New Delhi: Vikas, 1979) p. 866.
23. Kaul, n. 18, p. 115.
24. Top Secret, declassified notes on discussions between Chairman AN Kosygin and Minister of Foreign Affairs, AA Gromyko, with the Special Representative of India's Prime Minister DP Dhar, at Moscow, on August 5, 1971. PN Haksar Papers, NMML, New Delhi.
25. n. 6, Documents 252 and 256 (Declassified).
26. Ibid., Document 266 (Declassified).
27. Ibid.
28. Kissinger, n. 22, pp. 852-853.
29. Dixit, n. 10, p. 105.
30. n. 13.
31. n. 6, Document 45 (Declassified).
32. Ibid., Document 199 (Declassified).
33. PN Dhar, *Indira Gandhi, the Emergency and Indian Democracy* (New Delhi: Oxford University Press, 2000), p. 183.
34. n. 6, Document 309 (Declassified).
35. Dhar, n. 33, p. 184.
36. Jackson, n. 1, p. 42.
37. Dhar, n. 33, p. 179.
38. n. 6, Document 109.
39. Ibid., Document 239.
40. Denis Kux, *Estranged Democracies: India and the United States, 1941-1991* (New Delhi: Sage, 1993) p. 303.
41. Kaul, n. 2, p. 172.
42. PN Haksar, *India's Foreign Policy and its Problems* (New Delhi: Patriot Publishers, 1989), p. 158.
43. November 22, 2011 discussions with Satinder Lambah, then special envoy of the prime minister, on Pakistan.

13. Nuclear Weapons and Conventional War: Changes in Indo-Pak Dynamics from 1971 to 2021

Manpreet Sethi

> *Few other countries in the world face the full spectrum of threats to their security as India does, from low intensity conflicts to an unfriendly nuclearised neighbourhood.*
>
> – Pranab Mukherjee, Defence Minister
> Government of India, 2005

> *Escalation to a nuclear exchange naturally raises the spectre of tremendous destruction to levels where war loses any rational purpose. Our interests, therefore, require that nuclear weapons are available to deter a nuclear threat while war is kept restricted to conventional levels, fought and concluded on our terms. This naturally implies that we should have sufficient conventional capability to win at the conventional level so that we do not have to escalate to nuclear weapons use. And a strong Air Force is central to that capability.*
>
> – Jasjit Singh, *Defence from the Skies,* 2013

It is an unfortunate reality that two neighbours sharing the same history, geography, culture and language should have found peace to be such an elusive goal. India and Pakistan have lived under the shadow of war since 1947. The first encounter, in fact, took place over the state of Jammu and Kashmir (J&K) within months of their independence. During the seven decades that have since passed, periods of tension and crises have exceeded those of bonhomie and harmonious coexistence.

The overt nuclearisation of the region in 1998 brought its own complications into the relationship. Pakistan has since exploited the nuclear weapons as a shield from behind which to wage terrorism against India. Consequently, the possibility of war persists, including of its escalation to the nuclear level. If the latter eventuality is to be avoided, and the former has to be deterred, India needs to plan for employment of force in a manner quite different from the kind of war that the two countries fought in 1971.

Surprisingly, despite nuclear weapons having been in existence since 1945 and despite the difficult period of the Cold War, the US and USSR never gave much thought to the subject of conventional war between two nuclear armed nations. Perhaps this was because the two superpowers were mostly engaged in proxy wars in non-nuclear, third countries, away from their mainlands. A direct conflict between the two, if it were to happen, was expected to turn nuclear quickly. Hence, the planning shifted into the realm of nuclear war-fighting, not on how to fight and contain a war at the conventional level. The size and structure of their nuclear arsenals, targeting strategies and civil defence measures were all accordingly planned keeping a nuclear war in mind.

Consequently, little analysis is available on how to fight a conventional war without letting it escalate to the nuclear level. This is a unique challenge before India given that the possibility of war persists with both its nuclear armed neighbors with both of whom it has territorial disputes. Having to prepare itself for the eventuality of a conventional conflict has meant searching for a strategy that allows employment of the military to execute such a war prudently in a manner that minimises, if not obviates, the chance of use of nuclear weapons.

In view of the above, the chapter examines the relationship between nuclear weapons and conventional war. Divided into four broad sections, it starts with a brief historical survey of the conduct of military operations in 1971 in order to understand the objectives of war at that time and the scope of employment of force. The second section examines why Pakistan found it imperative to set out towards acquisition of nuclear weapons in 1972, and the strategy of nuclear brinkmanship that it has since followed. The third part then explains the constraints this imposes on India's conduct of conventional operations. A short analysis of the four crises since 1998 in which military force was deployed/employed helps discern the instruments that succeeded, and that did not. The concluding section highlights the special attributes of air power that are likely to make it the instrument of choice in future operations and the capabilities that should, therefore, be the focus of modernisation.

The chapter drives home the point that given the transformation in circumstances with the advent of nuclear weapons, India may no longer find it advisable to wage a war like the one that took place in 1971. While it remains an unfortunate reality that wars between India and Pakistan are still probable fifty years since then, most likely triggered by Pakistan's continued use of terrorism, India's response will have to be customised such as to be effective enough to punish, but to do so without causing a nuclear-armed Pakistan to feel the need to use its nuclear weapons. Only when India is able to signal a capability to do this, would it also be able to communicate the credibility of use of force in a nuclearised environment.

Conduct of Operations in 1971

In 1971, India found itself dragged into the internal situation of Pakistan created by its domestic politics and ethno-nationalist factors. Pakistan's national elections in 1970 yielded a political mandate in favour of the Sheikh Mujibur Rehman-led Awami League party from Bengali-majority East Pakistan. This mandate was rejected by the leaders of Punjab-dominated West Pakistan. Gen Yahya Khan, the martial law administrator since 1969, was encouraged by Zulfiqar Ali Bhutto as head of the Pakistan People's Party (PPP) to not appoint Mujibur Rehman as Prime Minister. Political instability grew in East Pakistan, which the Pakistan Army quelled with a repressive crackdown from March 1971. Ten million refugees poured into

India within months. As the situation became untenable, New Delhi leaned in favour of the resistance movement led by the democratically elected Awami League, supported by the Mukti Bahini, an irregular militia.

India was sucked into war when the Pakistan Army undertook hot pursuit into Indian territory and Pakistan aircraft violated the Indian air space in October-November 1971. In one such intrusion in November that year, the Indian Air Force (IAF) downed three intruding Pakistani aircraft. Thereafter, Pakistan launched preemptive air attacks on the IAF in the West on December 3, 1971. As India fought on two fronts, it was able to neutralise Pakistan Air Force (PAF) assets in the East to attain complete air superiority within two days of the first strike. This facilitated rapid advance of the Indian Army, ably supported by the IAF transport and helicopter fleets. Meanwhile, PAF strikes in the West attempted to degrade IAF capability, but without much success. The Pakistan Army too launched attacks to capture the Husseiniwala and Suleimanki headworks near Ferozepur and Fazilka, with larger plans to punch through into Punjab. But the Indian air attacks led to the loss of a large number of tanks that punctured the momentum and thereby foiled the planned 'Tikka offensive'. In his analysis of the 1971 War, a leading strategic expert of India, Jasjit Singh concludes, "Conventional air power had provided another proof of its role as a credible deterrent to aggression".[1]

The Indian military recalls the 1971 operations as a case of clear political guidance and successful planning and execution of defined military objectives. War aims were identified as: to assist the Mukti Bahini in liberating Bangladesh so that the refugees could return to their own government; to prevent Pakistan from capturing any Indian territory of consequence in J&K, Punjab, Rajasthan and Gujarat; to defend the integrity of India from a Chinese attack in the north.[2]

From these broad guidelines, each Service drew up its own priorities. For instance, the then Chief of the Air Staff (CAS), ACM PC Lal identified the primary tasks of the IAF to include air defence of the homeland and air bases; support of the Army and Navy;

bombing to neutralise or counter enemy air; and other operations like paratrooping and transport.[3] An extensive targeting strategy was evolved to ensure air superiority. The plan was to use "fighters to guard one's own air spaces and to attack the defences of the enemy, along with attacks by fighter-bomber and bomber aircraft on vital targets often deep inside enemy territory. This dangerous business, expensive in human lives and aircraft, was undertaken in full measure in 1971, covering virtually all known PAF installations in both West and East Pakistan."[4] Targets also included fuel storage tanks, gas plants, oil refineries, and power stations that severely disrupted the energy scenario in the country, as well as attacks on road and rail transport, even as the Indian Navy blockaded the only major seaport at Karachi which was the gateway for all imports and exports.

Such an extensive use of air and naval power in congruence with Indian Army advances created a rather difficult position for Pakistan. The starkness of the situation is thus described by Jasjit Singh:

> By the time the fighting ended, over 90,000 prisoners of war were in the custody of the Indian armed forces, large tracts of West Pakistan were under the occupation of the Indian Army and Pakistan was split into two, dealing a deep blow to the two-nation theory that formed the *raison d'etre* of Pakistan to start with. The traditional friends of Pakistan, the United States and the PRC, had been of little help, and great disappointment.[5]

As is evident, India had a free hand in the conduct of military operations in 1971. Neither the PAF nor the Pakistan Army were able to execute their premeditated plans. On the other hand, India managed to go beyond its planned objectives since it encountered no resistance. Expansive targeting across the nation wrought extensive disruptions. While the dismemberment of Pakistan was an outcome of its own internal contradictions and an inability to handle them through democratic processes, the war with India did leave Pakistan's military humiliated, and smarting for revenge.

What Changed in 1972?

Start of Pursuit of Nuclear Weapons

1971 left a scar on the psyche of the Pakistan military. In an important development that took place in the immediate aftermath of the operations, its leadership set out to acquire nuclear weapons to ensure security against India. As opined by a former Pakistani diplomat, Maleeha Lodhi, "1971 and the 'never again' paradigm that emerged after defeat and dismemberment proved pivotal in the decision to build the bomb."[6]

It may be recalled that in the 1960s, Zulfiqar Ali Bhutto, first as minister for fuel, power and natural resources, and later as foreign minister, had been quite vocal on the need for Pakistan to acquire nuclear weapons. In 1965, in an interview with the *Manchester Guardian*, he said, that if India built the bomb, "We will eat grass, even go hungry, but we will get one of our own."[7] However, Gen Ayub Khan, then Pakistan's president, did not hold the same view. In 1966, Bhutto left the government after the debacle at the 1965 War with India, which his Foreign Office had engineered despite advice to the contrary by Gen Musa as Army Chief. Bhutto created the Pakistan's People's Party, and ran for elections in 1970. Though the Awami League won the elections, the result was not acceptable to him and the elite of West Pakistan. War followed, resulting in the liberation of Bangladesh as a sovereign nation.

Bhutto took over as president of Pakistan in 1971. Having witnessed the dismemberment of his nation and given his strong views in favour of nuclear weapons from earlier, it was not surprising that in January 1972, he secretly assembled Pakistani scientists and engineers in Multan and challenged them to equip the country with nuclear weapons in three years. Domestic efforts were fortuitously supplemented with large doses of external help – through stealing of URENCO documents by AQ Khan, and through extensive material and technology proliferation from China. Consequently, in 15 years, the country declared itself nuclear capable when AQ Khan so announced in an interview in 1987.[8] This covertly developed capability then came out into the open with the conduct of nuclear tests in 1998.

Pakistan's Nuclear Strategy Post-1998

Since 1971, nuclear weapons have continued to be perceived as a security imperative for Pakistan. Many Pakistani analysts have described these as the 'strategic equalisers' to address the conventional asymmetry with India. They are seen as a shield that can protect the country from running the risk of confronting a superior conventional military even while indulging in acts of terrorism. Thus, they become the ultimate guarantor of national survival. This belief was well encapsulated in 1994 in a statement by former Chief of the Army Staff of Pakistan Gen Mirza Aslam Beg, "Oxygen is basic to life, and one does not debate its desirability ... *nuclear deterrence has assumed that life-saving property for Pakistan.*"[9]

Accordance of such centrality to nuclear weapons remains a Pakistani imperative, especially because of its policy of waging terrorism against India. The fact that Pakistan nurtures a large number of terrorist outfits has, by now, been openly acknowledged many times by the Pakistani leadership, as also the United States and others in the international community.[10] It is also clear that acquisition of nuclear weapons gave Pakistan's strategy of bleeding India through a thousand cuts a new lease of life, pace and intensity. Pakistan-sponsored terrorist activities wreak material havoc on India, and Pakistan's threat to use nuclear weapons is meant to psychologically terrorise the Indian political decision-making.

Therefore, Pakistan's nuclear weapons are less for 'nuclear' deterrence and more for providing immunity to the country to wage other modes of conflict. They are meant for deterring a conventional attack from India, besides magnifying the fears of the international community on the possibility of a nuclear exchange in the region. The Pakistan military works on the assumption that a 'concerned' international community would restrain India from using military force.

India's Conduct of Conventional Operations Post-1998

India has evolved four kinds of responses to Pakistan's strategy of covert warfare under the nuclear shadow: one, by building defensive measures such as better intelligence, better border fencing to block entry/improve interception of intruders; second, by reaching out to constituencies in Pakistan that are inclined towards peace with India and not in support of irresponsible actions of fomenting cross-border terrorism; third, by mobilising international public opinion and invoking global action through institutions such as the Financial Action Task Force (FATF); fourth, by taking military action to punish terrorists and their infrastructure and thereby degrade the credibility of national actors such as the Pakistan Army and Inter-Services Intelligence (ISI) which lend them support, space and resources.

In India's experience, fighting terrorism defensively and diplomatically has not been able to bring about a satisfactory change in Pakistan's behaviour. For Pakistan, proxy war against India is considered a low-cost strategy with high dividends. Deniability frees the country from responsibility, and projecting a low nuclear threshold protects it from the possibility of a conventional conflict. It is a win-win situation for Pakistan, while India is left searching for responses that can deter/defeat/punish such a strategy.

Amongst the other options available to India is that of use of military force. The employment of this tool, however, is impacted by the presence of nuclear weapons. It is a universally applicable reality that use of force against a nation possessing nuclear weapons must be done in a manner that achieves the political objective without endangering one's own self to the possibility of nuclear retaliation. As Martin van Creveld, a well-known analyst on war had astutely said in the 1990s, "From Central Europe to Kashmir, and from the Middle East to Korea, nuclear weapons are making it impossible for large sovereign territorial units, or states *to fight each other in earnest without running the risk of mutual suicide.*"[11]

This is where the difference lies between the war that could be waged in 1971 and which would not be possible in 2021. Even as military capabilities have grown, the possibilities for their 'safe' employment have shrunk. This lesson is not unique to India. It was also drawn by the US once the USSR acquired a nuclear arsenal. As explained by Jasjit Singh, "Soviet acquisition of nuclear weapons began to influence the operational doctrine from victory in war to include deterrence; and this progressively became a doctrine to prevent a direct war (by both sides) while maintaining a posture of strength and winning a war, if deterrence failed."[12] India's own experience from the manner in which the military instrument has been employed since 1998 underscores this realisation.

Kargil, 1999

Nuclear weapons had a role to play in both causing and containing the conflict at Kargil in 1999. Pakistan military's sense of abandon after acquiring nuclear weapons, which they believed had negated the possibility of an Indian military response, led them to execute the risky plan. Meanwhile, the Indian polity's recognition of the altered circumstances and the fact that the "nuclear factor played on the minds of the political decision makers"[13] helped contain the conflict. The political shadow of the weapon tempered India's response into choosing self-imposed constraints on the application of force. Even at the cost of bearing severe operational challenges and the risk of higher casualties, the Indian political leadership directed the IAF to limit its operations to own side of the Line of Control (LoC).

Speaking some months after the conflict at a National Seminar on "The Challenges of Limited War: Parameters and Options", then Defence Minister George Fernandes shed light on how nuclear weapons had changed the possibilities of use of military force, even though wars were unlikely to disappear for Indian military planners. He explained, "Nuclear weapons did not make war obsolete; they simply imposed another dimension on the way warfare was conducted ... conventional war remained feasible, though with definite limitations, if escalation across the nuclear threshold was to be avoided."[14] As is clear from the statement, conventional war when executed in the presence of nuclear weapons would have to be undertaken with 'definite limitations'. This had already been demonstrated at Kargil, but its inescapability was further driven home after the experience of the next Indo-Pak crisis in 2001-02.

Operation Parakram, 2001-02

This operation involved a full-scale military mobilisation in response to the terrorist attacks on the Indian Parliament on December 13, 2001, which itself had been preceded by a spate of other terrorist incidents. India's tolerance was breached and the need to wage war was openly expressed. Mobilisation ensued over the next few weeks and Indian forces were ready by January 2002. By then, Pakistan was yet to move its formations from the Western borders where they were engaged with the US war on terror against Afghanistan. India could have launched the offensive since it enjoyed a preponderant advantage in air and naval forces and a marginal edge in the Army too.[15]

However, mounting international pressure and a statement by President Musharraf on January 12, 2002, promising widespread domestic reforms to cleanse his country of militant and extremist groups stalled the launch of war. India decided to wait and watch, without demobilising, for tangible steps against terrorism. In response to India's ready forces, Pakistan also chose to mobilise its own forces. The two militaries remained in a high state of readiness for ten months, the longest Indo-Pak mobilisation. In the midst of heightened tensions, another Pak-sponsored terrorist strike took place at Kaluchak military camp in May 2002. While most would have thought that this would trigger decisive action, given that Indian forces were already at readiness, nothing more than rhetorical statements ensued. India threatened conventional war, while Pakistan hurled back threats of nuclear escalation. It also conducted flight tests of three types of nuclear capable ballistic missiles.

Why did India not wage a full-scale war – despite having a *casus belli* and the forces at readiness? The reason can, perhaps, be attributed to the difficulty that was found in defining precise politico-military objectives that were worth bearing the risk of war, especially when it included the possibility of nuclear escalation. Traditional war aims, especially with full-scale mobilisation, are assumed to be capture of territory or substantive attrition of military potential. These could have been achieved given India's preparedness across the three Services in 2002. But, the presence of nuclear weapons made such objectives risky to pursue and, hence, not considered politically prudent. On the other hand, more limited operational objectives that would be less risky could have been identified. But these were found to be insufficient to meet the political objective of forcing a change in Pakistan's policy of supporting cross-border terrorism.

Op Parakram, therefore, exposed the limits of coercive diplomacy with a nuclear-armed adversary. It also highlighted the perils of a large offensive under the changed circumstances. Despite the elaborate show of military preparedness, India could not effectively punish the adversary. It also found it difficult to de-escalate without achieving something. The 2001-02 episode, thus, forced the need to look for novel options of employing force against continued terrorist activity from Pakistan.

In April 2004, the Indian Army articulated the Cold Start doctrine that offered a fresh perspective on Army employment. Drawing upon the Warsaw Pact strategy of "swift advance [with] the ability to attack from a standing start",[16] the basic idea of Cold Start was to mount an offensive with a ready, mobile, lethal force (eight integrated battle groups) with integral logistics and air cover. The purported purpose was to avoid a long preparation time and to advance quickly into enemy territory for shallow penetration attacks so as to present him with "impossibly difficult choices at every turn".[17]

The doctrine, however, came in for much debate within the country and outside. It was criticised for focussing only on how to 'start' a military offensive without adequate thought to how to end the conflict since disengaging troops from enemy territory is never easy. Definition of politico-military objectives of such action was also seen to be problematic since it brought capture of territory, if not in large then in shallow chunks back into focus. But, to use territory as a bargaining chip in post-war negotiations to coerce Pakistan into giving up terrorism was considered to be a doubtful proposition. The idea of Cold Start currently stands shrouded in confusion with some senior military leaders denying it and others accepting it.

Imperative of Crafting New Military Responses

In the experiences of Kargil and Op Parakram, India found the building blocks to contour and war-game future military operations with Pakistan. It was clear that terrorist provocations were going to continue and that India had to evolve a credible conventional strategy for at least three reasons: one, to disabuse Pakistan of the assumption that its nuclear weapons had provided it with a free play on terrorism while tying India's hands; second, to turn around the view spreading within India that the country was unable to exercise credible deterrence against a smaller and weaker nation; and third, to expose the brinkmanship inherent in the Pakistani strategy. This required devising adequate conventional responses that could be 'safely' executed between two nuclear-armed nations without running the risk of nuclear escalation. India experimented along these lines with innovative use of military instruments in 2016 and 2019.[18]

Surgical Strikes, 2016

In September 2016, four operatives of the Lashker-e-Tayyebe (LeT)[19] mounted an attack on an Indian Army camp at 12 Brigade Headquarters (HQ), Uri. In view of the inflamed public opinion, the prime minister expressed in a meeting with his military commanders that "retaliation should be immediate to send an unambiguous message."[20] It was decided that covert cross-border strikes could meet the dual objective of imposing punishment and inducing fear to deter future actions. Surgical strikes were undertaken on the night of September 28-29, 2016, to signal "we know where you are based and where you launch your attacks from, and more importantly, we know where to hit you."[21]

With the successful conduct of this operation, India got its message across the border, literally and otherwise. New Delhi also realised the effectiveness of using a sharper tool against a nuclear armed adversary than the blunt edge of full mobilisation. The covertness of the action also offered the advantage of it being denied by the adversary, thus, freeing him from the requirement of retaliation. This, in turn, helped escape escalation. Far-sightedly, despite domestic and international pressure to show evidence of military action across the LoC, the Indian government decided against it, enabling the crisis to de-escalate.

This, of course, has not changed Pakistan's policy of using terrorism against India. But that was never the stated objective of the surgical strikes. These were meant to signal India's ability to hurt the terrorists and their supporters by hitting at will, even by entering and safely exiting enemy territory, thereby also denting the credibility of the Pakistan Army.

Operation Bandar, 2019

It was with a similar objective in mind that India decided to use another arrow in its quiver on February 26, 2019, when a dozen IAF Mirage 2000 aircraft equipped with the Israeli-built SPICE (Smart Precise Impact and Cost Effective) 2000 bombs flew across the international boundary between India and Pakistan to target a terrorist camp in Balakot in Khyber Pakhtunkhwa. This action was undertaken after the terrorist strike on Central Reserve Police Force (CRPF) personnel at Pulwama in February 2019. India dropped bombs on a Jaishe-e-Mohammed (JeM) camp where *fidayeen jihadis* were being trained. India's foreign secretary described this as a "non-military pre-emptive action"[22] and India took utmost care not to cause civilian, or even military casualties.

While Pakistan acknowledged the IAF's intrusion into its air space, and its own aircraft scrambled in response, it denied that any damage had been caused on the ground, except to some pine trees! Nevertheless, it chose to respond the next morning with 24 Pakistan Air Force (PAF) aircraft, a mix of F-16, JF-17 and Mirage-5. According to media reports, "Mirage-5 *tried to bomb* the Indian Army's 25 Division Headquarters, and an ammunition and logistics depot close to the Brigade Headquarters in Poonch."[23] But, whether deliberately so planned or as a matter of luck, the bombs did not hit Indian military targets. So, while Pakistan sent a message through day-time intrusion into India, escalation was, nevertheless, prevented. One of the Indian MiG 21 Bisons that scrambled in response to the PAF aircraft entering Indian air space, entered into a dogfight with an F-16, and suffered a hit, causing the pilot to eject. He fell across the LoC in Pakistan Occupied Kashmir (POK), and was captured by the Pakistan Army. His capture, and release after 60 hours, proved to be sobering developments. No further military action ensued and the relationship has since settled into an uneasy business as usual state.

India used air power in Op Bandar in 2019 for the first time since 1971. IAF fighters received political permission to penetrate Pakistani air space to hit at targets deep inside the country. This was a significant development since most war-games simulating Indo-Pak crises have popularised the idea that India's military response to a Pakistani terror act would likely be confined to POK since anything beyond that would be too risky. But, India's air strikes rewrote the template, opening new retaliation possibilities.

The Indian air action achieved two outcomes: one, it yet again trashed the assumption that Pakistan's nuclear weapons have tied India's hands on responding to Pakistan's provocations. Rather, it exposed the lack of credibility of Pakistan's projection that Indian military action would automatically trigger Pakistan's use of tactical nuclear weapons; second, the resolve exhibited in the conduct of the air strikes showed an appetite for risk taking which India had shied away from practising during past incidences of terrorism.

Put together, the Indian military actions in 2016 and 2019 have sought to communicate the message that India would not hesitate to hit back routinely to hurt the stakeholders of Pakistani terrorism. This also shows that India plans to make Pakistan a shareholder in the risks that could ensue instead of merely bearing the burden of risks created by Pakistan.

Air Power as an Instrument of Choice

India's experience with the Special Forces' surgical and air strikes have also brought out the importance of choosing the right military instrument that could calibrate the use of force in such a way as to send a message and yet minimise the chances of escalation. Cognisant of the need to employ force differently and to choose targets that would matter, but not threaten state survival, India experimented with tailoring its military actions in 2016 and 2019 to keep them well below Pakistan's nuclear threshold to extract maximum effect with least risk.

Balakot particularly showed the utility of air power, whose use customarily had come to be assumed to be escalatory. An impression had persisted since 1962 that air strikes widely expand the envelope of destruction, thereby magnifying the risk of escalation. Such a view was perhaps created because precision targeting was not the norm in 1971 and air strikes were far more indiscriminate in causing damage. But, with the advances now possible in precision air strike capabilities, as seen in Balakot, controlled air-to-ground strikes with a high accuracy actually offer the advantage of restricting collateral damage, and, hence, reduce the chances of escalation. Op Bandar, therefore, brought new insights on air power into the political and public imagination.

The air strikes were found to be particularly effective in meting out punishment with strategic reach, speed, surprise and calibrated lethality. They offered the advantage of flexibility of employment, of high precision targeting, of tight control over military engagement, and, hence, over escalation. In fact, a case for air power had been made by Air Cmde Jasjit Singh in 2013 when he wrote, "Land, naval and Air Forces are all capable of providing deterrence through denial. But it is only air power that can provide the added dimension of deterrence through punishment."[24] It was his prediction, "In the years ahead, air (and missile) power will be the central tool for conventional deterrence, as well as controlled punitive strikes for coercive diplomacy... India will need to depend more on its Air Force for defence of the nation than ever before."[25]

Indeed, in the case of Balakot, it was the IAF that deployed its assets since it had the best fit given the location of the target and the requisite firepower. The IAF exploited the element of surprise since its aircraft could take off from any airfield (air-to-air refuelling facilitated this), with any combination of weapon systems on board, use precision strikes to ensure calibrated use of force, and practise quick escalation and deescalation.

In future, strikes from the air may be executed by air assets owned by any of the three Services. They may even include long-range firepower vectors such as missiles launched from the ground, air or sea. The important point is not which military Service executes the action, but to recognise the unique attributes of air power that enable flexible response to cause maximum effect. A very important benefit of air power is its ability to quickly raise the tempo for strategic effect while also being able to equally quickly wind down in order to avoid the risk of further escalation. By transcending borders and terrain barriers, aircraft and missiles can punish an adversary without having to defeat him first. This is of particular significance in the presence of nuclear weapons where air power may actually prove to be less escalatory than sending armies across the borders.

Lessons for Conduct of Future Conventional Operations

A brief analysis of India's conflicts with Pakistan, pre- and post-nuclearisation has shown that conduct of conventional war is a challenging proposition that demands fresh thinking on politico-military objectives and operations. The first hurdle, in fact, is encountered in mindsets that have long been attuned to thinking about war, and war aims, in a certain way. It is difficult to alter thinking into accepting that the military instrument has to be utilised differently, with some restrictions, in order to resolve challenges like cross-border terrorism. Pursuit of traditional war aims such as territorial occupation and *blitzkrieg* for fast-paced attrition would not only not address the adversary's use of terrorism, but also end up heightening Pakistan's existential crisis. This would harm India in two ways. One, in moments of crisis, it could increase Pakistan's temptation to use nuclear weapon; second, it could, as one Indian military analyst said, play "into the hands of the Pak Army that uses such a threat to strengthen itself within Pakistan's political firmament."[26]

Therefore, it seems most prudent and credible to conduct military operations planned for a restrained and calibrated use of military force instead of an all-out employment of military capabilities. While armies do not like limits being placed on how or what resources they use, in the presence of nuclear weapons, certain political constraints on military choices are inevitable.

Once this realisation has been absorbed, a reprioritisation of military capability and future acquisitions becomes imperative. It seems natural that instruments that can offer high calibration possibilities, as well as the advantage of quick deployment and de-escalation will score over others. As seen in the cases of Uri and Balakot, the use of special forces and air power offered the advantages of secrecy and surprise, flexibility of employment and disengagement, calibration of force, and a perceived low risk of escalation. In contrast, a large-scale mobilisation of the Army, as undertaken in 2002 did not offer these benefits. Also, once deployed, it became difficult to disengage the forces without either conceding defeat or declaring victory. So, while land forces are best suited for territorial occupation or for deterrence by denial, they are not the best instruments to use when land grab is not the politico-military objective. As explained by a former Army officer, "The military must focus on accumulating capabilities to achieve limited military objectives for limited political outcomes instead of attempting to get ready for the 'big fight'."[27]

It then becomes imperative to prioritise feasible forms of force application keeping the nuclear environment in view. Air power, for all the advantages recounted above, would need to be high on the priority list of capability build-up. This would naturally have to include a number of aircraft in the right mix of high and less than high end aircraft,[28] equipped with the right weapon systems, particularly with Beyond Visual Range (BVR) capability, the right kind and number of force multipliers and necessary training to optimise utilisation of machines are the obvious requisites. Better stand-off capabilities of aircraft and weapon systems will ensure better reach as well as own safety. In fact, India should make use of its advantage of geographical expanse or strategic depth to deep base the aircraft. Better air defence will also ensure better protection of own assets. Neither can be ignored.

Also high on the priority list would be modernisation of reconnaissance, surveillance, and intelligence capabilities that can enable precise target acquisition and attack, as well as air attack capabilities with precision guidance in order to minimise risk of collateral damage.[29] Intelligence gathering should be able to utilise all possible systems and assets in space, at sea or on the ground. At the same time, high quality data fusion and analysis would offer better target selection, thereby enabling surprise and stealth for military operations.

Given India's long experience with Pakistan's repeated terrorist provocations, it is clear that it would be necessary to raise the costs across all spectra – economic, diplomatic, political, and military – especially to the Pakistan armed forces and intelligence establishment. These actions will also be repeatedly required since raising costs cannot be a one-action exercise. It will have to be sustained over time to have an impact. The Indian air strikes at Balakot, as also the surgical action across the border in 2016, managed to impose costs on Pakistan's military in terms of loss of face. In both cases, the armed forces were not able to 'save' their country from incursions from across the border and it caused a dent to their credibility.

India-Pakistan nuclear dynamics is unique. It has been described as the first case of a nuclear-armed underdog nation troubling another nuclear-armed nation with the tool of terrorism. Well explained by an analyst, "Terrorism is the classic underdog's tactic. Pakistan is clearly the underdog in any non-nuclear matchup with India, but it is certainly the world's first nuclear-armed underdog to successfully apply the tactic against a nuclear rival."[30] In such a situation, the possibility of war is obviously present. In fact, if India was to foreclose that option, it would amount to giving a free run to Pakistani terrorism. However, to successfully defeat and deter Pakistan, India has to alter the calculus of application of conventional force. The more options Indian military planners can find that fit the new circumstances, the greater will be the chance of success in forcing a change in Pakistan's behaviour.

Notes

1. Jasjit Singh, *Defence from the Skies: Eighty Years of the Indian Air Force* (New Delhi: Knowledge World, 2013), p. 168.
2. For more on this, see, ibid., p. 143.
3. Ibid., p. 145.
4. PC Lal, *My Years with the IAF* (New Delhi: Lancer International, 1986), p. 174.
5. Jasjit Singh, "Pakistan's 'Nuclear Deterrent'?: An Introductory Essay", in Shalini Chawla, *Nuclear Pakistan* (New Delhi: Knowledge World, 2012), p. xxiv.
6. Maleeha Lodhi, "We'll Eat Grass but Build the Bomb", *The Sunday Guardian*, June 19, 2021.
7. Feroz Hassan Khan, *Eating Grass: The Making of the Pakistani Bomb* (New Delhi: Cambridge University Press India Pvt Ltd., 2013).
8. Kuldip Nayyar, "We have the Bomb, Says Pakistan's Dr Strangelove", *The Observer* (London), March 1, 1987.
9. Gen Mirza Aslam Beg, "Pakistan's Nuclear Imperatives", *National Development and Security*, Vol. 3, No. 10, November 1994, pp. 29-41. Emphasis added.
10. Former Pakistani President and Chief of the Army Staff, Pervez Musharraf accepted this in an interview in November 2010 and US Secretary of State Hillary Clinton, too acknowledged the fact in the same month. Subsequent American Administrations too have admitted the same. More recently, the Financial Action Task Force (FATF) has been trying to coerce Pakistan to change its course. To little avail as of 2021.
11. Marin van Creveld, *On Future War* (London: Brassey's, 1991), p. 194. Emphasis added.
12. Singh, n. 1, p. 253.
13. Gen V P Malik, *India's Military Conflicts and Diplomacy* (India: Harper Collins, 2013), p. 127.
14. http://www.idsa-india.org/newpap-sph.html
15. Lt Gen Prakash Menon, *The Strategy Trap: India and Pakistan Under the Nuclear Shadow* (New Delhi: Wisdom Tree, 2018), p. 125.
16. As explained by Bharat Karnad, *India's Nuclear Policy* (West Port: Praeger Security International, 2008), p. 115.
17. Ibid., p. 126.
18. Prior to 2016 too, strikes across the border by Indian Border Action Teams have been known to have occurred, but they did not go as deep as the surgical strike. Also, after the Mumbai attacks, the option of air strikes had been considered and dropped by the leadership in view of domestic and international considerations. It was decided to punish Pakistan through economic and diplomatic measures while keeping India's own focus on economic growth and development.
19. The culpability of Pakistan was established through tracking of electronic signals, intercepted communications and other equipment and food items found on the terrorists.

20. Nitin Gokhale, "The Inside Story of India's 2016 'Surgical Strike'", *The Diplomat*, September 23, 2017.
21. Ibid.
22. "Text of Foreign Secretary's Statement on Air Strike". *Hindu Business Line*, February 26, 2019. Available at https://www.thehindubusinessline.com/news/textof-foreign-secretarys-statement-on-air-strike/article26372848.ece
23. R. Prasannan, Namrata Biji Ahuja and Pradip R. Sagar, "Inside Story of India's Air Strike and Pakistan's Counter Attack", *The Week*, March 2, 2019, https://www.theweek.in/theweek/cover/2019/03/02/stealthy-skydivers.html. Emphasis added.
24. Singh, n. 1, pp. 255-256.
25. Ibid., p. 257.
26. Menon, n. 15, p. 204.
27. Ibid., p. 202.
28. ACM Dhanoa, former CAS, was right in pointing out that a developing country like India, which would always suffer from resource constraints, it would be necessary to arrive at a mix of aircraft.
29. International and national legitimacy for actions will rely heavily on this. India's ability to undertake precision strikes enabled by accurate intelligence was a demonstration of its capability at Balakot. The action could garner the support of political leaders across world capitals only because of the choice of target, enabled by good intelligence.
30. Tom Hundley, "India and Pakistan are Quietly Making Nuclear War More Likely", Vox.com, April 4, 2018, https://www.vox.com/2018/4/2/17096566/pakistan-india-nuclear-war-submarine-enemies. Accessed on July 4, 2021.

Narratives and Interactions

Roaring MiGs of No. 28 Squadron: An Interaction with AVM BK Bishnoi VrC & Bar (Retd)

RR Chaudhary

No. 28 Squadron, was the first squadron of the Indian Air Force (IAF) to be equipped with the formidable MiG-21s when India started upgrading its military power and, hence, the name "The First Supersonics". The squadron was located at Tezpur in Assam when India launched its operations in response to the Pakistani provocation in December 1971. The Commanding Officer (CO) of the squadron was Wg Cdr Bhupendra Kumar Bishnoi. He had taken over command of No. 28 Squadron in May 1970 from Wg Cdr Surendra Kumar Mehra, soon after his conversion on to the MiG-21. A year and six months had passed since his command of the squadron and he was comfortable and well settled in his role. On December 3, 1971, the CO got a call from the Station Commander of Air Force Station Tezpur, informing him that the war with Pakistan had begun and the time of reckoning for his unit had come. He was ordered to move the squadron to Guwahati with all serviceable aircraft, men, pilots and equipment to position there by 2300 hrs, so as to undertake the next day's early morning missions. The saga of valour and professionalism that followed will always be remembered in the annals of the IAF's and India's history.

The Centre for Air Power Studies (CAPS) interacted with AVM BK Bishnoi VrC and Bar (Retd), to obtain an account of the courage and competence displayed by his unit during the 1971 operations. The narration that he provided makes one a part of the action that took place during those momentous days.

Moment of Reckoning

Question: Sir, how were you informed about your unit becoming part of the operations in East Pakistan?

AVM BK Bishnoi (Retd): It was December 3, 1971, about 1745 h. I was winding up the day's work after late afternoon flying; the dusk was fast approaching, when I got a call from the Station Commander, Gp Capt MSD Wollen (Mally). Much unlike him, he seemed excited. He said, "Bhoop (my nickname), war has started. Pakistan has attacked many of our airfields in the West a few minutes ago. Prepare to move the squadron to Guwahati with all serviceable aircraft, men, pilots and equipment to position yourself there by 2300 h to undertake the next day's early morning missions. An An-12 is being positioned in your dispersal within an hour to airlift your men, equipment and ordnance to Guwahati." By 2300 hrs, the full complement of No. 28 Squadron arrived at Air Force Station Guwahati, with 11 serviceable MiG-21 aircraft, along with pilots, weapons and technical manpower to mount operations the next morning. The fog had already started to set in, on the airfield.

Welcome at Guwahati

Question: How did Guwahati welcome you, and what was the support provided to you for your operations that were planned for the very next day?

AVM BK Bishnoi (Retd): On arriving at Guwahati, before I could switch off my aircraft, I noticed that the Station Commander Gp Capt Mankotia was already waiting to receive me in the dispersal area. I had never enjoyed such an honour ever before in my service. He straight away took me to his office. After some pleasantries, he said that war had broken out and he had got the code word and operations order for our missions tomorrow. He opened a red folder and took out some maps, and said, "These are the maps of the Pakistan Air Force (PAF) base at Tejgaon, Dacca. Your squadron's first task is to attack it next morning, Time over Target (TOT) of 0705 hrs, with rockets and guns and repeat these attacks for the next two days till we knock off the Pakistani fighters on the ground and in the air, and destroy the capacity of that base to support the war against India." It was a tall order, but then that was our purpose for being there. I had a closer look at the map, it was a regular 'million scale, map' showing the location of Tejgaon airfield next to Dacca, with no other details or photographs. I asked the Station Commander for a detailed map of the PAF operating area, showing the location of hangars, aircraft parking areas, dispersed location of fighter aircraft, pens/shelters and location of vital installations, including those of their command and control systems on the base. He looked at me and said, "That's all I have. You will find the rest after reaching Dacca tomorrow morning." I explained to him that from Guwahati, Dacca was 290 km which was at the extreme edge of the aircraft flying range. With limited fuel on board, there was no scope for tactical routing or performing a proper circuit for landing on return to Guwahati after allowing five minute's combat fuel for the attacks. How could I find additional time and fuel to loiter over Tejgaon, flying at a speed of 900-1000 km/h, with Pakistani Sabres on top and anti-aircraft guns below, hunting for us? I drew a blank. He threw his hands up and pleaded his helplessness by saying, "I can only give you what I have. Wish you and your boys all the luck and happy hunting." That's that, I said to myself.

VIPs of the Base

The Station Commander then briefed me on the accommodation arrangements made for the stay of men and officers in the mess, and the workplaces next to our parking area. He informed us that we would use 'Mountain Shadows' (VIP Cottage), located near our aircraft parking for conducting our day-to-day operations. I brought out that there would be many VIPs and dignitaries visiting the station during the war, and it might become embarrassing for him to lodge them in a hotel in the town. He instead humbled me by saying, "Today, there is no VIP more important than you and your pilots at this station. I want to ensure a congenial, comfortable and peaceful environment for you and your boys for the arduous job ahead." I thanked him and left.

Preparing for the D-day

Question: How did you go about preparing for the next day's mission?

AVM BK Bishnoi (Retd): I assembled all the pilots in our makeshift briefing room, a dug-out about 10 ft below the ground, and briefed them about the next two days' task. For the first mission the next morning, as CO I claimed the privilege and honour of leading the attack with four MiG-21s. The MiGs were armed with 2 × 32 × 57 mm rocket pods for counter-air strikes against the enemy Air Force set-up at Dacca; which was heavily defended by F-86 Sabres of the PAF and anti-aircraft four-barrelled Chinese guns. I would also take two MiG-21s with air-to-air missiles to escort us, to provide top cover during the attacks at Tejgaon and during exit. The attack profile was to be low-low-high, i.e., first leg from Guwahati to Tejgaon was to be flown at just about 100 m above the ground to avoid detection by enemy radars. As we approached the target area, we were to pull up to launch a shallow rocket attack. The last leg, that is, the return to Guwahati, was to be flown at high level. We did not have prior information about the precise location of various installations, aircraft dispersals, hangars and other vital areas on the airfield; therefore, to spot targets and aim at them well in advance, we had planned to pull up to a height of one kilometre, about 30 seconds earlier than usual. Fuel constraints did not allow us the luxury to fly back to Guwahati at the safer low level. If we climbed to 6 km soon on exit, it would make us vulnerable to the Sabres which would be on Combat Air Patrol (CAP),[1] either visually or directed by their radars. The two MiG-21 escorts were to cater for such an eventuality. Wg Cdr JV Gole, CO of No. 4 Squadron, was my roommate in the Officers' Mess on that night. He told me that he would be providing top cover to No. 17 Squadron's Hunters, which were to attack Tejgaon at 0700 h. I requested him that since he would be leaving Dacca just as my formation was to arrive over Tejgaon, if possible, he should give a simple radio call saying "Mad Dog", if he encountered a CAP of Sabres over Tejgaon.

D-day: The First Mission

Question: Tell us about the first mission that your squadron undertook on December 4, 1971.

AVM BK Bishnoi (Retd): At about 0200 h, I got a call from a worried Gp Capt Wollen, who was now appointed as the Chief Operations Officer at Guwahati (brought in from Air Force Station Tezpur), informing that a thick fog had settled over the airfield. He also enquired if I would be able to take off to make good the TOT of 0705 h. I assured him that even if half the runway was visible, we would take off. The weather looked grim when we reached the Flight Office at 0545 h. The tarmac was buzzing with activity. Aircraft were being readied and weapons were in the process of being loaded on the under-wing pylons. We walked to the aircraft at 0630 h. The men at work looked sombre and gave us a look which was somewhat emotional and patronising. The fact that it was not a routine training exercise for which they were loading the aircraft, but for a real war against an uncouth enemy, was reflected in their eyes. We entered the cockpits, started the aircraft and taxied out. Till then, even to me, all the activities seemed routine and the fact that we were going in for a real war had not registered or sunk in. It struck me like a bolt, when to my utter surprise and disbelief, I saw that No. 28 Squadron personnel had lined up on both sides of the taxi track leading from the dispersal to the runway. They were waiving at us, shouting "Bharat Mata ki Jai" and wishing us luck and success in our mission. It struck us then, "Oh boy, it is for real". The time to deliver was beckoning us; they all had high hopes and we couldn't let them down.

Action in the Air

On the runway, we found that due to the fog only a little more than a quarter of the runway was visible. At 0634 h all 6 MiG-21s roared down the runway for take-off. We took off and soon emerged above the thick layer of fog into a bright morning sun rising above the Garo Khasi hills, heading for Dacca. As soon as we crossed into the East Pakistan territory, I called the formation to make the weapons selections. I heard the sound of a swish and saw one rocket leave my aircraft and burst on a hill slope in front. Ah, a twitchy finger! I earnestly hoped and prayed that no one was hurt. Though the sky above was clear, the ground below remained covered with a thick layer of fog. With the ground below not visible, it was not possible to do map reading for navigation, and I had to rely totally on course steering and time.[2] It was calm, with a memorable sight of 4 MiG-21s streaking close to the ground at 780 km/h, and another 2 MiG-21s perched slightly above and behind, keeping a watchful eye for enemy interceptors. When we were 70 km short of Tejgaon, I heard garbled Radio/Telephony (R/T) transmissions (radio telephony transmissions from and to the aircraft), as if an aerial combat was in progress. Soon after, we received the R/T announcement of "Mad Dog" from Wg Cdr Gole, who was orbiting over Dacca. I informed my formation to expect a CAP encounter over Tejgaon.

It was only about a minute before reaching Dacca that the fog underneath suddenly vanished and I saw the chimney of a factory near the river bend spewing spiralling smoke. On the right side, the sprawling city of Dacca was approaching. I turned right towards the pull-up point, and gave an R/T call to the formation, "Switches on, pulling up to one kilometre, Tejgaon airfield to the left 11 o'clock, spread out for attack." The other aircraft acknowledged. The escort leader, Flt Lt Manbir Singh, confirmed that our tail was clear (there were no enemy aircraft behind us). I simultaneously saw two Sabres rolling half way down the runway '35' for take-off.[3] Obviously, the Pakistani radar had picked up our tracks, when we were about one and half minutes (20 km) short of Tejgaon, and ordered a 'scramble' of Sabres at the Operational Readiness Platform (ORP).[4] I drew the attention of the escort leader to the Sabres on take-off; he duly acknowledged by saying "contact". I then turned left towards the sprawling airfield of Tejgaon in front of me. It looked barren, devoid of any activity. My eyes searched hard for vital targets and aircraft on the ground; except large hangars there was nothing conspicuous and worth attacking. In a shallow dive, I aimed and fired a salvo of 16 rockets into the hangar. Smoke arose from it. Disappointed with the achievement, specially, after having travelled 290 km from Guwahati, I ordered the formation to turn around and make a second attacking pass on the airfield, though we had originally planned for a single attack. This time we saw transmitters, some fortified buildings and gun positions, and attacked those with the remaining rockets. While diving for attack on the transmitters, I saw a lone Sabre dangerously close and passing under me from right to left, with a MiG-21 in hot chase behind him. After the attack, I turned on course to Guwahati. While climbing, I informed the escorts that our formation was leaving Tejgaon, climbing and heading for home.

For a minute, I flew at low level and then pulled up to climb to 6 km on course to Guwahati. By then, the other three aircraft of my formation had joined me. The attacks had gone through without much trouble. All seemed well, and we were safely heading home. Manbir Singh, the escort leader had engaged the second Sabre in a dogfight over Dacca. He had fired two missiles at the Sabre which, while flying too low near the ground had suddenly pulled up in the easterly direction into the sun. The missiles had missed him. Our calm lasted only till I heard the escort leader call twice on R/T, "Dadu, (Flt Lt D.M. Subiya was Escort 2) where are you"? There was no response from Dadu. It raised my hackles. I presumed that Dadu and Manbir were at low level and, therefore, out of R/T contact with each other, so I called on R/T, "Dadu, report position". Dadu promptly came up and said, "I am in combat with a Sabre, over Dacca". It startled, and shocked me. He had apparently got too engrossed in combat and failed to keep track of the fuel on board, while forgetting that he was yet to fly 290 km back to base. If he waited any longer to shoot down the enemy aircraft, he would have no fuel to reach home. I immediately asked for his fuel state, to which he replied, "900 litres". We had left Dacca four minutes ago and he was still over Dacca, in all probability flying with full power or even reheats, burning up extra fuel. It spelled nothing but disaster. It would be difficult to make it back to home with that fuel. I ordered him to "disengage immediately, climb up to 6 km on course to Guwahati and fly for range; we will look out for you". I asked the formation to throttle back, spread out and look for Dadu. At the same time, I alerted our radar at Shillong of the situation, and asked them to lookout for Dadu's aircraft trailing somewhere behind us. Soon, the radar at Shillong called back, "Escort 2, 20 km, 6 o'clock, and his tail is clear". We reduced our speed to enable Dadu to catch up. I saw him come abreast. When I asked for his fuel state, he said, "It is 500 litres". It was a critical touch and go situation.[5] My first worry was that he may run short of fuel and may have to eject over enemy territory. I informed our base at Guwahati of the predicament of Escort 2. I asked them to get a rescue helicopter airborne to retrieve Dadu, if he had to eject due to engine flame out. I told Dadu to select power for maximum range and maintain height till he was sure of reaching the runway at Guwahati; and then make a direct high approach and land. His fuel state had dropped to 300 litres and then to 150. We crossed the Indian border, I asked Dadu to be ready to eject if his engine flamed out (engine stopping due to fuel starvation). On the finals of his approach to land, his fuel tank read zero. He said, "Sir, I will make it". I kept my fingers crossed with a prayer on my lips. It was the most tense five seconds of my life, till I saw with a sigh of relief, his aircraft touching down on the runway and the engine flaming out half way down its landing run. Fuel shortage by a few drops or a five second delay in breaking off the combat with the Sabre over Dacca would have made us lose a precious pilot and an expensive aircraft on the very first mission of the war. It was sheer providence that we did not. It was a great lesson learned by me and surely by Dadu. He is now well and happily settled with his family in the USA.

Air Strikes on December 4 and 5: Analysing the Effectiveness

Question: What was the further air effort after the first strike of the day and for the next day? How effective were these strikes in putting the PAF in East Pakistan out of action?

AVM BK Bishnoi (Retd): The squadron flew a total of about 30 sorties over Dacca with no tangible results. There was intense ground fire encountered over the target but the Sabres never came in sight of the MiGs for air combat. In the meanwhile, Hunters from Nos 17 and 37 Squadron and Sukhois of No. 221 Squadron also repeatedly attacked Dacca. Four Hunters and one Sukhoi were shot down – two by the Sabres and three by ground fire. The next day on December 5, 1971, we were asked to follow the same format as the day before, and we repeatedly showered rockets at the PAF base at Dacca. We hit some light aircraft in the hangar and a twin Otter standing in the open, followed by a strike on the fuel storage facility. Although the Sabres were getting airborne for the Hunters and Sukhois, they scrupulously avoided engaging the MiGs. At the end of the day, when we took stock of the last two days' effort over Dacca, we frustratingly realised that we had made no dent to the PAF flying effort and their operational capability, in spite of hundreds of counter-air sorties flown by the MiG, Hunter and Sukhoi aircraft. The Sabres were regularly getting airborne to intercept us, and were able to provide air support to their ground force to attack our troops. To preserve their aircraft assets, they only flew within their radar cover and attacked only when in an advantageous position, thereby shooting down the Hunters and Sukhois. They hardly flew beyond 25 km radius of their airfield. Their aircraft on the ground were well dispersed and camouflaged. They seemed determined to continue in the same manner to defend their airfield for a long time. The situation was utterly hopeless and unacceptable. We had to find an out-of-the box solution for this logjam.

A Daring and Brilliant Idea

Question: After you found that the air operations were not making much headway in keeping the PAF down, what did you do to provide a solution?

AVM BK Bishnoi (Retd): In the afternoon of December 5, 1971, I, along with Manbir Singh, went to meet the Chief Operations Officer,

Gp Capt Wollen, and expressed our woes of not achieving anything worthwhile in the last two days of conducting saturation attacks over Dacca. I mentioned that the PAF was defending only their airfield and not venturing beyond 25 km radius of that base. He agreed that the PAF had executed a well thought out strategy, to defend their airfield and the single fighter squadron's assets. Then he asked, "What do you suggest we do?" I said that we had been unable to destroy their aircraft so far either in the air or on the ground, while they had inflicted a loss of nearly nine aircraft and pilots in the last two days. Therefore, I proposed that we needed to deny them the use of the runway at Tejgaon and Kurmitola, by extensively bombing those airstrips, at the earliest. He asked me as to how we intended to do that. I explained the two available options. First was through conventional low-level shallow glide bombing, running in at 45 degrees to the runway; it was safe but could require almost 32 sorties to score a single hit on the narrow stretch of the runway. Besides there was a chance that the bombs hitting at a very shallow angle would not produce the desired results. Under the existing hostile environment over Tejgaon airfield, this mode of attack was, therefore, ruled out. Second was by attempting a high-level steep glide bombing along the length of the runway. Our training records of steep glide bombing, over the Daulang Mukh firing range had demonstrated that the average maximum line error i.e., undershoots or overshoot of bombs was about 200 yards, and the lateral error, 50 yards. With that in mind, I recommended steep glide bombing missions, along the length of the 3,000 × 150 yards runway, with four aircraft, armed with two Mark 62 Russian bombs each.

Mally (as he was called in the Air Force), appreciated my logic, yet he looked aghast and in a very sombre tone he said, "Do you know Bhoop what you are asking for? You are asking for suicide, hara-kiri. You would be climbing to 4.5 km to 5 km height in the sight of air defence guns and the CAP at Tejgaon before launching the dive. During the entire manoeuvre you will be exposed for more than 90 seconds to enemy anti-aircraft guns and Sabre CAP, under full radar guidance. Both will target you and your formation, one by one. Do you understand that?" He was a

Russia trained MiG-21 pilot, had commanded No. 28 Squadron during the 1965 War, and was an acknowledged authority on MiG-21 weapons. He was right in his apprehensions about the risk involved in attempting a steep glide bombing attack on a target such as Tejgaon, which was well defended. He would have failed in his duty if did not make us aware of what we were proposing. I explained to him that we had considered the risks during our discussions and also appraised him about the squadron's practice record for steep glide bombing during training. We further argued that our risk would be further reduced by the surprise and confusion that would be caused by the MiGs executing 'Stuka'-like near vertical dives on the airfield, never seen before, with high explosive bombs exploding all around. The reaction time required to comprehend the situation and react would be enough for us to push the attack through. Our biggest guaranty for success was the Sabre's reluctance to grapple with the MiGs. I assured him that we were bound to pull the strike off successfully, and even with some loss, it would be well worth the risk. I stressed that all the pilots of No. 28 Squadron wholeheartedly supported this plan and were sure of passing muster. 'Mally', grunted and said, "I will tell Command and discuss your suggestion. I will come back to you."

About half an hour later, he called and informed that Command Headquarters had approached Air Headquarters for clearance. Soon after that I got a call from the Senior Air Staff Officer (SASO), Eastern Air Command, AVM Charandas Gurudas Devashar, who asked, "What is that weird idea that you are peddling around?" It took me a little time to explain to him that we had worked hard and trained ourselves for this type of attacks. We were fully aware of the risk involved, yet willing to undertake the mission and were sure to deliver. The risk was well worth the gains obtained from grounding the PAF in East Pakistan for the rest of the war. Finally, he said, "All right, mount a two-aircraft mission for steep glide bombing of the PAF undefended airfield at Kurmitola near Dacca, to demonstrate your claim of proficiency." A two-aircraft mission led by Flt Lt Manbir Singh undertook the task. One set of bombs fell on the runway and the other very close to its edge. We got the clearance to go ahead with our plans, the next day.

The Most Decisive Air Strike

Question: The daring air strike by your squadron on the Tejgaon airfield was the pivotal point of the war. It resulted in air supremacy for the IAF over East Pakistan and enabled unhindered air operations in support of the ground forces, thus, hastening the end of the war. Will you describe that air strike which in all probability accelerated the defeat of the Pakistani forces?

AVM BK Bishnoi (Retd): You have rightly said that this air strike was the pivotal point of the war. On December 6, 1971, I led a formation of 4 MiG-21s, loaded with M-62 bombs for the attack on Tejgaon runway. We flew at low level to the left of Tejgaon, then turned right and approached the dumbbell '17' (one of the runway ends) at 11 o'clock to us. The formation was asked to stretch out in a stream and select bomb switches 'ON'. They confirmed the action. About 3 km short of the runway, at a speed of 900 km/h, I called on R/T, "RPM 100 per cent, pulling up ... pulling up to 5 km, for left hand attack." During the straight pull up, the air speed gradually dropped to 450 km/h. Turning left, I rolled on my back to align the aircraft axis along the runway length and then dropped the nose of the aircraft a little below the beginning of the runway, which looked like a thin ribbon from that height. The aircraft was now in a screaming dive of 60 degrees. The airspeed started increasing as I throttled back to 90 per cent RPM. It was very quiet on top of the trajectory, only the swishing air passing over the canopy. There was no anti-aircraft gun fire nor were Sabres in sight. The aircraft seemed suspended vertically by a thread over the runway. The altimeter was winding down crazily, the runway expanding rapidly, speed was 800 kmph and height 3.5 km; suddenly, the air space in front of me got filled up with ever exploding white and black puffs: air defence guns had opened up. Oh boy! You had asked for it ... hold your nerve ... speed 900 ... passing through 2 km ... approaching bomb release height; I steadied my aim on the first quarter of the runway ... steady ... steady ... wings level ... and pressed the released button. The aircraft's nose jumped up as the bombs left ... speed 1000 ... pulled the stick hard back to pull out of the dive, and threw a steep climbing turn to the left, generating 6+ 'g'; with guns still chasing me I climbed to 5 km. Nos 2 and 3 had finished their attack and the No. 4 was just pulling out of the dive. When I looked back on the Tejgaon runway, I could not believe my eyes. For a moment I thought I was hallucinating, when I saw eight smoking holes spread evenly across the full length of the runway. We had done it and we were safe and returning back to base. Someone from the Flying Control of Tejgaon, called on R/T on our radio frequency and said, "Good show". I thanked him. I looked up to God in the skies and thanked him and prayed that we remain blessed. While on the way to Guwahati, I informed our radar at Shillong to pass on the results of the strike to the SASO at Shillong. The SASO found it hard to believe. He ordered an immediate Canberra mission to photograph the damaged Tejgaon landing strip. After that strike of ours, all the efforts of the PAF to repair the damaged runway were thwarted by repeat bombing attacks by MiGs. The PAF 'retired hurt' for the remaining period of the war. We had obtained total air superiority over the skies of East Pakistan. It made possible the free and fast advance of our troops towards Dacca; uninterrupted helibridging across the rivers and marshes, and mass para-drop near Dacca to clinch its surrender in record time, with 93,000 Pakistani prisoners of war.

Wg Cdr BK Bishnoi (2nd from left) in the Crater on the Tejgaon Runway

Photo courtesy AVM BK Bishnoi VrC and Bar (Retd).

Air Strike that Ended the War

Question: The attack on the Governor's House on December 14, 1971, brought an end to the war in East Pakistan. It caused the Governor to resign and the Pakistani military to surrender. How was the tasking done and how was it executed?

AVM BK Bishnoi (Retd): This air strike was a study in smart diplomacy and clever application of war psychology by incremental raising of the threat level from the common soldier of the Pakistan Army to levels which now included the highest echelon of the civil bureaucracy and the Army brass. The fear of God was put across to the dignitaries sitting in the security of their ivory towers and they were made to feel that none of them was secure any more. The fear of the Mukti Bahini was also looming large.

On December 14, 1971, around 1145 h, when I was walking towards the crew room after a mission, I saw the ops commander waiting outside my office. He said, "Bhoop, there is a very important and crucial task from Air Headquarters, which I want you to undertake." He continued, "There is a meeting to be held at 1200 h, at the Circuit House, Dacca, chaired by the East Pakistan Governor, Mr. Malik, and attended by his cabinet, Gen Niazi, and some important foreign embassy diplomats. You are to strike the Circuit House at 1230 h, with rockets." I looked at my watch and said, "Sir, it is already 1145 h. The time required to plan and reach the target does not give me enough time to meet the time line of 1230 h." He said there was no choice and handed me a tourist map of Dacca showing the location of the Circuit House. The building was located in the centre of the town's thickly populated area, surrounded by tall buildings. I expressed my fears that attacking it would involve heavy collateral damage to civil life and property. He said it was not my business to worry about those issues.

After briefing the other three pilots on the mission profile and attack pattern, we moved to the aircraft. As I began to taxi out, I saw an officer running towards me waving a paper. I stopped the aircraft and opened the canopy; he said, "Sir, there is a change of target. It is not the Circuit

House but the Governor's House, repeat Governor's House." When I asked him about the location of the Governor's House, he shrugged his shoulders and said, "You find out". There was no time to change the planning. I did not want to inform the other three pilots on R/T, for security reasons. We took off and flew low to Dacca. Enroute, I pulled out the tourist guide map from my pocket and searched for the Governor's House. It was a difficult task to fly, navigate and read a map all at the same time. However, I concluded that it was somewhere Southeast of the Tejgaon airfield.

We reached Dacca and after we crossed the airfield on to our right, I called the other three pilots on R/T, informed them about the change of target and asked them to scan on their left to look for the Governor's Palatial House. I climbed to 300 m for a better view and easier spotting of the target. Barely a minute or so later, No. 3 called out and said, "Look 11 o'clock, 4 kilometres." We saw a sprawling set-up with huge open spaces and lawns and a large 'Raj' (British era) type building with a big dome in the centre, like the ones we often see in India. We flew at a distance to retain surprise and were sure that it was the one we were looking for. After doing a wide left 'U' turn, I ordered a stream left hand attack on the building. When in position, I pulled up sharply to about a kilometre and half, then got into a shallow dive and aimed at the base of the dome, below which I presumed was the conference hall. There was no anti-aircraft gunfire. From about a kilometre away, I fired a salvo of 32 rockets, which hit on the roof top below the dome and a huge cloud of smoke, dust and debris flew all around. I turned around and saw the other MiGs scoring hits on the building. The whole complex had erupted into a turbulent pall of dust which engulfed it. It was 1200 h on the clock; the mission had been accomplished. The Indian Air Force had delivered the last fatal blow and the countdown for the fall of Dacca had begun. The formation climbed to 6 km and headed home.

It would be pertinent to narrate at this stage what happened after the rocket smashed through the roof and walls of the Governor's House. The attack was recorded by an American journalist, who was present inside the Governor's House at that time, and was telecast by the American network a few months later from the USA. It also appeared as a BBC report in the *Times of India* a week after the attack. The journalist stated that, as rockets struck the place, Governor Abdul Motaleb Malik ran into the nearby trench, pulled out his hankie and covered his head with it. Then he went down on his knees and said his prayers. Soon came another burst of rockets, which made Mr. Malik take a final decision, which he had been avoiding for some time. He asked for pen and paper and with shaking hands wrote down his and his Cabinet's resignation from the Government of East Pakistan. He gave that paper to the American councillor crouching next to him, with a request to immediately forward it to Gen Yahya Khan in Rawalpindi. Thereafter, he gathered his family and left for the Continental Hotel which was located in the protected Red Cross area.

The American Councillor, instead routed the message through his government in the USA: "Civil government at DACCA falls". Gen Niazi was now in sole command of East Pakistan and he surrendered to the Joint Command of India and Bangladesh two days later, which brought down the curtains on the 13-day war. After the surrender ceremony on December 16, 1971, one journalist asked Gen Niazi, about his claim made a day earlier, that he had enough ammunition, rations and military force to defend Dacca for the next two months, and to fight to the last bullet; then what made him change his mind and surrender in less than 48 hours after that? He got up, turned around and touched the 'wings', worn by an Indian Air Force officer on his uniform and said, "It was this which made me do that". A rare and memorable tribute by the vanquished Army commander of the Pakistan Army to the Indian Air Force.

Postlude

We thanked AVM BK Bishnoi VrC and Bar (Retd) for his accounts of the exploits of his squadron. The squadron led by him was instrumental in significantly accelerating the pace of operations in the 1971 War in the Eastern Sector. When conventional counter-air operations against the PAF were not yielding the desired results, his squadron's unconventional and daring bombing of the Tejgaon runway effectively grounded the PAF operations in East Pakistan and provided the IAF complete air supremacy. It enabled the IAF to launch full spectrum air operations in support of the Indian Army, including utilising its helicopter and transport aircraft without fear of enemy counter-air operations. The squadron was also fortunate to get an opportunity to undertake the strike on the Governor's House which ended the civil government in East Pakistan and became instrumental in forcing the surrender of the Pakistan Army. The saga of No. 28 Squadron in the 1971 War is one of utmost courage and professionalism with its CO leading from the front.

As a Sqn Ldr, Bishnoi had been awarded a Vir Chakra (VrC) in the 1965 Indo-Pakistan War, for his 16 operational close air support missions, and for leading a mission that destroyed a Pakistani train carrying ammunition and tanks. Now, as a Wg Cdr, Bishnoi was awarded the Vir Chakra again (VrC bar), for leading the very daring raids over Dacca.

Notes

1. Combat Air Patrol (CAP) is an air defence operation carried out by fighter aircraft flying in own pre-designated area to protect from enemy aircraft attacks.
2. During those days, in the absence of modern equipment, following course steering and time was a method of navigating the aircraft from one place to another when the ground below was not visible.
3. Runway '35' or runway '17' is the nomenclature of the runway in a particular direction for flying operations.
4. Operational Readiness Platform (ORP) are fighter aircraft waiting on the ground at the runway to get airborne at short notice to intercept incoming enemy aircraft.
5. A 'touch and go' situation is one in which you have barely enough fuel to reach your destination.

Operation Kilo Flight: Night Attack by Otter Aircraft

Shamsul Alam

For this mission Flt. Lt. Shamsul Alam and Capt. Akram received the highest gallantry award "BIR UTTAM" of Bangladesh and the bombardier and gunner received the gallantry award "BIR BIKRAM". After this mission, both Otter aircraft and the Alouette helicopter flew over 48 operational missions, destroying vital targets of military importance in the Liberation War of 1971.

Prologue

I, Gp Capt Shamsul Alam (Retd), then flight lieutenant, am one of the pioneering officers in the formation of Bangladesh Air Force (BAF) Kilo Flight at Dimapur, India, on September 28, 1971, with three ex-Pakistan Air Force (PAF) officers and six licensed civilian pilots of ex-Pakistan International Airlines (PIA) and the Plant Protection Department.

I graduated from the PAF Academy, Risalpur, in July 1967. During the course of my flying career, I flew the T-37, T-33, F-86, B-57 and, finally, C-130 transport aircraft. I escaped from West Pakistan on June 3, 1971, while serving in No. 6 Squadron, PAF Base, Chaklala, to join the Bangladesh freedom struggle. While making my escape, I was captured upon landing at Dhaka airport while arriving by a PIA flight from Karachi. I was sent to a military concentration/prison camp at Dhaka cantonment where I underwent severe physical torture during the process of my interrogation. After prolonged interrogation, I was issued a chargesheet under MLR 39 (c) July 1971. If I had been tried by the Pakistan Military Court, I would have been awarded the death sentence for an act of treason.

In mid-August 1971, I made a second desperate but successful attempt to escape from the Pakistan military prison camp, crossed over to Agartala and, finally, reported to the Bangladesh government in exile in Kolkata. This is in itself a long, gruelling story!

Genesis of Kilo Flight

The Kilo Flight was inaugurated on September 28, 1971, by ACM P C Lal in the presence of Gp Capt A K Khondker who was second in command of our armed forces/Mukti Bahini during the Liberation War of 1971, Sqn Ldr Sultan Mahmood, Flt Lt Shamsul Alam, Flt Lt Badrul Alam, Capt Khaleque (ex PIA), Capt Sattar (ex PIA), Capt Muqueet (ex PIA), Capt Shahab (ex PIA), Capt Akram (ex Plant Protection Pilot), Capt Sharfuddin (ex Plant Protection Pilot) plus 58 airmen of various technical trades of the PAF.

The Kilo Flight started its journey with one DC-3 aircraft, one Otter aircraft and one Alouette-111 helicopter. For the conversion training, the DC-3 aircraft had Capt Khaleque (late), Capt Sattar and Capt Muqueet as the flying crew, with Flt Lt Chowdhury of the Indian Air Force (IAF) as the flying instructor. The Alouette-111 helicopter had Sqn Ldr Sultan Mahmood, Flt Lt Badrul Alam and Capt Shahab as the flying crew with Flt Lt Singla (IAF) as the flying instructor. The Otter aircraft had Capt Akram and Capt Sharfuddin (late) and myself as the flying crew with Flt Lt Ghoshal (IAF) as the flying instructor.

With brief technical training on the aircraft type, the Otter conversion flying training started right away from the beginning of October 1971. After completion of solo stage flying, the long day and night navigation training sorties were flown in which more concentration was given to long low level night flying missions covering a flying duration of up to 7 hours.

By the first week of November 1971, the Otter aircraft was fully modified with armaments in which two under wing fixed rocket pods each carrying seven air-to-ground rockets were installed, the right door was removed and twin barrel 303 browning guns were installed and at the tail end, the floor was cut open to install three bomb racks with each rack carrying 4 × 25 pounds incendiary type bombs i.e. a total 12 bombs. All these modification works were completed at the IAF base in Jorhat, India, under the direct supervision of Gp Capt Chandan Singh, base commander.

Without wasting much time, our live armament training missions started with maximum emphasis given on me to achieve almost 90 per cent rocket hits in the inner circle of a parachute during day and night. This was achieved through the trial and error method, without any gun sight. I had to achieve this after a long navigation flight of 6-7 hours duration at very low level night flying, identifying the parachute target after the end of a long night navigation mission, spread over various hill tops, and firing rockets in pairs. Night after night, these missions were flown to achieve the highest accuracy, safety and reaching a target at a given time.

D-Day

During mid-November 1971, both Otter aircraft and Alouette helicopter crews were called by Gp Capt Chandan Singh at the IAF base, Jorhat, to announce the 0-Day and assigning our targets. The D-Day was November 28, 1971, and for the Otter aircraft the target given was to destroy Chittagong fuel refinery storage tanks of the Eastern Refinery, Chittagong, and for the Alouette helicopter, the target was to destroy the Godnail aviation fuel storage tanks, Narayanganj. The Time on Target (TOT) for both aircraft was fixed at 10 minutes past midnight, with my night recovery at the IAF Kumbhigram airfield. A full intelligence briefing was given to us with target pictures and Chittagong airfield pictures. We were further briefed that there were no "ack ack" (anti-aircraft) guns positioned at Chittagong airfield and we would experience no black-out of Chittagong city and port areas. This made our night attack planning very easy since our targets of fuel storage tanks of the Eastern Refinery, Chittagong, were located very close to the Chittagong airfield. We were further told that the target pictures shown to us were taken three days earlier by Canberra aircraft of the IAF.

For this mission, the assigned air crew for the Otter aircraft was Capt Akram (co-pilot), Sgt Nurul Haque (bombardier) and Cpl Rustam (gunner) and myself. As per our final briefing, the Otter aircraft was to be positioned at Koilash Shahar, a 3,000 ft plant protection airstrip and the Alouette helicopter was to be positioned at Teliamura for the final mission. Both aircraft left Dimapur on November 26, 1971, for their respective staging posts.

I prepared my flight plan to reach my target at 10 minutes past midnight and my start up time was fixed at 7:45 pm. The Otter aircraft was fully refuelled manually at Koilash Shahar by the contingent of the IAF. We passed the uneventful nights of November 26 and 27, 1971, and had a good breakfast on the morning of November 28, 1971, in our tents. While I was giving my final briefing to my crew for our night mission of November 28, 1971, at about 4:30 pm, suddenly I saw an IAF flying officer who entered my tent and handed over a copy of a typed signal which read, *"Operation Kilo Flight Mission is postponed till further order. Remain at your station"*. This was shock to us!

Our long wait got over when, on December 3, 1971, the same IAF flying officer entered my tent at about 5:30 pm and handed over another signal copy which read, *"Operation Kilo Flight Mission is 'On' Tonight. All other briefings are as before"*. At Koilash Shahar, we had no idea that the PAF had already launched their strikes in the Western Sector on December 3, 1971, at around 4:30 pm.

We got airborne at about 8 pm in the darkness of the night, initially flying at 1,000 ft. The route planned was simple during the outbound journey. Till we hit our first outbound check point i.e. the Bay of Bengal shore line, this flying segment was shared between myself and Akram at the control monitoring our flying parameters jointly. We were only depending on our 'directional gyro' and 'standby compass', maintaining our planned accurate heading, speed and height. During this journey, we had no ground check point to compare with our map and our track was well covered by the winter fog, passing through hilly jungle terrain. We flew due south till we hit the coastline of the Bay of Bengal. We kept on lowering our altitude from 1,000 ft. to 500 ft. to avoid PAF radar detection and by the time we hit the coastline, we were about 100 ft. Thereafter, we turned left for Chittagong. By then, the half moon had already risen, meeting us head on which improved our visibility. Upon hitting the coastline, I took over the control and turned left heading towards Chittagong port, lowering our height further to about 50 ft. Contrary to the intelligence briefing that we received at IAF Jorhat, we found no city lights visible. On our right, we saw a few ocean vessels berthed/tied together at outer anchorage point, throwing out some lights. Now I was maintaining my heading, speed, height and monitoring my elapsed time!

After crossing our zero hour, I started gradually pulling up and Chittagong airfield was clearly visible in the shining moonlight. Just a few seconds later, I could see the shining fuel storage tanks of the Eastern Refinery, Chittagong! Identifying my first attack target, I pulled up the aircraft with full power and went into dive for my first attack, and aiming clearly on the fuel storage tank with a steady attack dive, I fired my first pair rockets. I clearly saw our rocket pair hitting the target as I pulled up from the dive of my first attack. There was no explosion! I came in for a second attack, fired the second rocket pair, hitting the targets and pulled up for the third dive. Again, there was no explosion! As I was preparing for my third attack, my co-pilot, Akram was distracted by streaks of light gushing past our right wing. We were under fire from deadly "ack acks" from Chittagong airfield. To our utter surprise and horror, the entire Chittagong airfield was fortified with Air Defence (AD) guns and these were firing at us in random with no stoppage.

Crossing my fingers, I pressed on with my 3rd attack, dodging the "ack ack" fire, aiming at the fuel storage tanks, and fired a pair of rockets which hit the tanks directly. As I pulled up from my 3rd attack, I heard a loud thundering noise of the explosion of the tanks. With a left bank, as I was coming for my 4th attack, a huge ball of fire lit our entire cockpit. Thrilled with joy, we pressed on with our 4th, 5th and 6th attacks, hitting our targets persistently and headed towards the sea, making a few orbits to see for ourselves from far the towering inferno of the Eastern Refinery fuel storage tanks. During the course of our rocket attacks, I did not hesitate to give my command to my bombardier to drop bombs in pairs and asked my gunner to continuously strafe guns from his side at random during every recovery from our dive. We accomplished our given mission successfully. As we set out for our return journey, both our gunner and bombardier came to the cockpit to watch the fireball on our right which still lit our entire cockpit as we were heading West to our next turning point for Kumbhigram airfield.

After hitting our inbound check point, we turned right to our planned heading for Kumbhigram airfield. The easy part was over. Now we had to get back to our home Kumbhigram! By this time, we had already flown over 4:30 h. The mighty Otter had just destroyed a major enemy target at night, achieving complete element of surprise, which neutralised the entire fuel supply of the Pakistan Army, Navy and Air Force; and was flying back home with a bare 'directional gyro' and 'standby compass' and the blessings of the Almighty! We had hardly any ground reference point to check with our map on this pitch dark foggy night in hilly jungle terrain other than simply flying on track, speed, height and hoping that God would take us back home safely! In 1971, the 'seven sister states' of northeast India did not have adequate electricity supply. So, in our inbound route, we did not experience any well lit city or township.

As we were approaching our Expected Time of Arrival (ETA) at Kumbhigram airfield, I kept on looking out and giving calls on my Crystal radio set, switching on to the pre-set VHF frequency of the Kumbhigram tower. But in spite of my frantic calls to the Kumbhigram tower, I did not get a reply, and as my ETA was fast approaching its end, I was getting worried. Suddenly, I heard a God sent faint voice in my earphone *"Kilo Flight this is Kumbhigram Tower"*. For the second time, I screamed with joy. I requested Kumbhigram to switch on their 'pundit light'. As it flashed, in a second, I saw we were about five miles right of track. I put a left bank and headed for the 'pundit light' – this scene is still flashing in my heart to this date! After orbiting over the Kumbhigram airfield for about 20 minutes till the 'goose neck lamps' were laid on the runway, I made a beautiful kisser landing. It was a mission of over 8:15 night flying hours beating the 'dam buster' night mission of the UK's Royal Air Force (RAF)!

Epilogue

As I disembarked from the Otter aircraft in my sweat soaked overall, I was received by my hero, Gp Capt Chandan Singh, the base commander of the IAF base, Jorhat, who literally picked me up from the ground saying *"Oh boy, oh boy, you have done it"*. I asked him, *"Sir, how did you know I had done it"*. He said they had heard a news report from BBC Radio a few minutes earlier that one unidentified aircraft had destroyed the Chittagong fuel refinery on the midnight of December 4, 1971. Gp Capt Chandan Singh further lovingly scolded me by saying, *"Bloody man, you have even delayed our prime minister from declaring her war against Pakistan which she declared at 00:23 hours on 4th December, 1971. She agreed to do this to maintain our element of surprise at the request of Air Chief Marshal P. C. Lal"*. We are all indebted and grateful to the Late Prime Minister Indira Gandhi and the IAF. LONG LIVE INDIA BANGLADESH FRIENDSHIP TILL ETERNITY!!!

Chronology of Air Action: Indo-Pak War of 1971

Compiled by TH Anand Rao

From early 1971, as the political situation in the subcontinent deteriorated, the IAF was alerted to the possibility of another armed conflict.

In the months preceding the 1971 War, the An-12, Packet and Dakota aircraft of IAF flew 2,386 h, lifted some 3,700 passengers and 1,034 tonnes of load as transport support missions for Indian Army's buildup in the East.

June 1971: The IAF had flown reconnaissance flights over East Pakistan since June 1971.

September 28, 1971: Nine Bengali pilots (three former PAF and six civilian pilots) and fifty technicians – formerly of the PAF and serving with the Mukti Bahini in various capacities – were gathered for a special mission at Dimapur in Nagaland. The mission included use of a DC-3 Dakota, 1 DHC-3 Otter plane, and 1 Alouette III helicopter which were weaponised to launch hit-and-run attacks on sensitive targets inside Bangladesh from the air. This tiny force was dubbed Kilo Flight, the first fighting formation of the nascent Bangladesh Air Force.

November 1971: In early November, both Indian and Pakistan governments protested violations of national airspace along the Western border.

November 22, 1971: The Battle of Boyra. Aerial interception that was fought between the Indian Air Force and intruding Pakistani Air Force jets that had crossed into Indian Airspace. 03 Sabres of PAF were shot down.

November 23-
December 11, 1971: Air support for the battle of Hilli-Bogura

December 2, 1971: First missions by BAF Kilo Flight on targets at Chittagong and Narayanganj. These missions continued till 16 Dec 71.

December 3, 1971: Full-scale war began.

- Pre-emptive strikes were launched on 03 Dec 71 by the Pakistan Air Force (Op Chengiz Khan) on 11 IAF bases. Retaliatory strikes launched by IAF over PAF airfields in West and East Pakistan. IAF attacked Chander, Shorkot, Murid, Mianwali, Masroor, Risalewala, Changa Manga and Sargodha, hitting a no. of PAF aircraft on ground & setting petrol tanks on fire.
- Seven Canberra aircraft of No. 35 Squadron struck the storage area at Drigh road and oil storage tanks at Karachi, destroying about 60 per cent of Pakistan's oil reserves.
- The Mukti Bahini Air Force (Kilo Flight) with Otter and Alloutte attacked oil installations at Narayanganj and Chittagong and set them on fire.

This air action marked the official start of the Indo-Pakistan War of 1971.

December 4, 1971: Eastern Sector.

- Indian air units commenced operations in the Eastern theatre.
- Canberra bombers struck Tejgaon repeatedly in the early hours.
- Hunters attacked Chittagong in the morning and Narayanganj fuel depots in the afternoon.
- Tejgaon was repeatedly attacked by Hunters, SU-7s and MiG-21s throughout the day.
- PAF was on full alert and Sabres flew Combat Air Patrols, resulting in several dogfights.
- IAF attacked several other targets, including the Teesta Bridge, Chandpur and Goalanda Ferry Ghats and flew several ground support missions.

Western Sector.

- Night bombing mission over Changa Manga forest by An-12s of 44 Sqn.
- Deep penetration bombing of Mianwali airfield by Canberra of 16 Sqn.
- A 2 aircraft strike over Chaklala airfield by a Hunter piloted by then Lt Arun Prakash [now Admiral (Retd)] destroys a passenger plane of USAF positioned for Brigadier General Charles Elwood Yeager (Chuck Yeager)
- Su-7s from Adampur attacked the intruding Pakistani forces close to Dera Baba Nanak area.
- Jaisalmer based Hunters attacked enemy positions at Islamgarh to the North.
- HF-24 from Uttarlai attacked enemy fortifications on the border at Ghazi camp.
- Hunters from Jamnagar were over Karachi. A number of PAF aircraft were destroyed on ground & oil tanks near Karachi set ablaze (Kiamari oil tanks).
- IAF fighter-bombers also attacked Sargodha, Wagowal, Shorkot & Murid.
- Eight Canberras attacked Masroor by day and night, making a significant contribution towards the success of the naval missile attack on Karachi harbour later the same night.
- PAF B-57 and one F-104 were shot down by anti-aircraft fire over Amritsar & the pilot captured.

December 5, 1971: Western Sector.

- IAF Counter Air Ops were limited to attacks on those PAF airfields which could be used to mount raids against Indian Army positions in the North. This led to PAF withdrawing many of its combat aircraft from forward airfields - Murid, Chander & Risalewala.
- Air strikes in the Battle of Longewala.

- Bombing raid over Haji Pir Pass by An-12 & Canberras.
- Long-range radar at Sakesar was attacked by Hunters & Su-7s. One of the antennas was hit & the radar put off the air for the rest of the War.

Eastern Sector.

- MiG-21's bombed Tejgaon and Kurmitola leaving the runways unusable.
- The IAF switched tactics. Ground support and attacks on Pakistani targets continued, including the first use of Napalm in combat by IAF near Jessore.

December 6, 1971: Eastern Sector.

- R/T intercept led to discovery of an improvised landing strip at Barisal, which was then attacked with bombs, guns & made unusable.
- Air raids over Tejgaon, Comilla, Sylhet, Jessore and Barisal airfields.

Western Sector.

- Chander & Risalewala struck during daylight hours, while Sargodha & Chaklala were struck at dusk by Su-7.
- 04 Hunters from Pathankot struck the Attock Oil Refinery, leaving the refinery in flames.
- 08 Canberras of No. 35 Sqn attacked a major PAF maintenance base at Drigh Road near Karachi. Hangers were hit & thick smoke was seen rising from this area.

December 7, 1971: Eastern Sector.

- Tejgaon airport was put out of operation, grounding the PAF in East Pakistan.
- Air raids continued on Kurmitola and Barisal airfields.
- Caribous converted to bombers carried out bombing raids over Tejgaon airfield.
- First major heliborne operations of the War, troops of 4/5 GR were heli-lifted from Kalaura to a DZ behind enemy lines, near Sylhet.

Western Sector.

- PAF bases at Risalewala & Chander were attacked at 1st light.
- Kohat airfield was attacked by Hunters & hangar destroyed.
- Counter-Air missions by IAF were reduced & Close Air Support missions for Indian Army on Western front were launched.
- 04 Hunters of No. 20 Sqn from Pathankot attacked the power house at Mangla dam. The power house was hit & destroyed.

December 7-9, 1971: Airlift by Mi-4s of 110 HU of a Battalion from Kailashahar to 'N' of Surma near Sylhet. The first ever night SHBO was planned on 8 Dec from Kailashahar.

December 8, 1971: Eastern Sector.

- Air strikes on Joydebpur Ordnance Factory.
- Night bombing of Tejgaon by Caribous of 33 Sqn.

Western Sector.

- Hunter aircraft from the Pathankot based 20 Sqn, attacked the Pakistani base in Murid and destroyed 05 F-86 aircraft on the ground.

December 9, 1971: Eastern Sector.

- Air strikes on Joydebpur Ordnance Factory.
- Canberra, Hunters & Gnats operating from Dum Dum, Hashimara & Kumbhigram attacked coastal vessels, motorised barges, gunboats, ferries, etc. destroying a total of 100 vessels in Narayanganj, Khulna & Sirajgunj areas.

Western Sector.

- 40 Su-7 & Hunter sorties were flown in Chhamb sector destroying more than 20 enemy tanks.
- Su-7s flew 20 search and strike missions against tanks and gun positions against Pak armour and guns in Bahawalnagar, Chistian Mandi, Amroka and Jalwala areas.

- 24 sorties were flown by Hunters in the general area of Longewala and Gabbar which destroyed 8-10 tanks & nearly 20 vehicles. An ammunition dump at Gabbar was also destroyed.
- Pak positions in Bahawalnagar, Sulaimanki, Chhamb, and Jassar were attacked by six Canberras and two An-12s. Interdiction targets were the marshalling yard at Lodhran and the railway stations at Kasur and Raiwind. Six aircraft took part in these raids.

December 10, 1971: Eastern Sector.

- Meghna River Airlift – IAF heli-lifted troops of the IV Corps from Ashuganj to Raipura and Narsingi in what came to be termed Operation Cactus-Lilly (also known as the Helibridge over Meghna).
- Su-7 dropped Napalm on Bhairab twice.
- Fratricide - Gnats fired at BNS ships near Khulna on Passur river.

Western Sector.

- Air Battle over Chhamb.
- HF-24 of 10 Sqn attacked Mirpur Khas railway marshalling yard damaging 40-50 wagons.

December 11, 1971:

- Tangail Para Drop. The Tangail airdrop involved several An-12s, C-119s, 2 Caribous and Dakotas from various squadrons airdropping 700 troops.
- Thirty Su-7 and Hunter sorties were mounted in Chhamb sector.

December 12, 1971:

- The first aerial victory when MiG-21FLs of No. 47 Squadron shot down a PAF F-104 over the Gulf of Kutch and this was followed by three more victories in quick succession.
- Bombing of Skardu airfield by An-12 and Canberras.
- MiG-21s and Hunters carried out 15 CAO missions against Tejgaon and Rangpur.

December 13, 1971:

- Air strikes on Joydebpur Ordnance Factory.

	• Three converted An-12s from the No. 44 Squadron struck the Jaydebpur Ordnance Factory in East Pakistan, while the Caribous carried out regular night raids on Tejgaon.
December 14, 1971:	• Governor's House struck by MiG-21s of No. 28 Sqn. • Air strikes on Dhaka University. • Air combat over Srinagar. Fg Offr NJS Sekhon shot two Sabres.
December 15, 1971:	• Bombing mission over Sui Gas Plant by An-12 of 44 Sqn. • 40 sorties of MiGs and Hunters were flown to target enemy troops occupying the Decca University campus, with no collateral damage caused to any of the buildings or structures outside the target area.
December 16, 1971:	Instrument of surrender of Pakistan forces was signed in Dhaka.
December 17, 1971:	• MiG-21FLs of No. 29 Squadron escorting HF-24 Maruts, shot down intercepting F-104s near Uttarlai in the Rajasthan desert in gun-missile encounters, while a third F-104, on an intruding mission, was shot down by another MiG-21FL of No. 29 Squadron. • Canberras and An-12 raided Skardu airfield. • Hostilities in the West ended at 2000 h.

The data has been compiled from multiple sources including IAF website, print and visual media, web articles and official twitter sources.

Notes

1. Sorties flown by IAF: 4,000 in Western Sector and 1,978 in Eastern Sector.
2. IAF established a highly credible serviceability rate which exceeded 80 per cent.
3. Sorties flown by PAF: 2,840 in the West and 30 in the East.
4. Losses - IAF-45 aircraft, PAF-75 aircraft.
5. IAF inducted 6 squadrons (~140 frames) within a span of 18 months, from 1968-1969. Just in time for 1971.

The List of IAF Gallantry Award

(PVC, MVC and VrC) Winners – 1971 Ops

Compiled by RR Chaudhary

Param Vir Chakra

1. Fg Offr Nirmal Jit Singh Sekhon

Maha Vir Chakra

1. Wg Cdr Vidya Bhushan Vasisht
2. Wg Cdr Cecil Vivian Parker
3. Wg Cdr Ramesh Sakhram Benegal
4. Wg Cdr Man Mohan Bir Singh Talwar
5. Wg Cdr Allan Albert D'costa
6. Wg Cdr Harcharan Singh Manget
7. Sqn Ldr Madhavendra Banerji
8. Sqn Ldr Ravinder Nath Bhardwaj
9. Wg Cdr Swaroop Krishna Kaul
10. Wg Cdr Padmanabha Gautam
11. Gp Capt Chandan Singh

Vir Chakra

1. Flt Lt Manjit Singh Dhillon
2. Flt Lt Manbir Singh
3. Flt Lt Parvez Rustom Jamasji
4. Flt Lt Vijay Kumar Wahi
5. Gp Capt Man Mohan Singh
6. Flt Lt Rajendra Singh Wahi
7. Flt Lt Lawrence Fredric Pereira
8. Flt Lt Syed Shahid Hussain Naqvi

9. Flt Lt Pushp Kumar Vaid
10. Flt Lt Partha Das Gupta
11. Flt Lt Andre Rudolph Da Costa
12. Flt Lt Nitin Gajanan Junnarkar
13. Fg Offr Sudhir Tyagi
14. Flt Lt Dilip Kamalakar Dighe
15. Flt Lt Pradip Vinayak Apte
16. Flt Lt Harbans Perminder Singh
17. Flt Lt Gurdev Singh Rai
18. Flt Lt Aruna Kumar Datta
19. Sqn Ldr Ramesh Kumar Sachdeva
20. Flt Lt Shivinder Singh Bains
21. Sqn Ldr Mohinder Kumar Jain
22. Flt Lt Jagdamba Prasad Saklani
23. Sqn Ldr Jiwa Singh
24. Flt Lt Mohinder Singh Sandhu
25. Flt Lt Ashok Kumar Singh
26. Sqn Ldr Jal Maniksha Mistry
27. Flt Lt Govind Chandra Singh Rajwar
28. Flt Lt Mandepanda Appachu Ganapathy
29. Sqn Ldr Farokh Jehangir Mehta
30. Flt Lt Mahabir Prasad Premi
31. Flt Lt Hemant Sharat Kumar Sardesai
32. Sqn Ldr Arya Bhushan Lamba
33. Sqn Ldr Iqbal Ali Syed
34. Wg Cdr Harsern Singh Gill
35. Fl Lt Somar Bikram Shah
36. Sqn Ldr Ramesh Chander Kohli
37. Flt Lt Ramesh Chander Gosain
38. Flt Lt Bharat Bhushan Soni
39. Wg Cdr Murari Lal Trehon
40. Flt Lt Surinder Singh Malhotra
41. Fl Lt Aspari Raghunath
42. Wg Cdr Ramanathan Sundaresan
43. Sqn Ldr Charanjit Singh
44. Flt Lt Arun Laxman Deoskar
45. Wg Cdr Arun Kanti Mukherjee

46. Sqn Ldr Gursaran Singh Ahluwalia
47. Flt Lt Robindra Kumar Sinha
48. Wg Cdr Ravindar Nath Dogra
49. Sqn Ldr Allan David Alley
50. Wg Cdr Donald Melvyn Conquest
51. Sqn Ldr Krishan Kumar Bakshi
52. Flt Lt Dinesh Chander Nayyar
53. Wg Cdr Narinder Chatrath
54. Sqn Ldr Suresh Damodar Karnik
55. Flt Lt Cherry Hassanand Raney
56. Wg Cdr Krishan Kumar Badhwar
57. Sqn Ldr Ravindra Nath Bali
58. Flt Lt Chidambaram Sarangapani Chandrasekaran
59. Wg Cdr Keshav Chandra Aggarwal
60. Sqn Ldr Jasjit Singh
61. Flt Lt Niraj Kukreja
62. Gp Capt Robert Arnold Weir
63. Sqn Ldr Anil Kumar Bhadra
64. Flt Lt Prem Bhushan Kalra
65. Sqn Ldr Vinod Kumar Bhatia
66. Sqn Ldr Kirpal Singh
67. Fg Offr Kariyadil Cheriyan Kuruvilla
68. Sqn Ldr Dinesh Chandra Bhandary
69. Flt Lt Aditya Vikram Pethia
70. Flt Lt Vinod Kumar Neb
71. Sqn Ldr Sindhaghatta Subbaramu
72. Flt Lt Roy Andrew Massey
73. Wg Cdr Bhupendra Kumar Bishnoi
74. Sqn Ldr Kalyan Kumar Dutta
75. Flt Lt Sukrutaraj Jayandra
76. Fg Offr Satish Chandra Sharma
77. Sqn Ldr Charanjit Singh Sandhu
78. Flt Lt Kuldeep Singh Sahota
79. Fg Offr Sukhdev Singh Dhillon
80. Sqn Ldr Ashok Prataprao Shinde
81. Flt Lt Yogendra Prasad Singh
82. Fg Offr Mohan Dikshit

83. Sqn Ldr Vishnu Narain Johri
84. Flt Lt Winston Rabinder Sanjeeva Rao
85. Fg Offr Harish Masand
86. Fg Offr Jai Singh Gahalawat
87. Sqn Ldr Jagbir Singh
88. Flt Lt Apramjeet Singh
89. Flt Lt Parminder Paul Singh
90. Fg Offr Bartan Ramesh
91. Sqn Ldr Sanjay Kumar Choudhury
92. Flt Lt Kukke Sreekantasastry Suresh
93. Fg Offr Sankarnarayanan Balasubramanian
94. Sqn Ldr Ghanshyam Singh Thapa
95. Flt Lt Shivinder Singh Bains
96. Flt Lt Melvinder Singh Grewal
97. Fg Offr Ballachandra Chengapa Karumbaya
98. Sqn Ldr Dilip Kumar Dass
99. Flt Lt Arun Vasant Sathaye
100. Flt Lt Manjit Singh Sekhon
101. Fg Offr Kishan Lakhimal Malkani
102. Sqn Ldr Preet Pal Singh Gill
103. Flt Lt Chandra Mohan Singla
104. Sqn Ldr Dhirendra Singh Jafa
105. Fg Offr Donald Lazarus
106. Sqn Ldr Iqbal Singh Bindra

The list has been compiled from data obtained from Ministry of Defence, Government of India website for gallantry awards.

Contributors

Air Marshal **Anil Chopra**, PVSM, AVSM, VM, VSM (Retd) was a fighter pilot, test pilot, and a pioneer of the Mirage-2000 fleet. He commanded a Mirage-2000 Squadron and the Aircraft and Systems Testing Establishment (ASTE). He was the Team Leader of the MiG-21 Bison upgrade project in Russia. He has commanded operational air bases in both the Western and Eastern Sectors. He was head of the IAF in Jammu and Kashmir (J&K), and head of the inspections of the Indian Air Force (IAF). He retired as Air Officer Personnel. He has been a member of the Armed Forces Tribunal, and a member of the Executive Council of Jawaharlal Nehru University (JNU).

An avid writer, he has had more than 500 articles published in various magazines, newspapers, and books. He has recently written books titled *China – The Rising Aerospace Power – Implications for India*, and *Greatest Air Aces of All Time*. Air Mshl Chopra runs "Air Power Asia" https://airpowerasia.com/, a website that puts Asia's aviation and military power into the correct perspective. He is invited for panel discussions and intellectual discourses by think-tanks, on television, and by eminent universities and colleges for lectures. He is currently Director General, Centre for Air Power Studies (CAPS).

Air Marshal **Vikram Singh** VSM was commissioned into the IAF's fighter stream in 1984. He went on to become a Flying Instructor and Experimental Test Pilot. He has served in the Plans Branch at Air Headquarter and various field and operational appointments. His earlier works include a detailed history of the Spitfire in IAF service *Spitfires in the Sun* published in 2014. He is now completing a mammoth history of the December 1971 air war with Pakistan. It is from this research that he has authored his article "Balance of Forces".

Air Marshal **VK Bhatia**, PVSM, AVSM, VrC & BAR, during his service career spanning more than 40 years, has flown close to 5,500 hours on 35 different types of aircraft which, apart from all types of fighters, also included transport aircraft and helicopters.

A double Vir Chakra awardee, Air Mshl Bhatia has had the rare distinction of being the Commander-in-Chief of three (Central, South-Western and Western) operational commands of the Indian Air Force. He was awarded the PVSM and AVSM Presidential medals in recognition of services of the highest order to the nation. Presently, besides being the president of the RCDS Association of India, he is serving on the Executive Councils of the Institute for Defence Studies and Analyses (IDSA) and The United Service Institution of India (USI) premium think-tanks. He is also a Distinguished Fellow at the prestigious Centre for Air Power Studies (CAPS).

Air Marshal **Harish Masand** VrC VM (Retd) was commissioned as a fighter pilot in December 1967. He soon saw action in the liberation of Bangladesh in 1971 while flying Hunter aircraft from Hasimara and won a Vir Chakra for gallantry. He inducted the MiG-29 as a Squadron Commander in 1987 and the Su-30s as the Base Commander in 1997. He is well-known for his displays on the MiG-29 and accident-free flying for all his subordinates through his career. He is a Flying Instructor, Fighter Combat Leader, a graduate of the Defence Services Staff College (DSSC) and an alumnus of the Air War College in the USA, Class of '93. He has also served as an instructor in many training institutes.

After retirement in 2006, he settled down in Mhow and keeps busy writing and speaking on defence and national security matters.

Air Vice Marshal (Dr) **Arjun Subramaniam**, AVSM (Retd) is a retired fighter pilot from the IAF who has flown MiG-21s and Mirage-2000s. He currently occupies the President's Chair of Excellence in National Security at the National Defence College and is an Adjunct Faculty member at the Naval War College. After retirement from the IAF in 2017, he has been a Visiting Fellow at Harvard and Oxford Universities and a Visiting Professor at the Fletcher School of Law and Diplomacy, Ashoka and Jindal Universities. He is the author of *India's Wars: A Military History: 1947-1971* and its newly-released sequel titled *Full Spectrum: India's Wars 1972-2020.*

Air Marshal **Bharat Kumar**, PVSM, AVSM (Retd) is an alumnus of the National Defence Academy, Defence Services Staff College and General Staff College, Voroshilov. A veteran of the 1965 and 1971 Indo-Pakistan conflicts, he commanded a MiG-21 Squadron, two operational bases, including Air Force Station, Gwalior, housing Mirage-2000 aircraft. He has held with credit many staff appointments, including Air 1 and Senior Air Staff Officer at headquarters of operational commands, Director (Ops), Director (Plans), and ACAS (Inspection) at Air HQ. He was AOC HQ Maritime Air Operation and reached the pinnacle of his service career when was appointed the AOC-in-C Southern Air Command in 1995 from where he retired in 1997. Air Mshl Bharat Kumar has authored several books on the Indian Air Force.

PVS Jagan Mohan, a historian of the Indian Air Force, has authored three books on the Indian Air Force and its conflicts, and assisted in several other history projects over the years. He has served as one of the editors of Bharat-Rakshak.com, a defence portal since 1999, and in 2007, was awarded a 'Chief of Air Staff Commendation' by the Indian Air Force for his contributions to the IAF's history. In 2013, he received a fellowship from the Centre for Armed Forces Historical Research (USI) under the General Palit Military Studies Trust to carry out research into the early history of the Indian Air Force. His publications include *The India-Pakistan Air War of 1965* (Manohar, 2005), *Eagles over Bangladesh* (HarperCollins, 2014) and *The Westland Wapiti in Indian Air Force Service 1933-1943* (CAFHR/USI, 2015).

Air Vice Marshal **Rajesh Isser**, AVSM, VM (Retd) is an experienced military aviator with extensive operational and combat in Sri Lanka (IPKF), Siachen Glacier, Kargil War and Congo (UNPK 2003-04). He has been a Task Force Commander in many rescue and relief operations all over India including Uttrakhand 2013, Ladakh 2010, Andhra-Karnataka 2009 and Arunachal Pradesh 2000. He has also done much operational rescue work in South Asian and African countries.

As a Director of net assessment at HQ Integrated Defence Staff, he has coordinated numerous strategic projects and authored strategy reports on many critical issues. An author of three books, he has more than 50 articles to his credit in national and international journals on diverse subjects such as disaster response, peacekeeping, counter-insurgency, irregular conflicts, etc.

Group Captain **HK Bajaj** VSM (Retd) was commissioned into the fighter stream of the Indian Air Force in June 1971. He has approximately 3,000 hours of accident free flying experience on single-engine aircraft. He is an A2 Qualified Flying Instructor (QFI). During a career spanning 32 years, he flew the HT-2, Harvard (T6G), Vampires, Kiran (HJT-16), Hunters, S-22 and MiG-23 (BN) aircraft. He raised and commanded an OSA-AK (M) missile squadron, was Chief Operations Officer of a premier fighter station and attended the Higher Command Course with the Indian Army. He commanded an Air Force Station for three years and was last posted as Senior Instructor at the Defence Services Staff College, Wellington.

Air Marshal **Diptendu Choudhury** AVSM VM VSM is an alumnus of the Royal College of Defence Studies UK, a Post Graduate in Strategy and International Security from King's College, London, a Master of Philosophy on Defence and Strategic Studies, and is pursuing his PhD on Air Power. An experienced pilot with over 5,000 sorties on fighters, he has commanded a fighter squadron, the prestigious Tactics and Combat Development Establishment (TACDE), two frontline fighter wings, and extensive experience in planning and execution of air operations at command at all levels. He has been Air Officer Commanding (AOC) Composite Operational Battle Response and Analysis group, Assistant Chief of the Air Staff (ACAS) Inspections and Director Air Staff Inspections. He has been extensively involved in planning and execution of air operations at strategic, operational and tactical levels, as well as policy formulation and strategy development. He has vast experience in air operations and exercises, having planned and executed several IAF and Command level exercises. He has also led the IAF in three international air exercises. An avid air power scholar, he is a regular writer and speaker on strategy, air power and security matters. Presently, he is the Commandant of the National Defence College, New Delhi.

Dr **Shalini Chawla** is Distinguished Fellow at the Centre for Air Power Studies (CAPS). She joined CAPS in 2006 and has published more than 100 research articles/chapters in national and international journals/books on a wide range of issues relating to Pakistan and Afghanistan. She lectures regularly at various universities, think-tanks and leading institutions of the Indian armed forces and Indian Foreign Service. She is actively engaged in India's Track 1.5 initiatives. She received a Commendation and Badge from the Chief of the Air Staff in October 2020 for her praiseworthy contribution to the service. She has authored four books titled *Pakistan's Military and Its Strategy* (2009), *Nuclear Pakistan* (2012), *India's Sentinel* (ed.) (2014) and *Strategic Advantage of Air Power* (ed.) (2019).

Air Vice Marshal **Kapil Kak**, AVSM VSM (Retd) participated in both the 1965 and 1971 Wars, and in the latter, took part in bombing operations in both the Western and Eastern Sectors. He worked as Deputy Director, Institute for Defence Studies and Analyses (IDSA) and Founding Additional Director, Centre for Air Power Studies (CAPS), and has authored over 50 book chapters and journal articles on a variety of strategic, national security, defence and air power issues, and edited the books *India and Pakistan: Pathways Ahead* and *Comprehensive Security for an Emerging India.* He is closely associated with the initiatives of public policy think-tanks and concerned citizens' groups on the India-Pakistan peace process and conflict resolution in Jammu and Kashmir. He is on the Council of Cluster University, Jammu, and on the Board of Studies (National Security), Central University, Jammu.

Dr **Manpreet Sethi** is Distinguished Fellow at the Centre for Air Power Studies (CAPS), where she heads its programme on nuclear security. She is the recipient of the K Subrahmanyam award in 2014 and Commendation by Chief of the Air Staff in 2020. Since receiving her doctorate in 1997, she has worked on nuclear issues ranging from energy, strategy, arms control to disarmament. She is the author/co-author/editor of eight books and over 100 papers. She lectures regularly at the National Defence College and other establishments of the Indian armed forces, police, Foreign Service, and universities. Dr Sethi is a regular at flagship nuclear policy conferences, Track II initiatives and the UN. She was Member, Prime Minister's Informal Group on Disarmament in 2012, and on the Executive Board of the Indian Pugwash Society. Currently, she is on the Board of Directors of the Asia-Pacific Leadership Network (APLN) and a consultant with the Nuclear Abolition Forum.

Group Captain **Rajesh R Chaudhary** is a serving officer of the Indian Air Force. He was commissioned in the Flying Branch of the IAF as a navigator. He has extensively flown strategic and tactical airlift aircraft in all their operational roles including disaster relief and the aerial refueller aircraft of the IAF. He has commanded an air defence missile squadron and tenanted the appointment of Director Aerial Refuelling Operations at Air Headquarters. A graduate from the Defence Services Staff College (DSSC), he is presently a Senior Fellow at the Centre for Air Power Studies (CAPS) involved in research on national security, civil-military relations and the Higher Defence Organisation of India.

Group Captain **Shamsul Alam** (Retd) is a veteran of Bangladesh Liberation War of 1971. For his bravery in the war, the Government of Bangladesh awarded him the second highest gallantry award, the Bir Uttam. Subsequently, he was awarded the Independence Day Award in 2017 by the government. In 1971, then Sqn Ldr Alam was posted to the Pakistan Air Force (PAF) Base in Rawalpindi and on hearing the call of freedom by Sheikh Mujibur Rahman, he left Pakistan as a civilian and travelled to Dhaka, where he was immediately arrested by the military intelligence.

Sqn Ldr Alam was part of the first air raid that attacked the Chittagong oil refinery by the Otter aircraft and the near simultaneous attack by the Alouette helicopter on the Narayanganj oil depot. Post the war Sqn Ldr Alam served in the Bangaldesh Air Force, wherein he was instrumental in setting up the Transport Flying Squadron, Flying Training Academy and Flying Instructor's School of the nascent Bangladesh Air Force. Gp Capt Alam now lives a retired life and is settled in Dhaka, Bangladesh.

Group Captain **TH Anand Rao** is a Senior Fellow at the Centre for Air Power Studies. He is an alumnus of the Defence Services Staff College (DSSC). Wellington, with a Master's degree in 'Defence Studies' from Madras University. He has researched extensively in the field of 'space security' and has written many articles on the subject. He has also authored a book titled *India's Space Security Dilemma* (KW Publishers, 2021). Gp Capt Anand Rao has flown various fighter and trainer aircraft and is experienced in a variety of operational roles. He participated in the Kargil War. He is also a Qualified Flying Instructor (QFI). He has served in many operational field and staff appointments in the IAF and was awarded the Chief of Air Staff Commendation in 2011.

Index